Teacher Education and the Challenge of Development

In developing countries across the world, qualified teachers are a rarity, with thousands of untrained adults taking over the role and millions of children having no access to schooling at all. The supply of high-quality teachers is falling behind: poor status, low salaries and inadequate working conditions characterise perceptions of teachers in numerous countries, deterring many from entering the profession, and there are strong critiques of the one-dimensional, didactic approach to pedagogic practice. Despite this, millions of teachers are dedicated to educating a newly enfranchised generation of learners.

Teacher Education and the Challenge of Development is co-written by experts working across a wide range of developing country situations. It provides a unique overview of the crisis surrounding the provision of high-quality teachers in the developing world, and how these teachers are crucial to the alleviation of poverty. The book explores existing policy structures and identifies the global pressures on teaching, which are particularly acute in developing economies.

In summarising the key policy and research issues and analysing innovative approaches to teacher supply, retention and education, this book:

- establishes an overview and conceptual analysis of the challenge to extend and improve the teaching force in developing contexts;
- sets out and analyses the quantitative and qualitative evidence around teacher contexts and conditions;
- provides a series of national studies that analyse the context of teachers and the policies being pursued to improve the number and quality of teachers;
- looks at a range of significant issues that could contribute to the reformulation and reform of teacher policies;
- provides an overarching analysis of the nature and challenges of teaching and the possible interventions or solutions, in a form accessible to policy and research communities.

This book will be of interest to educationalists and researchers in education, teachers, policy makers and students of development courses at both undergraduate and postgraduate levels.

Bob Moon has published extensively in the fields of curriculum, teacher education, school reform and international education. Over the last two decades he has had direct experience of leading major projects in the field of teacher education, most notably in Sub-Saharan Africa. He has also acted as an advisor to many national governments and international organisations such as COL, DfID, UNESCO, UNICEF and the World Bank.

Education, poverty and international development series

Series Editors

Madeleine Arnot and Christopher Colclough
*Centre for Education and International Development,
University of Cambridge, UK*

This series of research-based monographs contributes to global debates about how to achieve education for all. A major set of questions faced by national governments and education providers concerns how the contributions made by education to reducing global poverty, encouraging greater social stability and equity, and ensuring the development of individual capability and wellbeing can be strengthened. Focusing on the contributions that research can make to these global agendas, this series aims to provide new knowledge and new perspectives on the relationships between education, poverty and international development. It offers alternative theoretical and methodological frameworks for the study of developing-country education systems, in the context of national cultures and ambitious global agendas. It aims to identify the key policy challenges associated with addressing social inequalities, uneven social and economic development, and the opportunities to promote democratic and effective educational change.

The series brings together researchers from the fields of anthropology, economics, development studies, educational studies, politics, international relations and sociology. It includes work by some of the most distinguished writers in the fields of education and development, along with new authors working on important empirical projects. The series contributes significant insights on the linkages between education, economy and society, based on interdisciplinary, international and national studies.

Selected volumes will include critical syntheses of existing research and policy, work using innovative research methodologies, and in-depth evaluations of major policy developments. Some studies will address topics relevant to poverty alleviation, national and international policy-making and aid, while others will be anthropological or sociological investigations of how education functions within local communities, for households living in poverty or for particular socially marginalised groups. In particular, the series will feature sharp, critical studies that are intended to have a strategic influence on the thinking of academics and policy-makers.

Education Outcomes and Poverty

A reassessment
Edited by Christopher Colclough

Forthcoming titles

Education Quality and Social Justice in the South
Challenges for policy, practice and research
Edited by Leon Tikly and Angeline Barrett

Learner-centred Pedagogy
Education for democracy and development
Michele Schweisfurth

**Professional Education, Capabilities and Contributions
to the Public Good**
The role of universities in promoting human development
Edited by Melanie Walker and Monica McLean

Nomads, Development and the Challenges of Education
Caroline Dyer

Gender, Education and Poverty
The politics of policy implementation
Edited by Elaine Unterhalter, Jenni Karlsson and Amy North

Teacher Education and the Challenge of Development
A global analysis
Edited by Bob Moon

Teacher Education and the Challenge of Development
A global analysis

Edited by
Bob Moon

LONDON AND NEW YORK

First published 2013
by Routledge
2 Park Square, Milton Park, Abingdon, Oxfordshire OX14 4RN

Simultaneously published in the USA and Canada
by Routledge
711 Third Avenue, New York, NY 10017

First issued in paperback 2014

Routledge is an imprint of the Taylor & Francis Group, an informa business

© 2013 Bob Moon

The right of the editor to be identified as the author of the editorial
material, and of the authors for their individual chapters, has been
asserted in accordance with sections 77 and 78 of the
Copyright, Designs and Patents Act 1988.

All rights reserved. No part of this book may be reprinted or reproduced
or utilised in any form or by any electronic, mechanical, or other means,
now known or hereafter invented, including photocopying and recording,
or in any information storage or retrieval system, without permission in
writing from the publishers.

Trademark notice: Product or corporate names may be trademarks or
registered trademarks, and are used only for identification and
explanation without intent to infringe.

British Library Cataloguing in Publication Data
A catalogue record for this book is available from the British Library

Library of Congress Cataloging in Publication Data
Teacher education and the challenge of development : a global analysis /
edited by Bob Moon.
    p. cm. – (Education, poverty, and international development)
    Includes index.
    1. Teachers–Training of–Developing countries. 2. Teaching–Developing
    countries. 3. Economic development–Effect of education on–
    Developing countries. I. Moon, Bob, 1945–
    LB1727.D44T37 2012
    370.71'1091724–dc23
    2012013212

ISBN: 978–0–415–60071–2 (hbk)
ISBN: 978-1-138-79315-6 (pbk)

Typeset in Galliard
by Swales & Willis Ltd, Exeter, Devon

This book is dedicated to the memory of Liz Bird
1958–2010

Contents

Notes on contributors	xii
Preface	xiv
Acknowledgements	xvi

SECTION 1
International dilemmas in teacher education and development | 1

Introduction | 3

1 **Teachers and the development agenda: an introduction** | 5
NHLANGANISO DLADLA AND BOB MOON

2 **The context for teacher education in developing countries** | 19
LIZ BIRD, BOB MOON AND ANNE STOREY

3 **A Sisyphean complex? Economic and cost constraints in filling teacher quantity and quality gaps** | 32
LEE E. NORDSTRUM

SECTION 2
Addressing the teacher challenge in large population countries | 51

Introduction | 53

4 **China: strengthening the quality of teacher education in rural communities** | 55
YAN HANBING AND BOB MCCORMICK

x *Contents*

5 **India: committing to change** 76
FRANK BANKS AND PREMAKUMARI DHERAM

6 **Nigeria: balancing federal and local initiatives** 91
MOHAMMED IBN JUNAID AND BOB MOON

7 **Brazil: building national regulatory frameworks** 101
BOB MOON AND FREDA WOLFENDEN

SECTION 3
Teacher quality and good quality teaching 111

Introduction 113

8 **Professional development and female teacher morale in rural communities** 115
ALISON BUCKLER AND AMANI IBRAHIM ABDEL GAFAR

9 **Investigating teacher capabilities in Tanzanian primary schools** 129
SHARON TAO

10 **The lived experiences of women teachers in Karachi** 150
JACKIE KIRK

11 **How teachers' pedagogic practice influences learner achievements: a study from the Punjab, Pakistan** 164
MONAZZA ASLAM AND GEETA KINGDON

12 **Pedagogical renewal and teacher development in Sub-Saharan Africa: challenges and promising paths** 183
MARTIAL DEMBÉLÉ AND BÉ-RAMMAJ MIARO-II

SECTION 4
New strategies for teacher education and teacher development 197

Introduction 199

Contents xi

13 New modes of teacher pre-service training and professional development 201
JOPHUS ANAMUAH-MENSAH, FRANK BANKS, BOB MOON AND
FREDA WOLFENDEN

14 The 'new' new technology: exploiting the potential of mobile communications and open educational resources 212
TOM POWER

15 Reorientating the agenda around teacher education and development 227
BOB MOON AND ABDURRAHMAN UMAR

References 239
Index 263

Contributors

Jophus Anamuah-Mensah, formerly Vice Chancellor, University of Education, Winneba, Ghana.

Monazza Aslam, Research Associate, Centre for the Study of African Economies, University of Oxford and Visiting Research Associate, Institute of Education, University of London, UK.

Frank Banks, Professor of Teacher Education, Faculty of Education and Language Studies, The Open University (UK).

Liz Bird, formerly Senior Lecturer and Head of Education, Faculty of Education and Language Studies, The Open University (UK).

Alison Buckler, formerly Research Assistant, Teacher Education in Sub Saharan Africa (TESSA) Programme, The Open University (UK).

Martial Dembélé, Associate Professor, Faculty of Education, Université de Montreal, Canada.

Premakumari Dheram, Professor, School of English Language Education, English and Foreign Languages University (formerly CIEFL), Hyderabad, India.

Nhlanganiso Dladla, formerly Dean of Education, University of Fort Hare, Eastern Cape, South Africa.

Yan Hanbing, Associate Professor, Vice-Dean of Distance Education College, East China Normal University, China.

Amani Ibrahim Abdel Gafar, Lecturer, The Open University of Sudan, Sudan.

Mohammed Ibn Junaid, Professor and Executive Secretary, National Commission for Colleges of Education, Nigeria.

Geeta Kingdon, Professor of Education Economics and International Development, Institute of Education, London, UK.

Jackie Kirk, formerly Adjunct Professor of Education, McGill University, Canada.

Contributors xiii

Bob McCormick, Emeritus Professor of Education, The Open University (UK).

Bob Moon, Emeritus Professor of Education, The Open University (UK).

Lee E. Nordstrum is a research consultant based in Geneva, Switzerland.

Tom Power, Senior Lecturer in Education, Faculty of Education and Language Studies, The Open University (UK).

Bé-Rammaj Miaro-II is an Education Consultant based in Canada.

Anne Storey, formerly Senior Lecturer, Faculty of Education and Language Studies, The Open University (UK).

Sharon Tao is a doctoral student at the Institute of Education, London.

Abdurrahman Umar, Education Specialist, Teacher Education, Commonwealth of Learning, Vancouver, Canada.

Freda Wolfenden, Senior Lecturer and Associate Dean, Faculty of Education and Language Studies, The Open University (UK).

Preface

This book originated in the formal and informal networks that have developed across a range of research and development projects concerned with teacher education. Most have been carried out in developing countries with low and middle income economies. Many have involved international organisations such as COL, DFID, UNESCO, UNICEF and the World Bank. The book is primarily concerned with teachers in the primary and secondary phases of government funded schooling, although many of the issues discussed are relevant to teacher provision in the private sector and in other phases of education (pre-school, vocational, for example).

The views presented here are those of the individual authors. There are, however, some key issues that have been the subject of discussion over a number of years between many of the contributors. Of particular importance, in the context of this book and the series 'Education, Poverty and International Development', is the idea that the research and development agenda around teacher education must explore new modes of and approaches to provision. The sheer scale of expansion to meet Education for All (EFA) targets and the development of secondary education has, and is, putting enormous pressure on traditional modes of educating and training teachers. Such pressures will continue for the foreseeable future and well beyond current policy planning timescales. Any new agenda will also have to engage with the issue of the quality of teachers and, in particular, the impact this can have on the life chances of the millions of children experiencing schooling denied to their parents and grandparents.

These ideas are explored more fully in Chapter 1 but are mentioned here because it is this sort of analysis that has fostered the networks from which contributors have been drawn. The Open University (OU) in the UK has been playing a particular role in fostering these networks for many years. The university was established in the late 1960s. Not many people are aware that the founding policy paper for the university explicitly set out a role that included a contribution to international development. The Open University has been involved in the creation of 'Open University' type institutions in many parts of the world. Over the last two decades the Open University has given special attention to programmes for education and health professionals and this is now a priority in the university's international work co-ordinated through the International Development Office.

Preface xv

Teacher education has been a particular focus. The Teacher Education in Sub Saharan Africa (TESSA) programme, extending over eleven countries (www.tessafrica.net), has helped build the networks from which some of the contributors of this book are drawn, as has the Bangladesh-based English in Action programme (www.eiabd.com/eia/). Both are large scale initiatives. A number of smaller projects, such as the Digital Education Enhancement Project (DEEP), which was one of the first research initiatives to investigate the potential of mobile technologies for teacher education, have also provided a stimulus to the ideas in a number of the chapters. The Research Group on International Development in Teacher Education (RITES), part of the OU's Centre for Research in Education and Education Technology (CREET), has provided the research base to these sorts of activities.

The Open University projects and programmes have provided the stimulus to some of the rethinking in this book, but a wealth of other research and the wider literature around teacher development is drawn on. The information and analysis in successive UNESCO Global Monitoring Reports, and the University of Sussex's MUSTER study, for example, have been of particular importance. The success of the global commitment to educate all children depends crucially on teachers. This book is written as a contribution to the ongoing debate around teacher development and, in particular, the implications for future policy and research.

Acknowledgements

The Research Group on International Development in Teacher Education (part of the UK Open University Centre for Research in Education and Educational Technology) has, over the last two decades, provided the basis upon which the debates and networks represented in much of this book are based. The book is dedicated to Liz Bird, formerly Head of Education at the Open University, who died in a road accident shortly after helping draft Chapter 2. Successive Vice-Chancellors of the Open University have supported, and given priority to, the role of the university in fostering international development in teacher education. Acknowledgement of the support of Sir John Daniel, Brenda Gourley and Martin Bean is given here.

Acknowledgement is given to Elsevier for permission to use the material which forms the basis of Chapter 11, and Chicago University Press for permission to reprint Chapter 10. The author of Chapter 10, Jackie Kirk, formerly Adjunct Professor of Education at McGill University in Canada, was killed when the convoy of aid agency vehicles in which she was travelling in Afghanistan was attacked in August 2008. The Children's Investment Fund, and Peter Colenso in particular, are thanked for permission to use Figures 1.1–1.3 in Chapter 1. Sabine Detzel of UNESCO very kindly gave permission to use the unpublished country survey reports used at meetings of the E9 Ministers of Education in Bali (2008) and Abuja (2010). Dr Hamidou Boukary on behalf of the Association for the Development of Education in Africa (ADEA) gave permission for the use of an original ADEA conference paper as the basis for Chapter 12.

Professor Madeleine Arnot and Professor Chris Colclough, series editors, provided wise guidance in the planning and development of this book. The manuscript was prepared, as skilfully as ever, by Julie Herbert of the Open University.

Section 1

International dilemmas in teacher education and development

Introduction

Teachers are central to the ambition to provide an education for all children. The global commitment to ensure a basic education for all by 2015 has seen a significant expansion of primary education in many countries with a consequent rapid increase in teacher numbers. There has been a parallel mobilisation of international activity around the 2015 target, something unique in education policy. How to give every child a school place is by far the most daunting educational problem faced by the world community. In other aspects of social policy similar challenges exist. In health the campaigns to eradicate malaria and to combat HIV/Aids have been international in terms of politics and research. In education a similar global focus, realised through the UN Millennium Development Goals and UNESCO's Education for All programme, has been more recent but the commitment seems sustained. Other international agencies have universal basic education as a major concern and increasingly, the social and economic pressures to provide universal and equitable access to secondary schooling are becoming part of the discourse. This discourse has also evolved to take in the growing worry about the quality and overall achievements of these newly expanding education systems. The UNESCO 2005 Global Monitoring Report (UNESCO, 2005) provided a strong critique of the issues around quality and highlights teachers central to this concern. The World Bank has created eight policy goals necessary to ensure the improvement of teacher effectiveness (World Bank, 2010a). The UK's Department for International Development has called for the prioritisation of teachers in education development initiatives (DFID, 2010). In this context the way teachers are educated becomes an important part of the education and development agenda.

This first section of the book analyses a number of the assumptions that underpin the present structures of teacher education. Large scale teacher education systems are fairly recent in origin (fifty or sixty years in some countries) although many have longer antecedents that reflect European influences. The capacity of such systems to educate enough teachers to an appropriate level has been the subject of a number of critical reviews and these are examined in Chapter 1. The evidence shows that rich and poor countries share an agenda for teacher development but in developing country contexts the differences between the best and the worst are acute, the extra numbers needed more extreme in scale and the resources

4 Introduction

available to address the problems more limited. The first chapter looks at the relationship between educational achievement and subsequent life chances and draws on a range of studies to show how important teacher characteristics and qualities are to improving pupil achievement. The chapter then identifies a number of key concerns about the organisation of many teacher education systems.

Chapter 2 provides more data on the challenge to find enough teachers and provide them with some form of professional preparation. The chapter also looks at the parallel challenge to retain teachers in the schools and the working conditions they experience. A key argument of this chapter is that teacher education systems could be much more responsive to the present conditions of teachers. The numbers of teachers requiring education and training now exceeds the capacity of many systems. The needs of existing teachers for professional support are urgent if improvements in levels of achievement are to be brought about. And, the chapter suggests, conventional ideas about the curriculum of pre-service preparation and in-service professional development needs to be much more sensitive to the working lives of teachers. Finally Chapter 3 shows how economic and cost issues are strongly constraining the ways in which the 'quantity and quality gaps' can be filled in many developing countries. The chapter draws on a range of studies from different parts of the world to consider what are the main options for addressing these constraints, what positive lessons can be learnt from governments that have undertaken reform, and what seems the most promising way forward. Taken together the three chapters are beginning to highlight key concerns that subsequent chapters return to and which constitute questions for further analysis by those concerned with policy, research and the practice of teacher education.

1 Teachers and the development agenda

An introduction

Nhlanganiso Dladla and Bob Moon

Good teachers stay long in the memory. We define good teachers in a multitude of ways. Good teachers can be humorous, serious, conscientious, charismatic, even self-deprecating. But we can usually recognise them. Commitment, even vocation, are terms that come to mind.

In writing this chapter we thought of the teachers in Samira Makhmalbaf's classic film *Blackboards*. In the brutal mountains of the Iraq–Iran border two nomadic teachers, Reeboir and Said, climb through the bleak landscape to reach children in the remote village communities. Who can forget the opening scenes when the large band of teachers set out, carrying their blackboards on their backs, sometimes using them as shelter, camouflage or even shields from gunfire?

We think also of the teachers in the tent schools of mountainous Lesotho waiting for the bricks and mortar and builders to arrive. We remember the teachers who (working for the Nigerian Nomadic Education Commission) follow the communities who move across the southern Sahara. There are those informal teachers in Chad's 'école spontanée' created by village communities impatient for formal state education to arrive. In Chile, village teachers looking across huge mountain ridges see colleagues a mile or so away who can only be reached in a week. In Bangladesh, teachers staff boat schools. In China, teaching in a rural school obviates military service.

Teachers have an ambiguous status in many communities. Partially looked up to for the traditional respect the word teacher conveys, partially suspect for the realities of contemporary school life. The absent teacher, the late teacher, even the teacher demanding bribes for examination success can dent community confidence in education.

National education systems and national politics can be rough on teachers. The Teacher Service Commission in Kenya, we are told (Transparency International, 2009), is one of that country's most corrupt bodies. Teachers can be in the front line of conflict. Uganda's Lord's Resistance Army, as reported by Human Rights Watch, has allegedly surrounded remote schools on the eastern border of the Democratic Republic of Congo, attacked teachers and marched the children off into captivity and military service. Brendan O'Malley has documented the tribulations of teachers across the globe (O'Malley, 2007). His reports as a Special

6 *N. Dladla and B. Moon*

Representative on Children and Armed Conflict have warned the United Nations that schools, places that should be safe havens for children, have increasingly become the prime target of attacks. In Iraq between 2004 and 2007 seventy-three teachers died through such attacks. In Colombia in the first decade of the century an average of forty-two teachers were murdered each year. UNICEF has been in the forefront of monitoring violence towards teachers and schools. A press release on 23 January 2009 quotes UNICEF's regional director for South Asia, Daniel Toole, as condemning attacks on schools. UNICEF reports that in the period 2007–10 more than 170 schools, particularly girls' schools, had been blown up or burned down in northern Pakistan.

Reports on the problems associated with teachers regularly feature in the local and international press. *The Express Tribune* in Pakistan, for example, gave prominent coverage to a report that suggested that in the province of Balochistan over 5,000 'ghost teachers' were receiving salaries. Thousands of government schools, the report indicated, were receiving government funds but failed to operate at all (*The Express Tribune*, 27 January 2011). In Nigeria, the education commissioner of Kwara state sent 20,000 primary teachers the tests in English and Mathematics given to nine and ten year olds. Less than 10 per cent passed. The Nigerian *Guardian* newspaper commented in an editorial that the Kwara scandal was 'a symptom of a decadent system where favouritism, corruption, compromise, incompetence and the like hold sway' (*The Observer*, 2010).

The Nelson Mandela Foundation research, *Emerging Voices*, describes the commitment of many teachers in rural South Africa. But it also reports the despair of many communities at finding (or receiving) inadequate teachers. A parent is quoted as saying:

> Educators [teachers] came late to school. Sometimes they do not teach. School sometimes breaks early without parents' knowledge. Sometimes the school breaks for educators to do shopping in town. Parents do not have any say in decision making. They [teachers] just do as they wish.
>
> (p.16)

These concerns, of course, raise the whole issue of teacher status and we will return to this later in the chapter. It is, however, important to reflect on the ambiguous status of teachers. Whilst the notion of the village school teacher, the missionary teacher, the 'instituteur' of fabled French republican virtue has acquired folkloric status (and still, we believe, influences community perceptions of what a teacher should 'be' and 'stand for') the doubts about teachers go back a long way.

Charlotte Bronte's heroine, Lucy Snowe, in *Villette*, receives a sharp reminder of her status as she begins to move in society:

> she fixed on me a pair of eyes wide with wonder – almost with dismay. 'Are you a teacher?', cried she. Then having paused on the unpalatable idea, 'Well, I never knew what you were, nor even thought of asking, for me you were always Lucy Snowe'.

Chimamanda Ngozi Adichie, in her short story, *Jumping Monkey Hill*, has one protagonist arguing strongly that it's better to be a writer than 'a dull teacher in Arusha'.

These uncertainties around teachers represent one of the biggest challenges in the quest to improve education systems in the most impoverished parts of the world. The last two decades have seen a unique international movement to expand access to basic education. The World Declaration on Education for All (EFA) proclaimed at Jomtien, Thailand in March 1990, sought an expanded vision and a renewed commitment to ensuring that everyone 'be able to benefit from educational opportunities designed to meet their basic learning needs' (Article 1). The declaration also gave recognition to the importance of the quality of school and other educational provision. 'The focus of basic education must . . . be an actual learning acquisition and outcome, rather than exclusively on enrolment' (Article 4). The significance of teachers for this challenge was recognised in Article 7:

> The recognition of the vital role of both families and teachers is particularly important. In this context the terms and conditions of service of teachers and their status, which constitute a determining factor in the implementation of education for all, must be urgently improved in all countries in line with the joint ILO/UNESCO Recommendation concerning the Status of Teachers (1966).

The 1966 ILO/UNESCO document, nearly fifty years on, has stood the test of time well. It was an attempt at recognising 'the essential role of teachers in educational advancement and the importance of their contribution to the development of . . . modern society'.

The document is explicit in saying that 'Teaching should be regarded as a profession: it is a form of public service which requires of teachers expert knowledge and specialised skills, acquired and maintained through rigorous and continuing study'.

The document sets out the sorts of professional entitlement and responsibility associated with pre-service and professional development programmes. It also stresses that 'the proper status of teachers and due public regard for the profession of teaching are of major importance' for achieving all educational aims.

The Jomtien declaration created the agenda for a range of national and international activities around expanding provision and improving the quality of basic education. But progress was slow and the turn of the century provided a further milestone opportunity to restate commitments. The declaration of the meeting in Dakar, under the auspices of UNESCO and the specification of a series of comparable Millennium Development Goals (MDGs) in 2000 gave renewed and expanded impetus to Jomtien's ambitions.

The Dakar framework for action spoke of the need to 'enhance the status, morale and professionalism of teachers' and in what over the last decade has become a recurrent theme spoke of the importance of harnessing 'new information and communication technologies to help achieve EFA goals'.

8 N. Dladla and B. Moon

The UN's Millennium Development Goals embracing poverty and health and gender issues as well as education had as Goal 2 the achievement of universal primary education by 2015. There is little reference to teachers. Teachers, however, have been the focus of increasing interest and discussion as the debates around achieving Education for All and realising the Millennium Development Goals have evolved. Although a concern with quality was central to the Jomtien declaration the identification of the significance of teachers has only slowly emerged, not the least because of the availability of increasing evidence about the problems of teacher supply, retention, training and status. There are significant problems that appear to jeopardise any meaningful achievement of EFA.

Successive Global Monitoring Reports from UNESCO have focused attention on teachers. The 2005 report 'The Quality Imperative' (UNESCO, 2005) established something of a benchmark in giving prime focus to teacher pedagogic practice as an important determinant of the quality of schooling: 'In many countries, present styles and methods of teaching are not serving children well' (p. 230).

The multi-country 'MUSTER' research programme led by the University of Sussex was more strident in its conclusions (Lewin and Stuart, 2003):

> Teacher education appears to be one of the most conservative parts of many education systems. It seldom is the source of curriculum innovation, theorised pedagogy, or radical reconceptualisations of professional learning. It often lags behind schools in the adoption of new practice and patterns of learning and teaching. This is a signifier that political will and bureaucratic coverage may be needed for the implementation of real changes designed to improve efficiency and effectiveness.
>
> (p. 86)

The MUSTER programme represented a major study and critique of policies and practices towards teacher education. Many of the same researchers returned to the issues raised through the projects initiated under a DFID-funded consortium research programme CREATE (Consortium for Research on Educational Access, Transitions and Equity) which reported in 2011 (CREATE, 2011). The Consortium continued to find concerns about the deployment and quality of teachers. In a twelve-point development programme the recommendations echoed the earlier concerns set out in the MUSTER analysis, which included the need to 'review the teacher education systems and reform to prioritise skills and competences linked to more effective learning: upgrade subject and pedagogic knowledge and skills and consider less emphasis on initial training and more on in-service support' (p. 60).

One observer analysing the growing critique of teacher education policy has quite boldly suggested that 'business as usual' in the structure and process of teacher education systems is just not an option (Birdsall *et al.*, 2005) and the evidence from the MUSTER and CREATE research programmes gives strong support to this contention. (For an earlier country-specific analysis see Zeichner and Dahlstrom, 1999.)

Teachers and the development agenda 9

An interest in the quality of teaching and its consequences for pupil achievement and social and economic development goes beyond the discourse between academics, governments and international agencies. As we have suggested, press coverage frequently picks up the theme. On 9 March 2010, under the headline 'High Illiteracy Rate a Threat to Development', the Tanzanian *Guardian* carried an article by Sinde Ndwasinde, who wrote:

> it is totally unacceptable for a child to go through primary school and at the end of it not be able to write his name. It means there is something wrong. Whatever it is, we definitely need to improve the methods employed in the classroom.

In this context of growing concern there has been national and international responses. Governments have increasingly come to regulate or legislate. Such interventions can sometimes challenge the autonomy enjoyed by universities or colleges of education to set their own quality standards in the education and training of teachers. In South Africa, for example, the Higher Education Quality Committee selected teacher education as one of its priority areas of evaluation. Despite vocal protests from the teacher educator community within higher education, some courses and programmes were deemed inadequate. In other parts of Arica, and in other parts of the world, there has been less determination to take on higher education lobby groups. This phenomenon is not unique to low income countries. A comparative study of teacher education in Europe (Moon, 2003) found that the vast majority of European governments had tried to intervene in higher education to improve the quality of teacher education in the previous two decades.

National intervention can also occur where local, regional state control results in differential teacher education standards. The case studies of Brazil, China, India and Nigeria in this book illustrate this, although other countries (Pakistan, for example) have similar national–regional tensions. And in some situations the traditions of autonomy in higher education and the devolved powers of regional states intermingle in complex responses to attempts to reform, and raise the quality of, teacher education.

Many of the international organisations concerned with the improvement of education in low income countries are giving increased attention to teacher education. UNESCO, for example, launched its Teacher Training in Sub-Saharan Africa (TTISA) initiative in 2006. One of the early TTISA unpublished concept papers was explicit about some of the perceived shortcomings in teacher education:

> It is only now that people are starting to listen to those who saw the shortage of qualified teachers as a major impediment to national development and that national and international authorities are beginning to realise that the achievement of the Millennium Development Goals and the Education for All objectives depends on the training of professionals capable of the long

10   N. Dladla and B. Moon

term effort to promote education effectively, in particular through the training of teachers and managerial staff in the education system.

The UK based organisation, Voluntary Services Overseas, has produced a series of reports on teachers (VSO, 2002, 2007, 2008, 2009):

> In the developing world, a deficit model for understanding teachers' professionalism and status tends to prevail in academic and policy discourse on teachers. In other words, discussion, and to some extent policy interventions tend to focus on the attributes perceived to be lacking in teachers, principally knowledge of a range of pedagogic methods and approaches, subject expertise, professional commitment and work ethic. At the same time the public regard for teachers has deteriorated. Both these trends have developed in the recognition that teachers do not receive the conditions and support to enable teaching to take place, much less learning.
>
> (VSO, 2002, p. 14)

The UK's Department for International Development has recently (DfID, 2010) called for the prioritisation of teachers and teaching: 'bringing together the conditions for quality only bear fruit when interventions reach into classrooms, and impact on teaching – which requires above all a focus on teacher practice and pedagogy' (p. 30).

Many of the critiques of the current policy contexts around teachers have focused on primary teachers and the achievement of EFA and MDG targets. Similar analyses, however, are increasingly focusing on the growing secondary school sector. A World Bank study (Mulkeen *et al.*, 2007) has demonstrated that in many parts of Africa, the demand for secondary school teachers substantially exceeds the supply due to factors such as bottlenecks in the teacher preparation system, and perceived unattractive conditions of service. In 2011 the World Bank, recognising the significance of teachers to the development agenda, established an information base (SABER-Teachers) which seeks to accumulate data and research around eight core teacher policy goals.

The eight goals were selected because they are related to either student or teacher performance, they are priorities for resource allocation and they are actionable, that is government policies can make a difference. SABER, which stands for System Assessment and Benchmarking for Education Results, is part of the World Bank's focus, at least over the coming decade, on learning and the need to address the low levels of attainment in many developing countries (World Bank, 2010a):

> For too many students . . . more schooling has not resulted in more knowledge and skills. The results of substantial resources spent on education have been disappointing in terms of outcomes . . . Several studies illustrate the seriousness of the learning challenge. More than 30 per cent of Malian youths aged 15–19, who completed six years of schooling could not read a simple sentence. The same was true of 50 per cent of Kenyan youths.
>
> (pp. 6–7)

Teachers and the development agenda 11

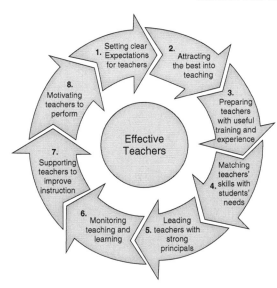

1. Setting clear expectations for teachers
2. Attracting the best into teaching
3. Preparing teachers with useful training and experience
4. Matching teachers' skills with students' needs
5. Leading teachers with strong principals
6. Monitoring teaching and learning
7. Supporting teachers to improve instruction
8. Motivating teachers to perform

Figure 1.1 The World Bank eight core teacher policy goals

UNICEF has a particular role in supporting education during emergencies and in post-crisis transitions. Teacher training has been identified as a concern and weakness in these contexts (UNICEF, 2010): 'Teacher training is a key element of an effective emergency response and perhaps even more crucial in post-crises and transition contexts. However, the relevance and effectiveness of teacher training (in such contexts) was inconsistent' (p. 41). These issues are also addressed in a recent analysis of the way children are educated in conflict zones (Mundy and Dryden Peterson, 2011).

The continuing critiques of the quality of teacher education and the perceived slowness to change is leading some economists to challenge the investment in EFA. Elizabeth Caucutt and Krishna Kumar (Caucutt and Kumar, 2007) argue that alternatives to universal primary education may deliver faster alleviation of poverty whilst educational attainment is so poor:

> our findings indicate that the idea of universality may have been oversold, especially in the context of SSA. At the current stage of development of these economies, and the continued low quality of their educational systems likely to prevail in the near future, policies that insist on full enrolment need not be welfare improving. Policy debates therefore need to focus on improving school infrastructure and quality as much as increasing enrolment.
>
> (p. 296)

If policy responses to this challenge are slow, evidence still mounts that teachers do matter and can make a difference. This is taking different forms. For example, the Global Monitoring Report for 2005 reports evidence that pupil attainment

12   N. Dladla and B. Moon

improves the better qualified the teacher. Other evidence indicates that it is the way the teacher teaches rather than years of experience or qualification levels that matters. Monazza Aslam and Geeta Kingdon formerly of the Centre for the Study of African Economies at the University of Oxford, suggest that improving weak teaching may be one of the most effective ways of raising pupil achievement (Aslam and Kingdon, 2007). In a study of teachers in government and private schools in the Punjab they looked not only at teachers' qualification levels but also at what they term 'process variables', that is the teaching strategies used. The findings suggest that the way teachers teach is more significant than fixed characteristics such as qualifications. Although cautious in presenting the findings they suggest that: 'the usually un-measured teaching "process" variables impact student achievement strongly – lesson planning, involving students by asking questions during class and quizzing them on past material, all substantially benefit pupil learning' (p. 23).

Albert Park and Emily Hannum have also (Park and Hannum, 2002) explored within-school variation in teacher and pupil attainment in Maths and Language. The study was carried out in the rural Gransu district in northwest China. They found that the way teachers taught made a difference. As with Aslam and Kingdon they acknowledge the problems that can go with establishing such linkages. They point to omitted variables and measurement difficulties as the major obstacles in this sort of work. But in this study they 'cautiously infer that much of the variation in test scores (at least about one fourth) is likely due to teacher differences'.

There is, therefore, evidence for a link between teacher quality and attainment. Which variables within the quality concept are most significant, however, prove more difficult to pin down (Glewwe and Kremer, 2005). But it does appear that the way a teacher teaches is more significant than experience or level of qualification.

These findings raise questions about the priorities and resourcing of existing systems of teacher education. In most countries pre-service (with an expansive infrastructure of campuses and staffing) accounts for the vast majority of teacher education expenditure. Yet it would seem that investment in effective professional development programmes for existing teachers is likely to reap the most reward in raising levels of attainment. The imperative to raise standards is backed by growing evidence that establishes a further link between teaching and attainment to social and economic outcomes. The 2005 Global Monitoring Report pointed to the link between the quality of the school experience and social and economic factors: 'years of education and acquisitions of cognitive skills – particularly the core skills of literacy and numeracy – have economic and social pay-offs as regards income enhancement, improved productivity . . . and strengthened efficiency of household behaviour and family life' (p. 43).

Data from internationally benchmarked tests (such as PISA, TIMMS) now goes back over a considerable period of time. This is allowing researchers to look even more analytically at the link between learning outcomes and the relationship with economic growth. Drawing on this data Hanushek and Woessman (2007) have demonstated a firm correlation between average student learning levels and long-term economic growth. A country with average test performance one standard deviation higher than another will have enjoyed a 2 per cent higher average annual growth rate in GDP over the period 1960–2000. This research suggests strongly that it is the quality of learning outcomes rather than the length of time in school that correlates with economic gains. Such findings indicate just how significant improving teacher quality could be in meeting the challenge of poverty alleviation.

In 2008 the report *Education for All by 2015. Will we make it?* also drew on recent research to suggest that:

> recent studies have examined the economic impact of the *quality* of education (using aggregate pupil test scores, mainly in mathematics and language), not just quantitative expansion: some studies find that measures of quality have a stronger association with economic growth than measures of quantity.
>
> (p. 189)

The Children's Investment Fund Foundation (2009) has carried out an extensive review of evidence on the social and economic consequences of raising educational achievement. Figures 1.2–1.4 summarise this analysis and the sources from which it is drawn.

As the Children's Investment Fund analysis shows, the benefits of higher levels of educational achievement go beyond economic gains. Gender mobility, changing demographic patterns and marked improvements in health and nutrition are

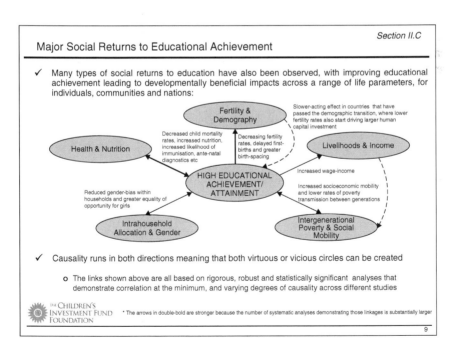

Figure 1.2 Major social returns to educational achievement

Figure 1.3 Strong linkages with other priority impact areas

Figure 1.4 Educational achievement, earnings and economic growth

significantly linked to educational outcomes. Priority areas for development such as child survival also point to the value of education, even where the levels of achievement do not stand the scrutiny of international comparisons. However, as Figure 1.4 shows, falling levels of achievement at the primary phase over the last two decades are impacting on economic opportunities.

Across each of the analyses set out in Figures 1.2–1.4 there is a strong linkage between educational achievement and a range of social factors, most notably health, diet and fertility. It is a two-way ongoing process. Higher levels of attainment lead to healthier people, healthier people (especially the children of more educated parents) go on to achieve even higher levels of achievement. Improving education quality also impacts on earnings, perhaps a 10 per cent increase for every extra year of schooling (Figure 1.4). Teachers, and their education, are central to this process.

The focus on teachers, teacher quality and teacher education goes with the grain on some recent theorising around education and development, in particular the work of Amartya Sen and the concept of capabilities which offers a distinct lens through which teacher quality can be conceptualised.

The capability approach appears particularly relevant to the issue of teacher education because so many issues go beyond quantitative measures and are linked more closely to well being and agency – a point made by Sharon Tao (Tao, 2009) in a study of the way in which school improvement strategies can be understood within a capability model. The capability approach also offers the opportunity to bridge the rather separate research fields of education and development. Unterhalter and Walker (2007) suggest that:

> what is new about the capability approach is that it combines a normative idea with consideration of how to link this with practice, not just in education, but in a wide range of political, economic and social fields that bear on education.
>
> (p. 239)

In the context of teachers this perspective makes it possible to look beyond particular issues and problems and locate analysis in a wider conceptual framework of the teachers' role. Research around teachers in low income countries has, as Buckler (2011) has indicated, been dominated by largely descriptive studies of specific issues such as qualifications, absenteeism, HIV/Aids. These often emphasise the problematic nature of the teacher's life and work. As Buckler points out, the prism through which teachers are understood can be relentlessly negative, even in contexts in which the data suggests a majority of teachers received positive attitudes to their role. In looking particularly at rural areas Buckler suggests:

> there is a need for policy makers in rural education to know more about these rural teachers' lives and have a better understanding of personal, environmental and social contexts that impact on their ability to acquire new qualifications and skills. While there is much to be found in the literature about rural

teaching environments, there is very little written about teachers' perceptions of how these environments impact on their teaching and learning.

(p. 2)

We believe that any improvements in the education of teachers requires sensitivity to the context in which teachers live and work. Change also requires questioning the assumptions and accepted wisdoms through which policies and practices are formulated. But, as Lewin (2002 and 2011) has suggested, policy structures around teachers and teacher education are often too weak to do anything other than replicate conventional modes of working. There are a number of issues that now make the lack of change untenable. We suggest five major concerns.

The first is the issue of numbers. We make the very simple assertion, repeated for more than a decade now (Moon, 2000), that the institutions created in the twentieth century to train teachers will be insufficient to meet the needs of the present century. In country after country the shortfall between capacity and need can be extreme. In India one million extra teachers are needed in the coming five years. In Indian states like Bihar and Orissa, high population states where poverty is most prevalent, the shortfall between training capacity and need is considerable. Inevitably these are the states with the highest proportion of unqualified teachers.

So we raise the question that if the traditional institutional structures for educating and training teachers cannot cope, what alternatives can be put in place? And here we have a further concern around the issue of numbers. Most policy systems focus on pre-service qualifications or upgrading qualifications. Despite the strong rhetoric around the need for a career-long continuing professional development programme for teachers, forms of provision are, almost always, inadequate and frequently non-existent. If inroads are to be quickly made into the problems of low achievement, then action on this front seems essential. It follows that most education and training will be based in the school with significant implications for modes and forms of education and training.

A second concern is the issue of rurality and, in particular, the conditions of women teachers in rural areas. In many countries on almost all measures, teachers in rural areas experience larger classes, lower levels of resourcing and poorer living conditions than those in towns and cities. And, with a few national exceptions, the majority of these teachers are women. Attempts to deploy teachers to rural communities are often met with resistance and hence the recruitment of local, mostly female, unqualified teachers. We believe that an analysis of the lives of female teachers in rural communities offers important insights into ways of building new forms of education and training.

A third concern is where the locum of responsibility for teachers lies. In almost all countries this involves some balance between central and regional authorities. In Nigeria, for example, provincial state governments have significant responsibilities, defining different entry qualification levels to teaching, different scaling levels and with sometimes markedly contrasting approaches to deployment and

Teachers and the development agenda 17

teacher development. The routinely collated national statistics that inform international debate and education progress often mask significant internal variations across a range of quality indicators.

We believe that the governance associated with central and local control is a major issue impacting on policies towards teachers and teacher education. And we are aware that the local has many different dimensions to it. Some of the states in Nigeria (as also, for example, in India and Pakistan) have populations larger than those of many countries. Two or three levels of governance lead to the administrative level where teachers are regularly paid and training provided. How these different levels interact and interrelate can be a crucial part of a teacher's life.

A fourth issue relates to the extent to which the discourse around teachers is capturing and synthesising the innovations, research and experimentation around teacher supply, retention, education and training. Despite the formidable challenges, well grounded attempts are being made, sometimes with associated evaluation data, to introduce new policies and practices. There are attempts to collect such information. The Global Monitoring Reports for UNESCO have been doing this for more than a decade although the changing profile of teacher need is not addressed as systematically as EFA targets.

We are particularly concerned that the evidence about the importance of the practical preparation of teachers, the development of key skills and knowledge needed in the classroom, are not leading to substantive changes in the curriculum of teacher education. The evidence for, and rhetoric around, the need for reforming what teachers are taught goes back at least two decades and yet, with the exception of some notable experimental projects, the institutional structure and systems responsible for training teachers seem very slow to change.

Our fifth premise relates to community and values. Teaching, as a vocation, a profession of sorts, has invariably been associated with moral and social advancement. Millions of teachers in low income countries work in communities that exist in or on the edge of poverty. The rhetoric of national and international discourse sees education as a major means of poverty alleviation. Yet teachers generally and specifically in their education and training rarely, if ever, discuss or consider this. These concerns seem external to the everyday life of a teacher and yet may be at the heart of reforming teacher education. Paulo Freire published his seminal *Pedagogy of the Oppressed* (Freire, 1970) over forty years ago. His books and his ideas rarely feature in teacher education and training programmes today. Yet his concern with the disadvantaged and the ways that education in general and pedagogic practice in particular can serve the cause of social justice resonate with the vast majority of the world's teachers. Freire, however, was clear that pedagogy was not something you did to people but rather a process worked through with them. He used the phrase pedagogy of the oppressed to refer to: 'a pedagogy which must be forged within, not for, the oppressed (whether individuals or peoples) in the incessant struggle to regain their humanity' (p. 36).

More recently Freire articulated his vision for teachers further (Freire and Macedo, 1999):

18   *N. Dladla and B. Moon*

> Teachers who engage in educational practice without curiosity, allowing their students to avoid engagement with critical readings, are not involved in dialogue as a process of learning and knowing. They are involved instead, in a conversation without the ability to turn the shared experience and stories into knowledge . . . one of the difficulties often confronted by a teacher in assuming an epistemological curious posture is that, at certain moments, the educatory falls prey to the bureaucratisation of the mind, becoming a pre-methodologist . . . it is not easy to be a dialogical teacher because it entails a lot of work.
>
> (pp. 51–2)

We believe that teacher education needs to embrace the development agenda more fully. It is difficult to conceive of who, other than teachers, can act as the guardian of children's rights and entitlement to education in many of the developing world economies. And it is difficult to disassociate the social justice perspective of development from the challenge to raise educational standards.

There is substantive evidence that existing investments in teacher education are failing to achieve the qualitative reforms expected in most countries. At a recent national conference in India, held in the state of Orissa, the Chairperson of the Indian Council for Teacher Education, Professor Md Akhtar Sidique, spoke of the national failure of in-service programmes to improve conditions in schools (*Bhubanestar Sunday Express*, 24 October 2010). Similar observations could be made across the range of national systems. It is our argument that the cultures of policy development and practice that characterise most teacher education systems need to reflect changed values and new purposes if ambitious goals for improving educational opportunities and educational achievement are to be realised.

This book seeks to critically analyse the key elements of teacher policy and practice, particularly teacher education. The views presented are those of the individual authors who come from a variety of cultural and geographical contexts. Many, however, have worked together on teacher development projects and have come to share some key ideas and approaches. These include the need to strengthen, within the development community, recognition of the role and significance of teachers. As this chapter suggests, there is now considerable evidence that children's life chances, socially and economically, are enormously advantaged if they do well at school and this feeds through to wider issues of social well being and economic prosperity. One central argument shared by all the contributors is that a child's school success, especially where wider informal community support is scarce, depends crucially on how well teachers teach. The quality of teacher education and training, therefore, becomes fundamental to the development process. The chapters that follow explore the assumptions and understandings that inform this process. They also provide evidence of the directions that the reforms of policies and practices might follow.

2 The context for teacher education in developing countries

Liz Bird, Bob Moon and Anne Storey

There are significant challenges to the creation of effective teacher education systems in the developing world. These vary in nature and scale from one context to another. There are, however, many issues that are shared and these have generated analyses over time from international organisations and through a range of research-based publications. The annual Education for All (EFA) Global Monitoring Reports (GMRs), for example, have given particular attention to teachers and made repeated suggestions for system reform in the structure, styles and content of teacher education. This chapter will look at the suggestions and comments made in the reports as well as scrutinising the wider literature, including a number of unpublished national reports that have provided the background to international meetings. In doing this, we want to suggest that the conceptualisation, planning and practices of teacher education will need to become more sensitive to the contextual challenges faced by policy makers, teacher educators and, most importantly, the teachers themselves. School systems have expanded rapidly, and will continue to do so for the foreseeable future, and yet the process of building policies and practices to recruit, educate and retain sufficient teachers struggles to keep pace.

The problems faced by existing teacher education systems in keeping up with demand has been identified for some time (Moon, 2000; Lewin and Stuart, 2003). India, for example, needs a million more teachers in the next five years with the training capacity as most states are unable to cope. In Bihar, for example, where 300,000 teachers are needed, the training college annual capacity is 7,500. Much of the debate has focused on the capacity of pre-service education and training, the major structural and institutional dimension of existing systems, to meet demand. In this chapter we want to look more broadly than this and suggest that initial pre-service training can only be one element in the rethinking and reform of teacher education. There has to be, we argue, some accommodation between preparation for teaching and career-long professional development, and that the context in which teachers work today points inexorably towards the need for new, restructured forms of provision that are not framed by existing institutional and resource structures. We also suggest that any reform needs to have a well-rooted understanding of the actual – rather than idealised – conditions under which teachers live and work. Subsequent chapters in the book look at this

20   *L. Bird* et al.

in some detail. The central concern of this chapter is teachers in primary and secondary schools, although it is important to note that similar challenges are faced in preschool provision, and in vocational and higher education.

In looking at the context for teacher education we consider teacher supply, teacher retention, teachers' working conditions and effectiveness, and policy formulation for professional development. These four concerns provide the structure to the chapter.

Teacher supply

The challenge to educate and train the additional teachers worldwide needed to achieve Education for All (EFA) is prodigious. The 2011 UNESCO EFA Global Monitoring Report (UNESCO, 2011a) estimates that an additional 1.9 million teachers are required by 2015. More than half of these are required in Sub-Saharan Africa where, in many countries, pupil-teacher ratios are high. In this region alone it is estimated that a third of all primary teachers are unqualified or under-qualified, a percentage that adds a further million teachers to those needing pre-service training. At a conservative estimate, at least two million unqualified or under-qualified teachers are working in the primary school systems of developing countries (UNESCO, 2006). A similar pattern is emerging from data on expanding secondary school systems (Mulkeen *et al.*, 2007).

The most consistent monitor of the teacher supply needed to achieve EFA has come from successive UNESCO EFA Global Monitoring Reports. These use a wide range of evidence, including data from the UNESCO Institute of Statistics. The 2005 report, which took quality as a major theme, gives particular attention to the importance of teachers to the EFA process. The report provides a critique of existing programmes of teacher education and training and sets out evidence to suggest that much existing pre-service training fails to provide new teachers with the necessary skills and knowledge to work effectively. Subsequent reports return to the number and quality of teachers. The 2006 report (UNESCO, 2005) is explicit in saying: 'Teacher numbers are generally too low and PTR's generally too high in the countries furthest from attaining universal primary education . . . a major teacher shortage is looming' (p. 87). The report goes on to highlight the large numbers of primary teachers with inadequate academic qualifications who lack pedagogic training, particularly in Sub-Saharan Africa and South and West Asia. The 2007 report (UNESCO, 2006) describes teacher supply and quality as 'seriously inadequate' (p. 79), the 2008 report (UNESCO, 2007) talks of 'serious teacher shortages' (p. 78) and, as with other GMRs, calls for special attention to be paid to the impact of HIV/AIDS on teacher supply. The 2009 report (UNESCO, 2008) reiterates concerns about teacher recruitment:

> Excessive PTR's, shortages of trained teachers and questions about teacher skills point to wide ranging problems in governance. Teacher shortages often result from inadequate investment in education and questionable incentive structures for teacher recruitment and retention. At the primary level, in

Teacher education in developing countries 21

particular, teacher training is often fragmented and incomplete, in some cases non existent.

(p. 119)

The 2010 report (UNESCO, 2010a) notes that 'teacher shortages remain a serious concern' (p. 115) and this is repeated in 2011 (UNESCO, 2011a): 'Sustained progress in education quality depends on making sure that all schools have sufficient teachers, that the teachers are properly trained and supported, and that they are motivated. None of these conditions is currently being met' (p. 83).

It is clear, therefore, that both the number of teachers and their levels of professional expertise are persistent concerns globally and that national governments have also come to recognise the problem. Teachers, for example, were the focus of a 2008 ministerial meeting in Bali, Indonesia, of the E9 countries.[1] In preparation for that meeting, UNESCO designed a survey that was completed by each national ministry. Some of these surveys were updated for a subsequent ministerial meeting held in Abuja, Nigeria, in 2010.[2] We have drawn on some of these surveys to further illustrate the contemporary situation around teacher supply and related issues.

All the E9 countries surveyed expressed concern about providing adequate numbers of teachers. Two indicators are shown in Table 2.1. The Net Enrolment Ratio (NER) gives the percentage of all children in the appropriate age range who are enrolled in primary school (commonly the 6–11 age range). The Gender Parity Index (GPI) for these enrolled pupils is the ratio of females to males.[3]

The table indicates a range of positions for the E9 countries, with a number of countries having high NER and GPI values within the acceptable 0.97–1.03 range. It is clear, however, that even in those countries with high NER values, significant numbers of additional primary teachers will be needed in order to meet Universal Primary Education (UPE) goals. Table 2.2 gives the estimated numbers of additional teachers needed by each country between 2004 and 2015 if goals are to be met. Figures are provided on the basis of different attrition rates (teachers leaving the profession). Even for low rates of attrition, the scale of recruitment needed is very high in every case, with enormously high numbers of teachers needed, in particular, in India.

Analyses of teacher supply over time tend to focus on the primary years. Increasing attention is now being given to the expansion of secondary education. In Sub-Saharan Africa, for example, as EFA provision grows, many countries are experiencing significant demand for both lower and upper secondary teachers (Alvarez *et al.*, 2003). Such a trajectory seems inexorable whilst economies grow and the transition towards more knowledge-based employment structures continues. One recent World Bank study (Mulkeen *et al.*, 2007) presented data which indicated that: 'In many parts of Sub-Saharan Africa the projected demand for secondary school teachers exceeds projected supply, in some cases by substantial amounts' (p. 9). The study goes on to suggest that in subject areas such as mathematics and science teacher shortages are particularly acute, and quotes evidence of very large numbers of unqualified teachers being recruited into the secondary sector.

Table 2.1 Net Enrolment Ratios and Gender Parity Index for E9 countries

	Progress towards UPE and gender parity								
	Bangladesh 2004	*Brazil 2004*	*China 2004*	*Egypt 2005*	*India 2005*	*Indonesia 2005*	*Mexico 2005*	*Nigeria 2005*	*Pakistan 2005*
NER 2004/2005	94%	95%	97%	94%	89%	96%	98%	68%	68%
GPI	1.03	1.00	0.91	0.94	0.93	0.96	1.00	0.88	0.76

Table 2.2 Expected numbers of teachers required between 2004 and 2015 to meet attrition and UPE goals (thousands)

Attrition rate	Bangladesh	Brazil	China	Egypt	India	Indonesia	Mexico	Nigeria	Pakistan
(low 5%)	335	277	908	283	1,612	611	205	NA	453
(medium 6.5%)	398	396	1,714	347	2,109	835	290	NA	536
(high 8%)	461	516	2,520	411	2,606	1,059	375	NA	620

Teacher education in developing countries 23

The scale of the need for additional and better-prepared teachers does suggest that the institutions of teacher education created to meet the needs of the twentieth century are unable, as currently constituted, to meet the demands of the twenty-first. The mathematics just does not 'stack up'. Millions of low qualified people are becoming teachers in primary schools. Teachers with limited subject knowledge are teaching key curriculum subjects in secondary schools. The demand for expansion (policy and consumer led) is likely to be matched by the employment of increasing numbers of teachers who lack the expertise required. It would seem crucial that the policies and structures of teacher education be reframed to take account of this new context.

Some change is taking place. A number of countries are, as successive GMRs have argued since 2005, looking to shorten the forms of pre-service education in order to bring larger numbers into preparatory courses. Most initiatives of this sort, however, are 'bolt-ons' to the dominant model of campus-based initial training and are often fiercely resisted by key stakeholders, such as the teacher trainers themselves or teacher unions, who see such a move as a dilution in standards and another threat to teacher status.

These are complex issues, which we do not seek to resolve in this chapter. We do suggest, however, that the current parallel track process (whereby a proportion of teachers enter the profession after relatively extended periods of training and an increasingly large proportion enter teaching with little if any preparation) is unacceptable, and training models will need to adjust. Such an adjustment, given the resources available in most countries, would inevitably require some realignment of pre-service and in-service provision. Policy systems, however, constrained by the assumptions based on existing arrangements, appear slow in appreciating the implications of these new dynamics around teacher supply.

Teacher retention

The problems of teacher retention are as challenging as those associated with teacher supply, if not more so. In a global review, UNESCO (2006) pointed to the inherent complexity in the management of teaching forces and the need for relevant monitoring data that captures the 'flows of teachers' into and out of and also 'within' the profession.

The problem of retention is not unique to developing country contexts. In the United States and the UK between 30 and 50 per cent of teachers leave within three to five years of entering teaching (Cooper and Alvarado, 2006). In both contexts data on attrition has proved difficult to access (Macdonald, 1999). In most developing country contexts a similar lack of data makes analysis very difficult. Nearly all the reports prepared for the E9 meeting mentioned retention as a major problem. Attrition rates are perceived as high, particularly in remote rural areas. The lack of monitoring systems makes it difficult to differentiate between attrition and migration (that is, teachers moving areas rather than leaving teaching). There is a perception that gaining improved qualifications through upgrading courses contributes to both attrition rates, as teachers use the higher

24   *L. Bird* et al.

qualifications to obtain other forms of employment, and migration rates as teachers move to other sectors (primary to secondary for example).

The balance between attrition and migration is difficult to establish and will vary from one context to another. One study (Bennell and Akyeampong, 2007) found that, in Zambia, one out of every three rural primary teachers and one out of four urban teachers moved job each year. There is strong evidence that it is often the least qualified and least experienced teachers who are posted to rural areas. In Namibia, only 40 per cent of primary teachers in the rural north are qualified, compared to 92 per cent in the capital, Windhoek (Mpokosa and Ndaruhutse, 2008). In Sierra Leone, the difference is even greater, with only 25 per cent of rural primary teachers in the north being qualified, compared with 96 per cent in Freetown, the capital (Bennell, 2004). In Peru, four out of five primary teachers are seeking to move (Fanfani, 2004). Planning professional development programmes and implementing school improvement strategies is extremely difficult in circumstances such as this. Similar issues affect the growing secondary sector, with attrition rates varying from 5 to 30 per cent in different countries. Malawi, for example, with a slow economy, has an 8 per cent rate, whereas in Liberia nearly one in three teachers leaves the profession each year (Mulkeen *et al.*, 2007).

In almost all developing country contexts a combination of factors is creating huge pressures for the school system. Attracting people to teach is difficult, retaining teachers equally so, and areas of most disadvantage (often rural communities) are subject to the greatest pressures. UNICEF estimates that in Uttar Pradesh in India there are 921 rural schools without a single teacher (UNICEF, 2012).

Successive GMRs have indicated the need for a more rigorous longitudinal collection of data. However, this has only materialised in a few countries. The responses from many countries to the E9 survey reinforce this perspective. The survey report from Pakistan, for example, indicated that there is no effective relationship between the supply and demand of teachers at any level of education, with teacher training being carried out without a viable policy and planning framework. India similarly pointed to the need for institutional mechanisms for forecasting long-term and short-term teacher requirements on a disaggregated basis in respect of geographical, phase and subject variables.

The Commission for Africa (2005) identified deficiencies in data as a major stumbling block to policy development in Sub-Saharan Africa:

> the quality of national data systems in many Sub-Saharan countries remains inadequate . . . few if any have the ability to disaggregate urban and rural development statistics. Important social, economic and environmental data – including, for example, data on gender or ethnic group – are often not available or of inadequate quality . . . even where data are available they are often not used in decision making.
>
> (p. 154)

Some countries, as responses to the E9 survey illustrate, have made moves to set up data systems. Brazil began carrying out school and teacher censuses in 2003,

Teacher education in developing countries 25

which have fed into policy decisions. Bangladesh is in the process of establishing a database with the capacity to record the over 300,000 primary teachers in over 80,000 schools. In China, following pilot programmes in Fujian and Guangxi Zhuang, a national system of teacher qualification registration is being introduced for the ten million teachers in primary and junior high schools. Indonesia began introducing a data collection system for teachers called NUPTK (Unique Number for Teachers and Education Personnel) and this, used in conjunction with a dating coding system for schools and pupils, is now part of the policy and planning process. In the post-conflict situation of Sierra Leone, a computerised Records Management Improvement Programme was established in 2005 and extended, in 2010, to include a teacher payroll element, perhaps one of the most significant aspects of data management for teacher policy (UNESCO, 2011a).

There has been little substantive research on the ways in which more accurate data could be collected and used in the development of local and national policies towards educating teachers. In many contexts, for example, the flows and movements of teachers are not factored into professional development programme planning. Few attempts are made to create 'portfolio' type opportunities, which would allow teachers to 'carry' a record of professional progress from one school to another. Where schools can become the focus for improvement strategies, the problems of teacher turnover are rarely considered. Our perception is that the professional development policy process often turns a 'blind eye' to the issue of retention with consequences for the coherence and effectiveness of provision.

Teachers' working conditions and teacher effectiveness

We believe that, alongside analyses of supply and retention it is also important to bring an understanding of teacher working conditions into the planning and practices of teacher education. The teacher with a very large class needs specific pedagogic advice, particularly where resources are limited. Teachers in remote areas distant from in-service training centres need provision that is different from the traditional 'course based' approach. There is some evidence (see, for example, Chapter 10) that female teachers, who may have to work around particular social and cultural community expectations, find access to professional development especially problematic.

There have been many studies around teacher status in developing countries. Voluntary Service Overseas (VSO), for example, has produced successive reports (2002, 2007, 2008, 2009). Other research-based reports explore this issue in some detail (Bennell, 2004; Mulkeen *et al.*, 2007). These provide evidence of a decline in teacher status in almost all parts of the developing world. In part this relates to salary. There are wide variations in remuneration between countries, but in many teachers have seen a decline in salary in real terms, particularly in the primary sector (Colclough *et al.*, 2003). Where salaries are low, teachers may take on additional work which, in turn, impacts on status (Rwanda has a special bank for teachers that provides loans for setting up part-time businesses).

26 *L. Bird* et al.

In many countries, teacher shortages have also led to the employment of contract teachers receiving wages significantly below those earned by qualified teachers. In India, for example, following a decision in 2002 to allow states to use central government grants to employ contract teachers, large numbers of teachers in this category entered the school system – half a million between 2002 and 2004. This recruitment was largely focused on remote, rural areas. In the states of Madhya Pradesh (which accounts for 46 per cent of all contract teachers) and Rajasthan (21 per cent) contract teachers make up half of all teachers in the former and a third in the latter. Their pay averages between one fifth and a half of that received by a civil service teacher (Govinda and Josephine, 2004; UNESCO, 2008). Whilst contract teachers may be the only way of providing schools to some communities, their remuneration is likely to reinforce negative images of teaching as a career.

There is, however, good evidence that pay is not the sole determinant of how teaching is valued. Research in the United States has demonstrated that a broader set of concerns impact on perceptions of status (Hanushek and Rivkin, 2004; Ingersoll, 2004). There is now a well-grounded literature that explores these concerns in low-income countries and these are explored in detail in Section 3 of this book. We want to briefly summarise the major issues, and suggest that the planning of teacher education needs to give far greater attention to the consequences of such issues for the types of provision made.

The first issue is deployment policy and practice, which features in the top two or three concerns raised by teachers, particularly female teachers, after pay (VSO, 2002). The 2005 GMR suggests that the perceived unfairness in teacher deployment is one of the most important reasons to explain why some teachers leave the profession. The report describes problems in Ghana where new teachers were deployed to remote rural areas where they did not have fluency in the language of instruction (Hedges, 2002). The GMR for 2010, looking at the educational needs of deprived areas, repeats the same concerns:

> Recruitment and deployment practices are at the heart of the problem. Many teachers, young women in particular, are understandably reluctant to move to remote areas, especially when they are characterised by high levels of poverty and lack transport, health services and other facilities. Teachers may be similarly reluctant, for career reasons, to serve in what are seen as failing schools. Experienced teachers may use their seniority to get assigned to the smallest classes (often in higher grades) leaving the largest classes to the least experienced or least qualified teachers.
>
> (p. 197)

A number of studies have confirmed the problems associated with deployment practice (Welmond, 2002; Mulkeen, 2006). In some countries, petty corruption around deployment can further erode teacher confidence in the system, as a recent investigation in Kenya revealed (Transparency International, 2009). Deployment to schools where teachers work double shifts can also raise problems, despite the additional remuneration that might be available.

The type of accommodation available to teachers is frequently as much a concern as the area they are deployed to. In looking at policies to achieve EFA, Colclough *et al.* (2003) suggest that, given the harsh conditions in some rural areas, mere persuasion will be insufficient and more direct incentives for teachers to work in remote schools will be required. These might include: 'better provision of teacher housing near to schools, transportation to towns from time to time and financial inducements' (p. 178).

School conditions are also a concern to many teachers. The Seventh All India School Education Survey (2002) found that one in five primary schools were in substandard accommodation, including some in tents or just open spaces, and one in five schools did not have safe drinking water. Less than 50 per cent of schools had urinal or lavatory facilities. The survey also found that thousands of schools had no blackboard.

Schools like this often have the worst pupil-teacher ratios. The failure to recruit sufficient teachers, even unqualified teachers, has led to significant national and regional disparities in pupil-teacher ratios. Progress to reducing class sizes can be seen in Latin America, but in Sub-Saharan Africa and South and West Asia not only has the pupil-teacher ratio gone well above the widely accepted international ceiling of 40:1 (Takala, 2003; World Bank Independent Evaluation Group, 2006) but the ratio of pupils to trained teachers has risen markedly (UNESCO, 2010a). Countries such as Chad, Mozambique and Rwanda have ratios in excess of 60:1 and the data shows marked increases in ratios in all the East African countries (UNESCO, 2008). Significant regional variations exist within such countries, which push some class sizes up to eighty or more.

Teachers, therefore, have important and often justified concerns about working conditions, but there is also increasing critical scrutiny of the way teachers work and their effectiveness in the classroom. In South Africa, for example, the Nelson Mandela Foundation (2005) has documented the decline of community confidence in teachers, particularly in rural areas. Absentee rates of teachers are a concern in many countries, with high levels of absenteeism showing links to low levels of pupil achievement in some regions (van der Berg and Louw, 2007). One quantitative study across a range of countries in different continents reported an overall teacher absentee rate of 19 per cent when research enumerators visited. In parts of India the figure was 25 per cent. The study also showed that between a third and a half of all teachers present in school were not teaching at the time of the enumerator visit (Chadhury *et al.*, 2006).

As more and more developing countries are agreeing to participate in international benchmarking of educational performance, political engagement with the quality of teachers and teaching is likely to increase. This is especially the case in developing countries, where poor attainment and low completion rates can be identified. Rapidly expanding school systems could be expected to show some initial declines but a number of studies have highlighted the extent and persistence of falling standards as problematic. The 2005 GMR, for example, noted the drop in performance of a number of Sub-Saharan countries between the first and second evaluations of the Southern and Eastern African Consortium for

28 *L. Bird* et al.

Monitoring Educational Quality (SACMEQ). Significant disparities exist within as well as between countries, and regional disparities are most acute in developing countries. A study of the mathematics achievement in Orissa and Rajasthan in India found that the difference between the best and worst schools was wider than the differences between most of the countries participating in the TIMSS evaluations (Das and Zajonc, 2008). Such differences raise important issues for improving the quality of teachers, particularly the structure and forms of teacher education.

There is evidence, however, that despite the difficulties there are attempts to address the working conditions of teachers. The E9 country surveys provide evidence of this. A federal regulation introduced in 2008 in Brazil requires that at least 60 per cent of education budgets devolved to states must be used for salaries in the basic education sector of achievement, and this appears to have boosted recruitment and status with a consequent impact on pupil attainment (Bruns *et al.*, 2012). In Pakistan, some local areas have introduced childcare provision to encourage women to carry on teaching. In Indonesia, a national four-stage career development plan is being introduced, including the provision of a mentored induction period. China has established a National Teacher Education Network and some improvements in primary teacher salaries (UNESCO, 2007). In India, a plethora of local incentive schemes have been introduced in different parts of the country. One initiative included the use of simple financial incentive programmes to reduce teacher absenteeism and raise levels of achievement. In a controlled trial, absentee rates in non-incentivised schools averaged 42 per cent, compared to 22 per cent in incentivised schools. Absentee rates of 22 per cent appear high, but in those schools student test performance improved significantly (Duflo and Hanna, 2005).

Incentive schemes focusing on student achievement have also been introduced into a number of Latin American countries. Mexico's Carrera Magisterial (Master Training) Programme has been shown to have a small but significant impact on achievement (McEwan and Santibanez, 2005). The same is true of Chile, which stands out as a country that has made a determined effort to improve the pay and conditions of teachers since the 1990s (Cox, 2003). In particular, the introduction of the Sistema Nacional de Evaluacion de Desempeno de los Establecimientos Educcacionales (National System of School Performance or SNED), which gives bonuses to the teachers in top-performing schools, has been shown to produce modest gains in test scores (Mizala and Romaguera, 2005). In both Mexico and Chile, however, the gains through such incentive systems were specific to small groups of schools and teachers and did not scale up to give system-wide improvements (Lavy, 2007).

The challenge in seeking to improve the quality of teaching is to make overall sense of the different ideas and programmes that attempt to influence the working lives of teachers. It would seem important that teacher education in some form is incorporated into change strategies but this is frequently not the case. Teacher education can provide support as well as development. Later chapters in this book explore the possibilities of conceptualising the teacher's role in terms of capabilities that need nurturing and safeguarding (see Chapter 9) with much more explicit links to ideas about self-esteem and well-being (Gough and McGregor, 2007). Such an approach would have implications for the curriculum and the structure of teacher education. Both, we would argue, need to be rethought if teacher development is to improve the quality of teachers' lives and their effectiveness in the classroom.

Policy formation for the education of teachers

Teachers themselves identify the lack of professional development opportunities as a major concern. There are, as we have identified, acute problems in providing sufficient pre-service training places including for those unqualified teachers already in schools. Successive surveys have also indicated the paucity of in-service support, particularly in the areas of most need, remote rural communities (VSO, 2007, 2008, 2009).

The UNESCO GMRs have tracked this problem. The 2005 report argued that: 'education policy has long put more priority on initial teacher training than continuing in-service education . . . balancing time and money spent on initial training and ongoing professional support is a critical policy question' (pp. 162–3). The 2008 report (UNESCO, 2009) picks up the same theme and argues that lifelong learning structures for teachers and ongoing professional activities are essential for improving professional skills. The 2010 report (UNESCO, 2010a) describes in-service training, which is vital to improving school quality and raising achievement, as poorly developed in many low-income countries. Substantial research programmes have pointed to weaknesses in pre-service training, in particular the lack of relevant and practical training in classroom methods (Lewin and Stuart, 2003). And there is a growing body of research, such as that reported by Monazza Aslam and Geeta Kingdon in Chapter 11, that provides evidence that it is the way teachers teach rather than their qualification level that determines effectiveness in the classroom, a point made in the 2005 GMR:

> What goes on in the classroom, and the impact of the teacher and teaching, has been identified in numerous studies as *the* crucial variable for improving learning outcomes. The way teachers teach is of critical concern in any reform designed to improve quality.
>
> (p. 152)

Given such analyses, the case for making professional development central to any reform initiative appears a strong one, but in many countries this is not the case. The World Economic Forum (2005) saw teachers as the most important constituency in education reform, but the forum notes that overall they continue to be largely ignored in policy dialogue, monitoring and implementation, a view confirmed by many studies (Lewin and Stuart, 2003; Mulkeen *et al.*, 2007; Vegas, 2007; Mpokosa and Ndaruhutse, 2008; Lewin, 2011).

30   *L. Bird* et al.

In some measure these policy weaknesses appear to reflect an inadequate conceptualisation of the policy process. One analysis, drawing on a series of World Bank studies of teacher recruitment, retention and training (DeJaeghere *et al.*, 2006), has suggested that policy makers need to analyse more comprehensively the way that 'multiple streams' of activity contribute to policy development. Three such streams are identified. First the problem stream, whereby all stakeholders come to recognise a problem exists, second the solution stream in which potential ways of resolving the problem are defined and refined, and third the political stream, when it is possible to build a consensus among various political forces about the feasibility of solution options. In looking, however, at the present and projected chronic teacher shortages in many countries and the continuing problems of teacher quality, such rigorous and conceptual policy analysis is rarely apparent. More often, the nature of the problem remains defined in limited terms (for example in terms of numbers rather than numbers and quality), solutions, where tried, frequently involve emergency, bolt-on approaches that fail to address systemic problems within established structures (for example the heavy resource emphasis on pre-service training), and establishing a consensus amongst stakeholders (teacher trainers, teacher union officials, politicians and the teachers themselves) is difficult.

The governance structures in many countries do not easily accommodate the building of consensus around solutions to the problem of educating teachers at scale, even if the problem can be accurately defined (UNESCO, 2008). Frequently, policy building is carried out through steep hierarchies, with decision making heavily concentrated at the top. While some countries are engaged in trying to decentralise education, there are many that have top-down structures in which teachers, school principals and local communities have little voice. Even in steep hierarchies, however, participants at each level have to choose the problems they wish to engage with, assess the feasibility of potential solutions and measure the impact that any decision might have for their own work and well-being (Elmore, 1979; Chapman and Miric, 2005). Support for such processes needs building into policy formulation. Jackie Kerr and Alison Buckler in Chapters 8 and 10 describe how many teachers have no involvement at all in decisions that affect their working lives.

The policy leverage between teacher supply, retention and education and training is inevitably, particularly given the lack of relevant and adequate data, very weak. Some countries are attempting to deal with this. Highly centralist interventions appear to be redressing the urban and rural imbalances in China (see Chapter 4) and Brazil, where deploying a contrasting mix of federal regulatory controls with a measure of local autonomy also appears to be having some impact on the effectiveness and quality of teachers (see Chapter 7). In both instances, a determined policy push to improve the quality of teachers and teaching has been seen through over a sustained period of time. In many other contexts such determination is less apparent. More commonly, however, in large parts of the developing world, the supply system operates independently of training provision and, given the often chaotic data available, even a willingness to coordinate policies would be

Teacher education in developing countries   31

unlikely to lead to improvements. The lack of any analysis of the inflows of teachers, the nature of the qualifications they have, the numbers of contract, volunteer or paraprofessional teachers, and the attrition and migration rates of qualified and unqualified teachers makes planning for initial education and training, upgrading and in-service professional development problematic. In many countries, however, despite the evidence of the scale of the contemporary and future problem, the policy response is partial. It is not yet clear if, in such contexts, any consensus is being established as to the most politically acceptable, technically feasible and cost-effective solution (DeJaeghere *et al.*, 2006).

It has been suggested that, although descriptive research on teacher behaviour and working conditions is strong, the research evidence around solutions is much weaker (Mulkeen *et al.*, 2007) and this is particularly true of solutions that work at scale. The need to provide more teachers and the urgency to improve the effectiveness of teachers is a problem involving very large numbers in most of the countries facing this challenge. (Chapter 13 explores the evidence for new approaches to providing teacher education at scale.) Equally, current analyses tend to be focused around specific issues (qualifications, absenteeism, reluctance to teach in remote rural schools) rather than try to gain more holistic understandings of teachers' lives and work, a theme addressed by many of the contributors to Section 3 of this book.

In this chapter we have suggested that policy around teacher education should take account of a much wider range of issues than is commonly the case. Initiatives to increase the supply of teachers that fail to take account of the conditions in which those teachers will work are unlikely to be successful. In 1966 UNESCO formulated a far-reaching series of recommendations concerning the status of teachers (UNESCO, 1966). These recommendations, which are reviewed by a UNESCO committee on a biannual basis, suggest the need to 'provide society with an adequate number of teachers who possess the necessary moral, intellectual and physical qualities and who have the required professional knowledge and skills' (p. 5). The EFA target date of 2015 is one year short of fifty years since this recommendation, and others describing the status of teachers, were formulated. The failure to improve the professional lives of millions of teachers, including the ways they are educated and trained, remains an enduring problem and deserves more attention perhaps than has previously been the case.

Notes

1 A UNESCO designation for the nine developing countries, with the highest populations: Bangladesh, Brazil, China, Egypt, India, Indonesia, Mexico, Nigeria and Pakistan.
2 Expected numbers of teachers required between 2004 and 2015 to meet attrition and UPE goals (thousands).
3 1 indicates parity, less than 1 indicates more males than females, and more than 1 indicate more females than males.

3 A Sisyphean complex?

Economic and cost constraints in filling teacher quantity and quality gaps

Lee E. Nordstrum

Introduction

Teacher quantity and quality gaps in developing countries

It is widely recognised that while the number and recruitment of teachers has grown significantly since 1970, recruitment rates have stalled and moreover have not kept pace with expanding enrolments (ILO, 2009, 2011). This has led to a worldwide shortage of teachers that is particularly acute in developing countries. Recent estimates posit that 1.9 million additional teachers are required to realise universal primary education, more than half of them in sub-Saharan Africa (SSA) (UNESCO, 2011a). As such, many countries in SSA must augment teacher recruitment growth rates by more than 6 per cent annually and the teaching workforce in South and West Asia must increase by more than 11 per cent if EFA is to be met by 2015 (UNESCO Institute for Statistics [UIS], 2011a).

This international teacher supply gap is substantially exacerbated when the inherent personnel requirements of expanding post-primary phases and the proportion of unqualified educators are taken into account (UIS, 2011b). To this end, the global adjusted net secondary enrolment ratio was 68 per cent in 2009 while pupil-teacher ratios (PTRs) remained relatively constant (UIS, 2011b). Assuming a constant PTR, this indicates that approximately 50 per cent more secondary educators (i.e. 15 million) would theoretically be needed to supply universal secondary education. Further, the proportion of the teaching workforce that meets national norms of minimum teacher qualification can be alarmingly low in some country contexts, as shown in Figure 3.1. Of 65 countries with available data in 2010, less than half of teachers meet national norms of adequate training in 21 (32.3 per cent). While in some cases this is likely due in part to evolving national norms of teacher preparation (e.g. Benin and Ethiopia), it is nonetheless indicative of shortages in 'quality' teachers and suggests that much of pre-service training in developing countries is ineffective (UNESCO, 2005).

At the same time, it has been progressively shown that characteristics typically associated with educator quality (and which largely determine salary structures), such as tertiary degrees, teaching certificates or years of experience, do not systematically produce desired learning outcomes or indeed guarantee

A Sisyphean complex? 33

sound pedagogical practices within the classroom (e.g. Hanushek, 1986, 2002; Kingdon, 1996; Ballou and Podgursky, 1997; Pritchett and Filmer, 1997; Glewwe, 2002; Hoxby, 2002; Michaelowa, 2002; Lazear, 2003; Loeb and Reininger, 2004; Umansky, 2005; Podgursky and Springer, 2007; Wößmann, 2010). This not only suggests that more and better qualified teachers are needed, but also that current policies and structures governing education investments (e.g. salary structures) need to be rigorously re-evaluated vis-à-vis the behaviours they sanction and incentivise among teachers on one hand and how they facilitate the recognition and reward of excellence on the other. In addition, the disconnect between formal teacher qualifications and performance begs serious questions of the quality of initial and in-service teacher education and training programmes.

The landscape of post-crisis education finance: fiscal shortfalls and ODA plateaus

Despite the evident need to tap into teacher labour markets and expand recruitment, the simplest and most obvious policy mechanisms for doing so (i.e. increasing personnel and total education expenditure) hang largely out of reach for most low-income countries (LICs), given contemporary spending patterns. According to recent assessments, the financial crisis of late 2008 left a budget revenue hole of approximately US$65 billion over 2009/10 in LICs (Kyrili and Martin, 2010a). By the end of 2010, government revenue in LICs was 1.1 per cent of GDP less

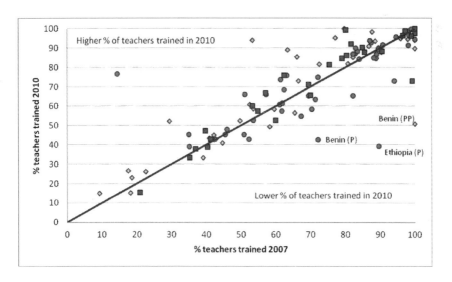

Figure 3.1 Percent of teaching corps trained 2007–10, 65 countries

Source: author's calculations based on UIS database.

Note: ◊ = pre-primary; ○ = primary; □ = secondary. Baseline values taken from 2007 or closest available year.

34   L.E. Nordstrom

than 2008 levels, with particularly sharp retractions in South Asia, Europe and Central Asia, the Middle East and North Africa. Unlike previous crises, many LICs opted to increase government budget deficits through stimulus spending in 2009, funded through a combination of grants and borrowing. However, forthcoming external finance and grants filled only one-third of the fiscal hole in LIC budgets and most governments were forced to rely on expensive domestic loans or dig into fiscal reserves to maintain expenditure (IMF, 2010a).

As a result, government budgets have come under increasing stress, and counter-cyclical policies were already rapidly unwinding in 2010, with only one-quarter of LICs continuing stimulus spending into a second year (Kyrili and Martin, 2010a). Educational expenditure has fared particularly poorly when compared to other MDG categories (e.g. health, infrastructure, agriculture): on aggregate 2010 spending was below 2008 levels, a trend that has continued through to 2012 in more than one-half of SSA countries (IMF, 2010b; Kyrili and Martin, 2010b). At the time of analysis, Kyrili and Martin found that only nine of 54 LICs had sufficiently 'high' fiscal space to increase expenditure, whereas 59 per cent had no space to raise domestic revenue, 57 per cent had critical levels of debt and 9 per cent had excessive aid dependence, rendering aid grants as the primary and most feasible means of MDG spending.

Nevertheless, necessary external finance is unlikely to be forthcoming from the international community. International aid stagnated in 2009 and the OECD has pointed to a \$20 billion shortfall in 2010 (OECD-DAC, 2010), meaning that previous aid targets (i.e. doubling by 2010) were missed by some \$16 billion (UNESCO, 2011a). After a strong increase to 2008, programmable aid increased diminutively in 2009 and plateaued in 2011.

It is in this context that we situate the economic and cost issues that strongly constrain what can be done to address the aforementioned teaching quantity and quality gaps. In this vein, this chapter seeks to articulate the overarching cost and resourcing issues that constrict the upgrading of the teaching profession in low- and lower-middle income countries. In particular, focus is given to salaries, their relative position in the overall education spend, as well as their traditional association with quantitative teacher qualifications and inelasticity to differentiated teacher practices or learning outcomes.

Four constraints to upgrading the teaching workforce in developing countries

Policy interventions designed to improve the quality of teaching in a given educational system are inherently subject to the 'fiscal space', not only within total government spending, but also within governmental education budgets. As such, the large share of educational spending consumed by teacher salaries is of fundamental concern for potential reforms. This is not just for benign reasons; rather, the structure of teacher remuneration rewards educators for particular behaviours and thereby provides incentives (or disincentives) for them to act in particular ways. This is the case irrespective of whether the salary structure in question is based on

A Sisyphean complex? 35

qualifications or performance. This section discusses these interlocutions in terms of how they constrain personnel investment and development.

Constraint 1: personnel remuneration as the lion's share of educational spending

In the majority of countries, salary expenditure constitutes more than 50 per cent of total education spending, though this proportion can swell to more than 80 per cent in developing countries (UNESCO, 2005; UIS, 2011b). This places significant limitations on other non-salary expenditures such as professional development, particularly as school infrastructure in LICs is also often weak and in need of improvement. Figure 3.2 presents recent data that show the proportion of total education spending consumed by salary costs relative to government spending levels in 94 countries.

There is substantial variation in the size of education budgets relative to total government spending (from more than one-quarter of all expenditure in Vanuatu, Indonesia, Morocco and Burundi to less than 9 per cent in Dominica, Jamaica, Zimbabwe, Sri Lanka and Panama) as well as in the proportion of the education spend allocated to salaries. In terms of the former, it is clear that education is prioritised, relative to other expenditure categories, in some countries more than others, though it must be noted that these data fluctuate on a yearly basis depending on needs in the education sector and spending patterns elsewhere. Regarding the latter, salary expenditure constitutes the lion's share of education budget spending in the vast majority of countries represented in Figure 3.2.

Figure 3.3 accentuates this relationship by expressing salary spending as a proportion of the total education budget for 108 countries with recent data available.

Budget allocations to salary expenditure varies extensively between countries and ranges from consuming the entire education budget in Zimbabwe to less than half in Guinea and Andorra (44.6 and 49.3 per cent, respectively). Nevertheless, it is clear that salary expenditure consumes the majority of education spending in many contexts: salary costs comprise more than 75 per cent of education budgets in nearly half of the sample (50 countries), more than 80 per cent of spending in one-third of countries and more than 90 per cent in 12 countries. Salary allotments over 80 or 90 per cent indicate marginal fiscal space within education budgets and a 'crowding out' of other current expenditures necessary to enhance the teaching workforce.

Figure 3.3 also differentiates by country income status: dark bars represent low-income countries, medium bars represent lower-middle income (LMICs) and light bars upper-middle and high-income countries. Though LICs and LMICs are found throughout the distribution, there is evident clustering towards the lower end: of 14 countries with the lowest relative allotments to salaries, ten are LICs or LMICs. This can also be problematic in that low spending on salaries does little to encourage high-quality candidates into the teaching profession in the first place (e.g. Delannoy and Sedlacek, 2001; López-Acevedo, 2002; Lazear, 2003; Coolahan *et al.*, 2004; Hoxby and Leigh, 2004; UNICEF, 2010).

36 L.E. Nordstrom

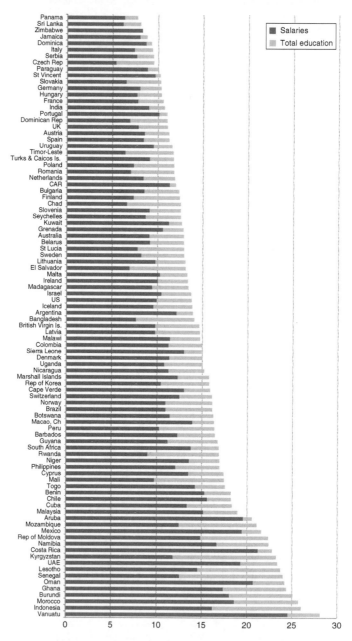

Figure 3.2 Total education and salary expenditure as a proportion of total government spending, 94 countries

Source: author's calculations based on UIS databases.

Note: data are from 2011 or most recent available.

A Sisyphean complex? 37

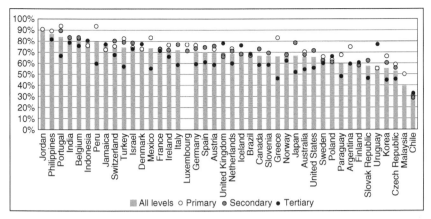

Figure 3.3 Proportion of education spending (ISCED 1–4) consumed by personnel remuneration, 108 countries

Source: author's calculations based on UIS databases.

Notes: dark bars represent low-income countries (n = 20); medium bars represent lower middle-income countries (n = 19); light bars represent upper middle-income and high-income countries (n = 69). Countries categorised according to World Bank classifications. Data are from 2011 or most recent available.

Figure 3.4 disaggregates salary allocations by school phase for 42 OECD countries and partner economies and displays marked heterogeneity between primary and post-primary levels, though not in a distinct or systematic fashion. It is sufficient to note that even in relatively wealthy economies salary expenditure claims a majority of the education budget, though the proportion tends to be lower at the tertiary level.

Constraint 2: increased unit costs of teachers in post-primary phases

Just as high salary budget allocations blunt governments' capacity to invest in other recurrent items and professional development, a second budgetary constraint is the increased unit costs of educators in post-basic schooling levels. Particularly in low-income countries, lower- and upper-secondary teachers tend to earn significantly higher base wages than counterparts in pre-primary or primary phases (UIS, 2011b). This wage structure constricts non-salary expenditure where the expansion of the education system is predominantly in post-basic phases (e.g. SSA, South and West Asia and the Arab States). Matching teacher supply to the rising demand for secondary and further schooling in these contexts implies an even more inflated salary bill relative to total education spending, further crowding out non-salary investments. Alternatively, countries with limited fiscal space to shoulder a ballooning teacher wage bill may opt to hire unqualified (and less expensive) contract teachers in lieu of traditionally trained candidates

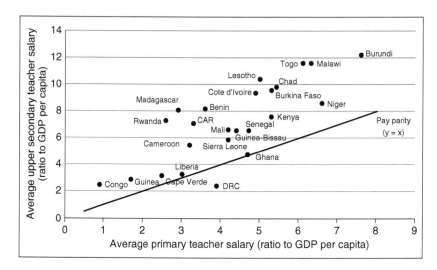

Figure 3.4 Proportion of education spending consumed by personnel remuneration, by school phase, 42 countries

Source: author's calculations based on OECD databases.

Note: data are from 2008 or most recent available.

(ILO, 2009, 2011). This has obvious negative implications for the overall quality and professionalism of the teaching workforce.

Data from UIS databases, presented in Figure 3.5, highlight this wage structure in 25 SSA countries. Nations are plotted according to average earnings for primary and upper-secondary teachers, expressed as a proportion of gross domestic product (GDP) per capita (see also Table 3.1). A reference line indicates pay parity (i.e. primary and upper-secondary teachers receive the same wage). In most SSA countries depicted here, upper-secondary teachers cost substantially more than primary, and are more than twice as costly in Congo, Madagascar, Rwanda, Central African Republic, Benin and Lesotho. Only Ghana and Liberia have base wage scales close to parity while the Democratic Republic of the Congo actually pays primary educators more than upper secondary.[1] On aggregate across 35 SSA countries, primary teachers' wages are equivalent to 4.1 times GDP per capita; lower and upper secondary average 6.3 and 7.2 times GDP per capita, respectively (UIS, 2011a).

From these data emerge another point: namely, that teacher salaries in many LICs are more expensive (relative to GDP per capita) than in most middle- and high-income countries: in general, OECD countries pay their teachers between 1.0 and 1.5 times GDP per capita (OECD, 2011).[2] This is not to suggest that educator wages should be pegged to country wealth, but rather that a high wage bill (relative to GDP per capita) represents an expensive and significant investment for LIC governments that are simultaneously attempting to expand access to primary and post-primary phases while enhancing the overall quality of the teaching workforce.

A Sisyphean complex? 39

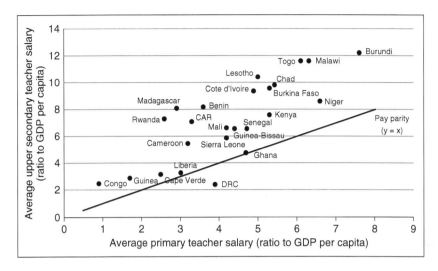

Figure 3.5 Primary and upper secondary teacher pay in 25 SSA countries
Source: UIS (2011a: 108). Note: data are from 2008 or most recent available.

Table 3.1 Teacher pay by school phase expressed as a proportion of GDP per capita, 35 SSA countries

	Primary	Lower secondary	Upper secondary
Angola (2003)	1.5	...	...
Benin (2006)	3.6	6	8.2
Burkina Faso (2006)	5.3	8.8	9.6
Burundi (2007)	7.6	8.4	12.2
Cameroon (2007)	3.2	5.2	5.5
Cape Verde (2009)	2.5	3	3.2
CAR (2007)	3.3	6.9	7.1
Chad (2003)	5.4	8.8	9.8
Congo (2007)	0.9	2	2.5
Cote d'Ivoire (2007)	4.9	8.8	9.4
DRC (2005)	3.9	2.4	2.4
Eritrea (2003)	7.7	...	...
Gambia (2003)	3.7	...	...
Ghana (2007)	4.7	4.7	4.8
Guinea (2005)	1.7	2.9	2.9
Guinea-Bissau (2006)	4.4	6.6	6.6
Kenya (2004)	5.3	7.6	7.6
Lesotho (2004)	5	10.4	10.4
Liberia (2008)	3	3.1	3.3
Madagascar (2008)	2.9	5.1	8.1
Malawi (2008)	6.3	11.6	11.6
Mali (2008)	4.2	5.6	6.6
Mozambique (2003)	4	...	...
Niger (2008)	6.6	7.4	8.6

40   L.E. Nordstrom

Nigeria (2003)	4.9	. . .	. . .
Rwanda (2008)	2.6	6.4	7.3
Sao Tome & Principe (2006)	2.3	. . .	. . .
Senegal (2004)	4.7	5.5	6.6
Seychelles (2003)	1.7	. . .	. . .
Sierra Leone (2004)	4.2	5.9	5.9
Sudan (2003)	2.2	. . .	. . .
Togo (2007)	6.1	8.9	11.6
Uganda (2007)	4.7	. . .	. . .
Zambia (2003)	2.7	. . .	. . .
Zimbabwe (2003)	6.1	. . .	. . .
Average (35 countries)	**4.1**	**6.3**	**7.2**

Source: UIS (2011a: 108).

Constraint 3: the qualification–salary connection and the performance–salary disconnect

It has been well demonstrated that in order to attract highly competent candidates into teaching, remuneration must at least be on par with that of other professions requiring similar levels of qualification (e.g. Psacharapoulos *et al.*, 1996; López-Acevedo, 2002; Umansky, 2005; UNICEF, 2010). As such, teacher wage structures typically reflect the assumption that effectiveness and quality increase progressively with years of schooling, teaching certificates and experience, and are therefore determined by rigid formulae of seniority, experience and education level (Ballou and Podgursky, 2002; Hoxby, 2002; UNESCO, 2005; Vegas and Umansky, 2005).

There is increasing evidence, however, that this assumption may be specious. A large number of studies on teacher effects point to highly heterogeneous impacts on desired learning outcomes that are idiosyncratic to the usual quantitative measures of teacher quality (e.g. Goldhaber and Brewer, 1997; Hanushek, 2003; Ballou *et al.*, 2004; Kane *et al.*, 2005; Rivkin *et al.*, 2005; Boyd *et al.*, 2006; Podgursky and Springer, 2007). In other words, teaching certificates, years of schooling, experience (beyond two years) and licensing exam scores have been found to be poor predictors of the classroom effectiveness of teachers. For example, Aslam and Kingdon (2012),[3] in their randomised sampling of 65 urban and rural schools in the Lahore district of Punjab, Pakistan, found that traditional teacher characteristics of teacher 'quality' (e.g. certification or training) have no bearing on students' standardised exam scores. On the other hand, 'process' variables (i.e. pedagogic classroom practices) affect pupil learning substantially. Kingdon (1996) arrives at much the same conclusion in her analysis of urban state-run schools in northern India: the quantity of teacher education, their formal training or experience have little impact on pupil achievement. These phenomena have also been observed in higher-income countries. Aaronson *et al.* (2003), using a large longitudinal dataset that linked student achievement with teacher characteristics in Chicago public schools in the United States, found that 90 per cent of teacher effects were not explained by any measured characteristics.

A Sisyphean complex? 41

This lack of systematic association between teacher qualifications and performance carries substantial implications for both education budgets and the quality of the teaching workforce. Ballou and Podgursky (2002) estimated that the United States spent approximately US$24.4 billion per annum (or 17 per cent of instruction expenditure) in the early 2000s on seniority pay despite the absence of evidence that teacher skills increase linearly with experience. This is indeed a sizeable proportion of the education budget to use on an evidently blunt instrument for increasing learning outcomes. Similar data do not exist in the majority of LICs, but their progressive availability could facilitate effective teacher management systems and inform human resource policy decision-making.

Other authors highlight several potential human resource effects stemming from qualification-based salary structures. First, rigid salary scales that reward distinct categories of teachers homogeneously may cause educational inequalities. Wages based on qualifications cannot favourably compensate educators, for example, who teach in more challenging settings (e.g. rural, low-achieving or low-income schools) (Loeb and Reininger, 2004) and therefore provide perverse incentives for better teachers to avoid such schools. Second, pay that is not responsive to actual teacher performance can also erode intrinsic motivation (Fehr and Falk, 2002; Muralidharan and Sundararaman, 2009). Kremer *et al.* (2005) found that rigid salary structures that did not differentiate between high- and low-performing teachers in India undermined job satisfaction and increased teacher absenteeism. Some educators in the study found that they could get by with little effort and were thus more likely to be absent while hard-working colleagues were frustrated by the lack of professional recognition for their work. Third, the absence of formal recognition (monetary or otherwise) of excellence in teaching will tend to discourage potential candidates who have the most to gain from performance-based incentive schemes (i.e. high-skilled, high-performing individuals) and instead encourage those who have the most to gain from qualification- and experience-based schemes (i.e. low-skill, low-performing individuals) (e.g. Kremer *et al.*, 2005; Dolton and Marcenaro-Gutierrez, 2008; Wößmann, 2010).

In developing countries, these effects manifest in numerous ways. For example, teacher absenteeism has been found to stem, at least in part, from lax professional standards as well as limited and ineffective support and control mechanisms (Michaelowa, 2002; World Bank, 2004). Attrition is more likely amongst higher-ability teachers than amongst those of lower ability (Podgursky *et al.*, 2004). Hoxby and Leigh (2004) have shown that the migration of high-ability women out of teaching from 1960 to 2000 is largely based on the 'push' factor of wage compression rather than greater opportunities outside of the education section.

Constraint 4: the necessity to undertake structural salary reforms to upgrade the teaching profession

Following on the previous constraint, current human resource policies and patterns of education investment do not systematically engender desired learning

42   *L.E. Nordstrom*

outcomes among students or incentivise desired pedagogical and professional behaviour among teachers (Pritchett and Filmer, 1997; Glewwe, 2002; Glewwe *et al.*, 2003; Crouch, 2005; McEwan and Santibáñez, 2005). Indeed, human resource investments in most educational systems, by rewarding years of schooling or experience and teacher credentials, still reflect the pervasive emphasis on an 'input' definition of school and educator quality (UNESCO, 2005). This is the case despite a wealth of research that indicates other aspects of teacher practices and characteristics matter just as much (e.g. Darling-Hammond, 2000; Kingdon and Teal, 2003; Lazear, 2003; Umansky, 2005).

In this vein, there have been many evaluations (mostly non-experimental) of performance pay schemes[4] based on principal-agent theory (Ross, 1973; Prendergast, 1999) that attempt to assess the extent to which incentives (monetary and non-monetary) can be employed to encourage specific teacher behaviours (e.g. participating in professional development) while limiting undesired side effects (see, *inter alia*: Figlio and Winicki, 2002; Lavy, 2002, 2004; Glewwe *et al.*, 2003; Jacob and Levitt, 2003; Clotfelter *et al.*, 2004). Many of these studies distinguish between programmes with teacher incentive schemes (which may or may not include pay-for-performance based on test scores) and traditional salary structures which are not incentive schemes. While this dichotomous nomenclature is understandable, particularly in experimental settings, it is misleading. Rather, all salary structures, whether traditional qualifications-based or performance-based, are in actuality incentive schemes in that they incentivise and reward particular behaviours. Qualification-based systems evidently value and reward formal teacher credentials and experience. Performance-based schemes may also value these characteristics, but may additionally reward, for example, achievement gains in student test scores, completed professional development or school leadership roles. Thus, the question posed to any given remuneration structure is not whether the introduction of incentives for teachers might be an appropriate policy intervention to elicit certain behaviours, but rather whether the behaviours desired are effectively incentivised and undesired moral hazard limited in the current structure.

In other words, national or sub-national education systems cannot assume that incremental and linear pay raises for their teacher workforces, allocated according to seniority and educational level, will inherently reinforce the desired behaviours present in professionals and pedagogues of 'good quality'. Indeed, given the proportion of educational spending allotted to teacher salaries, low- and lower-middle income countries, for which resource scarcity (and hence cost-effectiveness) is an important driver of policy, cannot afford to make this assumption. The literature discussed above suggests that the traditional determinants of teacher salaries (e.g. certification, years of schooling and experience) do not systematically predict positive teacher impact on learning or professional outcomes, which in turn implies that they also do not incentivise such outcomes. As such, LICs and LMICs literally cannot afford to be wasteful by adopting a human resource strategy that focuses solely on inputs that are not in themselves key determinants of desired human capital outcomes. While teacher education level, certification and years of experience should not be completely eschewed as indicators of teacher 'quality', it is clear from the above discussion that a much more robust definition of (and thus indicators for) teacher quality is needed.

This is constraining for national educational systems because the definitional expansion of teacher quality beyond degrees, certification and experience requires an altogether more complex data collection system of teacher characteristics, practices and student-level variables (including, but not limited to, outcomes). This is logistically out of reach for many countries, regardless of income status, and is financially impracticable for most LICs and LMICs. In contrast, teacher certification, tertiary degrees and years of experience are straightforward and inexpensive to monitor, and are therefore logical choices to base remuneration schemes upon. Nevertheless, difficult and protracted policy adjustments will be necessary to change traditional and inefficient remuneration structures into those that effectively reward excellence in teaching, and hence incentivise and encourage professionalism among the workforce.

Moderating the salary–qualification connection: options for linking salaries to performance

Alternative remuneration structures to traditional qualifications-based schemes exist and may provide a means to incentivise and systematise the hitherto idiosyncratic teacher effects seen in many studies. Most of these are founded on the tenets of principal-agent theory: namely, that the interests of principals (employers, schools or school districts) and agents (teachers) are not identical and sometimes conflict, leading to a loss of productivity and efficiency (Ross, 1973; Prendergast, 1999). To optimise production, it is incumbent upon employers to design incentives to motivate employees (teachers) to behave in certain ways that yield, it is believed, desired productivity gains and learning outcomes (Umansky, 2005). Such schemes are often, but not of necessity, monetary incentives that reward or sanction behaviour (Prendergast, 1999), the success of which is dependent upon the agent's level of risk-aversion, the risk involved, the desirability of reward offered or the aversion to the threatened sanction, and the employer's capacity to accurately determine and evaluated desired employee behaviour.[5]

As mentioned, the vast majority of performance-based schemes are merit pay structures (or pay-for-performance) that reward teachers based on pre-defined measures of quality learning outcomes (UNESCO, 2005). These can be disaggregated into at least four sub-categories. Individual merit pay programmes reward teachers with pay bonuses based on specific outcomes or behaviours, most often a combination of measures which includes student exam performance. Group performance-based incentives, in contrast, reward a group of teachers (e.g. a school) based on average performance measures across the group and are designed to take advantage of gains through teacher cooperation or production complementarities (Muralidharan and Sundararaman, 2009). Competition incentive programmes see individual or groups of teachers competing for limited prizes, such as job promotion or salary bonuses (Lavy, 2002, 2004). Automatic incentives provide teachers or groups with non-competitive monetary or professional (e.g. further

44   L.E. Nordstrom

education and training opportunities, increased decision-making authority) rewards for exhibiting certain behaviours or attaining a particular performance benchmark.

In principle, teacher merit pay schemes exert two effects on educator performance and the overall quality of the workforce. In the short-term, merit incentives offered to individual or groups of teachers can induce performance gains in incentivised outcome measures by motivating the current workforce to improve its level of productivity (Lazear, 2003). A wealth of empirical evidence attests to the potential short-term effectiveness of incentive programmes in realising achievement gains (e.g. Kingdon, 1996; Lavy, 2002, 2004; Glewwe *et al.*, 2003; Kingdon and Teal, 2003; Muralidharan and Sundararaman, 2009; Aslam and Kingdon, 2012). Over the long-term, performance pay will tend to attract teachers who are particularly effective vis-à-vis the incentivised activity (e.g. increasing student achievement) and repel those who are not, thereby enhancing the overall quality of the teaching workforce through a self-selection mechanism. This latter effect may be of particular importance to teacher labour markets as other studies have shown that higher-ability teachers are more likely to leave the teaching profession than lower-ability teachers (Podgursky *et al.*, 2004; Wößmann, 2010).

Theoretical and empirically supported short-term benefits notwithstanding, merit pay programmes have been criticised for engendering undesired and regressive side effects in many contexts. First, extrinsic incentives can undermine teachers' intrinsic motivation and perceptions of their own capabilities, thereby lowering actual productivity rates (Bénabou and Tirole 2000, 2003). Murnane and Cohen (1986) have argued that intrinsic motivation is particularly relevant to the work of teachers and that individual merit schemes may therefore harm the multidimensional and cooperative aspects of education. Second, weaknesses in both outcome measurement and teacher evaluation may introduce unwanted moral hazard into merit programmes (i.e. employee manipulation and 'gaming') (Prendergast, 1999; Heckman *et al.*, 2002). For example, even thoughtfully designed short-term programmes have been shown to induce cheating on exams (Jacob and Levitt, 2003), relocation of teacher effort towards test-taking (Holmström and Milgrom, 1991; Clotfelter *et al.*, 2004) and participant free-riding in the case of group incentives (Baker, 2002; McEwan and Santibáñez, 2005). Both Lavy (2002, 2004) and Glewwe *et al.* (2003), in the contexts of Israel and Kenya, respectively, found that financial bonuses based on student achievement gains resulted in teachers providing extra test preparation sessions after school hours, potentially to levy 'tutoring' fees on students. Third, achievement gains related to incentive programmes are generally short-lived and regress to pre-programme levels when the scheme expires (Prendergast, 1999; Glewwe *et al.*, 2003). Fourth, it is difficult to measure and quantify broader learning achievements and evolutions in teacher practices; thus teacher performance is often reduced to readily measureable student outcomes (e.g. test scores), especially in LICs and LMICs (Murnane and Cohen, 1986; Baker, 2002). When such measurement constraints exist, fixed qualification-based wage structures may be most optimal (Holmström and Milgrom, 1991).

As such, merit pay schemes may not be sufficient in themselves to appropriately align incentives of both principals and agents while limiting moral hazard and programme gaming (UNESCO, 2005). However, teacher incentive structures are not of necessity limited to merit pay. Rather, it has been argued that skill-based or condition-based pay schemes could potentially avoid some of the afore-mentioned critiques. Odden and Kelley (1997) have asserted that competency- or condition-based pay would reward teachers who expand and diversify their skill sets to include desired competencies or those who participate in certain activities. Competencies, which would be relatively straightforward to measure, certify and evaluate, may include pedagogical skills and practices or leadership and manage-rial techniques evidenced by the teacher. Remunerated activities may comprise, for example, participating in and completing professional development, assuming school leadership roles or classroom innovations. While there remains very little systematic research done on these types of programmes (Umansky, 2005), policy makers seeking greater efficiency in school resources would do well to directly incorporate desired teacher practices and competencies (beyond test scores) in the design of incentive programme interventions.

Addressing the constraints: positive lessons from country salary reforms

Evidently, the structure of remuneration schemes matters, as does the conceptu-alisation of any attempted salary reform that includes performance incentives. This section presents three examples of countries that have undertaken such reforms (i.e. India, Latvia and Mexico) and considers the positive examples that can be drawn from their experiences.

India: incentive framework facilitates experimental evaluation

A large-scale randomised teacher incentive programme was implemented in 300 rural government-run schools in Andhra Pradesh by the Azim Premji Founda-tion[6] on behalf of the state government from 2005 to 2007 (Muralidharan and Sundararaman, 2009). Teachers in incentive schools received salary bonuses[7] based on average student exam performance, conditional upon achievement gains from previous years being greater than 5 per cent. In their evaluation of the pro-gramme, Muralidharan and Sundararaman (2009) found that students in inter-vention schools performed significantly better than peers in control schools (0.28 and 0.16 standard deviations better in math and language exams, respectively), with a mean treatment effect of 0.22 standard deviations. A minimum average treatment effect of 0.1 standard deviations at every percentile across the distribu-tion of test scores suggests broad gains for low- and high-performing students. Test scores increased in both mechanical and conceptual aspects of the exam, as well as in non-incentive exams (e.g. science), indicating real learning gains (not just cramming or 'gaming') and positive spillover effects. Teacher behaviour also changed as a result of the programme, with programme teachers more likely to have assigned home and schoolwork, given extra classes outside of school hours,

46 *L.E. Nordstrom*

given practice exams and paid special attention to poor-performing children (Muralidharan and Sundararaman, 2009).

Arguably as important as the results of the intervention, however, are the inbuilt conditions of the programme that allowed for the estimation of treatment effects. The 300 schools involved were randomly allocated to one of three groups: individual incentive schemes, group incentive schemes or the control group. Mandal coordinators provided *ex-ante* information to all participating schools on student populations, classes, school performance reports, and oral and written communication about the intervention (Muralidharan and Sundararaman, 2009). Coordinators also made random visits to all schools to conduct surveys and collect data. As such, all schools operated under identical conditions of information and monitoring. Two other sets of 100 rural government schools were randomly selected to receive other resource inputs of similar value (i.e. extra contract teacher and cash grants for school materials, respectively) to statistically estimate if the incentive programme was a more cost-effective way of raising achievement. In addition, the experimental design incorporated safeguards against threshold effects (i.e. focusing instruction on students nearer to a performance target) and the exclusion of low-performing students.[8] Exams were invigilated by external teams of five evaluators.

Experimental designs such as this are important not only for confidently estimating treatment effects, but also for determining cost-effectiveness relative to other potential reforms and eventually building consensus around a given intervention.

Latvia: student test scores contribute to, but are not the main drivers of, performance-based remuneration

Latvia has recently undertaken salary reforms in wake of the economic crisis of late 2008 and subsequent wage bill cut in 2009, eschewing the traditional input-based financing of teacher salaries and adopting per pupil funding characterised by autonomy at the municipality and school levels to incorporate incentive schemes into remuneration structures (Hazans, 2010). Previously, teacher pay was determined by centralised statutes based on defined workloads, the number of teaching hours per week, complementary instructional tasks (e.g. lesson preparation, correcting written work) and pay supplements (e.g. for working with students with special needs). The financial reforms have greatly relaxed the firm regulations on compensated hours of complementary instructional tasks and have allowed school directors to use available funds as they see fit. This includes the autonomy to determine and vary base teacher salaries, as well as introduce performance-based pay (Hazans, 2010).

While the reform is too recent to allow for an evaluation of its impact on teacher practices, the composition of the workforce or student outcomes, Hazans (2010) reports a high incidence of performance pay schemes in municipalities and schools. Fifteen per cent of schools differentiate educator pay based on teacher reputation, work quality and innovation, student exam results and achievement, and approximately one in six schools take teachers' extra activities into account.

Over one-half of schools vary base salaries by 4 per cent, one-quarter of schools by 10 per cent and one in ten schools vary base salaries by 30 per cent or more.

Student exam results do influence teacher performance pay in Latvian schools and municipalities, but they are not central determinants of teacher performance. Indeed, only 1 per cent of municipalities reported encouraging the use of student test scores to determine teacher salaries and only 8 per cent of schools considered exam results (Hazans, 2010). More commonly cited criteria for determining performance salary echoed Odden and Kelley's (1997) earlier recommendation of skill- and conditions-based pay. Schools reported employing the following criteria for determining teacher base pay with greater frequency than student exam scores: extra teacher activities in school (15 per cent), reputation and work quality (14 per cent), non-test student achievement (12 per cent), innovation (11 per cent), methodological support to colleagues (10 per cent), weekly workload (10 per cent) and completed professional development (9 per cent). While specific permutations of these elements were not reported, the point remains that incentive pay structures are not forcibly limited to considering student achievement gains or even teacher value-added scores; rather, other characteristics and practices of teachers should be taken into account.

Mexico: taking a long-term approach to incentive reforms

Most performance-based pay schemes have been short-term programmes that last but one or two years before giving way to another remuneration structure (Umansky, 2005; UNESCO, 2005). While some temporary performance-based pay programmes have proved successful at enhancing specific learning outcomes and encouraging certain teacher practices as outlined above, they cannot greatly impact the aggregate composition of the teacher workforce in so short a time span. One exception to this is Mexico's Carrera Magisterial programme, which was instituted in 1992 and continues, 20 years later, to encompass the evaluation of hundreds of thousands of teachers and distribute millions of dollars in salary bonuses per annum (Santibáñez *et al.*, 2007).

Carrera Magisterial was designed jointly by federal education authorities, state education authorities and teachers' unions as a horizontal promotional system that rewards teachers with performance-based salary bonuses (Santibáñez *et al.*, 2007). Teachers participate voluntarily in the programme, which comprises five levels of promotion (bands A through E) that must be pursued sequentially. Awards are substantial, increase progressively with promotional level and persist for the teacher's entire career: band A teachers receive on average 24 per cent of the base salary as a bonus and band E teachers receive 197 per cent of the base salary (McEwan and Santibáñez, 2005). In an evaluation year chosen by the teacher, individuals are evaluated against a 100-point scale that assesses educational degrees (10 points), years of experience (15 points), federal and state professional development (17 points), peer review (10 points), content knowledge (28 points) and student performance (20 points). The nationally set cut-off score for promotion is 70 points. Evaluations of the programme have shown that its

48   *L.E. Nordstrom*

impact is greatest when teacher training is aimed at increasing teachers' practical experience and developing content-specific knowledge, and when supervision by school administration was rigorous (Lopez-Acevedo, 2004; McEwan and Santibáñez, 2005).

While numerous problems have been identified with the programme (McEwan and Santibáñez, 2005; Santibáñez *et al.*, 2007),[9] a positive aspect germane to our discussion is its long-standing duration. Unlike small-scale short-term interventions, Carrera Magisterial should, in principle, have made a substantial impact on the overall teacher workforce by attracting candidates who are particularly good at meeting promotion cut-offs and repelling those that are not (Prendergast, 1999; Lazear, 2003). This potential effect has unfortunately not been investigated by the few empirical evaluations of the programme and would be well-served by future research. Nevertheless, it remains a case in point that salary reforms and incentive interventions should be given sufficient time to elicit both short-term (enhanced teacher motivation and effort) and long-term (enhanced quality of teacher workforce through self-selection) effects.

Conclusions

This chapter has considered four factors that constrain attempts to fill teacher quantity and quality gaps in LICs and LMICs that have been caused by increased demand for schooling, insufficient teacher supply chains and inadequate pre-service training systems. First, the large proportion of total education spending consumed by teacher remuneration limits countries' capacities to allocate funds to teacher education and development systems, particularly in LICs and LMICs where school infrastructure is in a state of disrepair and in need of maintenance. Second, the wage bill is likely to increase further and command an even larger share of the education spend as LICs and LMICs expand access to post-basic school phases to meet demand, since educators in these phases tend to be paid significantly more than their primary counterparts. Third, this substantial spending allocated to teacher salaries is based largely on a reward structure that values teacher qualifications and experience, but these characteristics are only weakly associated with teacher effects and effectiveness in the classroom vis-à-vis learning outcomes and pedagogic practices. Moreover, qualification-based remuneration tends to attract low-quality and low-performing candidates into the teaching profession, thereby constraining attempts to upgrade the workforce through negative self-selection effects. Fourth, adjustments are needed in country remuneration structures to moderate the linkages between teacher qualification and salaries, and to promote greater linkages to teacher performance (broadly defined). However, such policy innovations require robust data collection and monitoring systems which are unavailable, for both logistical and financial reasons, in LICs and LMICs.

It is therefore evident that LICs and LMICs cannot simply spend more or hire more teachers in order to fill current educator quantity and quality gaps. While there is admittedly room for increasing resource efficiency in many low-income countries (thereby freeing up funds to support a larger wage bill), the dearth of 'qualified' educators produced by initial teacher training systems and the weak association between traditionally measured characteristics of teacher 'quality' and desired outcomes suggests that a fundamental restructuring of pre- and in-service training mechanisms are necessary. This, however, cannot be undertaken without a commensurate and rigorous evaluation and restructuration of teacher incentive and remuneration schemes.

As such, this chapter also highlights important areas for future research where evidence is currently lacking. Experimental evaluative analyses of current remuneration structures and potential alternatives are essential to identify desired, context-responsive characteristics of teacher performance that enhance learning outcomes and determine how these can be ideally supported. This is necessary for both 'traditional' and 'incentive' pay schemes, particularly in developing countries. Further research should investigate the suitable balance between student exam scores (or teacher value-added) and other teacher-level indicators to determine teacher effectiveness and performance in a way that is sensitive to context and which reinforces educators' intrinsic motivation. Finally, the evidence base surrounding the effectiveness and resource-efficiency of professional development programmes requires expansion, in order to meaningfully inform future discussion on the appropriate equilibrium between pre- and in-service training.

Notes

1 Primary teachers receive more than secondary teachers in the DRC as the latter phase relies heavily on user fees which are employed to supplement government funds (Bentaouet-Kattan, 2006; Nordstrum, 2011).
2 Korea is an outlier among OECD nations and pays teachers 2.11 times GDP per capita (UIS, 2011b).
3 See Chapter 11, this volume.
4 The vast majority of these have been short-term programmes (i.e. one to two years) which precludes the ability to monitor potential long-term benefits of performance pay schemes, which may be more significant than their immediate impact on teacher motivation.
5 For thoughtful and thorough reviews of principal-agent theory, see Prendergast (1999), Lazear (2003) and Umansky (2005).
6 Technical support was provided by the World Bank.
7 Bonus = Rs. 500 × [average percentage gain in test scores].
8 Specifically, average scores were used in both individual and group incentive programmes to guard against threshold effects. Zero gain scores were given to any student who took the pre-test at the beginning of the year but was not included in the post-test.
9 McEwan and Santibáñez (2005) have shown that the programme gives strong incentives to increase student achievement to a very small proportion of teachers (approximately 15 per cent). From the point system, it is possible for teachers to gain promotion despite very poor student performance (which only amounts to 20 of 100 points). In addition, teachers have little incentive to increase or maintain student achievement in non-evaluation years.

Section 2

Addressing the teacher challenge in large population countries

Introduction

This second section of the book provides four country case studies examining the way governments are responding to the challenge to supply teachers for large and growing school systems. Each of the countries (China, India, Nigeria, Brazil) has, in recent decades, developed explicit strategies to recruit and educate large numbers of teachers.

There are some important similarities in the strategies adopted. First in each of the countries there has been a significant level of involvement from federal governments. In Brazil, mandatory legislation to provide basic education for was introduced in the mid 1990s, in China a series of parallel 'projects' to modernise education, the National Project of Compulsory Education in Impoverished Areas for example, were introduced between 2004 and 2007, in Nigeria a 'Federal Teacher Scheme' was introduced in the early years of the century and in India the Right to Education Act came onto the statute books in 2009. Each case study illustrates the global trend towards ever increasing national government involvement in teacher policy, including interventions to make teachers and the professional preparation they receive more effective (Moon, 2003). Different strategies have been adopted. In Brazil strong rules in relation to funding appear to have secured significant improvements in the quality of the teaching force. In Nigeria important regional tensions and political instability have made federal action more difficult. In China central intervention has been strong and consistent whereas in India local responses to national legislation are much more contested. All four, however, have in different ways grappled with the challenge of establishing the best balance between national and regional responsibilities. In Brazil and, more recently, India governments appear to have taken back some of the responsibilities for teacher policy that traditionally rested with regional or state governments. The government of Nigeria is following the same path, although with rather less vigour. What is of interest, and could be of considerable value in looking at the issues more widely, is the forms of the structures and regulatory frameworks used. Data on this is not always easy to identify and there is a need for more empirical study in this area.

Each of the countries has very different demographic circumstances. But all the countries illustrate the acute inequalities between regions that exist despite the recent record of economic growth and, particularly in Brazil and China, genuine

54 *Introduction*

improvements in educational performance. These inequalities continue to be a major concern and are clearly manifest in the supply and quality of teachers to rural communities where the need is greatest. Each country is, however, trying to provide much greater access to teacher education and professional development opportunities and the case studies report the different ways in which school based training, open and distance learning and new information and communication technologies have been deployed to this end. Again this is an area where more precise comparative data than is currently available would be of value. Of interest, also, is the use of incentives to improve teacher effectiveness. The evidence suggests that such an approach, using a variety of forms of incentive, has been more characteristic of reforms in Latin America than other parts of the world (Vegas, 2007) but there is a growing interest in the schemes that appear to have been successful (Banerjee and Duflo, 2011). The extent to which incentive schemes have been applied in parallel with programmes of in-service professional development is of interest, but there is little evidence of this either in the four case studies or the wider literature. The case studies have been informed by the UNESCO E9 survey information referred to in Chapter 2 (see pp. 000–000). Each pair of authors, however, has independently chosen the particular perspectives adopted. Information and analysis is drawn from official documentation as well as the wider research literature.

4 China

Strengthening the quality of teacher education in rural communities

Yan Hanbing and Bob McCormick

Introduction

This chapter focuses upon rural education, and the role of teachers and teacher education in improving the situation in these areas. It is important to see the efforts to improve rural education in the context of China as a whole. The sheer scale of the educational enterprise and the role of government in it, particularly given its originally social to all enterprise, has to always be borne in mind when thinking of particular groups who might be disadvantaged. (A 'command' approach is where central edicts commanded change in the system, which local administrations then had to follow.) This remains true even although contemporary China has embraced many of the market approaches, not only to the economy, but to education as well. We therefore present general background on China and on its education system, as the frame to view rural education, rural teachers and their professional development from pre-service to in-service.

The picture is of a strong education system, but one that is still grappling with some severe but not widespread inequalities. It will be evident that the problems of size and diversity of the system represent special problems that overlay the usual rural–urban differences that exist in many countries. We aim to examine the inequalities, the sources of them, and the policies, particular of the government, adopted to try to deal with them, and the difficulties that remain. Some of these difficulties seem intractable or at the very least have inherent contradictions that may prevent the changes in the likes of pedagogy that are desired by the government and advocated elsewhere in the world (cf. Chapter 1).

Background on China

Characterised by geographic and cultural diversity, China also has a large population, which in 2011 was 1.347 billion (National Bureau of Statistics, 2012). Administratively it is made up of four municipalities (e.g. Beijing), 22 provinces and five minority nationality autonomous regions (e.g. Xinjiang). The age structure of the population is shown in Table 4.1 (National Population and Family Planning Commission of China, 2010).

China has enjoyed strong economic growth in recent years, with China's GDP in 2008 increasing by 16.8 per cent over the previous year (Ministry of

56 Y. Hanbing and B. McCormick

Table 4.1 China's population age structure

Age range	Percentage of total	Male	Female
0–14 years	17.9%	128,363,812	109,917,641
15–64 years	73.4%	501,987,034	474,871,442
65 years and over	8.6%	55,287,997	59,713,369

Education, 2010). The values added in the agriculture, industry and services sectors as percentages of national GDP were respectively 11.2 per cent, 48.2 per cent and 39.6 per cent (Ministry of Education, 2010). The total employed population of China in 2008 reached 774 million, and the employed populations in the three sectors as proportions of the total employed population were respectively 39.6 per cent, 27.2 per cent and 33.2 per cent, with more changes in recent years indicating a slight movement away from agriculture (Ministry of Education, 2010). The productivity of the agriculture sector is evidently lower than that of other sectors, which, to a great extent, determines the differential development of rural and urban areas. The relative poverty of rural areas remains a characteristic of conditions in China. However, it is important to realise that whereas rural and urban differences have been reduced, what is more enduring are the regional and social class differences (Murphy and Johnson, 2009).

Over the last decade, China's pace of urbanisation has accelerated, with large numbers of rural people migrating to cities, resulting in the urbanisation rate of China increasing, on average, one percentage point each year. In 2008, there were 745 million people in the countryside and 580 million people in cities, amounting to 56.1 per cent and 43.9 per cent of the total population respectively (Ministry of Education, 2010), by 2011 the National Bureau of Statistics indicated a reversal of these proportions with 51.27 per cent living in urban areas. There is also a large 'migrant' population, that is rural people who go to work in cities but are only granted temporary residential status (or may have no residential status), which results in a loss of rights and poorer access to education (Zhao and Hu, 2007).

China's regional imbalance in socioeconomic development is indicated by the different contributions to GDP; in 2006, East China (often referred to as the coastal region) created 59.7 per cent of GDP, though its population only accounted for 38.9 per cent of the total. As a culturally and economically developed region, Central China, with 31.8 per cent of the total population, is well-known for its agriculture, and it created 23.2 per cent of GDP and one-third of the national total agriculture value. West China, covering a vast territory, with poor natural conditions and infrastructure, and a scarce population (27.5 per cent of the national total), created 17.1 per cent of GDP (Ministry of Education, 2010). It is this latter area, with many remote as well as poor rural areas, which has been the subject of the government's recent efforts with regard to rural education.

China is a multi-ethnic country with many languages and cultures, including 56 nationalities, with 30 types of characters and over 80 kinds of languages (some only spoken), of which the Chinese language is the most common.

Modern Chinese can be divided into standard Chinese, that is Putonghua (the common language based on Beijing pronunciation) and dialects (e.g. Cantonese or Guongdonghua). Putonghua is the basic spoken and written (official) language throughout the country, however, research by the Ministry of Education (Xinhua News, 7 March 2007) shows that in fact only just over half the population can actually speak it; all literate people can of course read and write the common script (hanzi). The other 53 Minority Nationalities have their own languages, except Hui and Man. It is also the case that many of these nationalities live in the more remote and poor regions, exposing them to a double disadvantage. For example, it is often the case that schools in these areas cannot employ a teacher who can speak the minority language (Zhao and Hu, 2007) and, if the area is remote, it will in any case be difficult to get a good quality teacher to go there. Children in their early years are particularly disadvantaged, and of course this reduces the prospect of making all children 'educated' in their own culture. In any case the official position is that Putonghua is the language of instruction in all schools.

The education system

The national government and the local governments at various levels (e.g. cities, townships and counties) administer education. Secondary and primary education are administered by local governments under national guidelines (e.g. for the curriculum and general policy). Central and/or provincial governments of autonomous regions or municipalities directly under the central government, administer higher education. There are some 100 universities directly run by central government with the bulk of the universities being provincial institutions. Educational spending is 1.9 per cent of GDP and is failing to keep pace with the growth in the economy. Indeed it is lower than the government target of 4 per cent, which itself is less than the UN target of 6 per cent (Zhao and Hu, 2007).

China's education system has four components: basic education, occupational/polytechnic education, common higher education and adult education. Basic education comprises of pre-school education, primary with children starting at aged six (for six years) and junior senior (three years) and senior secondary (three years) schooling; compulsory schooling covers the first nine years.

By the end of 2008, nine-year compulsory education was just about universal, with 96 per cent of counties where illiteracy was basically eliminated among the young and middle-aged groups. The overall literacy rate for the population is 90.9 per cent (2000 census). In the same year, the gross enrollment rate of primary education was 105.7 per cent, the gross enrollment rate of junior secondary education was 98.5 per cent, and the gross enrollment rate of senior secondary school-age children (aged 15–17) was 74 per cent (gross enrolment rate expresses the number of students in school as a percentage of the number of those of school age in the population). The figures for secondary schools have shown an improvement in the last few years, particularly for senior secondary students, where the figure was 59.8 per cent in 2006. Table 4.2 shows the actual enrolment in the various sectors of schooling over the period 2005–2008, indicating that, as the birth

58 *Y. Hanbing and B. McCormick*

rate has declined (there is a rise in the population, but the birth rate is declining, along with the natural growth rate; National Bureau of Statistics of China, 2012, Chinese Government Official website, online at: http://english.gov.cn/2005-08/08/content_27315.htm; accessed 8 November 2011), the numbers in primary and junior secondary schools have also declined; the latest figures for senior secondary schools indicates that this decline has started there as well. Table 4.3 shows the figures for enrolment, schools and teachers in each of the sectors for the latest year available full statistics (unless otherwise stated all education statistics from this point are taken from Ministry of Education, 2009a; 2009 (incomplete) statistics indicate slight increases in teacher numbers: UNESCO, 2010b). The relative disadvantage of rural areas is indicated by the lower proportion of the school-age population in rural areas that attend secondary schools, compared with primary school attendance (in 2009 the proportions in rural schools are lower; UNESCO, 2010b).

As we will show, in western China during 2004–2007, various projects have aided the universalising of nine-year compulsory education, and the elimination of illiteracy among the young and middle-aged groups: 'National Project of Compulsory Education in Impoverished Areas', the 'Project of renovation of dilapidated school buildings in rural primary and secondary schools', the 'Modern Distance Education Project of in Rural Primary and Secondary Schools' and the 'Project of Constructing Boarding Schools in Rural Primary and Secondary Schools'. The conditions of primary and junior secondary schools in rural areas have been greatly improved and the teaching quality of these schools has been gradually enhanced. Nevertheless there remain substantial differences in

Table 4.2 The changes in enrolment in primary and secondary schools (2005–2008)

	2005	*2006*	*2007*	*2008*
Senior secondary	2,409.09	2,515.5	2,522.4	2,476.28
Junior secondary	6,171.81	5,937.38	5,720.9	5,574.15
Primary	10,864.07	10,711.53	10,564	10,331.51

Source: MoE (2009).

Table 4.3 Education statistics for 2008 showing rural elements

		Primary schools	*Junior secondary schools*	*Senior secondary schools*
Enrolment		10,331.5	5,574.15	2,476.28
(in ten thousands)	In rural	5,924.88	2,070.44	192.13
	areas	57.35%	37.14%	7.76%
Number of schools		300,854	57,701	15,206
	In rural	253,041	31,458	1,762
	areas	84.1%	54.5%	11.6%
Number of teachers		562.19	346.89	147.55
(in ten thousands)	In rural	333.73	134.39	11.89
	areas	59.4%	38.7.3%	8.1%

provision of both facilities (some very basic such as adequate furniture) and the quality of the teachers (in terms of qualifications and pedagogy). These differences reflect the differing social and economic conditions of rural and remote areas from those found in Central and East China. This has been exacerbated by the decentralisation of educational provision, one consequence of which has been to raise the costs of education (in terms of school fees) for rural families (Hannum and Adams, 2009).

Zhao and Hu (2007), in reviewing progress towards UNESCO's 'Education for All' (EFA) programme, conclude that China has made great efforts to achieve the six goals of EFA, in terms of primary and junior secondary school enrolments and the gender differentials in such enrolment, but that there remain key dimensions of disparity and barriers to education in terms of 'poverty, gender, social inclusion, people with disabilities and children in exceptionally difficult circumstances' (Zhao and Hu, 2007: 1). Their view is that the government has targeted poverty, but has been less focused on the other groups. They coin the phrase 'hard to reach' areas, where the government has targeted policy, but that there is a lack of funds 'to translate them into reality, or no practical guidance to solve problems raised during implementation . . . or no monitoring system to review the progress and adjust policy [that results in] many good policies [being] only effective on paper' (Zhao and Hu, 2007: 1). Later we will review these policies, but first it is necessary to explain the nature of the teaching force and how it is educated.

Teachers

The large teaching force arising from the vast scale of the education system represents a massive task for teacher education. Since the late 1970s, when China's economic development changed to emphasise markets, the focus was initially on increasing the supply of teachers, but as this has been achieved the emphasis has moved in the last decade to quality. The teacher-student ratio is relatively good, having first declined in 1990s and then improved in the last decade (Ministry of Education, 2009a: 17); in 2009 the ratios were: primary, 1:17.9; junior secondary, 1:16.1; senior secondary, 1:15.5 (UNESCO, 2010b). Rural primary and junior secondary school ratios are better than these, but despite these statistics, those for class sizes are surprising, as Figure 4.1 indicates. The explanation of the small class sizes for primary may relate to the numerous village schools with a catchment area of children within walking distance; urban schools will have a higher density population in their locality. Shi and Englert (2008) say that primary schools are over-staffed. On the other hand the distributions of class sizes for secondary schools are more equivalent (the exception is the relatively large number of rural senior secondary classes above 66 students; Figure 4.3). One of the reasons for this is that rural secondary schools have a boarding element to ensure that schools are viable for teachers to be able to support the curriculum range. However, for urban and rural secondary and urban primary distributions, the median class size (46–55) is very much larger than the teacher-student ratios published elsewhere in the statistical yearbook (Ministry of Education, 2009a). This may reflect the number of teachers in secondary schools who do not actually teach (e.g. head teachers) and also the fact that teachers have relatively light teaching loads, especially in urban areas (Paine and Fang, 2007), compared with other countries. (There are a small number of teachers who do not apparently have a teaching load: 2 per cent in primary, 4.5 per cent in junior secondary and 1 per cent in senior secondary.)

Quality was initially focused on ensuring properly qualified teachers entering the system. Primary school teachers are required to have at least a senior secondary school education, junior secondary teachers at least a three-year degree (diploma), and senior secondary teachers at least a four-year degree qualification. The percentages of teachers who have less than these qualifications in 2009 were:

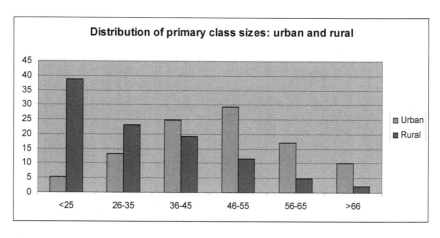

Figure 4.1 Primary school class sizes

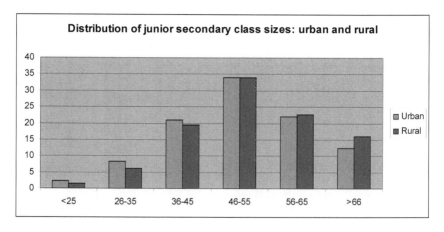

Figure 4.2 Junior secondary class sizes

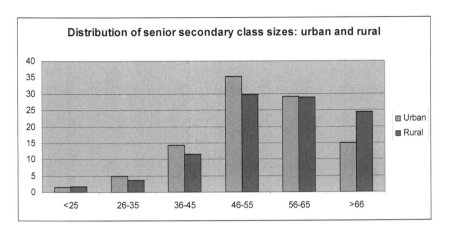

Figure 4.3 Senior secondary class sizes

primary 0.6 per cent; junior secondary 1.7 per cent; senior secondary 6.4 per cent (UNESCO, 2010b). Although teacher qualifications have been a source of problems in the past, the statistics indicate that even in rural areas the percentage of under-qualified teachers is low. Table 4.4 shows historical data for primary and junior secondary school teachers including a comparison of rural schools with all schools. This indicates both the improvement in qualifications over the years and, when compared with the current figure for junior secondary, a particularly great improvement. The differences between the qualifications of rural teachers and those for the whole country are decreasing. Nevertheless the absolute number of those without suitable qualifications is large. In arguing for e-learning to tackle the under-qualification of teachers, Gao and Zhang (2009: 99) claim that in 2007 some 300,000 teachers needed upgrading, giving percentages that are quite different from those taken from the Ministry of Education (2009a); they say there are 62 per cent qualified teachers in primary, and in junior secondary 41 per cent. In fact these latter figures would indicate over four million teachers with inadequate qualifications, ignoring those in senior secondary schools. (Later we examine the initiatives to improve quality of teachers in rural areas.)

The teaching population is relatively young, particularly in secondary schools: 88.6 per cent below the age of 45 in senior secondary schools, 84.7 per cent in

Table 4.4 Percentage of primary and junior secondary teachers with appropriate qualifications 2002–2006

	2002	*2004*	*2005*	*2006*	*2008*	*2009*
Primary schools	97.4	98.3	98.6	98.9	99.27	99.40
In rural areas	96.7	97.8	98.1	98.4	98.93	99.12
Junior secondary schools	90.4	93.8	95.2	96.3	97.79	98.28
In rural areas	86.6	91.3	93.2	94.8	96.86	97.52

junior secondary and 69.8 per cent in primary (2009). The rural figures are given for secondary schools (see Figure 4.4), although it is evident that there is little difference from the overall figures. One result of this age profile is that there are less experienced teachers in secondary schools to act as mentors to inexperienced ones (Paine and Fang, 2007; they were, however, using 1999 statistics), something that has important implications for school-supported professional development.

Given the historical tradition of reverence for teachers, in post-revolution China they have been less recognised than this tradition implies (Paine and Fang, 2007), although the government has done much to try to improve the status of teaching as a profession through increases in salary and living conditions. In recent times this was through the *Education Reform and Development in China* 1993 document (Zhou and Reed, 2005: 206), but there remain problems, with a 2008 report indicating that salary levesl are still relatively low and a performance salary system being instituted in 2009 (UNESCO, 2012). As with so many national policies that have financial implications, the implementation of this will still reflect the relative economic conditions in rural areas.

Shi and Englert (2008) quote from a survey published in 2004 showing high levels of dissatisfaction among a sample of primary school teachers about the desirability of becoming a teacher, even though they think their status will improve. (There are always problems about using such empirical data on China, as there is seldom any clarity about the sampling, making generalisation insecure, especially given the large numbers and variations across China.) This, Shi and Englert say, leads to difficulty in recruiting primary teachers and holding them after their initial appointment, exacerbated by the increased mobility that has come with the recent relaxation of regulations (Paine and Fang, 2007; Robinson and Yi, 2008). In many rural areas teachers are not government employees, but are recruited and paid for by the local village, being referred to as *minban* [民办]. Such teachers are more likely to be under-qualified and of poorer quality. Bai (2008) says that in Gansu (one of the poorest provinces), there are 9.7 per cent of such teachers

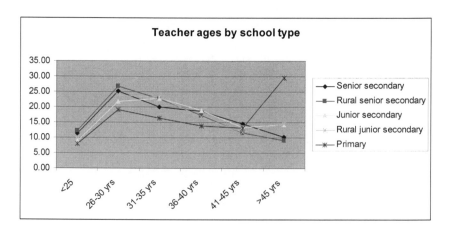

Figure 4.4 Ages of teachers in various kinds of schools (2008)

(he refers to them as substitute teachers [代课 *daike*]), but that in some areas it could be greater than 50 per cent. They might only receive 20–30 per cent of the salary of teachers employed by the government. The *Baidu baike* (online encyclopedia) says that *daike* are temporary teachers in rural areas who are not formally employed by the government, and that up until 1985 they were called *minban* teachers [http://baike.baidu.com/view/2066105.htm?fr=ala0_1_1, accessed 8 November 2011]. However, *minban* and *daike* teachers appear not to be the same, although the definition is somewhat confused. Robinson and Yi (2008) argue that such teachers were referred to as *minban* until 1986, and are now referred to as *daike*. However, the government statistics show that there is a category that are *daike*, but also *minban*, which we take to mean that, although they are 'substitute' teachers, they are employed in private, i.e. non-government, schools. Likewise there are *daike* who are employed in government schools. In discussing the employment of *daike* teachers where qualified teachers are not available, Robinson and Yi (2008) say this is only partly the case, and that in some cases qualified teachers are employed in government schools as *daike* because the local staffing quotas do not allow full government status (*gongke* 共课) to be allocated.

Robinson and Yi (2008) present detailed data on *daike* teachers in Gansu, showing that in the first five years of the twenty-first century they increased to about 14 per cent in primary schools (3.6 per cent in junior secondary; 2004), reflecting the needs of meeting nine-year compulsory education. They also show from survey data that *daike* teachers are paid about 20 per cent of government recognised teachers, but that they are actually younger and more recently appointed (as the statistics indicate). (Bai, 2008, claims that primary teachers are older, but this could reflect the large group who are over 45, as indicated in Figure 4.4. Nevertheless around 60 per cent of primary teachers are under 40.) However, although *daike* teachers are not as well qualified as government-recognised teachers, three-quarters of them are 'qualified' according to government standards. Appointing them is a cheaper way of providing qualified teachers. Table 4.5 shows the national statistics for *daike* teachers in urban and rural areas, but these of course hide provincial differences; as we indicated earlier they are more significant. Ironically they show that the use of *daike* teachers is higher in urban areas.

In an effort to try to improve quality, in 2006 the Ministry of Education declared that *daike* teachers were to be dismissed (at that time there were some 448,000

Table 4.5 Statistics for *daike* primary teachers in 2009 (MoE, 2009a)

	Rural		Urban		Overall	
	Number	%	Number	%	Number	%
Full-time	3,337,264	94.6	929,613	90.1	5,621,938	96.4
Daike	190,344	5.4	92,955	9.9	207,923	3.6
Total	3,527,608	100	1,022,568	100	5,829,861	100

Note that around 17,000 part-time teachers have been ignored. Also the 'Overall' figure includes those that are in schools in counties and towns, which are neither 'urban' nor 'rural'.

64   *Y. Hanbing and B. McCormick*

such teachers, 300,000 of whom were in rural areas). Although some provinces rehired them as formal teachers through an examination, many *daike* teachers did lose their jobs. This led to complaints from these teachers who thought that their dismissal was neither fair nor legal (Chen, 2010). This inevitably led to a reduction in supply as the 2009 figures show (Table 4.5). (In 2011 a pilot in Zhejiang and Hubei provinces was launched for a new teacher qualification examination and 29,000 teachers participated [Ministry of Education, 2011b].)

Teacher education

Structure and policy context

Teacher education since the 1950s has been based on specialist institutions for both pre-service and in-service training mainly administered at a local level. These teacher education institutions (referred to as 'normal' universities or schools, which has French roots; Hayhoe and Li, 2010), were segregated into normal universities for senior secondary teachers, normal colleges for junior secondary teachers, and normal secondary schools for primary teachers. (In Chinese the term 'shifan' [师范] is used to designate such institutions. Hayhoe and Li, 2010, give an historical account of the origins and development of these institutions. Only a handful of these are universities run by central government; Paine and Fang, 2007.) However, this segregation from other institutions of higher education was broken down with the 1996 reforms, to enable comprehensive universities (i.e. those not dedicated to teacher education) to prepare teachers for secondary schools (Shi and Englert, 2008). These reforms were part of the improvement in qualification requirements, with senior secondary school teachers needing a four-year degree (referred to as *benke* [本科]) from a university, junior secondary teachers a three-year degree (referred to as *zhuanke* [专科]) from a college, and primary school teachers a senior secondary level education from normal schools. Later targets were more ambitious with all primary and junior secondary teachers required to have a three-year degree and senior secondary teachers a four-year degree by 2010 (Zhou and Reed, 2005), with the eventual target in the next decade of all new teachers having a four-year degree (Shi and Englert, 2008).

With these reforms came a major reorganisation of the institutions, extending beyond just the removal of the monopoly of teacher education from the 'normal' institutions. The top-level comprehensive universities took on teacher education, rising to providing 30 per cent of all pre-service teacher education (Shi and Englert, 2008; Li *et al.*, 2008, say 35 per cent in 2005), and normal universities started to compete with comprehensive universities. Some moved into the more general higher education market hitherto the remit of comprehensive universities, which Zhong (2008) sees as a misuse of a special asset. Normal (teacher education) colleges were combined with specialised education institutes (run at township or county level), who traditionally were in-service institutions, and normal secondary schools are being phased out. The statistics are reported in many ways

China 65

(see Table 4.6 for 2006 data, and Figure 4.5 for data over the years 1999–2006), and various authors give data to show how normal secondary schools and junior education colleges are declining (as Figure 4.5 indicates), while those that offer three- and four-year degrees for teachers are increasing (including the provision

Table 4.6 Number of institutions and students of teacher education (2007)

	Types of institutions	Numbers of institutions	Number of students (10 thousand)
Universities/colleges (4-year degree)	Normal universities/colleges	97	66.59
	Others	244	47.36
	Subtotal	**341**	**113.95**
Short-term colleges (3-year degree)	Normal universities and colleges	68	10.55
	Short-term normal colleges	44	14.79
	Others	297	39.26
	Subtotal	**409**	**64.60**
Secondary normal schools	Secondary normal schools	196	20.52
	Other secondary vocational schools	2,002	48.52
	Subtotal	**2,198**	**69.09**

Source: *The Educational Statistics* of the official website of China's Ministry of Education: www.moe.edu.cn/ (accessed 8 November 2011).

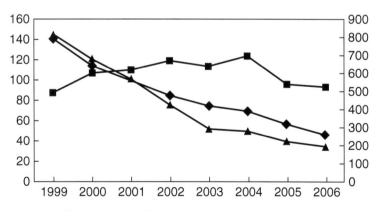

Figure 4.5 Trends in numbers of teacher training institutions (1999–2006)

by institutions not originally designated as 'normal'). Along with the dissolving of the divisions between teacher education and other higher education institutions, pre-service and in-service were combined. Traditionally in-service had been the responsibility of local education institutes and secondary normal schools that provided a very grounded and local system. Now all institutions provide in-service as well as pre-service. (The official statistics make it difficult to decide the number of institutions offering teacher education at the different levels, but 140 universities and colleges offering four-year degrees and 48 colleges offering three-year degrees provide teacher training. Other authors who provide various statistics are as follows: for 2005 Li *et al.*, 2008; Shi and Englert, 2008; for 2006 Zhu and Han, 2006.)

However, in the amalgamation of institutions there have been problems with the clash of cultures of the likes of universities that have a theoretical tradition to sustain, in contrast to the in-service institutes that are built on practice. In addition the loss of some of the lower-level institutions resulted in a dispersion of expertise (Paine and Fang, 2007). Not only was the creation of competition and the beginnings of a market a source of instability, but there was to some commentators too much diversity (Zhu and Han, 2006). For rural students this competition led to pressures on students and their families, and with it more responsibility upon them to bear the cost of higher education. This was alleviated by central government paying fees for teacher trainees who attend the six normal universities they controlled. In 2011 the first 10,000 pre-service teachers graduated and just over 40 per cent went to rural schools (online at: http://baike.baidu. com/view/1814113.htm). There were complaints that students did not realise this obligation to go to rural areas when they had their fees paid (Gu, 2008). Xie (2006) says that students have to pay first, but have the money reimbursed later when they take up their first teaching post. (The situation contrasts with earlier days, even as late as the 1980s, when all those in higher education had fees paid and living subsidised, with a guaranteed job on graduation.) For trainees who attend institutions funded by rural counties it is likely that guaranteed funding is more precarious, though there are schemes that target teachers who are supported through teacher training and who are then required to return to work in a rural area, as we will show later.

There have also been reforms to the teacher education curriculum, including strengthening the requirement for a period of teaching practice in schools as part of pre-service education. The recommendation is that students should spend one term in schools, but this may depend upon local conditions. In 2007 the policy of 'internship', as such an approach is called, was promulgated and in 2008 and 2009 modest numbers of colleges (124) and students (85,000) were involved through its implementation (UNESCO, 2012).

For all the reforms and rationalisation, the quality of teachers remains a concern, even though by and large basic under-qualification has been eliminated. For rural areas improving quality has to be done in the face of difficult working conditions. Paine and Fang (2007) give two vignettes of teachers, one from Shanghai, and the other from Inner Mongolia, which illustrate the contrasts that still exist (though in fact their field work was carried out at the end of the 1990s and beginnings of the first decade of the twenty-first century). A junior secondary mathematics teacher from Shanghai taught only 13 periods a week to two classes. Although she worked a long day, there was plenty of time to plan and develop lessons, including working with groups of other teachers in this planning and in lesson studies (we will come back to this on pp. 000–000). The *minban* teacher in a primary school in Inner Mongolia taught all the village children aged 4–12 years in a small cottage, with the pre-school children being in a small room, and the rest taught as a single class in the main classroom. This entailed, for example, older children being taught mathematics, while the rest of the children studied their textbooks and completed assignments and the pre-school children were drawing. Apart from school work there was tending to the four family pigs and chickens, and helping her husband in the fields and vegetable plot. These conditions were also reflected in their experience of in-service education to develop their professional skills.

In-service teacher education

The merging of in-service with the provision of pre-service education was part of the drive to improve the quality of teachers and to increase the status of in-service education. Paine and Fang (2007) describe the situation for teachers in Shanghai who could expect career education starting from pre-service, then probationary professional development and then professional development throughout the rest of their careers. Indeed it became both a requirement and an expectation for teachers to have 240 hours of professional development over a five-year period. This is not without difficulties, even in advanced urban areas such as Shanghai, where Paine and Fang (2007) reported teacher complaints about this requirement. In rural areas supplying good quality professional development, and attending it, proved difficult for rural authorities and teachers. The rural teacher in the vignette from Paine and Fang (2007) had to buy a bicycle to go to the local township for weekly training sessions, undertaken in her own time, and local authorities had difficulties in providing high quality resources of the kinds found in Shanghai. The demise of the normal secondary schools and local institutes has added to the difficulties of providing good quality professional development, because they represented a good link with practice. Nevertheless, at county level the transformation of teachers' colleges of continuing education into teachers' centres of learning and resources by reorganising them with local educational research institutions and audio-visual education institutions, enabled them to be multi-functional and serve a relatively larger number of teachers. The previous institutional arrangements provided smaller and more isolated organisations.

In spite of these local differences the government has a national teacher training plan with over a million teachers (98 per cent rural) participating in 2010 (Ministry of Education, 2012). Again these are national efforts to deal with local differences that result from long-standing differences in economic conditions.

68   *Y. Hanbing and B. McCormick*

Interestingly the use of multimedia approaches, including the use of ICT, both within schools in general and specifically for teacher education, has done much to both transform the distribution of resources for professional development to schools and to change the locus of such development. In the next section we look at how the new technologies are being used to provide teacher education, and then consider how professional development is increasingly school based.

Distance and online teacher education

One major and early provider of distance education was the Radio and Television Universities (RTVUs), which produces printed and audio-visual material centrally in Beijing (the Central Radio and Television University [CRTVU]), with students being organised into tutorial support groups through provincial RTVUs (there are several levels below this that organise and actually provide the support). In fact these universities focus on a wide range of students most of whom study three-year (*zhuanke* 专科) degrees in subjects other than education. In the 1980s those classed as having done 'teacher training' only represented about 1 per cent of graduates. (The total figure for 1980–1988 was 11,068 out of a total of 1,239,562; McCormick, 1992. There was a much larger number involved in non-degree in-service education; Wei, 2008: 53.) In a more recent account of the role of distance education and the CRTVU in general with regard to teacher education, Gao and Zhang (2009), argue (as do Yan, 2009, and Zhu and Gu, 2007) for a role for the CRTVU in trying to cope with what they see as an impossible task for conventional face-to-face institutions in trying to cope with the numbers of under-qualified teachers and the need to provide in-service professional development (which, as argued earlier in relation to their e-learning solution to under-qualification, may be suspect). Gao and Zhang (2009) go on to argue that, in addition to the use of satellite television transmission, this is now being supplemented by the Internet. They indicate the establishment of a National Teacher Education Network (by central government, not the CRTVU) and a general growth in online provision. Strangely they ignore the Teachers Television channel, which has broadcast programmes specifically for primary and secondary teacher since 1986 (McCormick, 1992). They also ignore the long tradition of teacher education universities running correspondence courses for teachers to upgrade their qualifications, and the numbers graduating this way in the 1990s far exceeded the CRTVU's graduates in teacher training (McCormick, 1992). In the 1990s teacher programmes were broadcast (using a dedicated education television satellite, which had many other educational programmes) in the mornings, evenings and weekends. Most teachers viewed recordings of these programmes in local in-service centres and indeed the support and study associated with them was provided at this local level with teachers in 'classes' of 30–40.

In fact what is now referred to as 'modern' distance education has been formulated into a number of policies, and most recently was part of the central government's primary and secondary teacher training plan (Ministry of Education,

2008), which focuses on rural areas. This includes the use of satellite reception and recording facilities, audio-visual materials and computers. Bai (2008) reviews this kind of provision, focusing upon Gansu, and indicates three models of provision, which in a sense reflect three kinds of centres that have been set up:

- *video replay centre*: sites with DVD player, television, recordings of excellent teachers demonstrating lessons, and teaching material;
- *video replay and computer centre*: this has a satellite receiver system as well as the equipment and material in the replay centre, along with a computer;
- *online centre*: where there is multimedia computer classroom.

Although Bai (2008) focuses on teacher education, Yu and Wang (2006) describe in the national context the same models, but their focus is on the use of such equipment in the classroom by students. (They give a history of the development of the 'modern distance education project rural schools' from a smaller project focused on female teachers.) These two foci of teacher and student use are not incompatible, but the latter requires more constant access to equipment than the former. However, it is evident that Yu and Wang do not consider the teacher education required to use ICT as part of classroom pedagogy. There appears to be no clear connection between the provision of such equipment for the two purposes. Indeed, Yu and Wang do not even mention the need for professional development for the teachers to use ICT as part of their classroom pedagogy.

Bai's discussion also includes an European Union funded project in Gansu (2001–2007), which established Teacher Learning Resource Centres (TLRCs) resembling Bai's second kind of centre (video replay and computer centre). Such centres were set up in schools to serve a cluster of schools, acting as professional development centres, hosting in-service activity, resources and even providing a source of teacher leaders who could go out to rural areas to support schools (Robinson, 2008). By the end of the project 85 per cent of these centres had some kind of Internet connection and 50 per cent had broadband. This enabled some 100,000 teachers and head teachers to undergo training on new teaching methods and curriculum (teachers) and management and administration (head teachers). (This figure includes: 10,308 backbone teachers [those who support other teachers], 78,931 teacher professional development [based in these centres], 688 head teachers trained as trainers and a further 8,900 trained by these peers [Robinson and Yi, 2009]. They claim that 80 per cent of teachers in the 41 targeted counties received training.) Robinson (2008) argues that this approach provides rural teachers with some way of meeting the requirement for 240 hours of professional development, and giving substitute teachers (代课 *daike*) access to professional development; they would otherwise not be entitled to it (as they are not government employees). She reports a survey in 2005 that indicated that, prior to the project, 28 per cent of teachers had had no professional development and the remaining 72 per cent had limited, intermittent and inadequate provision for their needs. In the 41 counties included in the project, 80 per cent of teachers in primary and junior secondary schools had access to a TLRC. Robinson also concludes that there remain challenges to maintain support and commitment from local government to fund future equipment needs and for renewal of materials.

Gansu, with its remote rural areas and large minority population (there are 44 minorities with Tibetan, Hui, Dongxiang and Mongolian being the largest groups), means that there remain, in the phrase of Zhao and Hu (2007) discussed earlier, 'the difficult to reach' or pockets of disadvantage. Thus the rural social and economic disadvantages, discussed in the first section, are replicated in digitally isolated communities that present difficulties for 'modern distance education', as for any form of teacher education. For example, the Internet was accessible to 28.9 per cent of the national population in 2009, which represents 40 per cent of the population in eastern China but only 21.5 per cent in western China; urban Internet users made up 72.2 per cent of the national total, leaving the other 27.8 per cent in rural areas. (The growth of Internet users is given in Figure 4.6.) According to the government document *The Internet in China* it is planned to increase this to 45 per cent by 2015 (State Council, 2010). This 'digital gap' will remain a problem that needs to be bridged.

School-based in-service

This is the kind of professional development that we might expect in European and other advanced countries, including peer coaching, and such collaborative activity within a school. In particular it contrasts with taking teachers out of school to attend lectures, which in the context of China might be somewhat divorced from practice. One of the features of the vignettes from Paine and Fang (2007) was the fact that the urban teacher in Shanghai was involved in lesson study and joint planning that essentially acted as school-based professional development. Gu and Wang (2006) give an account of such school-based professional development in Shanghai, which they characterise as an 'action education model', central to which is lesson study, a common approach in Asia (Fernandez, 2002).

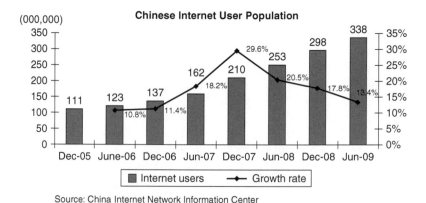

Figure 4.6 Growth in Chinese Internet use (CINIC, 2009)

Wong and Tsui (2007) carried out interviews in seven schools in four districts of Guangdong province (commonly known as 'Canton' province, southern China). This included 37 school administrators and 32 teachers in both public and private schools, of whom almost 70 per cent were positive (most positive in the elite public schools and least in the private schools). Most of this school-based work seems to be in urban areas, but it has been promoted in poor rural areas such as Guangxi Zhuang Autonomous Region (in the south-west border area), which has 40,000 primary and secondary teachers. The local educational department provided a free resource package on school-based in-service training, which included elements of school-based research, as well as more conventional study by teachers.

Interestingly none of this work seems to be linked to the developments in distance teacher education, where school-based resources are a focus. At the moment such centres within schools (e.g. the TLRCs in Gansu) are not available to all schools, and especially to those in remote rural areas. In judging school-based professional developments in China we should remember, however, that in countries such as the UK school-based collaborative professional development is far from universal (Pedder *et al.*, 2008), despite its promotion on an international scale as a model of how to work (Day and Sachs, 2004).

Reforms to support rural education

One element of rural education reforms is to give direct financial support to students, to overcome the increased cost to rural families noted earlier, along with the improvement of school buildings in rural areas. Thus in 2006, 52 million rural primary and secondary school students in West China and part of Central China were subsidised so that they did not have to pay tuition fees and, in 2007, this policy spread to rural areas nationwide. In 2005 and 2006, 37 million primary school and junior secondary school students from rural poor families were given free textbooks and allowances, which enabled them to pay fees of as much as 210 Yuan and 320 Yuan respectively; each of the eight million boarding students were also given annual allowances of 300 Yuan (equivalent of about £30 or $45). Similarly a school building programme for rural areas, particularly boarding schools, a requirement to serve western areas of China where distances to secondary schools in particular are large, enabled 5,000 schools to be built (Zhao and Hu, 2007). Clearly such schools are more expensive because of the need for student accommodation. Although school hardware and ensuring that students can attend school are important, training and capacity building are also essential, and hence the reforms that focus on teachers become significant. We have already indicated teacher quality as one element of this, and hence the focus on qualifications and professional development noted earlier. But evidence also shows that in rural areas employing someone who comes from the area is more important; in particular rural girls benefit in terms of achievement when they are taught by female teachers who are themselves local (Hannum and Park, 2006). Getting the right type of teachers to rural schools, where conditions are generally difficult for both living and teaching, is a challenge. A detailed account of the evidence

72   *Y. Hanbing and B. McCormick*

for the link of student outcomes and teaching quality in Gansu is given by An *et al.* (2007), in which they indicate that economic reasons (e.g. high cost of fees) are not the main reason for drop out of rural students (which is high), rather it is dislike of school. Establishing the link of achievement to teacher quality is more problematic, however (Hannum and Adams, 2009). Nevertheless the evidence indicates that pedagogy is important and the curriculum reforms by the government will help.

The reforms indicated above, of liberating institutions from traditional specialisms and reorganising the institutions to enable them to be upgraded, have produced a state of flux. This in turn may have disrupted the existing utilisation of teacher education expertise and perhaps dissipated it. Paine and Fang (2007) see challenges, from on the one hand a liberalising and decentralising of teacher education while wanting to control the quality of teachers, and on the other the difficulty of undertaking reform when the system is changing because of these reforms. There are no direct accountability systems for teachers who are currently serving, though the performance salary system noted earlier may help. There is also a desire to assess pre-service teachers more effectively. Inevitably, so Paine and Fang argue, the only existing national system of accountability of teachers is the student examination system. This reinforces traditional teaching, which reforms are trying to improve upon. They also argue that the stress on peer support, sharing practice and school involvement in professional development might reinforce traditional approaches, making this a difficult mechanism for reform. For rural teachers the concerns might be more prosaic, with the pressures of workload conflicting with in-service demands, the training costs falling on individual teachers and the practical difficulties of travelling to professional development sessions.

Although teacher quality remains a concern throughout China, it is particular so in rural schools. As noted a number of times, the differences between urban and rural conditions reflect their different social and economic development, and hence it is tackling the result of these fundamental differences that has been the focus of recent government efforts. A number of measures taken at various levels deal with these differences:

- *Attract graduates to rural areas and improve quality in rural areas*: in 2006, the Ministry of Education implemented a Special Teacher Recruitment Plan [STRP] (Ministry of Education, 2011a). This plan aims to recruit college graduates (especially those from comprehensive universities) to be teachers in rural schools. In 2011, the Ministry of Education implemented the Master Teacher Plan (Ministry of Education, 2009b), to complement STRP. This will develop backbone teachers from STRP-recruited teachers, through a Master of Education diploma.
- *Improve teacher qualifications*: in 2011, the Ministry of Education launched a teacher qualification and registration system. A pilot in Zhejiang and Hubei provinces was launched for a new teacher qualification examination and 28,000 teachers participated (China Broadcast Network, 2011). This for the first time clarified the qualifying standard for new teachers. Following this,

a public consultation on the 'Draft professional standards for kindergarten teachers, primary teachers and secondary school teachers' started in late 2011 (Ministry of Education, 2011b). These standards will be published in 2012.

- *Attract teachers to rural areas by using market forces*: for example outstanding graduates of junior secondary schools are targeted each year throughout Hunan province, and provided with free five-year education oriented to going back to rural primary schools where they would get a subsidised salary for five years.
- *Supplementing the budgets in rural areas* to enable teachers to take part in both full-time and school-based training (e.g. in Zhejiang, a relatively well-off province, where over 200,000 rural teachers were involved in such training).
- *Targeting particular shortage curriculum areas* where a newly qualified specialist teacher can make a difference, and supporting them with improved salary and professional development; in two years some 32,000 young university graduates worked in over 4,000 rural schools in the mountainous region of southern Ning Xia Province. (An example of a PE teacher in a Ning Xia school was given in the educational newspaper: *China Education Daily*, 20 October 2007: 1.)
- *Sharing of urban teachers with rural areas*, where teachers from a city like Shanghai visit sites in the suburbs, to enable interchange between urban and rural schools, as well as working in more remote areas such as Yunan (southwest China).
- *Increasing salary levels for rural teachers*, such that they can equal the salary of urban teachers; rural teachers (particularly *daike* teachers) not only can be paid less, at times they may not be paid regularly.
- *Improving housing conditions for rural teachers*, through targeted funds particularly for those western and remote areas.

Nevertheless there remain problems and, in 2008, a National Teacher Training Plan (Ministry of Education, 2008) contained similar measures to those above, in particular the matching of provinces in the eastern and central areas of China (e.g. Shanghai, Jiangxu and Zhejiang, with Yunan, Tibet and Xinjiang respectively), indicating a recognition of this. Also the major teacher education universities (controlled by central government) worked with such western and remote provinces. The 2010 plan allocated an unprecedented amount of money to support backbone teachers in central and western rural areas (www.gpjh.cn/cms). The accounts by the Ministry of Education in 2011 still indicate a concern with rural schools, but the focus seems to be shifting to controls and regulations as much as support to improve conditions locally. The former will suffer from being simply directives that require local finance and initiative, and the latter only a solution in particular instances which cannot provide a universal solution to rural education problems.

Another element was stressed in this 2008 training plan, namely distance learning, specifically targeted on rural areas. A programme for 23 provinces,

74　*Y. Hanbing and B. McCormick*

counties and towns was to use satellite television programmes, supplemented by the Internet, to train 200,000 rural teachers in language, mathematics and physical education. In addition there was to be set up a network of distance education for lead teachers who can then go out in turn to train other lead teacher in rural areas. However, as we saw earlier, despite the great achievements in reaching rural areas, there will remain pockets of disadvantage even using these 'modern distance education' means.

International lessons

Creating reform for the apparently intractable problems of dealing with the disadvantages facing rural areas provides a model for populous countries throughout the world. But as we have illustrated this still has limitations, particularly those related to funds for the implementation of policy and for monitoring its effectiveness, as indicated by our citing of the conclusions of Zhao and Hu (2007) earlier. The dilemma of moving away from a centrally controlled and organised system to harness market forces, while at the same time removing the levers of government that enable inequalities to be minimised, is ever present. This relies on some form of accountability and with it monitoring, which are both sensitive to the reforms to curriculum and teaching methods and do not produce backwash effects. China has much to learn about this, particularly because the student examination system (reinstated after the Cultural Revolution to engender a meritocracy) has become a conservative force running counter to the pedagogic reforms. It is well known that without reforming student assessment systems pedagogic reforms are inhibited and in some places doomed. If China can tackle this (given that it gave the world such centrally controlled examinations over 2,000 years ago), there would be a real lesson for the rest of the world. Despite some relaxation of an exclusive focus on the examinations for entrance to higher education, moves to change assessment have been minimal.

At the heart of the problems for rural education are inequalities that are both historical and existential relating to harsh geographical conditions typical in western provinces. Heavy policy and financial intervention by central government to support rural education shows the way for possible reforms elsewhere, but what is less evident is how support can be maintained when central government (or in some cases as we saw in Gansu, foreign countries) no longer intervene. The decentralisation of controls to local governments, as we indicated, has exacerbated rural and urban differences, and has led to the central initiatives and policy and legislative action, which in a sense undermine this decentralisation. Whether other countries can learn just from confronting this dilemma is unclear, but China offers no simple lessons to overcoming them.

Conclusion

There have been great achievements with such a colossal system, and as noted there will be enduring problems for some rural and remote areas as long as there remain social and economic differences from the rest of China. As a country it presents a situation that is quite different from the general picture of education and teacher supply depicted in Chapter 1, but nevertheless there remain problems of teacher quality particularly in these rural and remote areas. The best of teacher education, particularly in-service professional development (usually in urban areas), is as good as anywhere in the world. The collective tradition of working with colleagues in planning and reviewing lessons (formalised in 'lesson study' approaches) represents outstanding practice of professional development. Inevitably, in poorer rural areas, there remain problems in recruiting, training and sustaining good teachers, but there can be no doubt that many teachers show high dedication and professionalism in difficult circumstances. The issue will be the extent to which good quality is the norm, rather than the exception, and the extent of adoption of measures of teacher accountability that elsewhere in the world produce rigidities and lack of professional independence and self-worth. It is also evident that the introduction of 'market' elements in teacher education are likely to lead to less focus on practice (and a greater distance of teacher educators from local practice). The use of new technology could provide some way providing a school-based approach, seen in Chapter 1 as an important response to the first issue of the need for change in teacher education, but there is as yet no evidence that it is being seen in this way.

5 India

Committing to change

Frank Banks and Premakumari Dheram

A teacher can never truly teach unless he is still learning himself. A lamp never lights another lamp unless it continues to burn its own flame.
'The Ideal Teacher', Rabindra Nath Tagore (Poet: 1861–1941)

This chapter looks at the attempts to address the need for teachers to continue to learn throughout their career. It considers how India, with its huge challenges of scale of need and diversity of contexts, might through its renowned capability in the use of new technologies better exploit IT to address its educational aspirations – and indeed enable its teachers' 'lamp' to continue to burn.

In the period since Independence, the Government of India (GOI) has frequently legislated to construct shared responsibilities for education between national and state governments and funded a range of programmes to improve teacher supply and teaching quality. Before 1976, education was largely the responsibility of states, the central government being only concerned with coordination and determining standards but joint responsibility was established by a constitutional amendment. The most recent Right of Children to Free and Compulsory Education Act ('Right to Education Act') (GOI, 2009) sets out the latest commitment of the nation to improve significantly the access of all young people to a child-centred basic education. This Act, perhaps one of the most significant in India's history, is in part a response to the growing realisation that India's economic growth, whilst impressive, needs sustaining. And that sustainability is seen as crucial if parity is to be maintained with the neighbouring economic progress in China. India's foremost development economist has recently focused on this theme (Sen, 2011):

Expenditure on what is somewhat misleadingly called the 'social sector' – health, education, nutrition, etc. – has certainly gone up in India. And yet India is still well behind China in many of these fields . . . A fuller understanding of the real conditions of the mass of neglected Indians and what can be done to improve their lives through public policy should be a central issue in the politics of India.

(pp. 44–5)

The expansion in education institutions and the demand for teachers since independence has been huge, requiring a massive investment. There have been 11 five-year plans since Independence, and the development of the education system has been a central pillar of the social sector planning. The number of schools increased from 530,000 in 1950–1 to over one million in 2004–5. Similarly the challenges facing the implementation of the new 2009 Act are enormous; not only in its numerical scale and reach (about 20,000 new primary schools and the upgrading of about 70,000 primary schools are required (GOI Planning Commission, 2008)) but also in enacting the government's desire to reorientate the traditional teacher's role in the classroom towards more active student learning. The above quotation of Tagore goes on to lament that for many teachers, 'their subjects are like dead specimens of once living things'. Evidence suggests that these words are still relevant today (IBM, 2005; Dheram, 2007). Yet through the commitment of the GOI to new communication technologies, India is poised to exploit significantly new cheap hardware and a developing Internet infrastructure that could impact on both the numerical scale of the problem and on the qualitative changing nature of teachers' classroom life.

In terms of population, India is the largest democracy in the world. The 2001 census showed that although it is the seventh largest country in the world in terms of land area, India is the second most populous at 1,027 million people (531.3 million males and 495.7 million females). In 2008 the World Bank estimated that this had grown to 1.139 million, and with population annual growth at almost 2 per cent (15 million per year) it is likely to become the most populous country by 2050. Consequently India has one of the youngest populations among major countries in the world with almost 500 million of school age.

The country is divided into 28 states, seven union territories, 593 administrative districts, 6,496 sub-district level administrative units, and the 2001 census listed 5,161 towns and 638,665 villages. There are 22 recognised national languages and 844 different dialects used across the country. Hindi is the official language. The majority (80.5 per cent) are Hindus; Islam is the next most common religion at 13.4 per cent, followed by Christians, Sikhs, Buddhists, Jains and others (6 per cent).

Although behind countries like China with its high literacy rate of 94 per cent, compared to other counties in South Asia the adult literacy rate in India is relatively high at 63 per cent (70 per cent for males and 48 per cent for females), but it is very variable between states with Kerala at the top with a literacy rate of 90.9 per cent, while Bihar is at the bottom with 47.5 per cent. The GOI has established a succession of initiatives over the last 20 years to improve access to schooling for the 6–14 age group, as well as its quality. Today, more than 180 million children are taught by almost 5.02 million teachers, both trained and untrained, in more than 1.2 million primary and upper primary schools. It is estimated that over 98 per cent of children have access to primary schooling within one kilometre of their home, and almost 92 per cent to an upper primary school within three kilometres (Menon et al., 2010). Primary Gross Enrolment Rate (GER) calculated as a ratio of the gross enrolment of children as a proportion of the total children in the

78 F. Banks and P. Dheram

relevant age group, stands at 114 per cent for males and 109 per cent for females. Secondary GER however is significantly lower at 59 per cent for males and 49 per cent for females, an almost 50 per cent drop between primary and the secondary level (*info*Dev, 2010a).

Due to the structure of its economy, which favours manufacturing rather than financial services, India has not suffered the same aftermath of recession as many countries. In 2009–10 the economy grew by 8.6 per cent, fuelling a retail market that expands by 25 per cent annually. Every month 15 million people are acquiring mobile phones, for example, and in 2010 car sales stood at 1.5 million vehicles, an increase of 25 per cent in a year. Fifty-four per cent of GDP is contributed by the services sector and the acceleration of economic growth has reduced poverty both at state and national level. This growth, coupled with a large number of talented computer engineers, has created opportunities both in exporting software and for outsourced ICT, and also in the growing domestic market (OECD quoted in *Independent*, 2010). In this respect India is a leader in the ability to exploit new communication technologies for education and other purposes. However, access to the new technologies is not widespread and 25 per cent of people still live below the poverty line. A study by Oxford University suggests that more than 410 million people live in poverty in eight states of India; more people below the poverty line than in the 26 poorest countries of Sub-Saharan Africa (OPHI, 2010).

In India there is a balance of responsibility for education between the central and state administrations. At the centre it is administered by the Ministry of Human Resource Development (MHRD), and by the different departments of education at the state level. The GOI provides the overall policy framework, financial support and guidelines to ensure a national standard of education; however implementation is primarily done at the state level. The MHRD has two constituent departments, the Department of School Education and Literacy and the Department of Higher Education. Additionally there is a National Council of Educational Research and Training (NCERT) under the aegis of the MHRD to support both central and state governments in policy implementation.

For over 25 years attempts have been made to create a uniform pattern of schooling lasting 12 years – often called the 10 + 2 pattern, and all states have accepted a minimum of ten years to complete general education. However the primary, upper primary and secondary split is not consistent across states with 18 states splitting 5 + 3 + 2 and 12 others 4 + 3 + 3. Still other states have 5 + 2 + 3 and 4 + 4 + 2 schooling systems. Within a state, however, the schooling pattern is largely homogeneous. An outline of the education system is shown in Figure 5.1, which illustrates the 5 + 3 + 2 system.

Implementation of pre-school (kindergarten) is not compulsory although there have been government schemes since 1975 to integrate health support with early childcare. The attempts to establish universal primary education started almost as soon as India became independent. Through the new Right to Education Act every child in the age group of 6–14 years must now be provided with eight years of elementary education in a classroom appropriate to their age and in the

AGE	Alternative Education Stream	Years	Regular Education Stream
18+	Open Universities/ Distance Learning Institutions. (Government and Private)		Academic and Professional Degree Colleges & Technical/ Agricultural Universities (Government and Private)
17–18		Year 12	Senior Secondary Schools/Colleges, Vocational Training Institutions. (Government, Private and Religious Minority Schools)
16–17	National Institute of open Schooling	Year 11	
15–16	National Institute of open Schooling	Year 10	SECONDARY SCHOOLS (Government, Private and Religious Minority Schools)
14–15		Year 9	
13–14		Year 8	
12–13		Year 7	
11–12	Non-Formal Education Centres	Year 6	
10–11		Year 5	
9–10	FREE AND COMPULSORY EDUCATION	Year 4	PRIMARY SCHOOLS (Government, Private and Religious Minority Schools)
8–9		Year 3	
7–8		Year 2	
6–7		Year 1	
3–6	Pre-School, Kindergarten		

Figure 5.1 India education system (The Global Gateway, 2010)

vicinity of his/her neighbourhood. The planning for this provision is based on the number of children whose birth has been registered. However, it is estimated that only 38,000 out of the estimated 70,000 births that occur in the country every day are registered (Serrao and Sujatha, 2004). Although birth certification is not mandatory for school enrolment, the lack of accurate data on births makes the estimate of teacher supply requirements particularly difficult.

By 2001, the GoI, determined to address the 7.1 million children out of school and over 50 per cent dropping out at elementary level, had already launched a

80 F. Banks and P. Dheram

comprehensive and decentralised programme of Education for All named Sarva Shiksha Abhiyan (SSA) as a nationwide programme. SSA is implemented in partnership with state governments and is wide ranging. For example, the programme addresses infrastructure problems by opening new schools and improving the provision of additional classrooms, toilets, drinking water, and providing general maintenance. In curriculum terms, SSA seeks to enhance elementary education by including life skills and a focus on both girls' education and children with special needs (MHRD, 2010). The success of SSA has encouraged the government to proceed with further measures to improve access to secondary education through Rashtriya Madhyamik Shiksha Abhiyan.

Only about 50 per cent of the relevant age group attend secondary education. Secondary education is divided into two stages, 'Secondary Education' for classes 9 and 10 (14–15 years) and 'Senior Secondary' for classes 11 and 12 (16–17 years). After an increase in demand in the 1990s due to follow-on from increased completion at primary schools, there have been relatively little changes to secondary provision in recent years. Non-government organisations (NGOs) have increased their involvement in this phase with some financial support from state authorities.

The challenge to the supply of teachers for this system is formidable. It is estimated that there are 5.7 million available teacher posts at primary and upper primary levels, of which a little over half a million posts are currently vacant. The implementation of the Right to Education Act, which specifies a 1:30 teacher–pupil ratio, would require approximately another 500,000 additional teachers (over and above existing vacancies) to meet the new teacher–pupil ratios. This means that there is a need for 1.3 million newly trained teachers across the country, and the upgrading of about 772,000 current teachers who are untrained. However, these estimates are likely to change once the states undertake the redeployment process and calculate the exact requirement of additional teachers for each school. The implications of the Right to Education Act combined with the previous backlog in teacher recruitment and the numbers of untrained teachers (see Govinda and Josephine, 2005 and Kingdon and Sipahimalani-Rao, 2010) currently working presents a significant challenge particularly to states such as Bihar, Chhattisgarh and Jharkhand. Taken together the states of Bihar, Assam, Chhattisgarh, Jammu and Kashmir, Jharkhand, Orissa, Uttar Pradesh and West Bengal have 606,000 untrained teachers and need 973,000 new teachers.

However, there is considerable variation across the country. The 12 states of Andhra Pradesh, Delhi, Gujarat, Haryana, Himachal Pradesh, Kerala, Madhya Pradesh, Maharashtra, Punjab, Rajasthan, Tamil Nadu and Uttarakhand have very low levels of untrained teachers, which have a combined need for 233,000 new teachers and 94,000 in-service teachers that need training. Karnataka has no untrained teachers and Delhi, Gujarat, Kerala, Maharashtra and Tamil Nadu have less than 1 per cent untrained. The north-eastern states of Arunachal, Manipur, Meghalaya, Mizoram, Nagaland, Sikkim and Tripura together only need 3,161 new teachers, with an in-service training requirement for 72,000 teachers (*Times of India*, 2009; Menon *et al.*, 2010).

India 81

Taken overall, therefore, there is a need for over 1,300,000 new teachers. Of the nearly three-quarters of a million untrained teachers it is estimated 51 per cent are qualified to only higher secondary level or below (24 per cent secondary and 4 per cent with only primary level education) and about 31 per cent are graduates and 10 per cent postgraduates (IBM, 2005).

The preparation of these teachers has received ongoing governmental attention. The need for qualitative improvements in teacher education was noted by the Kothari Commission in the 1960s. In the 1980s the Chattopadhyaya report saw the role of the teacher as one who communicates to children: 'the importance of, and the feeling of, national integrity and unity; the need for a scientific attitude; commitment to excellence in standards of work and action and a concern for society'. The linkage of teacher role and nationalism harks back to the sort of republican responsibilities ascribed to the 'instituteurs' in the newly established state system in nineteenth-century France. But the same report goes on to say: 'if school teachers are expected to bring about a revolution in their approach to teaching . . . that same revolution must precede and find a place in the colleges of education' (GOI, 1985, p. 48). In 1993 the Yashpal Committee returned to the same theme in suggesting that a predominance of inadequate programmes of teacher preparation are leading to an unsatisfactory quality of learning in schools.

There is a significant level of provision for teacher preparation. Under the Right to Education Act, the central government is required to 'develop and enforce standards for training of teachers' (GOI, 2009, p. 4). Since 1995, the National Council for Teacher Education (NCTE) has been responsible for the planning and coordination of teacher education across the country. It regulates standards and has a very wide remit covering teachers for all levels of schooling and the non-formal sector and all methods of teacher preparation including part-time and open learning.

Table 5.1 Pre-service training of teachers

Preparation for:	Funding arrangements	Admission requirements	Length of the course	Diploma/degree awarded
Pre-primary education	Private unaided	12 years of schooling	One or two years	Certificate/ Pre-school in Education
Primary education	Government, private aided, private unaided	10/12 years of schooling	Two years	Certificate/ Diploma in Elementary Education
Secondary education	Government, private aided, private unaided	Graduate	One year	Bachelor of Education
Specialist courses in secondary science education	Government aided	12 years	Four-year concurrent course	Bachelor of Education

82   F. Banks and P. Dheram

In the early 1990s the government attempted to increase the opportunities for in-service professional development for teachers and facilitated enhancement to teacher education institutions at the state level. Developments include: District Institute of Education and Training centres (DIETs) and new Colleges of Teacher Education (CTEs) for improved initial teacher education for primary teachers, and improved State Councils of Educational Research and Training (SCERTs) and Institutes of Advanced Study in Education (IASEs). These, along with Block Resource Centres and Cluster Resource Centres, provide further in-service work for teachers.

Secondary teachers mostly prepare for their role by taking a one-year BEd degree, which can be studied for at university, or a CTE or IASE. For science teachers there exists a four-year concurrent university course where pedagogy and science subject studies are studied. Open and distance courses are also offered for the BEd under particular regulations set down by the NCTE concerning the level of face-to-face contact, audio-visual components, teleconferencing and so forth. Indira Gandhi National Open University (IGNOU), Karnataka, Kerala and Nasik Open Universities offer BEd course through this mode.

Despite a plethora of provision it is clear that the present institutional system is insufficient to meet either current or future demands. Innovation in respect of primary and secondary school pre-service training has primarily focused on new ways of presenting existing programmes rather than measures to address the shortfall in places illustrated in Table 5.2. The University of Delhi, for example, has offered an integrated Bachelor of Elementary Education since the mid 1990s. The programme is designed to integrate the study of subject knowledge, human development, pedagogic knowledge and self-knowledge. Students are introduced to a range of new approaches to primary schooling, including visits and teaching practice in schools adopting such approaches. In terms of time, however, this is at the luxury end of the training continuum with a four-year programme that could not be used in meeting the demands identified above. A similar integrated approach has also been offered in the four regional Colleges of Education in Ajmer, Bhubaneswar, Mysore and Bopal. An interesting trend in pre-service training has been to make students much more responsible for their own learning as a means of shifting their perceptions of pedagogy. This has been a feature of the new integrated courses and of programmes such as the 'Participative Teacher Education Programme', offered by the Department of Education, Banasthali Vidyapith, Rajastan. The approach is termed the 'Anweshana Experience' with tutors playing a much more facilitative role than is the case in most teacher education institutions (NCERT, 2005). Whilst these sorts of innovations have begun to influence the mainstream of training, they do not address the issue of supply and need that are so central to the concerns about teacher education and training.

Teaching is not the career of choice for most of the students progressing to higher education. However, the likelihood of obtaining a job attracts many to teacher preparation courses, and this is especially true of women. The proportion of women participating in teacher training has increased in recent decades. Potential entrants to teaching point to concerns about working conditions as a major issue. Whilst there are many schools with excellent facilities, the overall situation is very uneven. The most recent data from the seventh All India Education Survey of 2002 showed that nearly one in ten schools were in temporary accommodation, tents or even open spaces. Only four out of ten schools had lavatory facilities and a large number of schools had no blackboards.

A second issue of concern for entrants to teaching is the systems for deploying teachers. This is a state level responsibility and significant variations in policy exist. So in Bihar a newly recruited primary teacher is not posted to within eight kilometres of their home area, whereas in Karnataka attempts are made to deploy all teachers to their home areas. Some states, attempting to address supply issues, pursue policies that directly address acute problems but these are not always popular with teachers. Rajastan, for example, has a policy that appoints all newly qualified teachers (except certain categories such as widowed mothers) to rural areas. The endemic absenteeism of teachers in many parts of India, is, it seems, related to deployment policies.

A third area of concern is in-service continuing professional development. The need is acute yet studies have been critical of the capacity of DIETs to respond adequately to the huge challenge due to their generally poor technical infrastructure and their own similar low staffing levels (Menon *et al.*, 2010; IBM, 2005). Not all the problems with teacher professional development are due to such capacity problems. Poor teacher motivation and lack of 'ownership' of the training provided have been given as reasons why professional development initiatives in India have had limited impact on classroom practice (Dheram, 2007). Further, Dheram has suggested that a prevailing attitude of textbook-reliance and trainer-dependence has prevented teachers from taking responsibility and addressing their own specific needs. Additionally teacher education in India is seen as suffering from two interrelated major setbacks. First, teachers' mutual interaction with their professional community is limited; second, the restricted understanding or perception of the teacher's role.

The Sarva Shiksha Abhiyan (SSA) framework set out in 2003 seeks to support trained and committed teachers in all schools through improving the quality of pre-service and in-service training and by fostering and sustaining teacher motivation. The SSA requires teachers to receive 20 days of in-service training each year. Newly recruited teachers are expected to receive 30 days' orientation training and untrained teachers should have 60-day refresher courses. The National Council for Education Research and Training (NCERT) has produced guidelines for this training, published in 2006 under the title, 'The Reflective Teacher Organisation of In-service Training of Teachers of Elementary Schools under SSA'.

Implementation of these plans, however, is patchy. The NCTE has described how the school teacher in India may begin their career with a degree in education, attend perhaps half a dozen training programmes during a 30-year career, and learn to use the programmes on educational media offered by experts. This limited exposure to pedagogy leads the teacher to believe that teacher knowledge is 'given' by the trainer. Pedagogy is understood to be embedded in the curriculum materials and accepted without question. In other words, there is very

84 F. Banks and P. Dheram

little critical engagement and teacher reflection on their practice. Curriculum, syllabi and textbooks are rarely examined analytically by the student teacher or by experienced teachers. Teacher development programmes often ignore that the trainee knows their own classroom, which is different from context to context. Most institution-based teacher development programmes do not take the teacher's contextual awareness into consideration while designing the programme and as a result there is very little scope for an ongoing enquiry by the teacher into their teaching (NCTE, 2009).

The shortage of in-service educators is undoubtedly one of the reasons for such criticisms of professional development of programmes. At a 2010 conference held in Bihar the head of the Ministry's section on teacher training reported that 50 per cent of the teacher educator posts across India were currently vacant. In part this was an issue of states not using budgets for the purposes intended but it also reflected the difficulties of recruiting appropriately qualified and experienced staff to such positions. Teacher educators within the DIET 4 structure also appear to have been mostly recruited from the higher secondary school systems and have no experience of primary teaching (see Dyer, 2009).

India has developed a range of open and distance learning approaches to the challenge of educating teachers. The National Policy on Education formulated in 1986 expressed the view that: 'the future thrusts will be in the direction of open distance teaching' (p. 5).

The National Policy on Education was modified in 1992 but still retained the commitment to open and distance learning. The scale of provision is considerable. Over a third of Indian universities have Distance Education Institutes. There are currently 106 such Institutes. There are ten Open Universities of which the Indira Gandhi Open University (IGNOU) is the largest. IGNOU was given the responsibility of clearing the backlog of untrained teachers in Sikkiru and the North West States. It is estimated that there are at least 175,000 untrained teachers and IGNOU developed a six-month Certificate in Primary Education to cater for this group.

IGNOU has also worked with the NCERT to strengthen primary in-service provision within the DIETs and IGNOU has the prime responsibility for distance education activities under SSA. The scale of IGNOU's enrolment is considerable.

The quality of this form of provision has recently come under scrutiny. In part the very openness of IGNOU's offering and its national remit makes it accessible to evaluations not possible in more conventional institutions. Whilst there is concern about IGNOU's quality there is no way of assessing whether the scale of criticism is any greater than would be applied to the thousands of campus institutions. However the critiques of IGNOU do appear to reflect concerns about teacher education provision generally.

The deployment of new forms of information and communication technologies is seen by the Indian government as one way of addressing the challenge to improve and extend professional development programmes. In July 2010, at the launch of a 3,000 Rupee ($60) 'iPad-like' Aakash tablet, Human Resource

Development Minister Kapil Sibal said, 'The solutions for tomorrow will emerge from India' (BBC, 2010).

The solar-powered Linux-based laptop equipped with an Internet browser, video-conferencing capability and a media player was developed by the Indian Institute of Technology and the Indian Institute of Science. Linked to this hardware initiative is a decision by the MHRD to install broadband Internet at all of its 22,000 higher education colleges. The launch of such a high-profile device, at such a low price, attracted worldwide attention for a country keen to promote its competence in new technologies. It is often noted that 'by 2005, technology graduates in India outnumber the whole of the UK population' (Round and Lovegrove, 2005, p. 17) to illustrate the significance given to ICT by the Indian government. Further:

> India is adding about twice as many college graduates to its workforce per year as the United States (1.2 million in the United States versus 2.5 million in India). Of these Indian graduates, 250,000 earned engineering degrees, compared to 70,000 bachelor's degrees in engineering awarded here [the USA].
>
> (USA Economic Policy Unit quoted in Round and Lovegrove, 2005, p. 16)

Although these numbers look impressive in absolute terms, it must be remembered that the population of India is so large that these graduates are just the tip of a very large education pyramid. Of 100 schoolchildren enrolled in Year 1, only six young people complete senior secondary school at Year 12 (over 61 per cent dropping out at the secondary level) and qualify for a college education; and the grade repetition rate in some states is as high as 30–40 per cent (IBM, 2005). Although India produces so many computer specialists, the country still has considerable infrastructure problems, such as intermittent electricity and a very limited bandwidth per Internet user. This leads to a low participation in home computer use despite the price for Internet services being cheap compared to other countries in the region (*info*Dev, 2010b).

In India, the importance of using ICT to improve teaching and learning has been recognised for almost 20 years, and along with increased wealth is a GOI determination to address infrastructure problems. For example, the MHRD in collaboration with the Department of IT and Department of Telecom have instigated a National Knowledge Network that will implement the necessary increase in bandwidth for universities and colleges mentioned above.

The Indira Gandhi National Open University (IGNOU) is the major provider of in-service teacher education programmes through open distance education. IGNOU has been a major provider of training under SSA and for clearing the backlog of untrained teachers. IGNOU was based on the UK Open University and similarly has an established system for developing courses and producing print-based teacher education materials. There is a network of country-wide study centres where their staff provide teachers in training with face-to-face counselling and

86   F. Banks and P. Dheram

access to facilities like teleconferencing, computers and the Internet. Similarly, the Central Institute of Educational Technology (CIET) is the premier institute of educational technology at the federal level to develop and disseminate new approaches to teaching and learning including the use of ICT and conducts short in-service teacher training programmes. It offers short duration training programmes and workshops for making multimedia packages and material for teachers. CIET also uses national TV channels such as Doordarshan 1, DD Bharti and Gyandarshan to broadcast its programmes, and it has recently negotiated broadcasting time with commercial providers like Tata Sky and DTH.

There are currently a large number of ICT initiatives across India at all levels of education. Some are nationwide, such as through IGNOU and CIET, some set up by state governments, and many by NGOs and private companies. A number of ICT in education programmes that apply to teacher education, some well established, some at the pilot stage, are set out below as Table 5.2.

There have been a large number of initiatives to introduce computers into schools and to upgrade the skills of the teachers in the use of ICT. There are thousands of computer suites and SMART classrooms (rooms with TVs and multimedia equipment) that have been installed in schools in the last five years, but as in many countries, provision of equipment in schools does not guarantee its use by teachers (Ward, 2003). Commenting on Indian teachers' attitude to the use of ICT, a survey by PricewaterhouseCoopers India noted:

> To increase digital literacy levels among students and teachers, steps will need to be taken to overcome their technophobia. Teachers are typically wary of

Table 5.2 Summary ICT-based teacher development programmes 2010

Name of ICT-based teacher education programme	School level	Purpose	Extent
Intel Education Initiative Shiksha (Microsoft)	Secondary – train the trainers Secondary	Teacher training and informal training in rural areas Software and teacher and student training.	14 states – about 570,000 teachers Ten states – about 200,000 teachers, ten million students (by 2008)
Gyan Darshan and Gyan Vani	Schoolchildren, college students and young job-seekers	Gyan Darshan – an educational TV channel Gyan Vani – FM radio channel	All India
School Television in India	General non-formal and primary and secondary schools	General and curriculum programmes. For children and teachers	All India
Same language subtitling on TV	All population	Increase in literacy by combining speech and written word	All India

India 87

technology; this is the case for not only teachers in the rural areas but for those in urban areas as well. Unless teachers realize that training will help them rather than pose a threat to their jobs they will continue to remain hesitant. The first step therefore is to get the teachers on board. Raising awareness, about use of ICT in education and improving their teaching efficiency could help in developing positive attitude toward the use of ICT in education among teachers.

(*info*Dev, 2010b, p. 35)

Despite these concerns about Indian teachers' technophobia, the general involvement of the population in social network sites such as Facebook is growing exponentially, the numbers doubling to 20 million users in the last six months of 2010 (Socialbakers, 2011). Participatory programmes which encourage and promote interactive training through an ongoing dialogue between teachers and other stakeholders, including teacher educators, material developers, examiners, administrators and publishers, may be the key to successful teacher development.

In this context new technology could provide an appropriate medium that will create a sense of community for the teacher, provide various opportunities for interaction and raise their awareness of the ways in which they can play a more meaningful role in their own school-based professional development. An analysis of the use of ICT for professional development in India (see Menon *et al.*, 2010 and Bean *et al.*, 2011) suggests the need to consider two major strands for learning in the workplace. The first is the closeness of the learning, physically, to the work setting and pedagogically through work-based activities – making the learning 'local'. Making the school the site of learning for teachers and their practice a focus for that learning is much more likely to change the way that they teach their pupils than bringing them out of the school to a training centre. If the learning is local to where they work and focused on that work, the change in their day-to-day practice is more marked.

The second area is the extent to which the learning is becoming a communal experience. For successful school-based learning, moving from a focus on a tutor who 'knows all and teaches', to a learners' forum for the sharing of new ideas, problems and successes, is seen to lead to more profound and lasting change. Meeting locally as a 'cluster' of learners, or by using mobile phones and 'Web 2.0' technology such as Twitter and Facebook, learning becomes a meeting place like a village centre or local market where all can meet, share, compare and interact.

The developments in social networking have had a profound affect on the way we now look at learning. Putting it starkly, in many ways the past 150 years' one-to-many 'distant from practice' ways of learning have been an aberration. In the twenty-first century we have returned to a more informal and social view of learning; one that radically changes the way we now think about the potential role for higher education and human resource development.

In the following matrix (Figure 5.2), the horizontal axis indicates level of social interaction ('one-to-many' versus 'many-with-many' from one individual teaching large numbers of students to a communal view of teaching and learning). The vertical axis indicates the location of the professional development and learning ('close to practice' versus 'distant from practice' from learning in an institution to learning in the work setting). Looking at the bottom left quadrant, this represents conventional centre-based education such as currently offered by a DIET and in conventional higher education too. The efficiency of such learning needs to be evaluated more widely in a country of over one billion people as such models, although important for access to specialised high-tech equipment, can only have limited impact.

Greater impact in terms of numbers can be made with the use of guides and materials for use in schools as set out in the top left quadrant. Self-study materials have a long pedigree in India and work-based manuals and instruction books are commonplace. However, such manuals for state employees, at least, have had minimum impact. The suggested working procedures seem like merely recipes to be followed without question, and without real understanding of the underlying rationale. It is the 'Encyclopaedia Britannica' approach – looking up an answer and attempting to see how it might fit one's particular circumstance.

In the bottom right quadrant is where sharing general ideas and concerns through new technologies can facilitate learning. These are methods appropriate for large-scale populations: with so many people looking at a bulletin board, surely someone will know the answer to my problem even if they cannot know my context.

Finally, there is the complete opposite to the residential workshop, the highly localised work-based collaborative model that draws on new forms of social learning to help develop practice. Through the use of Open Learning it is possible to satisfy the huge demand that cannot be met by building bricks-and-mortar institutions and at the same time use the power of practice-based pedagogy to change

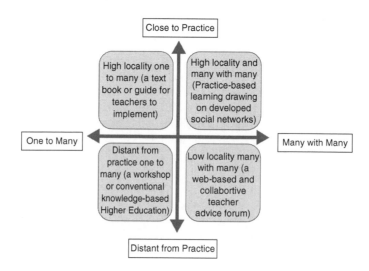

Figure 5.2 Teacher development matrix

and improve practice in schools. Even if India could afford to build sufficient new bricks-and-mortar institutions to meet the demand for teachers it would not be the best way to change or develop practice.

The passing of the Right to Education Act in 2009 and its implementation in April 2010 sets out a requirement for providing free, local, compulsory and quality education to all children in the 6–14 age group. Its mandate to have only trained teachers in schools, and the establishment in law of a pupil–teacher ratio of 30:1 with teaching through child-friendly and child-centred approaches have considerable implementation challenges for central and state governments. This bold commitment to education for all citizens must be matched against the current gross inequalities. As Reddi and Sinha (2003) have pointed out:

> India is a country of grand contradictions. While it is a global leader in the knowledge economy, it is also home to more than half the world's poor and illiterate people, most of whom are women. Urban India has problems of excess, while in the rural areas there is deprivation. The challenge that the country faces is to arrive at a policy that maintains its global position while also providing opportunities for access and services to the rural hinterland.
>
> (p. 245)

Whilst there is considerable activity to seek to improve teacher education and training, particularly to provide a more equitable distribution of qualified teachers across this large country, significant problems exist. A growing educated middle class, in part benefitting from the expansion of private rather than state schooling, is matched by a very large number of communities marked by disadvantage. Such communities are where the most endemic education problems persist, including low levels of achievement, poor completion rates, sometimes rampant teacher absenteeism. These are the contexts in which untrained teachers in inadequate school buildings are most likely to be found. It is the growing scale of need and demand that seems to defy and defeat the best intentions of policy makers. In analysing the Indian context this case study describes a number of opportunities where policy improvement needs to be made.

First there is the balance of power and responsibilities between national and state governments. The post-Independence history of education in India is replete with national pronouncements and initiatives inconsistently applied. There will, of course, be differences between states. The urgency, however, about addressing the acute crisis in teacher supply and training is not universally acknowledged.

Second, there is the issue of quality accountability systems at all levels. Here the issue is more than evaluation, monitoring and inspectorial structures, important as these are. Rather it is a question of creating a general acceptance, a culture of concern, around generally acceptable levels of provision. In pursuing quality, however, policy makers have to be realistic about the resources available. This leads to a third point. Current teacher education and training crucially involves someone playing the trainer role, the teacher educator. The lack of people with the experience and qualifications to play this role appears to be a major problem for pre-service and in-service training. In a system with acute teacher shortages and very large numbers of unqualified teachers it is likely that the teacher educator role will be problematic.

Fourth, given that the existing institutions of teacher education cannot fulfil the demand the importance of looking at new modes of provision seems paramount.

It is clear that the only way hundreds of thousands of teachers will receive sufficient ongoing training is through a school-based approach. Yet the infrastructure and assumptions seem firmly based on 'out of school' models of pre-service and in-service provision. To some extent, as has been shown, new forms of communication technologies are offering new possibilities for radically different models of training. Future planning and policy development needs to incorporate such new ways of thinking into the mainstream of policy development. Open University style courses, where the students are working close to their everyday setting, draws on a 'pedagogy of practice' that relates what they are learning through their study to their workplace, and brings examples from their workplace into their study. This local learning, combined with the social networks of others involved in similar study, supports practitioners in local communities in a sustainable way. Not only is the learning more convenient in terms of flexibility of time commitment and location of learning, it is more effective in developing people. Rather than being 'one-to-many' like Encyclopaedia Britannica it is 'many with many' like Wikipedia.

A final issue relates to the question of the teacher vocation. In many disadvantaged communities the teacher offers the major way in which children can overcome the impediment of poverty and seek a more socially and economically fulfilling life. This values dimension, however, to the education of a teacher, is rarely mentioned in official pronouncements or college syllabi. It could be argued that significantly strengthening the moral position and responsibility of the teacher could significantly impact on status and acceptance. This, perhaps above all, remains the biggest challenge for the development of the education system in India.

6 Nigeria
Balancing federal and local initiatives

Mohammed Ibn Junaid and Bob Moon

Nigeria, with a population of over 140 million, estimated to rise to 156 million by 2015, is Africa's largest country by population. Towards the end of the first decade of the present century the public teaching force comprised around 680,000 primary and 120,000 junior/secondary teachers. The 2010 UNESCO monitoring report estimates that expenditure on teachers will have to increase by over 300 per cent if EFA targets are to be met by 2015. Currently Nigeria has 10 per cent of the global figure of out-of-school children at the primary level (UNESCO, 2010a). These are daunting figures. Nigeria also has a currently buoyant private sector, although reliable figures in respect of teachers, teacher qualifications and learner enrolment are difficult to establish. The prevalence of unapproved private schools further compounds the problem of lack of accurate statistics on this sector. The education system in Nigeria has been seriously undermined by huge and persistent data gaps, making informed planning and effective monitoring and evaluation immensely difficult. The last time Nigeria sent education data to UIS was in 2005. Data gathered after 2005 has been so riddled with errors, gaps and contradictions that it was impossible to forward it to UIS. This was particularly evident in the data concerning teachers. To address this challenge, the Federal Ministry of Education has recently developed and adopted a new policy on Education Management Information System (EMIS) that calls for a decentralised, systemic and professional approach to EMIS. However, problems still remain.

Nigeria, given its size, embraces a wide range of socio-economic cultures and contexts. Wealth distribution is uneven with consequent impacts on educational opportunity. Both gender and geography are reflected in these inequalities. The average poor rural female teacher has less than 40 per cent the national average for years of schooling and around one-quarter the average for rich urban males (UNESCO, 2010a). Inevitably these disparities flow through to the make-up of the teaching force. In Lagos, for example, 98 per cent of primary teachers hold the Nigeria Certificate in Education (NCE), the accepted teacher qualification benchmark. In Kaduna in the north this drops to just over 60 per cent (Omo-Ojugo, 2009).

Regional inequalities are deeply rooted in the social and political evolution of the modern Nigerian state and have significantly influence the way teacher education has developed. The first teacher training college was established in

92 M. Ibn Junaid and B. Moon

Abeokuta by the Church Missionary Society in 1859. Other colleges, founded by missionaries of different denominations, were established towards the end of the nineteenth and early twentieth centuries. The first training college in northern Nigeria was founded by the colonial government in 1909.

The missionary, Christian model of teacher training was heavily criticised by a colonial office report, the Phelps States Commission Report of 1922, for its irrelevant and poorly conceived curriculum, inadequate supervisory systems and high pupil teacher ratio (Osokoya, 2010). In 1929 a federal, centralised system of education was introduced which merged the previously separate north and south departments into one national body. At the same time a system of two-year teacher training centres and colleges was introduced for lower and higher primary school teachers. In 1946 the regional structure was reintroduced and the country divided into East, West and North, each with a regional assembly that provided a powerbase for political groups that opposed each other at a federal level. The status of education as a regional rather than federal responsibility was strengthened by introduction of the 1951 McPherson constitution which devolved statutory powers over education to regional authorities. Differences in education policies were quickly apparent. Whilst the East and West regions embarked on free primary schooling for all in the mid 1950s the North region did not follow until required to by the military government two decades later (Osokoya, 2010).

The federal and regional divide in Nigeria, the basis for much political strife, including a civil war between 1968 and 1970, has been a dominant structural feature of developments in education. The structure itself has been subject to repeated changes. Four regions in the post-independence era were split up to become 12 in the 1960s. Subsequent local clamour for recognising social and cultural distinctiveness increased the number of states to over 20 in the 1980s and it currently stands at 36 (created in 1996) plus the Federal Capital Territory. These administrative dividing lines formalise some marked extremes in cultural diversity, most notably the Islamic traditions in the north and the more western, Christian society in the south, the richer and more urban parts of the country. Through much of the 1960s and 1970s individual states had considerable autonomy in how education was organised and resources (up to and including the university sector). However, during the period of military rule (1984–1999) centralist policies were increasingly adopted. Teacher colleges and universities, for example, were made a federal responsibility in the mid 1970s.

More recently moves to decentralise educational administration have created tensions within the federal structure. For example, whilst teacher salaries are set at a national level and linked to civil service pay structures, individual states may determine additional allowances and other conditions of service. Devolved education budgets also contribute to differential approaches to teacher supply with some states, making a discretionary judgement about budget priorities, failing to recruit sufficient teachers. In Nigeria, as in other Sub-Saharan African countries, the overall national picture masks significant regional inequalities (Omotor, 2004). There are teacher shortages and the employment of unqualified teachers in some states (sometimes in the Nigerian context termed 'PTA teachers' as they are recruited by parents) and an oversupply of qualified teachers in other parts of the country. In the last five years the federal government, recognising this problem, has twice recruited significant cohorts of teachers for what is termed the Federal Teacher Scheme (FTS). This scheme is aimed at addressing both the problem of shortages of qualified teachers in the basic education sector and that of a growing number of unemployed qualified teachers – a problem resulting from some states' seeming preference to employ qualified teachers at lower salary levels. This was revealed in a study conducted by the National Commission for Colleges of Education (NCCE) in 2004. The FTS is thus designed to attract unemployed qualified teachers. Under the scheme, these teachers are employed by the federal government on a two-year term and posted to states with shortages of qualified teachers. At the end of the two years, the benefiting states are expected to absorb these teachers into full employment. The first batch of 40,000 teachers completed the service in 2008 and 27,000 of them were absorbed into the workforce. A second batch of 34,000 were enlisted by the Universal Basic Education Commission (UBEC) in January, 2009.

Primary and secondary teacher preparation

The benchmark teacher qualification, decreed by the federal government in 1997, is the Nigerian Certificate in Education (NCE). This normally represents a three-year programme of studies in one of the over 80 Colleges of Education which are overseen by a federal agency, the NCCE. In some states it is possible to recruit NCE qualified teachers for all posts, in others this proves problematic. The Teacher Registration Council of Nigeria publishes data on the teaching force. The 2006 report showed that of the 640,000 teachers (in 60,000 schools) nearly four out of ten (38 per cent) did not have the NCE. Significant federal investment is being made to address this. The National Teachers Institute (NTI) based in Kaduna, but covering the whole country, offers school-based open and distance learning upgrading courses for far in excess of 100,000 teachers aimed at the achievement of the NCE qualification. A fast-track programme – 'The Pivotall Teacher Training Programme' (PTTP) has also been introduced. This course, providing for 18 months of college- and school-based training (and including a distance programme from NTI) has had only partial success. It has been rigorously opposed by some states, particularly those without NCE-level recruitment problems. More recently, in a bid to address, once and for all, the problem of under-qualified teachers in the basic education sector, the Federal Ministry of Education introduced a Special Teacher Upgrading Programme (STUP) aimed at providing specially packaged fast-track training for serving Grade II teachers to qualify them for the award of the NCE within a period of two years.

The modus operandi of the programme is based on a flexible approach, in which teachers are allowed to remain in their jobs even while they are on the course. It combines face-to-face lectures, tutorials and integrated school experiences. The entire block of study and teaching is to be completed within two years. In terms of content, the STUP programme uses the same NCE curriculum that is followed

94 M. Ibn Junaid and B. Moon

by full time pre-service students in the Colleges of Education. However, it differs slightly only in so far as it incorporates an additional component of school-based professional development through mentoring and internship. The curriculum of the NCE qualification has, in recent years, been extended to embrace more school related and pedagogic issues such as environmental or computer studies. The educational aspects of combating HIV/Aids are also addressed. All courses include the equivalent of three months of supervised school-based training.

Secondary teachers are primarily and formally prepared through the university sector and those Colleges of Education that run degree programmes in affiliation with approved universities. Of the 190,000 secondary teachers, nearly three-quarters (74 per cent) are qualified to teach at that level, that is they hold a relevant degree. Although data for subject breakdowns of these overall figures is unavailable it is clear that acute shortages of qualified teachers exist in mathematics, science and languages and both modern and indigenous languages. Federal Minister of Education, Rugayyatu Rufa'i, recently acknowledged:

> despite the monumental development in the education sector, the system is seriously being challenged by the inadequacy of qualified teachers in Science and Mathematics subjects. Moreover most teachers and pupils have very low skills on the use of ICT.
>
> (*Daily Independent*, Lagos, 8 August 2010)

As in the primary sector, upgrading courses seek to reduce the number of unqualified teachers.

There are additionally a sizeable (the figures are not recorded) number of teachers working in the Islamic and Koranic schools primarily in the north of the country. These religious schools have now been incorporated into the formal basic education system. At the moment, only the framework for the integration of the Islamiyyah and Quranic schools into the UBE scheme has been developed. The actual incorporation of these schools into the formal basic education system is yet to happen on a national scale. As such, there are no definite figures of teachers that are involved or clear guidelines for their engagement and training at the national level. However, there are disparate and uncoordinated attempts by some states in the north to integrate these schools into their formal education systems. Much of these state efforts revolve around advocacy towards attitudinal change in favour of integration, provision of funds for instructional materials, posting of teachers, payment of grants to proprietors, construction of classrooms and training of teachers and school managers. Very little data on these initiatives exist, making it difficult to say anything about numbers and the nature of provision for teachers to work in these schools.

Teachers within the public school system have few opportunities for continuous professional development (Adagiri, 2009). However, in recent years there have been attempts by both federal and state governments to provide opportunities for continuing professional development for teachers. The UBEC devotes 15 per cent of its intervention funds to states to teacher professional development.

This percentage of the intervention goes directly to in-service training of teachers in all states and the Federal Capital Territory (FCT). Under this arrangement, a total of 1,493,352 teachers have been trained to date (*Daily Trust*, Abuja, 30 September 2010).

Similarly, since 2006, the federal government through the NTI has engaged in in-service training programmes aimed at upgrading the skills of the current teaching force in the basic education sector on an annual basis. Under this programme, the federal government had trained 145,000 teachers annually in 2008, 2009 and 2010. A consequence of this is that considerable resources (an average of N3 billion a year) are directed at the in-service training of teachers already employed in addition to the financing of pre-service training of teachers going on in the Colleges of Education and universities. The Teachers Registration Council of Nigeria has also recently attempted to extend provision, particularly through programmes focused on information and communication technologies. UNICEF's 'Child Friendly School Initiatives' has a professional development component although this touches only a small percentage of teachers.

At secondary level provision has been very limited, although consideration is being given to awarding credits for active engagement with professional activities and establishing a linkage between such courses and promotion. There has also been discussion recently of making all registered teachers undergo an annual professional examination.

Perceptions of teaching

The status of teachers in Nigeria is problematic, particularly at the primary level. A range of factors appear to have contributed to what is perceived as a decline in teacher status. Teacher salaries at primary and secondary levels are perceived to be inadequate and compare unfavourably with other occupations. Conditions of service, particularly in the primary phase in rural areas, are rarely good and often wholly inadequate. For example, there are major structural issues around the deployment of teachers. A study by NCCE that looked at the situation of over 5,000 NCE qualified teachers found that just over half were unemployed (NCCE, 2004). This despite acute shortages of teachers in some areas and, in many parts of the country, high pupil-teacher ratios. In terms of deployment tensions exist between different levels of the federal structure. Thus local education authorities, who in the devolved structures are responsible for primary teacher recruitment, have to seek permission for appointments of the State Universal Basic Education Board which also, because of the way universal basic education is funded, may need to gain the agreement of the State Ministry of Education. Into this bureaucratic complexity delays and prevarication occur that impact significantly on the extent to which individuals, given the low pay, see gaining a teaching post as worth the effort. The 'balkanisation' of educational structures has also contributed to further dysfunctional characteristics. Some states, for example, will only give permanent posts to those trained within the state. 'Out of state' appointments are sometimes only made on a fixed term contract basis. This has a

96 M. Ibn Junaid and B. Moon

twofold effect on education. First, it deprives the schools of qualified teachers as many of these potential employees resist contract appointment. Second, the few contract teachers that accept such appointments view their position as unjust and discriminatory, being citizens of the same country as their 'within state' trained counterparts, and therefore are largely not committed to their job.

Once in post teachers face a well documented range of problems. Schools may be in poor conditions without books and other resources. Toilet provision may be rudimentary. Appropriate teacher housing may be unavailable. Opportunities for professional development usually do not exist and the location of the post may make access to upgrading courses difficult. Ogiebaen and Uwameiye (2005) carried out a nationwide survey of public attitudes to teachers and teacher education. Teaching was poorly perceived because of poor remuneration, the irregularity of salary payments, the poor working environment and the inability, given salary conditions, to obtain loans for housing. Public perceptions of teacher education were also negative with education facilities perceived as a 'last resort' option amongst parents with children about to enter university. Findings of this sort have been confirmed in a number of other studies (Afe, 2002; Edukuyho, 2002).

Promotion opportunities are perceived as limited and, where available, involve many moving into another occupation. Promotion for a primary teacher means moving into the secondary phase. Secondary teachers aspire to tertiary posts in Colleges of Education. The rewards structure has the consequence of devaluing the lowest phases of schooling with most of those who graduate from primary upgrading programmes moving to secondary schools or occupations other than teaching.

Reform strategies

A number of reform strategies have been put in place to address the systemic problems of teacher supply and quality. At the federal level is a multi-faceted reform programme, the National Economic Empowerment and Development strategy, which includes within its remit issues such as overcoming poverty amongst rural teachers, early years education, and commitments to overcome gender inequality. A Child's Rights Bill has been introduced which makes it mandatory for parents to send their children to school. National policies to promote literacy and numeracy exist and a Universal Basic Education Commission oversees local progress towards national goals.

In 2010 a National Teacher Education Policy was introduced. In launching the policy the Federal Minister of Education, Professor Rugayyatu Ahmed Rufa'i, talked of repositioning the education sector in general to improve pre-service and in-service teacher education in the country (Olatunji, 2010). The policy stipulates standards and teacher outcomes for education and training courses that are to be more rigorously linked to the age levels to be taught. Raising the standards for admission to teacher education courses are proposed.

The new policy incorporates the components of both pre-service (PSTE) and in-service (ISTE) training aimed at ensuring coherence and continuity of training opportunities throughout the career of teachers. It also focuses on standards to be implemented in both programmes with emphasis on the evaluation of teacher performance. A further dimension of the policy is its focus on lifelong learning through continuing professional development of teachers throughout their career and recognition of their achievements in a well-defined career path and reward system. It also aims to create adequate incentives to attract competent people into the teaching profession.

On 15 April 2010, the Honorable Minister of Education presented the new National Teacher Education Policy (NTEP) and its accompanying Implementation Guidelines to the public at the National Commission for Colleges of Education, Abuja. The national policy represents an increasing federal interest in regaining a measure of control and authority over teacher education policies and practices. The policy provides a structure around which both the Federal Ministry of Education (FME) and the states can address the teacher quality and development issues. It addresses the need to provide a supportive system for improving the quality of teaching and learning in both the public and the private schools, particularly at the basic and secondary education levels. It provides a basis on which to consider what kinds of initial teacher education programmes best suit the preparation of primary and secondary school teachers. It guides the development of education programmes that will optimise teacher opportunities to demonstrate knowledge and skills designated as important for them to engage with the demands of a highly competitive, rapidly changing and technologically oriented society.

For the first time, teacher educators and regulators in Nigeria have a comprehensive strategy that responds to the challenge of quality teaching and teachers. This is supplemented by some states (Kaduna, Kano and Kwara) who, with the aid of DFID, are undergoing significant teacher development reform processes of their own undertaking. Similarly, the FME has established partnerships with the Japanese International Cooperation Agency (JICA) to strengthen mathematics and science education at the primary level through in-service training for teachers of science and mathematics under the SMASE project in three states (Kaduna, Niger and Plateau). The new policy had sought to underpin and align these disparate efforts and processes to provide a comprehensive structure for developing teacher education programmes which optimise opportunities for both pre-service and serving teachers to develop knowledge and skills that will ensure quality outcomes for all students. In describing the standards for teaching in Nigeria, the Teacher Education Policy provides the structure that will allow teacher educators and regulators to achieve the teacher quality objectives of the National Education Framework and the Federal Education Sector Plan. The approval and adoption of the policy by the National Council on Education means that henceforth teacher quality and development in all states of the federation would be guided by the provisions of the national policy. The policy provides a clear definition of roles and responsibilities and harmonises operations of both federal and state governments in establishing a fully developed teacher development structure.

As in the university sector, the college of education sector has witnessed the emergence of large numbers of private providers of teacher education. From an

98   M. Ibn Junaid and B. Moon

initial small number of private Colleges of Education in 2000, the number of such colleges has risen to over 44 in 2010 with a growing number of prospective proprietors applying for approval to establish more colleges. Now numbering 44, the private Colleges of Education have outnumbered both the federal colleges and the state-owned Colleges of Education. No comparative data on the effectiveness of these different types of institutions exists. Recently the establishment of a Nigerian University Central Research Fund has provided the opportunity to focus research on teachers. However, not much has been achieved as yet. The fund has just been set up and the guidelines for accessing the fund have been published.

To give further momentum to the EFA process, Nigeria has embarked on the reform of its teacher education with a focus on the inclusive dimensions of the right to education as a fundamental human right, and with greater emphasis on making teacher education more relevant to the existing teacher needs in the basic education sector. The reform focuses on redesigning the teacher education programme along specialist teacher programmes in line with the new National Teacher Education Policy (2009) and the UBE Act (2004) both of which emphasise the production of specialist teachers for the basic education sector. Specialist programmes began in 2011. In the interim, the harmonised teacher education Minimum Standards are planned to ensure that pre-service teachers are given adequate exposure to the main elements of the basic education curriculum. Added to this are the modalities for the restructuring of the curricula as well as the internal arrangement of the schools, departments and programmes of the Colleges of Education that will take cognisance of the basic education structure comprising:

- Early Childhood Care and Education (ECCE)
- Primary Education Studies (PES)
- Junior Secondary Education (ANFE)
- Adult and Non-formal Education (ANFE)
- Special Needs Education (SNE).

As part of the restructuring process, Nigeria is collaborating with USAID on a Teacher Education Initiative (TEI) project aimed at improving the quality of pre-service teacher training in the Colleges of Education. The activities under this project will support the implementation of the National Teacher Education Policy developed with USAID assistance and first approved in January, 2009. The TEI will work with and through the National Commission for Colleges of Education (NCCE) in support of the policy and programme initiatives of NCCE. The specific objectives of the project include, among other things, the improvement of standards of practice particularly in the curricular and training methodologies for Early Childhood Education (ECE) and Primary Education Studies (PES), with a focus on reading and mathematics instruction in the early grades. The project also includes measures to increase the proportion of students at the teacher training institutions preparing for the ECE and PES specialisations and to increase the numbers of female students training to become teachers and actually obtaining positions as teachers. Collaborative work is also going on with DFID on the restructuring of the college of education system. This involves the development of Teacher Standards, the development and introduction of new college programmes as well as the concomitant new college structure and the minimum standards for college management.

The federal–state dimension

Attempts to reform and improve the quality of teachers have to be understood in the context of the tensions that exist between the federal government and the states. Some commentators (Anikweze, 2008) perceive the disparities that exist between states as an indicator of the problems of the move to embrace decentralisation.

> Constituted federalism in Nigeria has compelled roles and functions for the delivery of education to be excessively fragmented, reducing the level of interest and responsibility in some functions and paying little attention to others. The political instability in governance and the fluctuations in economic fortunes have not only adversely affected budgetary provisions for education but also introduced instability in the way education has been managed consequent upon inevitable decentralisation . . . decentralised teacher management has mitigated against full implementation of EFA by the injection of parochial and ethnic sentiments into the recruitment of primary school teachers . . . another drawback is poor supervision of instructions due to the high degree of familiarity that often exists among teachers and their headteachers.
>
> (p. 83)

In education policy discourse there has been much discussion around the issues of centralisation–decentralisation. International organisations have given much attention to this in recent years (Ahmad *et al.*, 2005). However, in many countries growing concerns about quality have seen increasing national or federal interventions in previously local affairs. This tension is one of the prevailing conditions of policy development in Nigeria with profound consequences for teacher education and training.

The concern about teacher quality has led to a number of federal initiatives aimed at improving the quality of teaching and teachers in the country including the development of a national teacher education policy, the special fast-track teacher upgrading programme, and a number of in-service professional development programmes. However, these initiatives have been shrouded in the tension that characterises the current nature of education as a responsibility for both the federal and state governments. Although the evidence reveals a genuine commitment by the federal government of Nigeria to support the professional development of teachers, such initiatives often appear to lack the full support of the states. Some states, for example, in addition to refusing to appoint 'out of state' trained teachers, have also resisted the setting up of improved unified salary structure for teachers, seeing it more as their exclusive employer responsibility (Anikweze, 2008).

Much of the information about federal state interactions and interrelations in respect of teacher policies is anecdotal, framed in terms of local political disputes and often reported in newspapers. There have been few studies of the ways the structures work in practice. International representations of the situation in Nigeria tend to mask very large regional differences. Many of the states in Nigeria, as in other large population countries, would exceed in size most of the long list of low-income countries. Important questions, therefore, are unresolved in seeking to improve the ways in which teachers can be managed and educated at such a large scale. There is a need for a better understanding of the range of functions associated with teacher management and the levels at which they are held in the system and which other levels are accountable for the effective working of such functions. There is also a need for more insight into the types of people needed to make such functions operative. The articulation of teacher education programmes between federal, state and local levels is of particular importance. There is, also, almost no understanding of what happens to the tens of thousands of primary teachers undertaking primary upgrading programmes. How many successful graduates are retained in the primary sector? And there is as yet no systematic evaluation of the extent to which the investment in such upgrading or professional development generally works through into improvements in the school system. This is a situation not unique to Nigeria, but it remains problematic if reform strategies, aimed at significant qualitative changes in the effectiveness of teachers, are to be successful.

7 Brazil
Building national regulatory frameworks

Bob Moon and Freda Wolfenden

In 2011 Amanda Gurgel, a teacher in the state of Rio Grande de Norte, became, almost overnight, a YouTube celebrity. Her presentation to a state conference on education, a strongly worded critique of state policies towards teachers, had two million viewers within just a few weeks. She complained bitterly about the low salaries that forced teachers to take on more than one job, the poor, overcrowded classrooms, the lack of resources and, to much applause, her view that education and teachers needed to become a government priority (www.youtube. com/watch?v=4xzfivgmlU0).

The population of Brazil is a little under 190 million. In recent years economic growth, as in other large developing countries such as China and India, has been strong. The number of teachers is large. Nearly 400,000 pre-school teachers, nearly one and a half million elementary level teachers and just under half a million secondary teachers. Although economic growth has been strong, wealth has been concentrated, most particularly in urban areas. The South East region accounts for over 50 per cent of GDP whereas the North region stands at around 5 per cent. These inequalities, however, are changing and it is estimated that the country, in the first decade of the present century, has begun to reduce these inequalities in parallel with educational improvement. Like many countries experiencing growth, the Brazilian population is predominantly a young one. Forty-nine million under 14, 35 million between 15 and 24. Nearly 70 per cent of the population is under 40 (World Bank, 2010b).

Amanda Gurgel's passionate outburst, however popular amongst teachers, has to be seen in a context of quite significant improvements in the overall performance of the Brazilian education system. What one World Bank report has termed the 'managed revolution' of Brazilian education (Bruns *et al.*, 2012) has led to some world beating improvements. A Brazilian child born in the second decade of the present century will complete more than twice as many years of schooling as her parents. The average educational attainment in the labour force since 1995 has improved faster than any other developing country, including China, which had set the pace in previous decades. The percentage of the population not completing secondary school has dropped from 70 per cent to 40 per cent in less than two decades. The 2009 results for PISA shows that Brazil had a 52-point increase in mathematics since 2000, suggesting that pupils have gained a full

102 B. Moon and F. Wolfenden

academic year of mathematics achievement in the first decade of the century, the third largest increase ever for countries participating in the PISA process (World Bank, 2010b). These two visions of education in Brazil, the polemical critique of Amanda Gurgel and the strong improvements in education performance recognised in the World Bank study are not incompatible. The country is large and diverse with extreme regional inequalities. Some historical contextualisation helps explain the challenges faced by Brazil today.

The aspiration to provide universal education came later to Brazil than many countries. In part this reflected the importance given to mass schooling in the years of colonisation. Unlike many European countries, Portugal, untouched by the Protestant reformation, was slow to embrace mass education and in Brazil the process was even slower. The first moves to create any form of basic education came in the early years of the new republic at the end of the nineteenth century and this was primarily in the emerging urban areas to the south. In the state of São Paulo, for example, previously scattered schools were brought together in 'school groups' with new school buildings in an attempt to create a model of public education. Parallel provision was made for teacher training schools (escolas normais) that sought to introduce new teaching methods into the schools (Tanuri, 2000) Through the period of the First Republic (1889–1930) primary and secondary education, a state rather than federal responsibility, expanded slowly. At the end of the republic barely one in four of the population had achieved basic literacy. It was only when a new government headed by Getulio Vargas came to power in 1930 that education became a priority with the Education Minister, Gustavo Capanema, using new central political powers to create a national education administration (Schwartzman, 2004).

Progress, however, was slow. Responsibility of schooling remained at the state level with extensive involvement from the Catholic Church, seen by many as resistant to reform. Even in the 1950s and 1960s, as the economy expanded and an urban society was created, education did not emerge as a national priority. The ambitious plans of President Juscelino Kubitschek in that period, which led to a new road infrastructure, the construction of dams, the modernisation of industry and the building of a new capital, Brasilia, paid little heed to schooling. In particular the country was seen as slow to develop any sense of a teaching profession outside the elite primary and secondary schools of São Paulo and Rio de Janeiro (Schwartzman, 2004).

The basis for the recent improvements in Brazil's education system is widely seen as the period between 1995 and 2002 when Paulo Renato de Souza, formerly a University Rector and an economist, became Minister of Education (Bruns *et al.*, 2012). Of particular significance was the establishment of a National Fund for Basic Education which sought to reduce regional inequalities in state expenditure and ensure that resources earmarked for education were used for that purpose. In parallel a national office for education research and statistics was established to provide policy makers with accurate data on the disbursement of funds and related issues.

This 'managed revolution' in performance also included a range of further federal level initiatives, most importantly a number of normative measures including the establishment of a national curriculum and regulatory frameworks directed at improving teacher quality, and the introduction of national programmes of pupil assessment that provided evaluative and comparative data on how effectively the education system was working.

This last measure has been of particular importance. In the early 1990s little or no information on student learning was collected at a federal level. Successive measures by the Cordero and Lula da Silva governments have systematically constructed one of the world's leading systems for measuring the outcomes of education. The Prova Brasil/Provinha Brasil student assessments and the IDEB (Índice de Desenvolvimento da Educação Básica) composite index of education quality system developed by the INEP (Instituto Nacional de Estudos e Pesquisas Educacionais 'Anísio Teixeira) is superior to many existing international systems in the quantity, relevance and quality of the student and school performance information it provides. This data has provided the basis for a range of new policies including those designed to creating a stronger incentive base to policy towards teachers.

The 1996 Law for Guidelines and Basis of National Education (LDB Law no. 9394) provides the legal reference point for the education system and is seen as a cornerstone of the education reforms. Through this the federal government distributes resources to states and municipalities to ensure that the constitutional rights of every child to education is met. The law also established a number of principles including:

- that education should be free;
- that equal opportunities to schooling should be provided;
- that there should be freedom to practice a plurality of pedagogic ideas;
- that the administration of school systems should be democratically controlled.

Subsequent to the promulgation of the law a series of national Educational Development Plans have been put in place. The development of education policy is the responsibility of the National Education Council (NEC) and this includes teacher supply and teacher education and training. There is an acceptance, however, that federal prescriptions have to be flexible and open to local interpretation. The NEC has, therefore, a wide consultative function with state authorities, the private sector, teacher unions and parent organisations. Many of these consultations take place at public hearings in different parts of the country. The NEC does not specify a national curriculum, but it has set out basic competence areas that all children should achieve whatever the form of curriculum experience. The specific requirements that relate to teacher quality date back to the education plan of 2001. This proposed a comprehensive improvement in the pre-service and in-service education and training of teachers.

In recent years there have been a number of policy focused investigations of teachers. The Aniso Teixeira National Institute for Studies and Educational Research carried out a teacher census that showed that teachers working in the basic education sector came from predominantly poor backgrounds. There is no bulge in any of the age groups for teachers but the teaching force is predominantly female (84.1 per

104   B. Moon and F. Wolfenden

cent). Brazil needs more teachers at all levels. Precise quantification is complex. The national method of counting teachers has been through function rather than the teacher as an individual. A teacher working in more than one school (for example in double-shift schools) can be counted more than once. There have been specific studies, however, that point to significant shortfalls. One study identified the need for 711,000 teachers in the 5th grade and above whilst the training output was only 457,000. The situation in specialist subject areas is particularly acute. Across the current secondary sector there is a minimum requirement of 23,500 physics teachers but only 7,200 teachers currently have graduate qualifications in the subject. The supply and demand context for teachers in Brazil is entering a complex period. There are significant shortages in many areas, but in other areas demographic change will see falling enrolment, particularly in the south and south east (56 per cent decline in fertility rates over the last 25 years). Up to 200,000 primary teacher posts may be at risk (Wong and de Carvalho, 2004).

The qualifications of existing teachers is also a cause of concern. The 2004 survey quoted above estimated that 17 per cent of the 835,000 teachers in grades 5–8 do not possess a higher education qualification. Of the half a million secondary teachers nearly one in ten have not graduated successfully from a higher education institution. Amongst teachers in the early grades, and in pre-school provision, the percentage is even higher, particularly in rural areas.

There have been improvements. The overall percentage of teachers with tertiary degrees has moved from 20 per cent in 1996 to 38 per cent in 2006 (Menezes-Filho and Pazello, 2007). However, research in Brazil has raised questions about the usefulness of using graduation and/or higher education teacher qualifications as an indicator of teacher quality. In Brazil teachers are recruited from the bottom third of those achieving secondary leaving certification. In 2005 only 11 per cent of the top 20 per cent of secondary leavers wanted to become teachers. Those intending to become teachers consistently come from poorer and less educated families than those wishing to enter all other professions (Louzano *et al.*, 2010). There is almost no competition to obtain places on pre-service teacher preparation programmes. On present enrolment it is estimated that 70 per cent of students have previous teaching experience and are upgrading their qualifications. A recent study of graduates from a range of programmes (Louzano *et al.*, 2010) showed significant inadequacies in major parts of the teacher education curriculum. Teacher selection in Brazil is highly decentralised and many states and municipalities hire on the basis of written examinations (concurso) without any use of interviews or any reference to evidence of practical competence.

The concern about teacher quality is reflected in research on the effectiveness of teachers in the classroom. Brazilian data shows that variations between teachers within schools are as great as variations between schools. At the same time, data on teachers' use of time in the classroom shows significant differences with international averages. The time spent on instruction is below 66 per cent (compared, for example, with an OECD average of 85 per cent of class time). Traditional teaching methods predominate with little use of co-operative active pedagogic strategies. These problems of teacher quality contribute significantly to the ongoing concern about the overall progress of pupils in key curriculum areas. Despite the impressive progress Brazil has made, 60 per cent of students, using PISA data, lack basic numeracy skills. On the basis of the national testing systems in 2009 50 per cent of primary school leavers lacked basic literacy skills, roughly the same as in 2003 (World Bank, 2010b).

Such concerns also extended to the proportion of high performers in the secondary mathematics curriculum, seen by some researchers as a key factor in ensuring the education system impacts on social and economic indicators (Hanushek and Woessman, 2007). Whereas 53 per cent of 15-year-olds in Shanghai, 28 per cent in Korea and 15 per cent across all OECD countries have high level mathematics skills (scoring over 600 in PISA assessment), only 1 per cent of Brazilian children could perform at this level.

The same World Bank analysis has pointed to encouraging signs that the interventions to improve teacher quality and teacher incentivisation working in parallel with increased use of data is beginning to work. Brazil's national testing system – SAEB and Prova Brasil – tracks learning levels of students in 4th, 8th and 11th grade. The newly introduced *Provinha Brasil* since 2007 also tracks learning of 3rd graders. Figure 7.1 shows the most important national trends. First, a clear decline in average learning levels from 1997–2000 has been identified, a period of rapid school expansion and improvements in primary completion rates. Second, there was a modest but encouraging uptick in learning outcomes from 2001 to 2003, which was also reflected in PISA (when Brazil registered the

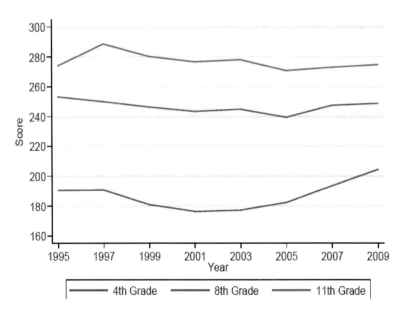

Figure 7.1 Brazilian math proficiency on SAEB/Prova Brasil, 1995–2009 (quoted in World Bank, 2010b, p. 28)

Source: SAEB (1995–2005), Prova Brasil/SAEB (2007–2009)

106   B. Moon and F. Wolfenden

strongest improvement in math performance in Latin America). Third, progress clearly slowed after 2003, but it appears to have resumed since 2005. This upward trend was reflected in Brazil's 2009 PISA performance. Attempts to improve the quality of teacher entrants has contributed to this.

The 1996 National Law of Education set out an aim to have 70 per cent of all pre-school and grade 1–5 teachers at graduate status by 2011 and all final elementary grades and secondary high schools require graduate level qualifications. Although these targets, as has been noted above, have not been achieved, significantly improved percentages of tertiary qualified teachers have been recruited.

The quality of higher education courses is assessed by a National System for Graduate Education Evaluation (SINAES). For institutions to be accredited or reaccredited it is necessary to receive a successful evaluation through this process. The structure of initial teacher qualification was simplified in the period 2003–6. Four categories come under the 'professional' (PRO) designation in relation to teachers:

- Pro-preschool (for professionals who work in day care centres or public and private pre-schools);
- Pro-graduation (for teachers in elementary and secondary high schools);
- Pro-formative (for teachers recruited into training who do not have adequate expertise in the subjects they wish to teach);
- Pro-employee (for people working in schools as technicians, administration, multi-media specialists and so forth).

This revised structure of initial teacher education is an example of the development of regulatory frameworks to raise standards and improve the consistency of provision. A series of such initiatives have addressed the quality of teachers. The federal ministry has introduced a new examination for all prospective teachers (the Exame Nacional de Ingresso na Carreira Docente) which gives considerable emphasis to high level content mostly in curriculum subjects, a process seen by some as reigning in the concern of university departments of education with social theory at the expense of pedagogic expertise (Bruns *et al.*, 2012). The federal ministry has also mandated that every district and municipality employing teachers should establish a formal teacher recruitment process (which shows demonstrated mastery of subject matter and pedagogy) and career pathways (which must be explicit about the performance requirements expected of teachers who progress from one grade to another). The impact of these changes has not been uncontested. Teacher educators, for example, have expressed concerns about the focus on competence and subject mastery and the 'surveillance' approach to enforcing reform (Figueiredo and Cowen, 2004).

In 2007 a further measure, the concept of a basic minimum salary for teachers, was introduced. This sought to address the large variations in teacher remuneration across states and municipalities. This was part of a new national approach to more equitable funding established through the 2007 Maintenance and Development Fund for Basic Education and Education Professionals (Fundels). There

Brazil 107

have also been measures to retain student teachers' interest in teaching as a career. The Institutional Scholarship Programme for Teacher Initiatives (Pbid) introduced 20,000 grants for this purpose. The overall investment in this intervention was 40 million US dollars in 2008. In addition to these national initiatives a number of state projects sought to retain a commitment to teaching amongst prospective and existing teachers.

The introduction of the federal Fiendeb initiative has seen an expansion of pre-service education and training programmes for teachers and a diversification of routeways. For example significant investment has been made in open and distance learning strategies to offer access to teacher training in remote localities. The Universidade Aberta do Brasil, the Brazilian Open University, opened 290 centres across the country in 2007 with priority being given to courses for prospective teachers. A Support Programme for restructuring the expansion of federal universities (Reuni) has recently been introduced which allows the expansion of teacher training places in higher education. Around 50 institutions have responded, representing an increase of 13,500 places in the post-2008 period.

In a country the size of Brazil overlapping programmes and projects seek to address similar problems. The federal ministry has introduced a Programme for the initial formation for Elementary and Secondary Education teachers in remote locations. Higher education institutions are invited to compete for funds to establish such outreach programmes. The programme gives a particular focus to qualification upgrading and to the preparation of teachers of mathematics and the three sciences (biology, chemistry, physics). Another example is the Proformacão programme operating in the north of Brazil (Bof, 2004). The Ministry of Education also introduced affirmative action to secure increased numbers of entrants to higher education from indigenous communities and teacher education courses through the Programme for Graduate Formation and Indigenous Graduations (Prolind).

Perhaps the most significant series of federal regulatory and enabling initiatives is in the sphere of in-service continuous professional development. A 2007 decree (Number 6094) set out an Everyone for Education Commitment, which whilst reaffirming already established principles also set out a number of goals relating to teachers. These included:

- the importance of career planning with appropriate remuneration and promotion prospects;
- valuing the work of education professionals through acknowledging their commitment to efficient performance of their duties, the dedication and responsibility of their role and the understanding of different forms of continuous professional development;
- recognising the importance of support within and outside the school;
- enabling all teachers to democratically engage in the political pedagogic project represented by the sector in which they work.

In 2007 the Ministry of Education introduced a National Network for the Continuous Professional Development of Teachers in Basic Education. Essentially this

108 B. Moon and F. Wolfenden

represented the establishment of a contract between federal government which provided technical and financial support and local providers (working in conjunction with state and municipal parts of the network) to provide education and training opportunities. The National Network objectives are focused on institutionalising and legitimising training opportunities across the country, establishing, what is termed, a dynamic interaction between universities, schools and teachers and building pedagogic communication of practice amongst teachers. The most recent priorities for the Network has been in the teaching of literacy, numeracy and science. The literacy and numeracy initiative is developed under the title Pro-letters: Mobilization for Education Quality. This is an in-service initiative focused on providing support to teachers in the early grades across the country. The Programme has adopted an integrated approach combining elements of open and distance learning through videos and printed guides as well as face-to-face tutorial sessions. Other related initiatives are now in place:

- The Programme for Inclusive Education: The Right to Diversity (which focuses on school leaders and teachers);
- The Programme for the Continued Formation of Secondary School Teachers (with a strong focus on improving subject teaching, particularly the teaching of Spanish which has recently been made compulsory in the school curriculum).

The federal ministry, faced with a large number of education sub-systems and with a higher education sector that jealously guards its autonomy in respect of the curriculum for teacher education, has recently developed a threefold strategy to improve teacher education and training. First a new examination (Exame Nacional de Ingresso na Carreira Docente) covering both subject content and pedagogy has been introduced for all new teachers. Although the ministry does not intervene in university course design this examination aims to steer teacher preparation towards a much more proactive focused structure. The ministry is not setting a pre-determined score that teacher entrants must achieve, this is left to local municipalities, but the entry levels accepted will be published.

Second, the ministry is embarking on an ambitious expansion policy towards secondary teachers of mathematics and science. Over 100,000 new additional training places are being funded at universities. And third, every teacher recruiting administration must establish a formal teacher recruitment process with an explicit career profile set out that shows the links between salary increase and improved performance. This third measure reflects initiatives already underway in some regions. São Paulo, the most recent World Bank study reports (World Bank, 2010b), has developed an innovative effort to upgrade teacher quality by creative a selective, highly recommended new career track comparable to Chile's AVDI (Asignación Variable por Desempenho Individual) and Peru's Carrera Publica Magisterial. Early outcomes suggest that teachers successful in achieving entry into this new career track produced high levels of pupil attainment even when results were controlled to take account of teachers' age and experience. The provision of this new career stream also appears to be impacting on overall teacher recruitment policies. In 2010 São Paulo had 270,000 candidates for 10,000 available teaching posts.

Numerous examples of incentivisation schemes can now be identified. Pernambuco, for example, has introduced performance targets for schools bonus payments for teachers when targets are met. Pernambuco's system is relative tough (less than 50 per cent of the target achieved results in no bonus awards) compared to other similar schemes (in São Paulo the percentage of bonus is related in the percentage achievement of target) but early results are deemed encouraging. In the first year of the programme 52 per cent of schools achieved bonus targets with an average teacher payment equivalent to 1.8 months salary. Research linked to this initiative has also provided more detailed analysis of the impact of a school-based bonus payment (Ferraz and Bruns, 2011). Key findings include:

- learning levels across Pernambuco's state schools improved considerably;
- the more ambitious the target the more progress the school made;
- strong acceptance of the initiative was found amongst school principals;
- schools that just missed the bonus went on to perform significantly better the following year;
- schools where teachers spent more time on instruction were more likely to receive the bonus (see Figure 7.2).

The implications of these sort of findings for teacher education programmes, both pre-service and in-service, could be significant although, as yet, there is little evidence of this having an impact on teacher development practices.

Teacher use of instructional time	OECD Good Practice Benchmarks	Overall PE sample	Subsequently achieved bonus for 2009	Didn't achieve bonus for 2009	Difference, bonus and non-bonus recipient schools
Learning activities	85%	61%	62%	53%	0.09 (0.04)**
Classroom management	15%	28%	27%	30%	−0.03 (0.03)
Teacher off-task	0%	12%	10%	17%	−0.04 (0.02)***
. . . o/w teacher out of classroom		8%	8%	12%	−0.04(0.02)***

Figure 7.2 Use of instructional time by teachers achieving and not achieving bonuses

Note: standard errors in parentheses.
* significant at 10% level; ** significant at the 5% level; *** significant at the 1% level.

Source: Bruns et al. (2011).

This chapter began by describing Amanda Gurgel's denunciation of federal and regional education policies. It is doubtful that she was aware of the accolades being bestowed on Brazil's 'managed revolution' by the World Bank and other international organisations. One of the major challenges for policy makers in Brazil is the establishment of a structured relationship, a basis for shared values perhaps, between the imperatives of system-wide reform and the needs and perceptions of teachers. Brazil represents a very large scale laboratory of substantive reform around teacher quality and teacher development and, given the significance of these reforms, it should command considerable attention from policy analysts and researchers as the varied strategies and initiatives evolve.

Section 3

Teacher quality and good quality teaching

Introduction

In the first two sections of this book concerns about the quality of expanding education systems have been looked at from a number of perspectives. Teacher quality has been identified as a key element in improving the quality of learning. But quality is not an easy term to define. It is clearly something more than being qualified (although qualifications are used as a proxy for quality in much of the official documentation about the teaching profession). The third section of the book addresses the quality dimension of teachers and teaching through a range of research studies, each of which seeks to give more substance to any analyses of quality.

A number of themes emerge, many of which are touched on by more than one contributor to the section. The first is the importance of looking beyond the statistics about teachers (important as these may be) to try to gain a richer understanding of their lives and motivations. This means, as the first chapter in the section suggests, the need to look beyond teachers as problems (the absentee teacher, the unqualified teacher) to teachers more generally, including the many who are successful despite, often, very challenging working conditions. In doing that it becomes quickly apparent how big a gap there is between teachers and the systems within which they work. The system, in its various manifestations (local education office, salaries department, teacher education institutions) often appears to be insensitive to the nature of teachers' lives.

The study of teachers' lives has featured in the educational literature for some time, but only recently have studies based on teachers and developing countries begun to appear. In the chapters that follow, the lives of teachers in Ghana, Pakistan, Tanzania and Sudan are examined to provide conceptually rich accounts of the way they make sense of their roles. There is particular consideration of female teachers and the challenges they face in combining other roles with their teaching tasks.

In exploring teachers' lives each of the contributors provides a conceptual focus to the data. One of the most interesting for future research and theorising, explored in Chapter 9, is the extent to which the ideas associated with capability theory could provide a framework for descriptive, situational analysis and a structure through which improvement and even the measurement of improvement could be conceived. This seems an important idea around which the policy and research discourse about teachers could be taken forward.

114 *Introduction*

The importance of looking beyond common indicators of equality is illustrated in the final two contributions to the section. The work of Monazza Aslam and Geeta Kingdon on teachers and pupil achievement in Pakistan first appeared in a working paper of the Centre for African Economies at the University of Oxford. It has been widely circulated in the development world as evidence that to understand teacher effectiveness requires looking beyond the formal qualifications of a teacher to the way in which they actually teach. In one sense this insight is not new, as the critiques of teaching styles and teacher education have suggested for many years. The study, however, has a distinctive methodological rigour which extends to identifying some of the teacher pedagogic practices that need to be fostered. As such the research has important implications for future research on this important issue, as well as offering grounds for some rethinking of the curriculum of many teacher education programmes. This theme is picked up in the last chapter of the section, a contribution that also began as a working paper, this time for the African Development Education Association and which has been widely circulating amongst those interested in the improvement of pedagogic practice.

The section has something, as the title suggests, of a dual lens on teachers, examining their lives as they conceive them and exploring the ways in which teachers can become more effective. Both, it would seem, are essential for further analysis of the qualitative dimension to teaching.

8 Professional development and female teacher morale in rural communities

Alison Buckler and
Amani Ibrahim Abdel Gafar

Introduction

Nkyen village, Central Region, Ghana.

The sun shines dimly through the mist that lingers over the salt ponds. It is 8 a.m. and around 80 of Nkyen's 300 pupils have made their way across the fields to school. The teachers send them to their classrooms. Instead of following them, the teachers drag chairs onto the veranda and chat in a circle, sliding lower in their seats as the sun rises higher in the sky. One teacher sets her chair away from the main group and hunches uncomfortably, balancing a Dip. Ed textbook and a notebook on either knee, oblivious to the teachers' chat and the rising commotion from the bored children. Two hours later a teacher checks his watch and calls out in Fante. A child rushes out of a classroom and into the storeroom and emerges, energetically pumping a hand bell up and down. Pupils troop obediently out of the classrooms where they have been sitting patiently, inactive and untaught, and break into a run towards the playing field and the food vendors. The Dip. Ed student looks reluctantly up from her books.

In the context of what UNESCO has termed 'the teacher issue' (the recruitment, training, deployment and retention of teachers in low-income countries) teacher morale and teacher motivation are often raised as concerns (UNESCO/TTISSA, 2008). Unacceptably high proportions of teachers are reported to be demotivated and suffering from low morale and low professional self-esteem; several authors have used the word 'crisis' to describe the state of teacher motivation across the continent (Adelabu, 2005; Bennell and Mukyanuzi, 2005; Black and Hosking, 1997; UNESCO, 2009; VSO, 2002). It is widely understood that teacher ability and resources are not the sole determinants of education quality; low morale and low self-esteem negatively affect teacher motivation and impact on the quality of teaching teachers are able to provide (Colclough *et al.*, 2003; Mpokosa and Ndaruhutse, 2009; VSO, 2007, 2008, 2009; World Bank, 1990).

This chapter draws on data from an ongoing, four-year study of female primary school teachers' lives in rural communities in Sub-Saharan Africa. One aspect of this study, carried out by the TESSA (Teacher Education in Sub-Saharan Africa) research consortium, is exploring teacher morale as it relates to teacher identity

116   A. Buckler and A. Ibrahim Abdel Gafar

and agency and how these are developed and influenced by rural and remote contexts. The data[1] suggests that teacher morale is more complex than is often acknowledged in existing literature; it is fragile, but also fluid and influenced by a complex interaction of personal, social, school and policy factors.

Some studies of teachers in low-income countries suggest that teachers' level of qualification, as well as their perceived and actual access to further education and training, impact on their professional identity, morale and self-esteem (Mackenzie, 2007; Nleya, 1999; Verhagen and Tweedie, 2001). Other studies have found little or no relationship between teachers' self-esteem and motivation and their level of qualification (Bennell and Akyeampong, 2007; Ramachandran *et al.*, 2005). This chapter contributes to this debate by exploring how teachers' morale and professional identity are influenced by pedagogical processes in professional development programmes. It focuses on two teachers coming to the end of the first year of an in-service diploma in education. Ruth is a student at the University of Cape Coast in Ghana and Sabeera is a student at the Open University of Sudan. The chapter is framed by Leach and Moon's (2008) assertion that pedagogy can (and should) build the identity, morale and self-esteem of learners.

Context

Most countries in Sub-Saharan Africa are experiencing a chronic shortage of qualified teachers, although the issue of teacher qualification is complex. Pupil enrolment at the primary level has been increasing since independence, galvanised by the Education for All (EFA) agenda and Millennium Development Goals for education and the removal of or subsidisation of school fees. Recent data estimates that Sub-Saharan Africa requires 1.2 million more primary school teachers (UNESCO, 2010a). In addition an estimated four million teachers are working in schools with no teaching qualification – to meet the demands of increased enrolment governments recruited thousands of unqualified teachers after a bare minimum of training, sometimes as little as two weeks. Many more, like the two teachers in this chapter, require further training as minimum qualifications for teachers are raised to improve education quality.

The vast and varied training needs of teachers in Sub-Saharan Africa means that teacher development programmes are 'at the centre of scrutiny' (Mestry *et al.*, 2009: 475). It has become increasingly clear that traditional, full-time campus-based courses do not have the capacity to deal with such large numbers of teachers. Part-time, in-service, school-based programmes have become an increasingly routine mode of educating and upgrading teachers at scale (Moon, 2007a; Moon and Nhalanganiso, 2002).

In-service teacher education in Ghana

In 1970 Ghana had one of the most highly developed education systems in West Africa. More than 60 per cent of primary school teachers were qualified and it was predicted that this would reach 100 per cent by 1975 (Akyeampong and Furlong,

2000; Konadu, 1994). By 1982 the percentage of unqualified teachers had fallen below 50 per cent (Akyeampong *et al.*, 2000) prompting a series of initiatives to raise the entry requirements for primary teacher training and strengthen provision for in-service teacher education.

In 2005 the minimum qualification for teaching at the primary level in Ghana was raised from a 'Certificate: A' (Cert:A) to a Diploma in Education. Teacher training colleges (TTCs) were upgraded to diploma-awarding Colleges of Education (CoE) (Ghana Ministry of Education, 2009). The combined annual output of Ghana's 38 CoEs is 9,000 compared to the country's 33,000 teacher vacancies and the need to upgrade existing Cert:A teachers (GNA, 2010). Until 2001, 10,000 teachers per year were awarded full-time scholarships to study for a diploma. The number of scholarships has since been reduced by two-thirds to ease the number of teachers leaving their classrooms and the burden of replacing them (Anamuah-Mensah and Benneh, 2009; Dawson-Brew *et al.*, 2009). Most Cert:A teachers now obtain their diplomas through three-year in-service programmes coordinated by the University of Education, Winneba and the University of Cape Coast.

In-service teacher education in Sudan

Until 1990 the minimum qualification for teaching at the basic level in Sudan was graduation from junior secondary school followed by a Diploma in Education. Most teachers acquired this diploma through a four-year, pre-service, college-based course. A smaller number of teachers who were unqualified but had at least a year of teaching experience obtained their diploma through a two-year in-service programme. This system produced 3,000 qualified teachers each year (UKNARIC, 2007; UNESCO, 2001; Willis, 2002). In 1990 teaching became a graduate profession and teacher training colleges became affiliated with universities to offer B.Ed programmes (UKNARIC, 2007).

By 2004 only 10 per cent of Sudan's 130,000 primary school teachers held a B.Ed (Sudan Federal Ministry of Education, 2004). To address the high numbers of under-qualified teachers, as well as cope with the pressures of training new recruits, a two-year, in-service diploma was introduced at 73 training centres across the country. Once teachers have completed their diploma they can enrol directly into the third year of the B.Ed course. The Open University of Sudan (OUS) was created, in part, to become the main provider of B.Ed and Dip. Ed qualifications. In 2008 over 100,000 teachers were studying with the OUS (Moon, 2008; Sinada, 2009).

Teachers, self-esteem and morale in Sub-Saharan Africa

Considering the potential morale-boosting effects of teacher education pedagogy in Sub-Saharan Africa seems a timely project; much of the literature about teachers on the continent paints a miserable, and relatively static, picture of teacher morale. A study by the National Professional Teachers' Organisation of South

118   *A. Buckler and A. Ibrahim Abdel Gafar*

Africa (2002) reported that one in four educators had a sense of low morale towards the profession. Over half of teachers in a study from Botswana and Malawi claimed that morale was low at their schools (Bennell, 2002). Low teacher morale has also been reported in Ghana (USAID, 2009; World Bank, 2011) and Sudan (Sudanese Federal Ministry of Education, 2004).

Low morale is attributed to a range of social, policy, infrastructural and management issues (Akyeampong and Stephens, 2000; Bennell, 2004; USAID, 2009; VSO, 2002). The status of teachers, for example, is said to have declined over the last 30 to 40 years (Bennell, 2004; UNESCO, 2009; VSO, 2002, 2009; Welmond, 2002), salaries are low and declining in real terms (Sumra, 2004; UNESCO, 2009) and pupil enrolment is increasing five times faster than in the 1970s leading to increased workloads for teachers (UNESCO, 2010a). Low morale is also attributed to poor working conditions, inflexible and impersonal deployment systems, a shortage of teacher accommodation, scarcity of resources and teaching materials, weak management structures, corruption, a lack of support in dealing with large-scale policy changes and both limited access to and the additional pressures of professional development and upgrading courses (Barrett, 2007; Buckler, 2009; Dos Reis, 2007; Mackenzie, 2007; Mestry *et al.*, 2009; Mulkeen, 2006; Shalem and Hoadley, 2009; Sudanese Federal Ministry of Education, 2004; Tao, 2005). Many of these issues are exacerbated in rural areas.

Low morale among teachers has been linked to low motivation, absenteeism, aggression, disinterest, lack of confidence to try new techniques, psychological withdrawal from work and early exit from the profession (Mwamwenda, 1995; Ramsey, 2000). It has also been coupled with a sense of weakened control over the pedagogical process and 'extremely poor schooling outcomes for students' (Shalem and Hoadley, 2009: 119).

Framework

While morale and self-esteem are regularly discussed in the literature around teachers in Sub-Saharan Africa there is ongoing debate over what they are and what they mean; they are rarely explicitly defined and are often used interchangeably. The *Oxford English Dictionary* (2010) defines morale as a 'moral condition as regards confidence and discipline' and self-esteem as to 'think favourably of self and regard as valuable'. From this it can be inferred that morale is a state of existence and self-esteem can be seen as an interpretation of this state. This study draws on a more holistic definition proposed by Wentworth (1990). Here morale is understood as 'the quality of lives within a community that involves being known and appreciated, having professional knowledge valued, and being given the freedom to act'. In this chapter this definition is presented as an overarching understanding of teacher morale, self-esteem and professional identity.

The framework for this chapter, linking identity and morale with education and pedagogy, has been adapted from Leach and Moon (2008). They suggest that, at its core, pedagogy must 'have the purpose of power for allowing children and others to forge their own ways and identities' (pp. 5–6). Pedagogy here is

Professional development and female teacher morale 119

understood as 'a dynamic process informed by theories, beliefs and dialogue . . . realised in the daily interactions of learners and teachers and real settings' (p. 6) rather than a specific formula or set of techniques to ensure effective teaching. In this chapter it is suggested that Leach and Moon's conceptualisation of identity-building pedagogy can be applied to the teaching and learning of teachers themselves. Indeed, the five attributes of pedagogy – voice, relationships, community, language and imagination – that Leach and Moon propose contribute to learner identity and self-esteem are especially interesting to consider in in-service education where the main learning environment is often not a lecture theatre, but learners' own communities and classrooms. They are also especially interesting when the learners are adult teachers with existing, highly developed identities, shaped by and for the communities and classrooms in which they teach.

If, as is suggested, a high proportion of teachers in Sub-Saharan Africa, and especially teachers in rural and remote areas, suffer from low morale and low self-esteem then in-service education programmes could offer a valuable provision by not only providing teachers with the skills and strategies to improve classroom practice but also by boosting their morale, self-esteem and sense of professional identity. In fact, studies from high-income countries show that teachers *need* to have high levels of morale and self-esteem to develop their practice (Craft, 2000). If morale, like identity, is imagined as dynamic and fluid, constantly shifting as a person develops through interactions with people and situations, it stands that it could be influenced by the pedagogical processes embedded in in-service teacher education programmes.

Teacher morale: two teachers from Ghana and Sudan

The data on which this chapter draws was collected during the 2006/7 and 2007/8 academic years in which Sabeera and Ruth were enrolled in the first year of their in-service Diplomas in Education with the Open University of Sudan (OUS) and the University of Cape Coast (UCC) respectively. The two teachers' experiences of their diploma courses will be explored in terms of three of Leach and Moon's pedagogical attributes: voice, relationships and imagination and how these intersect with their identities as women teachers in rural communities.

Ruth, February 2007

Ruth, now in her mid-twenties, was brought up in a small town in the east of Ghana. She wanted to be a lawyer but her family persuaded her to enrol at a teacher training college. After three years studying for her Cert:A at a residential TTC Ruth was posted to Nkyen school in Ghana's central region. When the fieldwork was carried out she had been teaching at Nkyen for four years. The school is a strip of three traditionally painted yellow and brown classroom blocks surrounded by a large field.

Ruth's pupils are the children of workers on the salt-farms that surround the village. Nkyen is less than a mile from the sea but has no fresh water supply.

120 *A. Buckler and A. Ibrahim Abdel Gafar*

Electricity is limited and sporadic. Ruth lives in a hostel next to the school and, because she is the only female teacher in the hostel, has her own room. It is just big enough for a bed, a desk and a small gas stove. The other (male) teachers sleep five to a room. None of the teachers stay in the hostel during weekends; Ruth travels home to be with her family.

In terms of Wentworth's (1990) definition Ruth's morale is low. She does not feel appreciated by the community, she does not feel that her professional knowledge is valued and she does not feel that the very basic school environment reflects her professional status. Pupil attendance is chronically low at Nkyen and the relationship between the teachers and the community has reached an impasse. The market women are hostile to the teachers, over-charging them because having a salary is rare in the village. The teachers have boycotted the market, preferring to shop in their home towns at weekends. When teachers have approached parents about their children's absenteeism they have met with indifference, aggression and even violence.

Ruth has a strong sense of duty and commitment to her post, although little emotional attachment. She feels over-burdened with the content-heavy curriculum and frustrated by the lack of textbooks; she spends a significant proportion of each lesson copying from the textbook onto the blackboard. She dreams of teaching in an urban school and her main reason for enrolling on her Dip.Ed is the prospect of promotion and the opportunity to move to a school in town: 'I don't want to be one of the ones who got left behind at the bottom.'

Sabeera, November 2007

Sabeera is one of 15 teachers at bab alnaher basic school for girls. Bab alnaher is on the banks of the White Nile and about an hour's drive from Khartoum. The village is large and sand coloured with flat-roofed buildings hidden behind high compound walls. The school is painted white and green and encloses a large tree-filled courtyard.

Sabeera studied law at the University of Khartoum but returned home after graduation to marry the local imam. Sabeera lives with her extended family, including her three small children, in a large, modern house with a separate tiled washroom. The compound's courtyard is dominated by an enormous satellite dish. When she returned to the village she started teaching English at bab alnaher, the school she attended as a child. Bab alnaher is headed by Sabeera's cousin; most people in the local area are descendants of the same tribe and the whole village is a close-knit family, related to each other in multiple ways. Though she has a degree, Sabeera has no teaching qualification and like several of her colleagues is studying for an in-service Dip.Ed with OUS at the request of the district education office.

Sabeera's morale could be considered to be high. She is a popular and well-respected member of her community and communicates regularly with her pupils' parents both professionally and socially. She is extremely proud to be a teacher. This pride is drawn from both the high value placed on education in the strongly

Professional development and female teacher morale   121

Islamic culture of the village – pupil attendance here is high and the teachers are revered – and her view that teaching is the best job for women because it enables them a professional status and an income but does not detract too much from their duties as wives and mothers.

Three attributes of pedagogy, in practice

Voice: 'the process by which we take control of our lives'[2]

Enabling learners to feel they have a genuine voice in the learning process is a key aspect of developing their self-esteem (Leach and Moon, 2008). Self-directed, constructivist approaches to learning are increasingly embedded in pedagogy at the primary level in Sub-Saharan Africa. In 2000 Sudan introduced a dimensions-based curriculum designed to encourage pupils to think critically, solve problems and take responsibility for their learning (Alarky, 2009). Ghana's curriculum revision in 1996 targets 'high-level cognitive objectives, values and practical skills' and emphasises critical thinking, problem-solving and pupil voice (Attar, 2000). Teacher education curricula in both countries is being adapted to help teachers move away from more traditional methods of 'chalk and talk', drilling and recitations and to facilitate learning environments that encourage pupil participation. However, just as other studies have identified that only a narrow range of teaching strategies are used in pre-service programmes for Sub-Saharan African teachers (Kanu, 2007; Stuart and Tatto, 2000) on Ruth's in-service programme there appears to be a tension between how she is taught to teach, and how she is taught.

Ruth is one of 350 students who receive their instruction through monthly lectures at the university campus. The course is highly structured with little opportunity for flexibility or choice, particularly in the first year before students move into their selected subject areas. A lecturer of in-service teacher education at UCC was asked if he felt there was a tension in lecturing teachers about the importance of allowing their pupils to have a voice in the learning process:

> In the university, I don't teach, I lecture. But in the classroom, you teach, you demonstrate . . . The teacher came here and said I am going to read education. But children, they don't choose. They are finding their way and you must help them direct themselves, listen to them and find the best way for them to learn. [As for] the student-teachers you give your lecture and go away . . . they have chosen to be here, they are focused on the exams, their path is already set.
>
> (Lecturer, University of Cape Coast, 2009)

Ruth shares the view of her lecturer that enabling learners to have a voice is a method for teaching children rather than adults, yet the limited opportunities for her to have a voice in her studies denies her a model of what facilitating pupil voice might look like in her own teaching. Ruth enjoys trying out new techniques but

122   A. Buckler and A. Ibrahim Abdel Gafar

her lessons tend to conform to a more traditional teaching style; lecturing from the front, writing long passages on the board for pupils to copy into their books and little pupil–teacher or pupil–pupil interaction. She feels participatory strategies 'work better in better resourced places and with children who have better English . . . here you have to go over and over things so they understand which means even if you start out with different plans you still end up lecturing'. Furthermore she is frustrated by the high levels of absenteeism and lack of ambition among her pupils. She feels that they, and their families, lack interest in and an understanding of education and she questions the pupils' ability to take responsibility for or their right to have a voice in their learning. Yet Ruth consistently scores A-grades in her teaching methods assignments; Freire might say that she was an excellent student but a 'meek receptacle' of her course content (2000: 72).

The hierarchical nature of the course structure further hinders Ruth's ability to have a genuine voice in the learning process and she feels unable to share the challenges of her classroom with her lecturers. 'You don't get personal time to talk to [the lecturers], you only see them in lectures [and] it would not be appropriate.' She has great respect for her lecturers and this acceptance of the educational hierarchy and her sense that 'the teacher knows best' also supports her justification for lecturing her pupils.

Ruth often talks about her teaching and her diploma as though they are separate entities: 'You feel torn because there is so much to learn, you want to study but you need to prepare lessons . . . you can't do both at the same time'. She feels that much of what she learns is not relevant in the context she works in and the disconnect between the assumptions of her course materials and lecturers and the realities of her classroom makes her feel she would have little to offer in a discussion: 'Because I hardly ever have a full class – it's different here . . . it's embarrassing'. If she felt more able to discuss the challenges she faces in an academic context it might not only help her to see synergies between what she studies and how she teaches, but also help her to see how she can have a positive impact on the challenges at her school.

The structure of Sabeera's course is very different. The remoteness of the village means that the Dip.Ed lectures consist of seminars where 30 teachers meet with their tutor three times a week. While the course curriculum is highly structured, students are encouraged to choose issues for discussion, for example if they have found an assignment particularly challenging or a strategy particularly useful.

Sabeera's tutor encourages her to reflect and comment on her learning and she appreciates the opportunity to feedback. She acknowledges that it is a different way of learning: 'It's not like the University of Khartoum . . . there we received lectures . . . you did not talk in the lectures, you just wrote notes . . . [the seminars] are more like discussions, we talk too' (Sabeera, 2007). A Professor of Education at OUS explained this:

> There is a belief that knowledge is enough and that it is possible to improve teaching through knowledge. Here at the Open University of Sudan we emphasise the distinction between learning and training. The **training** of

Professional development and female teacher morale   123

teachers and training teachers to develop the skills to **practice** concepts they learn, we believe, requires structured, supervised teaching practice and small, regular seminars.

(Sinada, 2009)

However, Sabeera also finds it difficult to maintain a classroom environment where pupils' voices are participatory rather than reciting. Like Ruth she enjoys trying new strategies but often reverts to a more traditional style. She suggested that this was because she mostly teaches English, which is new to the pupils, there is a 'lot to learn in a short amount of time . . . they have no basic knowledge [of English] before I meet them in the class'. Asking them to chant songs and poems is her preferred technique. While Sabeera readily admits that the format of her seminars, and being able to share her experiences with other teachers, have a positive impact on her self-esteem, she still lacks the confidence to embed child-centred pedagogies in her teaching repertoire. A boosted self-esteem may not always translate into better teaching when the pressures of a dense curriculum leaves little room for experimentation.

In-service teacher education, hypothetically, values the voices and experiences of its students since assignments are designed to be based on their own classroom practice. However, it is very difficult for tutors of in-service courses, with student cohorts reaching into the hundreds and with very limited contact time, to create a space where students' voices can be both heard and responded to. Leach and Moon (2008: 146) point to the 'dominant discourses' of curriculum which leave 'little space or time for the voice of the learner'. Ruth and Sabeera, as students of in-service programmes, have to manage two simultaneous curricula which compete for space in their classrooms. Sabeera tends to prioritise the pupil curriculum, reverting to tried and tested techniques to ensure she covers the syllabus. Ruth – because of low pupil attendance and lax supervision – often prioritises her studies over teaching her pupils. The pressures of these competing curricula leave little room for the teachers to reflect on or discuss synergies between the two. Admitting that they struggle to combine these curricula appears to be difficult even when the learning environment is conducive to discussion between the teachers and their tutors.

Relationships: 'a shared an open framework in which trust can be built'

The importance of relationships in education delivery is widely acknowledged (see for example Freire, 2000), in particular the establishment of a consistently trusting, respectful and supportive relationship between the educator and the learner. Less attention has been given to the pedagogical relationship between the teacher educator and the student-teacher. The development and maintenance of this relationship is crucial and especially challenging in distance education where contact between teachers and their tutors is limited and often infrequent. In some cases there may be no face-to-face contact.

124   A. Buckler and A. Ibrahim Abdel Gafar

The structure of Ruth's diploma leaves little time for student-teachers to develop meaningful relationships with their lecturers:

> You go there at the end of every month, Saturday and Sunday, you go in the morning, the lectures start at 6:30. During the break you prepare for the two papers. At 2:30 you move from the lecture room to the examination room. You are tested every month. 30 minutes for one paper and then they take it and bring you another paper and you answer everything and after that you can go.
>
> (Ruth, 2007)

Ruth has no one-on-one time with any of her lecturers, nor are there any small-group teaching sessions. Feedback of exams and assignments is reliable but impersonal: 'They are regular at marking our exams and our quizzes but they don't get time to discuss them with us.'

Ruth is largely unperturbed by the formal structure of her course: 'It's like, at college there is time for small groups but this is a university and lectures are more common.' Ruth's pride at being a university student and, again, her respect for academic hierarchy, facilitates her acceptance of this impersonal system of teaching and learning. This pride in itself boosts her morale. However, professional relationships are not unimportant to Ruth and the absence of supportive, personal relationships between lecturers and students has encouraged her and her peers to foster productive relationships with each other by setting up an informal study group.

> There is another teacher who is also doing this course and I found out about other teachers who are near to here . . . so after school we all meet up for discussions . . . we discuss the books that we are using . . . we take a unit per session, or perhaps two. Then the next time we meet we say 'how did it go?'.
>
> (Ruth, 2007)

The importance of feeling safe to share experiences and questions is an important part of the learning experience (Dillon and O'Connor, 2009). For Sabeera this is embedded in the course structure while Ruth has independently sought out opportunities for this.

In programmes like Ruth's, the difficulties of establishing meaningful relationships between a lecturer and 350 students who only have limited contact time once a month are clear. Dillon and O'Connor (2009) point to the large amount of literature and advice given to teachers about how to develop their relationships with their pupils compared to the dearth of advice for teacher educators about how to relate to and develop positive relationships with their adult students. In some areas communications technologies appear to be offering opportunities for interaction and engagement between students and tutors with the potential of enriching these relationships and boosting student-teacher morale. Evidence that mobile phones can enhance rapport, strengthen relationships between teachers on in-service courses and their tutors and reduce the student drop-out rate is

Professional development and female teacher morale   125

increasingly available (Hendrikz and Prins, 2009; Pouzevara and Kahn, 2007; Valk _et al._, 2010). Although in order to boost morale _and_ improve teaching it is important that tutors are familiar with the realities of their students' classrooms and that student-teachers feel able to share their struggles as well as their successes.

Imagination: 'That which allows us to envision what we, and our communities, might in the future become'

The final attribute of pedagogy considered here is imagination: 'our understanding of the world and our place in it' (Leach and Moon, 2008: 154) which is 'anchored in social interaction and communal experiences' (p. 155). Pedagogy, they argue, can develop a learners' imagination by raising awareness of future possibilities and allowing them to imagine what they, and their communities, might become.

For teachers on in-service professional development programmes, enrolment suggests they already hold an idea about what their new qualification will enable them to do or be. Both teachers in this study have a clear idea about where they hope the Dip.Ed will take them: Ruth – whose decision to upgrade was her own – imagines that her diploma will enable a geographical shift (out of the village) as well as a professional promotion to a job at a secondary school and enrolment on a B.Ed programme. Sabeera – whose enrolment was at the request of her superiors – imagines her diploma will raise her status in the community, enrich her experience of teaching and improve her skills in the classroom.

Ruth's approach to her professional development is often known as 'stepping stone': 'When I came out of training college I saw some teachers taking this kind of thing and they told me how I could apply . . . and that after three years you can start your degree course . . . I saw it as a path to the degree, really'. She believed that she had learnt all she needed to be a teacher at college. One key way her Dip. Ed has contributed to her professional imagination is by helping her to see how she can continue to develop her teaching skills.

> Now I have started distance education I see that I lack certain things. When you come out from college I think you should have to learn further because . . . It's not enough. When you study, you see that what you are doing is not all that perfect.
>
> (Ruth, 2007)

While the Dip.Ed has inspired Ruth, at this point she appears unable to transform her pedagogy in an environment that she sees as ill-equipped and unappreciative. Again the disconnect Ruth feels between what she is learning and the context in which she works limits her professional development. While the Dip.Ed is expanding her imagination about the type of teacher she could be, the morale boost this could potentially instil may be deferred until she is transferred to a school that she feels will value her skills.

In addition, Ruth's narratives imply an underlying belief that teaching at the primary level is for two main groups of people. The first are those who have an

126 A. Buckler and A. Ibrahim Abdel Gafar

innate love of young children and who see teaching as their vocation. The second group she imagines are those who are workshy and 'happy to be stuck at the bottom'. Because she does not associate herself with either of these groups she has imagined a new identity for herself as someone who is driven and moving up through the system to an urban school, into secondary level teaching and beyond. Ruth's Dip.Ed has had little effect on how she imagines the shape of the education system in Ghana and the low status she attributes to the primary sector. The pedagogical processes embedded in her Dip.Ed course and the social interaction between lecturers and teachers appear to be cementing her ideas around achievement, employment and status.

In this attribute of imagination it is important to look beyond the teachers' personal worlds and consider the social and cultural contexts in which they work. To understand how the pedagogical processes in their Dip.Eds might influence Ruth and Sabeera's imagination about what they may become requires a consideration of how they understand local and national expectations of the role of education and the role of women.

Teachers have a low status in Nkyen and education is little valued since most children will become farmers or work on the salt ponds. A key reason Ruth wants to leave is because her aspirations for her pupils clash with local aspirations. She has little confidence that she can – by herself – challenge this communal imagination and significantly impact their futures. Since she feels her newly acquired skills are unappreciated at Nkyen, her desire to be a better teacher is largely a personal endeavour.

Sabeera, on the other hand, is inseparably part of and involved in the maintenance of the communal imagination of her village which, in turn, reflects national views. When al-Bashir came to power in 1989 he announced that education should be, at all levels, based on Islamic values and and a new curricula was designed that incorporated the ideological-religious principles of an Islamic state (Breidlid, 2005; Sudan Federal Ministry of Education, 1999). Sabeera's job as a teacher maintains the local and national status quo both by embodying the village's imagination and by perpetuating it: 'The school teaches society really because society begins in the school. The role of the teacher is to carry out Sudan's educational aims by fixing the students for their futures as Sudanese citizens.'

Sabeera's enrolment on the Dip.Ed course seems to have strengthened the conviction she has that teaching is her vocation.

> I was a lawyer at the beginning. I didn't want to be a teacher. But when I began to practice teaching I refused to go back, even if they gave me my own special office to be a lawyer in Khartoum I would not want to go back . . . when I began the Dip.Ed I thought it would benefit the pupils most, but I have benefited almost as much because through teaching I realise that I can serve Allah, by teaching better I can serve better . . . The protection of national unity starts in the community – teachers build and protect the community, on all levels.

> (Sabeera, 2008)

Professional development and female teacher morale   127

Leach and Moon assert that pedagogy should 'most importantly raise students' awareness of future possibilities' (p. 144). Ruth's course has helped shape her professional goals – she dreams of being a university lecturer and sees no reason why she should not achieve this. As a rural woman in Sudan, however, Sabeera understands that her professional options are limited. She had 'no choice' but become a teacher when she married. Studying for the Dip.Ed is a way of developing her professional identity and contributing to her community without challenging their shared imagination about her role in that community.

Conclusion

Close behind the challenge of training and recruiting enough teachers to work in the classrooms of Sub-Saharan Africa is the challenge of ensuring these teachers are confident in and committed to their role as educators. This is important whether they see themselves as teachers forever or whether they see teaching as a stepping stone to another profession or another level within the education system.

Leach and Moon (2008) assert that: 'if we believe that learning is essentially a life-long process then identity must be at the heart of pedagogy' (p. 143). Teacher education in Sub-Saharan Africa, and indeed across the world, is increasingly imagined as an ongoing process of developing and reflecting upon knowledge and skills yet the identities of teachers in Sub-Saharan Africa have been little acknowledged as factors that affect how teacher education programmes are produced or consumed. Day (1991) explains how both personal and school factors impact on the quality of learning in continuing professional development for teachers. These two case studies show how for rural teachers enrolled on in-service programmes the local community and teachers' relationships with this community also influence the impact of professional development.

One reason teachers undertake professional development is to contribute positively to the development of their school (Craft, 2000). For Sabeera this is true; improving her teaching skills is a way of giving more back to the community which she feels honours and supports her role as their teacher. This has a cyclical effect on her morale. Ruth's participation on the Dip.Ed, however, has created a 'conflict of identity' (Eckert, 1995) – she is saving her developed teaching skills for a better resourced school in a community that she feels will appreciate and benefit more from them. Ruth's morale boost comes from her high grades and their promise of a better future, it has little effect on her teaching at Nkyen.

Increasingly teacher education initiatives train teachers from within communities, ensuring commitment to their schools (Gallastegi *et al.*, 2011). Where training local teachers is not possible, however, a key aspect of in-service teacher education could focus on building and maintaining relationships between teachers and communities. This could improve teachers' teaching as well as increase their motivation and ability to invest these skills locally. Without this, in-service education courses may have little impact in helping teachers to deal with the often overwhelming challenges of teaching, particularly in rural areas where enhanced

128   A. Buckler and A. Ibrahim Abdel Gafar

teaching skills are especially valuable but also where professional support for teachers is likely to be scarce.

The purpose of this chapter was to see if and how the pedagogical processes embedded in in-service programmes for teachers – the 'daily interactions of learners and teachers and real settings' (Leach and Moon, 2008: 6) can influence teacher morale. Sabeera and Ruth both feel that their morale has been enhanced and both feel their professional identity and skills have been developed. But their experiences show that while boosting teachers' morale should be an important focus of in-service teacher education courses, increased morale and an enhanced sense of what is possible in teaching does not necessarily lead to improvements, or even changes, in teachers' work. There is a gap between enhancing Sabeera and Ruth's professional identities and with them having the confidence to see how they can make deep and sustainable changes to their teaching repertoires that have a positive impact on the learning of their pupils. One important aspect here is ensuring that the content of the courses genuinely reflects the realities in which the teachers are working. Second it seems important that the pedagogical processes embedded in the programme allow teachers to reflect openly and critically on the challenges of their classrooms.

Rural teachers on in-service courses occupy several worlds despite often staying in one place; of teaching and learning, of practice and theory, of school and academia. If in-service teacher education is to have the desired effect of upgrading teachers' qualification, enhancing their skills and enabling them to make both subtle and substantial – but crucially lasting – changes to their teaching, it needs to focus on developing pedagogies that draw these multiple worlds together. Enabling a space for teachers to engage in honest and critical discussions about the challenging realities of their classroom and strengthening relationships between teachers and their tutors so these discussions can take place without fear or embarrassment appear to be important aspects. Finally it is interesting to reconsider Leach and Moon's definition of imagination: 'That which allows us to envision what we, and our communities, might in the future become'. In-service teacher education pedagogies that reinforce notions of a hierarchical education system risk handing teachers the tools to move 'up' and out of basic education. Pedagogies designed to enhance teachers' experiences of and commitment to teaching may help teachers to envision themselves as valued members of a highly qualified, motivated community of professionals.

Notes

1 Teachers' Lives is a qualitative research project using ethnographic and narrative approaches to explore the lives of female teachers in rural and remote schools in five Sub-Saharan African countries: Ghana, Nigeria, Kenya, South Africa and Sudan. For more information on this project and data collection methods see Buckler (2011) and Moon and Buckler (2007).
2 Quotes in the sub-headings of this section are from Leach and Moon (2008).

9 Investigating teacher capabilities in Tanzanian primary schools

Sharon Tao

Government primary schools in Sub-Saharan Africa are faced with a litany of problems, but one issue often discussed, dissected and debated is that of the poor quality of teachers. The global impetus for Education for All and the subsequent Dakar Framework for Action has brought the issue of teacher quality to the fore, as it has been widely researched and accepted that teachers are the strongest school level determinant of student learning (Lockheed and Verspoor 1991; Scheerens 2000; Hopkins 2001; UNESCO 2005). In Sub-Saharan Africa, scarce financial resources and the demand to expand the teaching force have exacerbated the poor provision of teacher quality, and much discourse has evolved around the determinants of quality teaching, as well as reforms needed to improve quality within the existing teaching force. To that end, a great deal of research has attempted to delineate teacher variables that affect student achievement (cf. Guthrie 1982; Fuller 1987; Heneveld 1994), which often entail lists of 'teacher competencies' (such as skills and content knowledge) and elements of 'teacher performance' (the use of knowledge and skills in the classroom) (Anderson 2002). I would like to posit that deficiencies in teacher well-being undermine efforts to both identify teacher quality variables and initiatives to improve them. First, lack of teacher well-being leads to opportunistic behaviour that runs counter to what is needed for quality teaching and learning to occur; and second, lack of well-being affects acceptance and adherence to reforms attempting to reconcile such behaviour.

That is why I shall examine the issue of teacher quality through the lens of the Capability Approach. I will suggest that the greatest barrier to teacher quality and success in reform is a lack of empathetic and realistic insights into their contexts, constraints and mindsets; as well as a lack of teacher consultation and participation in the planning process. I will also suggest that improvements in teacher quality come only with holistic improvements to teacher well-being, which is achieved when valued capabilities are expanded. These arguments will be supported by three applications of the Capability Approach:

1 in-depth situational analyses to explain current behaviour;
2 determining teachers' valued capabilities to guide improvement measures; and
3 evaluation processes to monitor overall teacher well-being.

130   S. Tao

I will first discuss the situational analysis framework that the Capability Approach offers, and will draw upon experiences and insights gleaned during nine months spent teaching in Arusha, Tanzania, to provide examples of how this framework can be operationalised. I will demonstrate that such a framework not only sheds light on the antecedents of teacher behaviour, but also provides reasons why improvement measures are not implemented. Second, I will discuss the methodology for capability selection that has been put forth in the literature and apply this to teachers. I will also discuss how the expansion of these valued capabilities can guide practice and policy to improve teacher quality in more substantive ways. Finally, I will investigate the monitoring and evaluation tools that the Capability Approach has to offer, and explore how these can be used to hold governments accountable to a holistic view of teacher development. However, before demonstrating these various applications, a discussion of the Capability Approach is in order.

What is the Capability Approach and how can it improve teacher quality?

The Capability Approach (CA) emerged as an intellectual response to various inequality measurements, as it critiqued the 'information base' in which comparisons were being made (Sen 1999: 56). For example, welfare economics looked at income as the basis for evaluating inequality and poverty, and although Sen (1992: 20) acknowledged that income was an important resource for well-being, he argued that there were components of well-being that were not directly acquirable with income (such as being healthy, or being able to make choices). Sen (1992: 33) also argued that current spaces for evaluation did not account for the fact that different human beings attained different levels of well-being when given the same income or bundle of goods. Thus, Sen (1999: 73) suggested that instead of focusing on the *means* that might facilitate a good life, we should instead focus on the *actual living* that people manage to achieve; and more importantly, the *freedom* that people have to achieve the types of lives they want to lead. This alternative view bore the information base of *functionings*, which are the 'beings and doings' that people have reason to value; and *capabilities*, which are the opportunities or substantive freedoms that people have for realising these functionings. Sen (1999: 36) argued that focusing on capabilities as an information base is paramount because they serve both 'instrumental' and 'constitutive' roles. Instrumentally, expanding capabilities can be viewed as a *principle means* of development both for an individual or a society; in addition to this, expanding capabilities could also be viewed as the *primary ends* of development, as Sen believes intrinsic capabilities such as being literate, nourished and enjoying political participation, amongst others, are substantive freedoms that enrich human life.

Before discussing ways in which CA can be used to understand issues of teacher quality, it should be noted that this is not the manner in which it has been previously linked to teachers. Instead, many authors have looked at the importance of teachers in regards to capability expansion within schools, such as Unterhalter and Brighouse (2007), who discuss the role teachers play in the well-being and agency freedoms of students; Bates (2007) discusses the responsibility of educators and educational administrators to foster the pursuit of capabilities as worthy educational goals; and Biggeri (2007) discusses how the expansion of children's capabilities are often subject to parent and teacher control and decisions. This body of work has provided many thoughtful and interesting entry points in which to think about teachers, particularly because it highlights the instrumental role that they play in the expansion of students' capabilities. Thus, I would like to build upon this work by putting forth the effort of investigating teacher well-being, as doing so would address teacher quality at two levels. First, expansion of teachers' valued capabilities would entail the improvement of working conditions that are at the root of counter-productive teacher behaviour. Much research has proven that teachers' professional efficacy, commitment, job satisfaction, stress, morale, engagement or disengagement (from school or profession) and pedagogical practice are all directly influenced by the conditions under which they work (Leithwood 2007). By using CA to investigate and subsequently alter working conditions that negatively affect teachers' behaviour, valuable mindsets such as efficacy, commitment and morale would no longer be at a deficit. Second, almost all interventions and reforms to improve teacher quality have targeted capacity building (such as in-service training and teacher resource centres, amongst others) (Anderson 2002; Dembélé and Lefoka 2007; Sifuna and Kaime 2007), however a lack of teacher well-being seriously undermines any potential these efforts may have in terms of acceptance, adherence and ability to execute. That said, I shall now explore the theoretical and practical applications of CA, not only because of the instrumental implications it may have on these two strands of teacher quality, but also because improving teacher well-being is also a primary end in itself.

How can the Capability Approach be used?

The Capability Approach (CA) is very relevant to evaluating the development of teachers because of its broad scope and highly interdisciplinary nature. 'Scholars use the Capability Approach for different types of analysis, with different epistemological goals, relying on different methodologies, with different corresponding roles for functionings and capabilities' (Robeyns 2005b: 193). Table 9.1 demonstrates CA's variety of uses.

Table 9.1 Modes of capability analysis

Epistemological goal	Methodology	Role of functionings and capabilities
Welfare/quality of life measurement	Quantitative empirical	Social indicators
Normative theories	Philosophical	Part of the philosophical foundations
Thick description/descriptive analysis	Qualitative empirical	Elements of a narrative

Source: Robeyns (2005b: 193).

132   S. Tao

A quantitative measurement provided by CA is the Human Development Index, which signalled an important paradigm shift in assessing countries' development by focusing on a broad set of social indicators such as health, education and standard of living, rather than the sole measurement of GDP (Sen 1999). Other applications of CA, however, are more commonly qualitative and theoretical in nature. Political and moral philosophers have used CA as a tool for normative theorising about what is fundamental for well-being and human flourishing (cf. Nussbaum 2000, 2003). As a result, scholars have devised lists that 'isolate those human capabilities that can be convincingly argued to be of central importance in any human life, whatever else the person pursues or chooses' (Nussbaum 2000: 74). Thus, careful selection of capabilities is done in order to create criteria for social justice that governments can be held accountable to.

CA can also be used as a descriptive tool 'to explain behaviour that might appear irrational according to traditional economic analysis, or revealing layers of complexities that a quantitative analysis can rarely capture' (Robeyns 2005a: 194). This is particularly important when analysing specific situations as it allows for deeper levels of understanding. CA achieves this by taking into consideration *conversion factors* (such as personal skills, social norms and logistics), which help to elucidate extenuating circumstances that can affect a person's ability to achieve certain functionings (Robeyns 2005a). This in turn provides a robust situational analysis that can more clearly guide subsequent policy and action.

Following on from these different applications of CA, it would seem possible to augment the list in Table 9.1 by making explicit Sen's implication of using it to guide policy. Hitherto, Sen has been adamant in his lack of endorsement of a specific 'list' of capabilities because he views CA as an approach in which participatory methods of capability selection and prioritisation should be applied (Sen 1999, Gasper and Van Staveren 2003). 'When the Capability Approach is used for policy work, it is the people who will be affected by the policies who should decide on what will count as valuable capabilities in this policy question' (Robeyns 2005b: 196). This implies a proactive and democratic use of CA amongst stakeholders to select capabilities that will determine actions based on their expansion. Thus, this application would be qualitative and participatory in nature, and the role of functionings and capabilities would not act as social indicators or elements of a narrative, but instead as goals to be achieved.

Given the different applications of CA, I believe its relevance to teacher quality are three-fold: first, it can act as tool for descriptive situational analysis in order to understand reasons behind low levels of quality in the existing teaching force, as well as reasons for lack of adherence to improvement measures; second, CA can be operationalised as a framework for improvement by utilising participatory measures to identify capabilities to be subsequently expanded; and finally, CA can be used as a measurement device to later monitor the overall expansion of teacher capabilities and development. I will demonstrate these various applications drawing upon insights gleaned from my time in Tanzania, and I shall start by using CA to provide a case study situational analysis of the teachers at the government primary school I worked in.

Using CA for situational analysis

As discussed in the previous section, CA can provide a very in-depth understanding of a situation through its use as a descriptive tool. This is particularly relevant to measures which examine and improve teacher quality because quite often the inequalities and social structures that set the conditions for teacher behaviour are not fully understood. This can lead to slippages and oversights that can render improvement initiatives ineffectual, which is why CA is useful as it accounts for a variety of factors that affect behaviour and acceptance of change. Robeyns (2005a) has put forth a concrete framework that acknowledges the cultural and social contexts in which capabilities are situated, by identifying *conversion factors* and *choices* that can block capabilities or functionings. Figure 9.1 outlines how these elements are related and can be used to analyse data.

This framework for analysis demonstrates the key areas between the initial inputs and the end outcomes that are imperative for understanding teacher behaviour. 'Knowing the goods a person ... can use is not sufficient to know which functionings he/she can achieve; therefore we need to know much more about the person and the circumstances in which he/she is living' (Robeyns 2005a: 99). Robeyns acknowledges that 'goods and services' are instrumental in the achievement of functionings, but states that it is not the market value of a resource that is important; instead it is the *characteristic* of the good that enables a functioning to be achieved. For example, a teacher is not interested in a textbook because it is an object made out of paper, but instead she is interested in it because it can make her job easier and more effective. However, a teacher's ability to convert such a good into a functioning is influenced by three conversion factors. These include, *personal conversion factors* (such as intelligence, training and skills, amongst others); *environmental conversion factors* (such as geographical location and logistics); and *social conversion factors* (such as policies, social norms and power relations). In order to understand the genesis of these conversion factors, we must also look at the broader social context and culture that surrounds a school and affects the teachers.

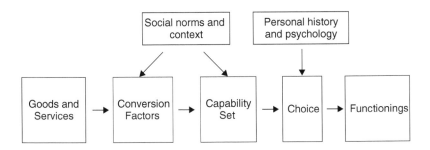

Figure 9.1 A modified rendering of CA factors

Source: Robeyns (2005a).

The elements in Figure 9.1 link together to provide an in-depth understanding of the antecedents to a problem or behaviour. I shall now bring this figure to life with an example of how conversion factors and choices affected the teachers I taught with at a peri-urban government primary school in Arusha, Tanzania. It should be noted that this data was not collected under the guise of research – it comes in the form of reflections that were recorded at the time. However, this method of retrospectively drawing on ethnographic insights is referred to as autoethnography (Ellis and Bochner 2000); and within this approach is 'participant observation' in which immersion into a culture allows for thick descriptions of social processes that can be reflective of reality and rely less on researcher inference (Cohen *et al.* 2007). I would identify myself as a 'participant observer' in that I was immersed in my village and school culture, lived in an orphanage and a *boma* (family compound) that allowed me to identify with the community, and was accepted by teachers and students more readily than other *wazungu* (Westerners) because I spoke Kiswahili and stayed for an extended period of time. Thus, the reflections that I gleaned will contribute to the following example (and others in the next section) to demonstrate teachers' capability (or lack thereof) of converting a good into a functioning.

Figure 9.2 illustrates the many factors that affected the use of textbooks at the primary school. The school had a plethora of teaching materials, storybooks and even a small library, made possible by the Western volunteers who often worked there. Some textbooks were bought in Arusha, and were in line with national curricula. However, many were bought in Western countries and subsequently brought over. Even though this was not ideal, these books could have easily served as teaching aids and extra teaching material. However, the Tanzanian teachers rarely used the Western books and, by looking at the conversion factors, we can understand why. First, the fact that teachers were not trained or had the confidence to use non-syllabus related material could be considered a personal conversion factor (PCF). Another PCF was the fact that most of the books were written

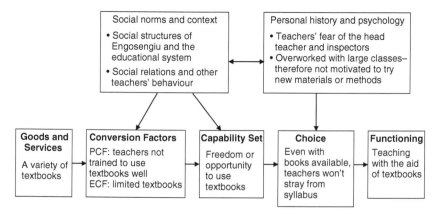

Figure 9.2 Descriptive analysis of factors affecting 'teaching with a textbook'
Source: Robeyns (2005a); data: Tao (2005)

in English (not in the teaching language of Kiswahili), in which most teachers were not fluent. An environmental conversion factor (ECF) was that many books came in limited amounts (20–30 for a class of 70). Finally, social conversion factors (SCF) included the fact that it was not a social norm for Tanzanian teachers to use foreign materials, nor did the head teacher encourage it.

After identifying the conversion factors that affect teachers' capability of using textbooks, CA also highlights the choices that teachers make in turning their capability into a functioning. In this case, the teachers did have a slightly expanded capability to use textbooks as they were readily available, along with Western volunteer teachers who were willing to assist. However, many of the teachers still refrained from using the books because of personal and psychological factors that influenced their decision-making. Generally, teachers did not often seek assistance from volunteers, as most did not have trusting relationships with them (due to language barriers and high volunteer turnover). So even if a teacher was interested in the new books, many were too apprehensive to ask volunteers for help with them. A more significant factor, however, was that most teachers feared the somewhat autocratic head teacher who was adamant that staff strictly follow the scheme of work given by the Ministry of Education. With such an environment, most teachers did not dare use a new book or set of exercises for fear of reprimand. A final key factor that influenced teachers' choices was the fact that using new materials would create more work. It takes time to plan a lesson that is creative or not outlined on the syllabus; and for teachers who are overworked and under-motivated, taking extra time to plan a lesson with new material is a choice most would not make.

Thus, the functioning of 'teaching with the aid of textbooks' was not achieved, even though the potential was there. Before discussing measures that would reconcile these conversion factors and choices, I would first like to give a more complete situational analysis of teacher behaviour vis-à-vis CA and reflective data from my time at this school. This will touch on a variety of actions that run counter to teaching and learning processes, and thus allow for a more informed idea of how to navigate change.

Descriptive analysis of teacher behaviour

The following is a common description of state schools in developing countries:

> First, teachers often do not show up to teach at all. Second, when they do show up, they often do little real teaching, because they are waiting to offer 'private tuition', when the richer families hire them for after-school instruction . . . Third, even when responsible teaching is done in the classroom, it is still primarily focused on rote learning, as students are crammed with facts and routinised answers for the various examinations they are going to sit.
>
> (Nussbaum 2006: 387)

A great deal of classroom research supports this observation and, given my experiences, I too witnessed such behaviour. However, instead of vilifying teachers for

136 *S. Tao*

these actions, I would like to use CA to offer reasons why these examples (and others) exist. The following Tables 9.2 and 9.3 address two strands of teacher behaviour: commonly criticised actions that are seen to impede learning and student capabilities (such as those offered by Nussbaum 2006); and behaviour that demonstrates a lack of acceptance and adherence to teacher quality reforms. By using conversion factors and personal choice variables that were observed whilst teaching at my primary school, I will attempt to elucidate the constraints on capabilities and functionings that are often overlooked when discussing and planning for teacher quality. It should be noted that although the examples in these tables address 'negative' behaviour, it is *not* meant to imply that that all teachers are deficient or behave this way. Nor does it imply that improvement measures should be premised on a deficit model. The intention of this exercise is purely to explain behaviour that is often perceived as 'unprofessional', as well as demonstrate how CA can be used to provide a rigorous analysis of a situation.

In analysing the various conversion factors associated with teacher behaviour, we can start to consider areas of capability deprivation, and how they can be reconciled. It seems that many of the personal conversion factors (such as lack of training, being tired and hungry) are results of poor teacher education and factors that lead to feeling overworked. Many in-service training interventions have attempted to alter rote-teaching methods (Dembélé *et al.* 2007); however, these initiatives often suffer from lack of acceptance because planners do not consider the new set of conversion factors that surround them. Unfortunately, training to address other issues such as non-violent classroom management and gender sensitisation have been slower to come, and interventions to reconcile teacher hunger or tiredness are paltry at best.

Environmental conversion factors such as excessive workload (due to class size, poor remuneration, lack of teaching resources) lead to stress, reduced morale, reduced commitment to the school, and increased likelihood of attrition. These ECFs are the result of planning at national levels and have proven slow to alter due to states' lack of capacity, resources and finances. However, more nimble school-level initiatives such as scheduling lunch breaks, creating non-monetary incentives and gender-sensitising teachers to previously published texts may help to mitigate some problems.

Social conversion factors that entail norms within the wider community may also prove difficult to alter, however, head teachers can directly influence a school's culture. The principal is often the locus of control for changing SCFs, and research indicates that training of management can positively affect teacher behaviour (Rizvi 2008). For example, head teachers can instil codes of conduct (such as not missing class or withholding content); as well as create environments that promote agency as opposed to fear. However, altering head teachers' behaviour (in order to benefit the teachers within their school) is no easy task, and also requires a separate investigation into conversion factors and choices that affect them.

To be honest, many of these solutions are not new, but the difference here is that efforts are underpinned with the intent of enhancing teacher well-being and

Table 9.2 Descriptive analysis of 'commonly criticised' teacher behaviour

Perceived problem	Goods and services	Conversion factors (Reasons why 'the problem' exists)	Capability	Choice	Functioning (or lack thereof)
Absenteeism (or being extremely late for class)	n/a	PCF: Hungry, tired (not enough breaks so teachers feel entitled to be late or miss their last classes of the day). ECF: Too many classes, too many students, too many papers to mark. SCF: Other teachers skip class and it is 'overlooked' by management – in fact, the head teacher often schedules staff meetings during class time.	Freedom to come to class	Many teachers are overworked and thus resentful. This low motivation affects their choice in coming to class.	Teaching for the maximum allotted time (but not the case)
Rote teaching methods	Teacher training	PCF: They are satisfied with current methods and grew up with rote teaching as well; not trained in or convinced by child-centred pedagogy. ECF: 70 students in a class and no supplementary teaching materials. SCF: Teachers view foreign innovations with scepticism; and rote teaching is considered the best method for preparing students for national exams.	Freedom to teach with a child-centred pedagogy	Most teachers believe rote teaching is very effective for large classes, and taking on new methods would add to their workload.	Teaching with child centred-methodology (but not the case)
Withholding content during class	Content from syllabus and textbooks	PCF: They have the content and time to teach after school tuition classes. ECF: Low salaries warrant secondary income generation and there are students willing to pay for the tuition. SCF: It is a common practice among other teachers and not condemned by management.	Freedom to maximise the teaching of content in class	Many teachers withhold content because they've chosen to put their needs first (by generating more income through tuition).	Teaching all subject matter during class (but not the case)
Lack of preparation for class	Teacher training and teaching materials	PCF: Lack of training means that lesson planning consists of finding exercises in textbooks and having students copy from the blackboard. ECF: Busy with secondary jobs and chores, scarce	Freedom to be prepared for class	Lack of time, financial incentive and motivation means that most teachers would	Being prepared for class

		teaching materials. SCF: It is not a common practice among other teachers and not demanded by management.		rather not add to their workload.	
Corporal punishment	Teacher training	PCF: Tired, daunted by large classes, have not been trained in any other form of classroom management. ECF: 70+ students per class. SCF: Corporal punishment conveys teachers' authority, teachers experienced it themselves, it is 'overlooked' by management.	Freedom to manage and discipline a class in a non-violent manner	Corporal punishment makes a teacher's life easier as it is seen as the easiest and fastest way to discipline.	Managing a classroom without using violence (but not the case)
Gender bias in treatment of students	Teacher training	PCF: Not trained with gender sensitive pedagogy. ECF: Textbooks and materials are highly gendered. SCF: Social reproduction of gender bias in teacher training and society.	Freedom to teach with equity and enhance girls' learning	Most likely an unconscious choice (to cater to boys and assign gendered tasks) due to social norms.	Equitable treatment of students and enhancement of girls' learning (but not the case)

Teacher capability in Tanzanian primary schools 139

agency. By addressing conversion factors that demonstrate an appreciation and acknowledgement of teachers, it is possible that the ever elusive element of teacher motivation might in fact rise. This is particularly relevant in regards to interventions which attempt to bolster teacher capacities, as acceptance of change is often contingent on motivation and morale. A small but significant body of literature is drawing attention to the fact that teacher motivation is paramount for reform implementation, and addressing these links requires just as much thought and planning as creating reforms themselves (Chapman 1997; Fry 2002; O'Sullivan 2002; Davidson 2007). For example, the Tanzanian government outlined several initiatives to improve teacher quality such as:

1   improve pre-service and in-service training;
2   improve teachers' methods by introducing child-centred techniques;
3   ask teachers to use double-shift and multi-grade teaching systems as an interim measure;
4   increase teacher-to-pupil contact time by having a minimum instructional week of 20 hours (MOEC 2001).

These are laudable intentions, however the plan did not identify how these improvements would be implemented. The reforms are understandably geared towards improving student learning, however, they do not acknowledge teachers' needs, nor make provision for factors that affect teachers' acceptance and adherence. That said, Table 9.3 attempts to illuminate problems associated with reforms such as these, by giving a descriptive analysis of the conversion factors and choices that mediate implementation.

The data in Table 9.3 does not represent reforms that directly affected teachers at my school, however, the conversion factors and choices are extrapolated from an in-depth understanding of the teachers that I knew, and are augmented by research that has investigated working conditions, interventions and behaviour change (cf. Hurst 1981; Carron and Chau 1996; Chapman 1997; O'Sullivan 2002; Davidson 2007; Sifuna *et al.* 2007).

In analysing the various personal conversion factors associated with teacher acceptance and adherence to reforms, we can see that teachers' attitudes have a huge effect on their training, skills and willingness to change. Clearly, if teachers do not see a problem with their methods, they will not see the need to adopt a new pedagogy. However, even if they are willing to change, they still do not have the adequate training, time and classroom conditions to implement child-centredness. A teacher's feeling of being overworked is also a very influential PCF because any new reform that adds complexity and planning to her duties will be understandably met with resistance. Some possible ways of navigating these PCFs is to consult teachers directly when creating reforms, not only to determine feasibility, but also to engender a sense of ownership and accountability. More often than not, teachers are not included in this process and cannot inform planners of realities, achievability and personal opinions. With teacher participation, more implementable reforms could be developed such as *learning-centeredness*

Table 9.3 Descriptive analysis of 'lack of acceptance and adherence' to reforms

Goods and services (new reform)	Conversion factors affecting acceptance of and adherence to reforms	Capability (intention of reform)	Choice	Functioning (or lack thereof)
Improved pre-service and in-service training	PCF: Many enter the teaching profession as a last resort, thus motivation to learn (even at an 'improved' pre-service course) is lessened. Also, some in-service courses are not free, and thus teachers cannot afford to attend. ECF: In-service courses are often taught in urban centres making attendance difficult for teachers in rural areas. Also, even 'improved' courses teach outdated content and are didactic in nature. SCF: Attending in-service courses is not a common practice amongst other teachers at school and is not expected by head teachers	Freedom to teach with improved content knowledge and pedagogy	There is no professional or financial incentive to seek extra training so many teachers choose not spend the time or money.	Teaching with improved content knowledge and pedagogy
Training to introduce child-centred pedagogy	PCF: Training is hindered as teachers are satisfied with their current classroom practice and do not see the need to change methods. Also, many teachers have varied interpretations of this pedagogy. ECF: Not many courses are available, especially in rural areas; some courses are taught in the second language of English; 70+ students make child-centredness extremely difficult to implement. SCF: Teachers are dismissive of foreign teaching methods as they don't account for realities in the classroom; pressure to cover the syllabus for exams does not allow time to master a new, complicated and 'slower' method.	Freedom to teach with child centred pedagogy	Teachers resist innovations that increase the complexity of their work and run counter to their beliefs about effective teaching.	Teaching with child-centred pedagogy
Double-shift and multi-grade teaching systems	PCF: Teachers are not trained in multi-grade techniques and view it as adding complexity and planning to their workload. ECF: Already have too many students to take on more. SCF: Other teachers view and reinforce the notion that double-shifts or multi-grade classes are a burden. If it is an interim measure, most teachers will not feel pressure to change their behaviour.	Freedom to provide instruction to more students	Teachers might not have a choice if they are assigned a multi-grade class, but they can choose not to cater to different learning levels.	Providing instruction to a greater number of students

20-hour instructional week	PCF: Teachers already feel overworked without enough breaks in the day. More work makes them resentful. ECF: Too many classes, too many students, too many papers to mark SCF: Other teachers are unhappy and feel entitled to skip extra classes; the head teacher does not usually monitor such behaviour.	Freedom to maximise time with students	Teachers are overworked and if there are no incentives to work extra hours, they would most likely skip extra classes.	Maximising teaching time
Teacher resource centres to aid in class preparation	PCF: Teachers don't have the skills or motivation to seek out new materials and plan new lessons. ECF: Limited number of centres makes them difficult and time consuming to get to. SCF: A foreign innovation that is not completely understood or appreciated by teachers. No other teachers use the centres, and the head teacher does not encourage it.	Freedom or opportunity to prepare for class	Teachers instead choose to use the centre's photocopy machines for personal reasons, as they view this as a small form of extra compensation.	Ability to prepare for a class

142 *S. Tao*

pedagogy (cf. Verspoor 2005: 175) or refined *performance mode* practice (cf. Barrett 2007), which both acknowledge current pedagogies used by teachers and the constrained working conditions that affect them.

Many environmental conversion factors also have their root in excessive workloads, and as mentioned in the discussion of Table 9.2, factors such as class size, lack of resources and poor financial incentives are national planning issues that have proven slow to change. However, if government planners could see the direct link between excessive workloads and how they form barriers to improvement measures, perhaps they would be more apt to address workload issues as a strategy for ensuring reform implementation.

Many social conversion factors that stem from collective teacher attitudes and behaviours also come from resentment brought on by working conditions and lack of appreciation. This resentment leads to teachers feeling justified in the social norm of not accepting or adhering to reforms. It also plays a large role in teachers' 'choices' to alter reforms to suit their needs (as in the teacher resource centres). Again, principals can play a large role in creating environments that counter such beliefs. However, it seems that the overall pattern in the conversion factors and choices discussed, points towards a much larger reform—one that tackles teacher working conditions in a holistic fashion, not only to aid implementation of reforms, but to improve the motivation and morale that ultimately mediates teacher quality. Davidson (2007: 160) expands:

> Teacher motivation is related to a long list of variables, including whether an enabling environment exists and whether teachers are equipped to carry out their roles. However, at a basic level, teacher motivation is linked to how teachers feel they are being treated and to the way they perceive their own working and living conditions. For example, if a teacher feels that she is being asked to teach too many periods per week, the problem needs to be addressed, regardless of whether or not others in the education system perceive the teacher's workload is too high.

Teacher participation is what is needed in order for planners to understand teachers' perceptions of working conditions – a subtle yet significant linchpin for teacher motivation and quality. This is where CA offers many interesting possibilities. Thus, I shall now discuss CA's application as a 'framework for action' to ameliorate teacher working conditions on a more holistic level.

Selecting valued capabilities of teachers

The Capability Approach (CA) was deliberately left underspecified because Sen believes that it is the role of those being affected by capability expansion to in fact have the freedom and agency to select the capabilities that are worth expanding (Sen 1999; Robeyns 2005b). Sen has not held a view towards capability selection within schools, however, there are certain theoretical processes put forth in the literature that can be applied. As well, we can look towards research that has

Teacher capability in Tanzanian primary schools 143

attempted capability generation in education (cf. Unterhalter 2003b and Walker 2006) in order to apply their methods to the specific scenario of improving the well-being of teachers.

As mentioned previously, Sen does not endorse any specific 'list' of capabilities needed for agency or well-being (as he believes these are contextual and should be determined by people themselves). However, Sen has alluded to the necessity of *basic capabilities*, which allow people the opportunity to do things that are necessary for survival. The relevance of basic capabilities is 'not so much in ranking living standards, but in deciding on a cut-off point for the purpose of assessing poverty and deprivation' (Sen 1987: 109). Some examples of basic capabilities are to be nourished, to have shelter, and to be in good health. In regards to teacher well-being, the notion of basic capabilities could potentially be scaled along the same dimensions. We would evaluate teachers' *unfreedoms* and if there were no facilities for clean water, sanitation or nourishment (or rather, appropriate lunch breaks for nourishment), action would need to be taken to expand those basic survival capabilities. Such conditions obviously do not contribute to teacher well-being on very basic levels, so it can be argued that a set of basic capabilities is necessary.

Determining a list of basic capabilities is fairly straightforward, however as soon as we move beyond these examples, the task of selecting capabilities that are less central to survival (and are tied to the type of life that teachers value) is much more complex. Moreover, once selection has been made, prioritising or weighting these capabilities depends on another set of value judgements by its constituents.

Sen is adamant towards a democratic and public process of selecting and weighting capabilities, however does not go into detail about the methodology behind it. Fortunately, much theorising regarding such a process has ensued. Robeyns (2005b: 204) posits that CA 'needs to be supplemented with methodological tools that would enable us to correct for biases in the selection of functionings that result from the social positioning of the researchers'. Thus she has put forth several criteria for selecting capabilities that mitigate bias, which may stem from a researcher's values, views or personal constructions of well-being. These include:

1 explicit formulation of a list that can be discussed and defended;
2 justification and scrutiny of the method that has been used to generate the list;
3 differentiation of 'ideal' versus 'pragmatic' capabilities; and
4 capabilities that cover *all* relevant dimensions that are not reducible to each other (Robeyns 2005b: 205–206).

I shall now discuss two authors who have acknowledged this methodology for generating lists of capabilities, particularly in the realm of education.

Examples of educational capability selection

Although those being affected by capability expansion should have the agency to select capabilities themselves, it would be of due diligence to create a provisional

144   S. Tao

list of capabilities in order to be cognisant of areas that may come up. Thus, I will look at examples of educational capability generation in the literature, in order to guide preliminary lists that may be used for teachers. Unterhalter (2003b) provides an interesting example of educational capability formation through a method of cross-referencing aspects of education with the evaluative aspects of capabilities. This created a starting point for identifying relevant conditions needed to secure certain functionings within the realm of female adult education.

Unterhalter posits that many evaluations of gender equality in education look at very narrow indicators of well-being achievement (such as test results). However, by using CA, we instead examine 'how conditions in education relate to wider social processes and the issue of the exercise of agency' (Unterhalter 2003b: 7). Thus, the conditions necessary for well-being and agency form the beginning of a capability list that can be later discussed and debated by relevant participants.

Walker's (2006) work did in fact include discussion with relevant participants in an effort to determine a list of gender equitable capabilities for South African secondary schools. The discussions began with a set of preliminary capabilities that were attached to agency, choice, and constitutive of South African educational policy. She then used interviews to ground her list in context and help extrapolate further capabilities. Her final step involved discussing the list with other academics by using a publication as a forum for debate. Examples of the selected capabilities include autonomy, knowledge, social relations, respect and recognition, aspiration, voice, bodily integrity and emotional integrity (Walker 2006).

These two lists were formed specifically to create social justice criteria for gender equity in adult literacy classes and South African secondary schools. Although they are directed towards students, many of the valued capabilities can prove helpful as a starting point for interventions for teachers.

Selecting capabilities for teachers

As discussed above, it is not uncommon for teachers to be vilified for their behaviour in schools. However, expanding teacher capabilities not only mitigates some of the conversion factors that are the root of such behaviour, but also promotes conditions needed for behaviour change and reform. Let us look to Unterhalter's (2003b) matrix to generate a starting point for teacher capability expansion. The difference here is that agency and well-being for teachers should not only be predicated on capabilities that are expanded within schools, but also within the teaching profession itself.

Through this exercise we can see that many teacher capabilities are broad in nature yet encompass many of the conversion factors discussed in above. We can see that expanding certain teacher capabilities would have a knock-on effect towards expanding student capabilities (such as being able to concentrate in class without hunger or tiredness would certainly benefit the teaching process). However, some capabilities could also conflict with those of students. For example, 'being able to manage a classroom' to some teachers may mean using corporal punishment as a management tool, which would obviously violate a student's

Teacher capability in Tanzanian primary schools 145

Table 9.4 Capabilities related to teacher development

Aspects of capabilities	*Aspects of teacher development*
Well-being achievement	Acquiring employment as a teacher with consistent job security (this would promote consistent income, a sense of belonging and respect)
Well-being freedom	The conditions needed to keep and enjoy the job: 1. Basic survival capabilities (such as clean water, sanitation and shelter) 2. Emotional/mental well-being: to not be in fear of violence, discrimination, or harassment from the head teacher or other teachers 3. Bodily integrity: being able to concentrate in class and not be hungry, tired or ill 4. Being able to manage a class (not to feel overwhelmed or overworked) 5. Being able to feel respect and recognition (self-confidence and self-esteem) 6. Being able to enjoy social networks and feel a sense of belonging 7. Being able to teach in a well-managed school with sufficient resources (time for class, salaries paid on time, materials and building) 8. Being able to access in-service training to upgrade qualifications (without gender bias, or extra cost to one's self) 9. Being adequately remunerated (in order to live comfortably and not need secondary income)
Agency achievement	Exercising individual agency within the school and being able to live the type of life they value (choosing to teach at the school of their choice, choosing the profession, and contributing to school decisions)
Agency freedom	The conditions needed to exercise agency in the school: 1. Being able to have a voice and participate in decision-making with confidence 2. The freedom to act without repercussion or shame 3. The ability to aspire and strive to do well (to be encouraged and expected) 4. Being able to feel respect and recognition (self-confidence and self-esteem)

Framework: Unterhalter (2003b).

capability for bodily integrity. Thus, discussion, interpretation and scrutiny of these capabilities amongst teachers is necessary. Another concern I have with this list is that some capabilities suffer from the assumption that the presence of certain conditions (such as in-service training and sufficient resources) are enough alone to ensure improved teaching. This, of course, is not true. The nature of the in-service training and conversion factors that affect the use of resources need to be addressed. That is why more discussion with participants is paramount in order to qualify some of these capabilities with specifics. For example, 'being able to feel respect and recognition' could mean 'being able to use textbooks not assigned on the syllabus' in more specific terms. Thus, proper grounding of this list needs to be done amongst the teachers and head teacher within an individual school. The importance of participatory measures will also highlight the different

146 *S. Tao*

capability deprivations between rural and urban schools, and male and female participants.

Once valued capabilities are identified, policy measures can be designed for their expansion. Addressing all the capabilities in one comprehensive reform would be ideal, as teacher well-being would thus be improved on a holistic level. However, such a reform would be extremely broad, costly and thus problematic. One solution would be to have teachers prioritise 'ideal' and 'pragmatic' capabilities, and work with government planners to determine which improvements are possible. This exercise may not expand all capabilities at once, but it would demonstrate levels of respect, acknowledgement and consultation that have been absent until now. This type of reform is also clearly situated around teachers, which may be cause for concern, as many would argue that student learning should be the 'ends' of any teacher quality intervention. What needs to be understood here is that improvements to teacher well-being bring changes in internal states, such as morale, motivation, efficacy, professionalism and an openness to change (Leithwood 2007). This in turn mitigates many of the conversion factors and choices that impede the teaching and learning process, as well as initiatives to improve student learning outcomes.

Monitoring teacher development

Thus far, I have attempted to generate a provisional list of capabilities for teachers situated around their well-being and agency at the classroom and school level. As discussed in Robeyns' criteria for selecting capabilities, the explicit formulation of these lists, along with the justification and scrutiny of my methods (which this chapter reflects), are just the first two steps in operationalising CA. What is still needed is delineation of 'ideal' versus 'pragmatic' capabilities (as mentioned above), and rigorous coverage of *all* relevant dimensions. I believe these last two steps should be grounded by the actual conditions, contexts and people in which the interventions will be applied. Thus, these steps will be omitted here, as their outcomes will be determined in context. However, this does not preclude a discussion of a final application of CA that is central to any educational planning process: monitoring and evaluation.

As discussed previously, one of CA's applications is quantifying evaluations of well-being (Robeyns 2005a). An example of this is the Human Development Index (HDI) and the many subsequent indices that have been created in its wake (most notably the Gender Development Index, the Gender Empowerment Measure and the Human Poverty Index). The annual publication of these indices is widely publicised, which encourages countries to be cognisant of and improve their ranking (Unterhalter and Walker 2007).

Initial critiques of the HDI as a measurement tool pointed to the difficulties of capturing the complexity of human development in a single index; but even with its simplifications, the HDI has had the intended effect of focusing policy makers' attention to basic human capabilities rather than GDP (Fukuda-Parr 2003). Also,

The ranking of countries has provoked policy-makers to examine how each country fared and to ask why some countries managed to achieve much higher levels of 'human development' in comparison to countries with similar income levels.

(Fukuda-Parr 2003: 305)

This comparison has been criticised for breeding a competitive culture that impedes mutual support and contribution (Unterhalter *et al.* 2005). There have also been general criticisms of indices in that they are based on poor quality data, inappropriate levels of aggregation and crude instruments (Unterhalter and Brighouse 2007). However, such problems should not preclude attempts to improve indicators, especially if the net result is a refocusing on human well-being and an increased awareness of topics that have not otherwise been addressed. Robeyns (2003a: 27) adds:

> Although using just a few functionings and perhaps in a somewhat crude way, [the HDI] is probably the application which has had the largest impact on policy making. Perhaps this is one of the best illustrations of the usefulness of the Capability Approach.

That said, I cannot help but extrapolate towards a Teacher Development Index (TDI), which could bring issues of teacher development to the fore in an attempt to improve the living and working lives of teachers. Some preliminary thoughts are that it should not exist as a gender-blind index. Research suggests that women teachers experience not only the constraints that all teachers face, but also gendered constraints that result from social structures (such as discrimination, harassment and child care responsibilities) (Komunte 1996). However, distilling such complexities into a single index would prove difficult, as would trying to render qualitative capabilities (such as self-esteem, the ability to have a voice, and being free from fear) into quantitative measures. Alkire (2002) attempted methods of quantifying qualitative capabilities in relation to three different Oxfam projects in Pakistan. This entailed focus groups in which women discussed the intangible effects stemming from their income-generating projects, such as learning that they could make their own decisions, that they were able to discuss their problems with others, and that they could save money and time. During these discussions, focus group facilitators had the responsibility of ranking these qualitative impacts on the women's lives (5 = intense impact and 0 = no impact); and these rankings were later used to indicate the most significant effects of the project as identified by participants. One could challenge such a methodology by arguing that the evaluators' taxonomy of valued capabilities was subjective and was in essence 'imposed' on the participants. Alkire (2002: 292) acknowledges this problem, yet also counters by stating that, 'the case studies began by asking open-ended questions, and only introduced the strategic questions about unmentioned dimensions of impact if the respondents had systematically excluded them'. Nevertheless, it was concluded that further research was necessary in order to determine how to minimise ranking bias.

148   S. Tao

How does this bode for evaluating the capability expansion of teachers? In looking at the provisional list of capabilities generated in Table 9.4, here are some preliminary suggestions for creating quantifiable indicators that can be later aggregated into an index (see Table 9.5).

These are very preliminary suggestions for indicators and much work has yet to be done in finalising an overarching list of indicators, creating data collection methods that are reliable and cost-effective, and applying appropriate statistical and aggregation methodologies. These tasks are beyond the scope of this chapter, however, the overall goal of creating a TDI is clear: to recognise and reconcile constraints on teacher capabilities. The achieved functionings of such actions would not only lead to the improved well-being and morale of teachers, but as argued thus far, would also lead to improvements in overall teacher quality via its positive reactions. Moreover, a TDI could serve as a much-needed advocacy tool for teacher's unions, as well as a standardised measure for the monitoring and evaluation of teacher development within districts and regions (as opposed to methods used by the Inspectorate). On a larger scale, it could also indicate how different countries fare in their treatment and development of their teaching force.

Conclusion

This chapter has been an exploration of the Capability Approach and how it can be used to approach teacher quality in government primary schools. My interest in pursuing a new framework was born from experiences whilst teaching in Tanzania, and from my hypotheses that solutions firmly entrenched in context, teacher empathy and participatory measures would ameliorate teacher quality

Table 9.5 Preliminary indicators for a TDI

Capabilities	Suggestions for creating a quantifiable indicator
1) Basic survival capabilities	Water, sanitation and shelter can be observed and ranked on a normative scale
2) Mental well-being, bodily integrity, social networks, respect and recognition, voice, freedom to act and freedom to aspire	These capabilities can be gauged using Alkire's (2002) focus group methodology to rank impactful qualitative functionings
3) Having a well-managed school with adequate resources	Resource availability can be observed and ranked on a normative scale, or reflected in spending per pupil
4) Teacher capability to manage a class	Teacher workload can be extrapolated from pupil/teacher ratios and number of classes per day
5) Teacher capability of accessing in-service training	Enrolment ratios of teachers for in-service training sessions
6) Teacher capability of being adequately remunerated	Teacher salary relative to cost of living

reforms. These tenets were closely linked to those of CA, so it seemed appropriate to utilise retrospective data in order to demonstrate the many ways in which CA can be used to improve teacher quality.

Overall, this study has used the theoretical framework developed by Sen as a basis for shifting the teacher quality discourse, and has demonstrated how it can be used to improve quality in the following manner:

- By using CA as tool for descriptive analysis of teacher behaviour to fully understand reasons (or conversion factors and choices) that lead to low levels of quality.
- By operationalising CA as a framework to identify and expand capabilities that reconcile conversion factors and thus improve teacher well-being.
- By using CA as a measurement device to later monitor policy and practice aimed at expanding teacher capabilities.

It should be noted that two caveats have been cited in regards to the scope of this study:

1 final capability lists must be relevant to context and thus grounded in discussions with teachers themselves; and
2 further research is needed to establish and test a Teacher Development Index that would function on a larger scale.

I believe this framework for improving teacher quality is ambitious and will prove problematic when governments are faced with executing policies needed to expand teacher capabilities. I am not naïve to the financial and capacity constraints that many governments face. However, my hope is that this study has created a new nexus – one that rethinks the determinants of teacher quality and challenges top-down views of development in education. In sum:

> Academic and policy debates focus on teachers' deficiencies, and seldom take into account the difficulties under which they live and work. The fundamental importance of the teachers' role in ensuring effectiveness of education must be recognised, understood, and taken into account if these international efforts to achieve development targets in education are to be successful. Further, the rights of teachers must be realised in order to secure and strengthen their own commitment to achieving quality education for all.
>
> (Fry 2002: 1)

My hope is that utilising the Capability Approach will contribute to, and further, these important efforts.

10 The lived experiences of women teachers in Karachi[1]

Jackie Kirk

Teachers are recognised as key actors in processes of educational development and quality improvement, and teacher education has been made a priority by many different governments and agencies. However, teachers are rarely consulted on issues of policy and education reform (Villegas Reimers and Reimers, 1996). A recent study by Education International highlights the lack of teacher involvement in the assessment of Education for All (EFA) and national strategy development. In particular, teacher unions have been excluded from policy consultations and negotiations (Education International, 2003). According to a Voluntary Services Overseas study, this failure to involve teachers and the apparent lack of interest in teachers' opinions are major factors in the 'fragile' and 'wavering' levels of teacher morale and motivation in development contexts (VSO, 2002). Few ministries of education and large development agencies have systemic ways for senior policy makers to learn about what is happening at the school level or for classroom teachers, many of whom are women, to inform these policy makers about their experiences. Although not specifically documented, it seems likely that in many contexts women teachers participate even less than men teachers in policy dialogues and consultations. Women are often underrepresented at all levels of educational decision making, and, although women do much of the teaching, 'most theorizing about schools and classrooms and teaching and learning has been done by men' (Miller, 1995).

In the language of programme reports, agency policies and research studies, teachers are often narrowly defined in terms of their pedagogical roles, with little attention to other dimensions of their lives. As Ibrahim Makkawi writes, 'When social scientists discuss the concept of teachers' role they often limit their scope of analysis to the roles performed by teachers in the classroom or within the school as an organization' (Makkawi, 2002). Research tends to focus more on the material conditions of teaching, teacher education, and specific interventions, practices and programmes. Furthermore, the gender neutrality of such literature can conceal the particular experiences that women have of the profession.

In this chapter, I discuss data from a study of women teachers in Karachi, Pakistan, that present their alternative perspectives so as to inform educational policy development and to develop more explicitly gendered theories of teaching. I begin with a brief introduction to the positioning of women teachers within the

The experiences of women teachers in Karachi 151

international context of gender, education and development. I then introduce the study from which I present data and the organising concept of *impossible fictions*. Using the words of women teachers, I discuss experiences of becoming and being a woman teacher, as well as women's experiences and perspectives on teaching girls and boys. I end with a brief discussion of the implications for policy and programming, especially for teacher education.

Gender, education and development

In the policy and programming literature, gender issues for teachers are given some attention but primarily in relationship to women's access to teacher education programmes or teacher training and sensitisation to girls' education. Both of these are seen as effective means to encourage girls to attend school and to ensure more appropriate, quality learning experiences for them. Gender equality in education has become an international priority issue, one that is inscribed within the EFA targets and the United Nations' Millennium Development Goals. One of the EFA targets articulates the need to close the gender gap in education and, more specifically, to achieve gender parity in education by 2005 and gender equality by 2015. Similar aims are also articulated in the Millennium Development Goals; the third of the six goals deals with gender equality and the empowerment of women, expressing the need to eliminate gender disparity in primary and secondary education, preferably by 2005, and in all levels of education no later than 2015. International commitment to these interrelated development goals is having a considerable impact on policy development in education and shaping the priorities for national governments and international and local agencies.

With regard to achieving gender equality in and through education, attention is particularly focused on the number of girls enrolled in school and completing their studies. Recruiting and retaining women teachers have become priority strategies for improving girls' education for a number of reasons. Especially in rural and more conservative areas, parents are usually more likely to allow their daughters to go to school if female teachers are present. Women teachers are also thought to be more supportive of girls' academic and personal development and are often considered important role models for girls in school. A study in Nepal indicates that mothers feel more comfortable talking about their children with a woman teacher, and in India women teachers are considered 'more sincere' as they are less likely to be involved in local politics (UNESCO, 2000). Such studies confirm anecdotal evidence of the appeal of women teachers and the positive impact of their presence in schools. Particularly in Africa and South Asia, there is a significant amount of attention paid to finding solutions to the constraints women may face in accessing training and upgrading opportunities in order to ensure there are more women teachers in schools to attract and support girls.

Despite the importance of women teachers to educational policy, there is only a limited literature on the experiences of women teaching in development contexts. Sandra Stacki has investigated issues of female teacher empowerment within a programme for women teachers in India (Stacki, 2002), and Linda Schultz has

152   J. Kirk

looked at the gender experiences of Nepalese women entering teaching (Schultz, 1998). Gloria Bonder and Cecilia M.B. Sardenberg discuss innovative forms of professional development for women teachers that involve reflection on their personal and professional experiences as teachers but also as women, wives, mothers, daughters (Bonder and Sardenberg, 2000). Such studies highlight how gender affects teacher experience, and how different male and female perspectives and priorities on teaching may be. Although such scholarship implies that gender should be an explicit issue to be addressed in teacher education content and process, in general there is little explicit attention to issues of gender as lived and perceived by teachers in development contexts.

The study

My study interweaved feminist theory and methodology with theories, policies and practices of gender and development around a central focus on women teachers' lives in Karachi, Pakistan. The data came from a combination of individual interviews, group discussions and written questionnaires from women teachers working in predominantly nongovernment schools (private, church or Aga Khan network affiliated). During fieldwork in Karachi in September 2001, I conducted in-depth interviews with four women teachers and held informal discussions with three groups of between five and ten women teachers. Two of these discussion sessions were held in the schools and the third at the hostel where the women were staying during their professional development programme. After a forced departure from the field after September 11, 2001, I was able to develop a written questionnaire that was distributed through two teacher development programmes and subsequently completed by a further 19 women teachers. No attempt was made to create a representational sample of women teachers; rather, the emphasis was on seeking out participants for whom the subject of the study was of interest and who were keen to discuss their experiences of gender and teaching. The findings of the study cannot be generalised to the general population of women teachers, but they do provide some insights into issues that have not been addressed before in the context of gender equality and education.

Girls' education is a particularly important issue in Pakistan, and closing the gender gap in enrolment (currently 24 percent) has become a national and international priority. Different international donors and financial institutions support gender and education programmes, including teacher education for women. Most recently, Pakistan has been included in the United Nations Children's Fund's (UNICEF) 25 by 2005 initiative, which targets countries with particularly large gender gaps for accelerated action. There are particular measures in place to recruit new women teachers, especially in the remote, rural areas of North West Frontier Province and Balochistan, where the low number of female teachers has been a significant barrier to girls' educational access. Incentives offered have included a relaxation of the academic requirements and widening of the age range for entry into teacher education.

Impossible fictions: an organising concept

Notions of impossibility, tension and contradiction in the experiences of women teachers are richly documented in literature from North America and Europe. Valerie Walkerdine refers to the 'impossible fiction' of being a woman teacher in today's society, to the tensions and contradictions that are inherent in an identity that asserts power and status and commands respect (teacher) at the same time that it speaks of subordination, marginalisation and repression (woman) (Walkerdine, 1990).

As a conceptual organiser for this study, *impossible fiction* has several interconnected layers. It is important to recognise that *impossible fiction* articulates not a straightforward impossibility but a constant tension between possibility and impossibility. It also articulates the dialectical relationship between fact and fiction that characterises women's experience of teaching in relation to policy aims and objectives. Clearly, it is quite possible to be a women teacher in Pakistan, and there is much fact relating to that experience to be explored. The data presented are testimony to the very real possibilities of being and doing everything the term 'woman teacher' might imply. However, they also reflect the complexity of the social worlds in which the women teacher participants live and in which the position of a woman teacher is a particularly tricky one. The concept of impossible fiction focuses attention on the tensions and contradictions created through women's multiple positions in families, communities, classrooms and schools. It also highlights the ways in which women reconcile these different positions. The women teachers' narratives presented are certainly shaped by sometimes quite contradictory expectations and limitations, and the dissonance between what they might want to do and what is feasible for them to do can be quite tangible. However, within the concept of impossible fiction, resistance to these limitations and to other people's expectations is also very possible.

To analyse data of different forms I use a combination of both close reading and a more holistic, impressionistic technique in which the narrative as a whole is considered for its thematic elements. I problematise the stories told to me of becoming and being a women teacher through the lens of impossible fiction, using an analytical approach that probes disjuncture and highlights dissonance. Doing so allows me to draw attention to the ways in which powerful societal and individual narratives work to produce certain perceptions and narratives.

Although the participants in this study speak Urdu as their mother tongue, all but one of the interviews and all discussions and questionnaires were conducted in English. This was considered to be quite appropriate as all the women concerned are teaching in English medium schools, taking professional development courses and activities in English, and are quite used to reading, writing and talking about educational issues in English. Furthermore, interviewing and working in English facilitated a direct communication between researcher and participants that was more comfortable than working through an interpreter. As far as possible I quote the exact words spoken or written by the participants in the study, but in some instances I have made the meaning clearer for the reader with slight edits; additions are indicated by brackets and omissions by ellipses. Listening closely

154   *J. Kirk*

to the women participants, presenting direct quotations, and reflecting on the meaning of these words in the context in which they are situated is a method I use for 'making problematic' the everyday worlds of women teachers. In the following sections I consider women's experiences of becoming a teacher, being a woman teacher, and teaching girls or boys.

Becoming a woman teacher

'Even we are common with God – in the past – and nowadays . . . I have heard it from lots of people, that people go into teaching that, you know, can't do anything else.' This is how, in an interview context, one of the participants described the general position of teachers in Pakistani society. As in other countries, teaching is a profession that can command some respect and elevate the teacher to a position of some status within a community. In the past it may have been particularly important and had certain resources attached to it. Yet today, where state resources for education are limited, working conditions are generally poor and classrooms underresourced, someone who works in the sector may not be viewed particularly positively. Especially in the cities of Pakistan, where apparently more glamorous, better respected, and better remunerated career opportunities may exist, this woman indicates how teaching is now often seen as a profession for those who have no other options.

The reality for many women is that there is little else they can do. In many families, teaching is still considered a worthy profession, one that is acceptable for women, and one in which the working environment is relatively safe for them. Tasneem, another teacher participant in the study, explained to me in an interview how she fell into teaching, 'by default really'. Her story of becoming and being a woman teacher is one with multiple layers. Teaching was not a profession she explicitly chose, and yet it is one in which she feels she can develop her own maternal understandings of child development. She can also use her creative talents and interests to the fullest. Although she had done some teaching before her children were born, it was her involvement in her children's school that drew her back into the profession when they were old enough for her to return to work. Her husband insisted that she stay home when they were young and, although she questions this now, at the time she accepted his decision. Tasneem described with enthusiasm the projects, activities, and professional development programmes she is involved with now, but her tone remained wistful as she reflected back on the choices that she had to make or that were made for her.

In face-to-face interviews and the written questionnaire I asked participants how and why they became teachers. I was interested to know more about the reasons women would give for their entry into the profession and about the extent to which these reflected personal aspirations and/or family or societal expectations of appropriate careers for educated women. One woman replied, 'I chose teaching because it is a noble profession and I thought that I would be able to teach easily to the younger group of children. Yes, there are lots of teachers in my family. Yes, my family wanted me to become a teacher'.

The experiences of women teachers in Karachi   155

Within this short text three distinct reasons for becoming a teacher coexist. First, the notion of teaching as a noble profession is articulated, a notion that, according to the earlier quotation, may no longer be quite as true as in the past. Nonetheless, the notion clearly retains some value and may be an account into which women invest and gain an important sense of the significance of their work. At the same time, also articulated is the belief that this woman will be able to teach younger children, reflecting a common perception that women are predisposed to working with young children and therefore particularly suited to primary school teaching. Any 'comparative advantage' that women may have in caring for young children is a somewhat problematic, essentialising discourse that can become a means of limiting the range of professional opportunities open to women. Taking up and enacting such a discourse may represent an act of agency for individual women, inserting themselves into a professional domain that does command some respect and status. Yet it remains an agency that is circumscribed by traditional gender roles. A third reason for becoming a teacher expressed in this short text is one of family expectations and perhaps limitations; teaching is clearly an acceptable profession and one into which this woman is encouraged. These three ideas are potentially contradictory and may be understood as a reflection of the tensions between quite different perceptions of women teachers in the Pakistani context. Yet they coexist within a very brief extract of text, and they are all quite valid. For the woman teacher they are all three very viable discursive resources from which she can construct her story of becoming a woman teacher.

In other responses, teaching was also described as a career that can be compatible with the heavy family and household commitments that most women deal with every day. Women teachers are able to work a morning at school and then return relatively early to prepare the food and the home for the evening. Alternatively, they may first complete chores at home before coming to school for an afternoon shift. Although one woman in particular asserted the active choice she made to become a teacher, and another even defied her family's opinion, most narratives reflected family approval if not encouragement. Rather than a specific vocation to be a teacher, it may be the realities of family expectations and household commitments that channel a woman into the profession.

> I thought about other careers as well and worked as an accountant for two months in an office. But being the eldest of three sisters and having no mother, I have many responsibilities at home to fulfill so it was not possible for me to work for 12 or 13 hours in an office and my father also objected to it, so I chose teaching where I have to spend seven to eight hours in school and sometimes 11 to 12, when I go for workshops, but I can easily come home and complete my assignments at home, which was not possible while working in an office.

Another woman wrote, 'I had to choose this job as I was in financial crisis. I thought of other jobs such as office but the timing did not suit me'. And indicating the way in which teaching may be more of an accommodation than a vocation, one woman wrote, 'This profession suits me, because in Pakistan whole responsibility of house and children is mostly of women, due to short working duration it suits me, I can easily balance my both duties'. These extracts attest to the situation of many urban Pakistani women. They may need and want to contribute to the family income and yet, as women, be able to do so only in a certain number of acceptable ways. Teaching may be considered a suitable profession, one that can be combined with other responsibilities. As I discuss later, however, this apparent ease with which women teachers can combine their professional and household duties is not that simple, either. I learned how much time and energy have to be invested by teachers in order for them to make the most of their career. In interviews and group discussions I heard about the long hours and, especially in the nongovernment schools, of the multiple professional development and school activities that take place after regular hours. A constant negotiation of a comfortable and feasible balance between home and school activities may be just one of the challenges that women teachers face in their daily lives.

Responses to this question about becoming a teacher are especially interesting in that they encapsulate the tension for the woman teacher. The teacher is expected to facilitate the individual, rational development of each child and yet has to do so within the confines of a classroom, in which her role is considered similar to that of a nurturing mother. The importance of education in building the future of Pakistan is articulated not only in the discourse that is present in the government's educational policies, but also in those of the country's major investors, such as the World Bank. The responsibility of women teachers to contribute to building a competitive society is, however, somewhat paradoxical, in that it seems to depend on the traditional roles (family and community building) that women have played. The students are projected as privileged subjects into a future society within which women teachers are not necessarily assured a more powerful position. Tensions inevitably exist. Is the achievement of a 'competitive society' actually at the heart of women teachers' aspirations for their work? Is it even possible for them to achieve it from positions defined by 'inborn characteristics' of women? Essentialist descriptions of women teachers, and any 'comparative advantage' they may have based on so-called natural abilities for child rearing, are, as mentioned above, quite problematic. Yet it has to be acknowledged that, in the context of Pakistan, this narrative is one that can position women into educational development and allow them to claim an important role within its processes. In this way, it represents a significant and very viable discursive resource for a woman teacher to draw on.

Being a woman teacher

Career satisfaction

Even when they entered the profession by chance or not exactly by choice, women teachers also indicated how their profession can be highly fulfilling. However, for this very reason teaching may make heavy demands on individuals. In the

The experiences of women teachers in Karachi   157

questionnaire I asked, 'Can you tell me what you enjoy most about teaching in your school and why?' Replies included, 'Teaching is a fun-loving profession but it requires full attention and full devotion. The future youth is dependent on you'. Another teacher wrote, 'Teaching is a respectable profession so I think it's enjoy[able] only when [you] are totally devoted to it'. Yet another wrote, 'Teaching depends upon the interest of the teachers. The more you are involved in it, the more [you]'ll find interest in it'.

It may seem that, like any other activity, the more one puts into teaching, the more one will get out of it. However, an analysis of the phrases in which women use words such as 'but', 'only' and 'depends' draws attention to the paradoxical situation in which they may be placed. Teaching can be a very stimulating and rewarding career for women, and it can gain one respect, yet the extent to which it can provide this sort of satisfaction depends on one's interest and commitment. The word 'devotion' is used, a word that implies heavy demands on the individual. It reflects not only the dominant narrative of women's natural love for their classrooms and their students discussed earlier but also a sense of self-effacement. As women devote themselves entirely to their teaching and to their students, and are perhaps expected to do so, we have to ask whether they as women and as teachers are not lost from view.

Equally problematic is that these women may want to invest more time and energy in their teaching but are unable to do so because of family and other commitments. As one participant in a workshop articulated, 'Well yes, I wanted to make a difference – and I am trying – even our students they are doing so many more activities and things than we were doing. But still, I have . . . boundaries. I can't do everything'.

Having to respect the boundaries and not being able to do everything may create a frustration and a tension and may in fact detract from the appeal of the teaching profession. Drawing on feminist critiques of education, I suggest that these women's comments speak to the social and political construction of a profession that relies heavily on women's devotion, energy and input while at the same time perpetuating the subordination of this female commitment, engagement and action within male-centred processes and systems. Traditionally, education depends on and further entrenches particular gender relations and expectations. Teaching is, in the words of many of the respondents, a profession that is primarily about caring and loving. Women may be expected to show devotion to their teaching, to work hard, and yet not to push the boundaries or rock the boat too hard.

Despite these issues and limitations, though, teaching does bring certain satisfactions. As one woman wrote:

> I enjoy the extra-curricular activities like class projects and dramas, etc., because through these activities the children are motivated to show their inner qualities, which in normal routine remain hidden. Although we have to work extra hard with the children . . . I feel proud of my students when they put up their work with great enthusiasm.

158   *J. Kirk*

Again, the enjoyment derived from teaching is tempered by the 'extra hard work' that is involved.

Although the responses tend to reflect a more selfless enjoyment derived from the students' achievements, one woman's response to the question about enjoyment of teaching clearly indicates the possibilities for teaching to create a space for women to be creative, experiment, take leadership, and feel they are making a difference: 'I enjoy the most when my students' response is [good] and they are anxious to know more about the subject. By this I am aware how successful I am.'

Teaching may also allow women to develop attitudes and skills that then affect their lives outside the classroom. Responses to my question, 'Please describe any changes teaching has made in your life', indicated some of the ways in which teaching, although not necessarily a preferred career choice, has contributed to personal development, fulfilment and some economic advancement:

> Teaching has made many good changes in my life . . . I am always aware of new educational systems taking place around me. It always helped me in my children's education, naturally money improves our social status.

> [Teaching] broadens the vision, build[s] confidence in women. Women also learn to deal with the opposite sex on equal levels . . . My social circle has enhanced, I've become more social. I have learned to handle difficult and tough situations. Time management has improved. I use my time in more productive ways as compared to the time period when I was a housewife.

Although such narratives may be very positive and inspirational, they remain somewhat problematic in that they are premised on a somewhat deficit model of the nonteacher woman. In the second narrative especially, the pre-teaching housewife appears as a socially inept individual who is unproductive with her time. From what I learned about the workload of Pakistani women within the home, it is hard to imagine how they might be considered unproductive, but this comment may reflect prevailing perceptions of housewives' lives. Notions of productivity and reproductivity are especially contradictory for the woman teacher, who, on entering the workforce, apparently becomes a productive member of society. At the same time, her productivity is premised upon her reproductivity (i.e. her innate talents as a woman for raising children). In any case, if a teacher's role in society is characterised as productive, it appears we arrive back at the problematic notions of women teachers' complicity in education to build a competitive society, discussed earlier. Alternatively, resistance to models of education as serving economic development ends appears to be evident in the emphasis placed by the respondents on, for example, 'the children's inner qualities' and on their 'anxiety to learn more about the subject'.

Women teachers, authority and participation

Data collected in this study indicate that authority is also a complex issue for women teaching in Pakistan. Participants in the study were quite candid in discussing the authority over them, especially in relation to needing the permission and approbation of their families (particularly their fathers and husbands) in order to take up a teaching career. In the questionnaire, I asked about the extent to which they were involved in educational decision making in order to gain insight into women's participation in educational issues beyond the classroom. I was interested to know if and how they were involved in curriculum development and selection, for example. However, I was aware that by posing the question I inevitably set up certain expectations and thereby, to some extent, framed the responses provided. Respondents described being the subjects of higher school authorities. They indicated the lack of teacher participation in decision making beyond the classroom but also their respect for the authority of the school administration; in most of the nongovernment schools, the head teachers are also women but the power of the governing board is predominantly in the hands of men. One woman wrote, 'We are only involved in school activities and school events only . . . I think teachers in Pakistan are not allowed to participate in any school decisions'. Another woman wrote, 'School policy and school rules are totally based on the administration. However, we can always give our suggestions about the curriculum and activities and events [that] take place in the school. I am not involved in any education decision-making. I only obey them'.

Although these responses may be somewhat disappointing, they have to be understood within a context where, as one woman states, it is believed teachers are not allowed to participate in school decisions. Another teacher wrote, 'Frankly I do not have any idea about our level of participation in educational decision-making because it has been only 5 years for me to be a teacher'. Such responses also have to be read in relation to responses to my probing of the level of satisfaction with the extent to which they are involved, such as: 'I think the current level of participation in educational decision-making is just right – neither is it too less nor is it over-burdening'. And, 'I am totally satisfied with [the] present situation'.

If a woman is already giving her 'full attention and full devotion' to classroom instruction and assuring the development of each individual for a role in competitive society, and if she has multiple domestic responsibilities to fulfil as well, is it at all feasible to imagine her having the time, energy or inclination to be involved in higher-level decision making? The answer is apparently yes. One woman was especially adamant about the inappropriateness of the school administration's approach: 'As such we are not at all involved in the school policy, curriculum, school rules or any events! We are just given the final outcome!! . . . I would like to be more involved because I am a part of this institution and I must be given some value! By taking my ideas and views for all this.'

And another woman wrote, 'We are involved in giving ideas only. The decision is made by the administration . . . I would like to be more involved in decision-making by giving more ideas and putting them into practices as well and not just working on what is assigned to me'.

Women teachers may feel frustrated about their lack of authority in the school and the authority that is exercised over them in the school context. However, as indicated earlier, it may at the same time be very possible for them to appreciate

160 J. Kirk

the authority they can and do command in their classrooms, families and communities. In the questionnaire, I explicitly asked if becoming a teacher had brought about any changes in these women's lives outside of the school. One woman wrote, 'A major change that teaching has made into my life is that I've started giving advice to everybody'.

Women teaching girls and boys

Programming strategies to recruit and deploy women teachers have proved to be an effective and very relevant response to expressed barriers to girls' education. Yet we know very little about the lived experiences of women teaching boys and girls. The teachers involved in this study were teaching either girls or boys, and they had attended all-girls schools themselves. I was therefore interested to find out more about this distinctly gendered experience of education. The data were then read 'within and against' the context of the development imperative to increase and improve girls' education.

Women teaching girls

Interviewing a woman named Hina, I became even more aware that the seemingly obvious connection between women teachers and girls' education may, in reality, be a more complex issue. A primary school head teacher who has raised a large family, is involved in community work, and has also entered local politics, Hina may be a powerful role model for younger girls and women. Yet when I asked her about her beliefs concerning education for girls, she concentrated on traditional, gender-stereotypical skills such as sewing and cooking, albeit insisting on the need for up-to-date, quality equipment.

In the questionnaire, another woman replied thus to the question about what she enjoys most about teaching in her school: 'I enjoy teaching girls and making friends with them. I love to share their experiences, joys, games, ideas, etc.' This is a response that suggests that she positively enjoys working with girls. She identifies closely with those she teaches, but her relationship with them, and the activities they engage in together, are very much constructed within the gender status quo. The 'making friends with girls' may be a way to develop a closer relationship with her students or an expression of her devotion to her profession, but when read in relation to educational policy documentation that positions girls' education as a strategy for gender equality, it becomes more problematic. Contained within this sort of relationship between woman teacher and girl student, the potential for transformation of patriarchal structures and processes and for the shifts in power relations required to bring about gender equality appears quite limited.

Women teaching boys

In an interview setting, Farida talked about her gender choice and the preferences of other staff in a school that is split between mornings for girls and afternoons for boys, with a different set of teachers and of administrative staff for each.

The experiences of women teachers in Karachi   161

FARIDA: Mostly the teachers choose girls.

INTERVIEWER: And why do they choose the girls?

FARIDA: [laughing] Because boys are more energetic – and because afternoon time is a tough time – for teaching. And girls are mostly shy and quiet and disciplined, and boys are slightly – like – so that is why peoples like coming on girls' shift.

INTERVIEWER: And when the teachers are talking together, and you're talking together, what emerges as the main challenges for teaching the girls? . . . And how does that compare with the challenges of teaching the boys?

FARIDA: In a girls' [section] – teachers are saying they are not participating very much – not group discussions, not in group work, so how can we improve this? And, in the boys' section, we are mostly working with discipline, for discipline.

INTERVIEWER: What made you decide to choose the boys?

FARIDA: [after thinking for a while] Because even I start in a boys' [school], and I [am] comfortable with boys. I think so. I like boys, boys are participating and they are communicating, and they want more, more, more – like enhancement . . . I think so, it's better than in a girls' school – girls like . . . in a one part they are, 'Stop, okay miss, it's enough'. Boys, – they is not, they want more, more, more.

INTERVIEWER: And . . . you find that more enjoyable as a teacher?

FARIDA: Yes.

What is interesting here is the reasoning Farida gives for why other women teachers may prefer to work with girls rather than boys. It is not necessarily a question of gender identification or of particular concern for the rights of girls to quality education. Nor is it a particular awareness of gender policy and the need to promote girls' participation in the education system. It is primarily the fact that the girls are easier to work with. Later in the interview she explains that teaching the girls' shift, which is the morning session, is more convenient for many women in that they can complete their household chores in the afternoon and prepare for the evening. Ironically, the gendered expectations of household responsibilities for the women teachers and the socialisation of girls to more passive and less demanding classroom behaviours converge in the school context in a way that appears to neither disrupt nor challenge the prevailing patterns of gender relations in society.

From talking with these women I also gained fleeting indications (rarely captured in interview or discussion transcripts) of a somewhat sexually charged classroom environment in which a woman is teaching boys. This is an element of the classroom experience, and of being a woman teacher, that is quite absent from any policy or programme description. I was fascinated when in one discussion Ghazala started to explain her early days as a teacher.

GHAZALA: I was only 17 or 18 [when I started teaching] and there were some of the boys who were maybe 14 or 13 and there was definitely a special twinkle

162   *J. Kirk*

in their eyes, and they would be working very hard at their religion [the subject she was teaching] – no other subjects, only religion was so important.
INTERVIEWER: And how did you feel about that?
GHAZALA: Well, I was scared – I was only new to teaching and I was a little bit scared, I didn't know how to handle these boys.
INTERVIEWER: But did you enjoy it at all too?
GHAZALA: Yes [smiling], I liked it.

The situation Ghazala describes resonates with Erica McWilliam's theorising of the 'corpor/reality' of the classroom, of the embodied and somewhat erotic nature of the teaching and learning process. Ghazala's candid description embodies both the power and the powerlessness of the novice woman teacher. She is quite aware of the hold she has over these somewhat flirtatious boys, who work harder for her classes than for those of any other teacher. And yet this power is tentative and somewhat problematic. She is scared, and she is aware that the expectation is that she will 'handle them'. Is an acknowledgment of one's sexuality, and of the sexually charged nature of the classroom, an acceptable means of 'handling' such students? Apparently not, as Ghazala needs to find alternatives. However, traditional and acceptable modes of discipline may jeopardise the positive relationships she has with the boys and may also mean a regulation of her own pedagogical pleasure.

The satisfaction women may gain from teaching appears, ironically, to be dependent on the ways in which the boys they teach are socialised into more outgoing, active, and perhaps somewhat flirtatious behaviours in the classroom. As Farida commented, it is the passiveness of girls, the ease of classroom management with girls, and the less demanding and less challenging behaviours of girls that appeal to many girls' school teachers. The data presented reflect theoretical tensions in development planning and programming between the practical and the strategic gender interests of women and girls. They signify a more complicated relationship between girls and women teachers in schools than might be assumed, suggesting the need for a more critical gendered analysis of women's and girls' multiple positionings inside and outside the classroom. Also significant in discussion of gender issues in education is the relationship between women teachers and boys, a subject that has so far received very little attention in development contexts.

Discussion

Taken literally, being a Pakistani woman teacher is clearly very possible, and there are thousands of women who embody that description every day. However, the data suggest that taking up and acting out a narrative as a woman teacher in Pakistan may nonetheless be an inherently contradictory experience. It is an experience that is characterised by a dialectic of agency and submission – power and powerlessness – and by a delicate balancing of what is doable within quite rigid boundaries, the possible with the impossible. The concept of *impossible fiction*,

The experiences of women teachers in Karachi   163

originally used to describe the complex experience of being a woman teacher in Western contexts, is powerfully resonant in this Pakistani context, too. It highlights the dissonances between official truths and individual women's realities. We have to think about multiple identities and subjectivities, shifting positions, and ever changing power dynamics within complex discursive fields, and we must acknowledge and work with the complex experiences women may have of becoming and being teachers in Pakistan.

To develop 'gender-redistributive' education policy (policy that is intended to transform existing divisions and distributions to create more balanced relationships between men and women), in-depth understandings are required of the multiple ways in which women teachers experience and interpret their work. We need to know more about the choices women can and do make to become teachers, about how they perceive their relationships to boys and girls. We need to know more about personal and professional relationships of women teachers with each other, men, girls and boys. We also need to be able to theorise the connections and disconnections between women's positions in the classroom and their positions in their own families and communities. This study is significant in that it looks in detail at women teachers' lived experiences of gender *and* the roles they play in the formation of the gendered identities of boys and girls. In a context where much attention has been focused on gender disparities in rural areas, it highlights the importance of studying urban women who are teaching more privileged children in nongovernmental schools.

Working with either boys or girls, and occasionally with both, women teachers in Pakistan clearly have very significant roles to play in achieving gender equality in education. The Education for All imperative to address gender gaps in enrolment, achievement, and outcomes in education has to be taken seriously in Pakistan and the roles of women teachers in achieving the targets carefully considered. This study indicates that there are complex gender dynamics in operation in classrooms and that possibilities exist for women teachers to reproduce traditional patterns of gender socialisation for boys and girls *and* to be agents of change. Teacher training should not sidestep these issues and should make explicit linkages between improving girls' education and the actions and implications of women teachers' activities in the classroom and beyond. Alternative approaches need to be developed that connect with women teachers' own gender perspectives, concerns, experiences, and challenges. The influence of women teaching boys should also not be forgotten. Linkages have to be made between the personal and the professional, the public and the private, with a recognition of the fact that women's participation in the public realm of education does not necessitate a denial of their own experiences within the private sphere.

Note

1 This chapter is an edited version of an article that first appeared in *The Comparative Education Review* 48 (November 2004).

11 How teachers' pedagogic practice influences learner achievements

A study from the Punjab, Pakistan[1]

Monazza Aslam and Geeta Kingdon

Identification of the characteristics and practices of teachers that contribute most towards improving pupil achievement has often eluded researchers even though the most effective means of improving school quality may be through addressing weak teaching (Glewwe and Kremer, 2006, p. 995). The objective of this chapter is to delve into the black-box representing 'teaching' to uncover the teacher characteristics and teaching practices that matter most to pupil achievement.

Past literature probing teacher quality has adopted one of two approaches. In the first, an educational production function links measurable teacher characteristics to pupil achievement, controlling for student characteristics. The methodologies adopted in this approach vary, from Instrumental Variable (IV) approaches (Hoxby, 1996; Kingdon and Teal, 2007; Sprietsma and Waltenberg, 2005) to panel data studies (Clotfelter *et al.*, 2006), to randomised experiment studies (Glewwe and Kremer, 2006). The consensus from this wide array of studies is that many of the standard teacher characteristics such as certification, training and experience do not matter to pupil achievement (Hanushek and Rivkin, 2006). As these résumé characteristics often underpin teacher compensation policies, these findings are controversial and widely debated.

A second approach calculates 'teacher quality' as a teacher fixed-effect in an equation of student achievement gain where different groups of students (in a given year or over time) are taught by the same teacher. The resulting 'total teacher effect' enables the researcher to define a good teacher as one who consistently produces high achievement growth for pupils. This approach, in estimating total teacher effects, does not require identification of specific teacher characteristics that generate student learning. A number of studies have used this approach (Aaronson *et al.*, 2003; Hanushek *et al.*, 2005; Rivkin *et al.*, 2005; Rockoff, 2004) and they conclude that teacher quality matters substantially to pupil achievement. However, when they regress this teacher fixed-effect on teachers' observed characteristics, their findings are consistent with those from the more direct achievement production function approach: observable characteristics such as certification and training explain little of the variation in teacher quality.

This study takes the direct approach linking teacher characteristics to student outcomes in an achievement production function, but with two innovations. First, we use a methodology that overcomes the biases associated with the

How pedagogic practice influences achievement   165

non-random matching of students to schools and, within schools, to teachers. Second, we also test the importance of classroom practices and teaching techniques rather than confining attention only to teachers' résumé characteristics, i.e. qualifications, experience and training.

The key empirical challenge in identifying teacher effects arises due to the potential non-random matching of students to schools and, within schools, to particular teachers. For instance, if higher-ability students sort into classes with better qualified/trained/experienced teachers within their grade or if teachers possessing these characteristics are systematically assigned to teach the classes with higher performing pupils, a positive coefficient on a given teacher characteristic could not be interpreted as causal. Our approach to address such endogeneity is to estimate a pupil fixed-effects equation of achievement using cross-section data. Across subject rather than across time differencing is used. The idea is exactly the same as in panel data estimates of the achievement production function but we will show below that our approach is superior to the panel data approach both methodologically and in terms of cost-effectiveness. Apart from Kingdon (2006) and Kingdon and Teal (2010), the studies adopting this technique use data from the United States or Europe and look exclusively at teacher gender effects on pupil achievement (Ammerm ller and Dolton, 2007; Dee, 2007; Holmlund and Sund, 2005). Kingdon (1996) for India is the only study to our knowledge that applies this empirical methodology to study the effect of wider teacher characteristics.

The second innovation in this chapter is to test the importance of (typically unobserved) teaching 'process' variables in determining pupil achievement rather than only of observed teacher education, experience or training. If unobserved teaching methods are correlated with both observed teacher characteristics and pupil achievement, included teacher characteristics variables suffer omitted variable bias. The inclusion of measures of teaching methods should mitigate such bias. We are fortunate to have data on measures of various important aspects of the class teaching process.

Finally, it should not be presumed that the achievement production function is a universal constant, applicable to all school types and all settings. The way in which teacher characteristics or teaching practices affect student learning may differ across school types. In particular, private and public schools operate under very different sets of incentives. Pakistan has a large and growing private schooling sector which experienced an almost 800 per cent increase at all education levels in the past few decades (Andrabi *et al.*, 2006; Aslam, 2008). We will ask whether the pupil fixed-effects achievement production function differs in public and private school systems.

Data

The data for this study come from a purpose-built school-based survey conducted by one of the authors in Lahore district in Punjab province, Pakistan, in 2002–2003. Using stratified random sampling on 65 schools (25 government and 40 private) in urban and rural Lahore, the survey collected detailed information on

166   M. Aslam and G. Kingdon

1,887 pupils in any one section of grade 8 in each sample school. Each pupil filled out a questionnaire with questions on personal characteristics (age, motivation, gender, etc.), parental and family background (parental education and occupation, family structure and size, wealth and income, etc.), and schooling (books prescribed in school, length of the school week, family expenditure on schooling in the past year, hours of home tuition taken, etc.). Each child was also weighed and his/her height and arm circumference measured. In addition, the Raven's Standard Progressive Matrices test and tests of numeracy and literacy were also given to each sampled child. The former was administered with the view to obtain some measure of innate ability. The literacy and numeracy tests were developed by the Educational Testing Service (ETS) for use by Knight and Sabot in their study in Africa (see Boissiere *et al.*, 1985) and have been discussed extensively in Knight and Sabot (1990). We adapted these tests to the Pakistani context, reduced the number of questions to test within limited time, and translated them into Urdu to administer them to children in the national language when the medium of instruction in the school was Urdu. Availability of standardised tests is a unique feature of the dataset and avoids biases faced when relying on national test scores.

In addition to the above, data on school resources and expenditures was also collected by interviewing head teachers of the schools through a school-level questionnaire. Also, mostly for consistency checks and for some additional information, each child was sent home with a 'parents' questionnaire' which was filled out by the parent (or the child asking the parent questions if parent was illiterate) and returned to school authorities the next day. Information on 1,770 parent questionnaires was collected and collated.

Some additional unique features of our data allow us to go beyond what extant studies have been able to achieve in Pakistan. First, in addition to the rich individual and school-level information, detailed information was also elicited through a teachers' questionnaire from *all* teachers who taught the pupils in the section of grade 8 that was sampled in each school. This included information on personal attributes (gender, age, family background, education) and characteristics such as experience, tenure and salary, etc. As pupils were tested in two subjects – mathematics and a language (Urdu or English depending on the medium of instruction of the school), in all schools where these two subjects are taught by different teachers, for each student-subject row corresponding information on the subject's teacher is available. This allows exploitation of an identification strategy which effectively controls for all subject invariant student unobservables.

The second rare quality of the dataset is that in addition to the standard teacher characteristics, information about 'teaching methods and techniques' was also obtained. This was done by asking each sampled teacher to answer a series of questions such as those recording the minutes/week spent on average in giving 'surprise tests' or quizzes, maintaining discipline and order, writing material on the blackboard and reviewing homework given to the students previously. Teachers also noted whether they used lesson plans, asked students frequent questions and read out aloud from notes or textbooks, etc. while teaching to the sampled pupils in grade 8. Given the policy debate surrounding the most effective inputs to improve student learning, the availability of these process variables is fortunate. For instance, a recent news report on a study in the UK argued that what matters most to student achievement is the quality of the teacher, i.e. how effective the teacher is in teaching her subject. The variables used in our study are a step closer to assessing teaching effectiveness. These 'process' variables also provide some insight into teacher 'unobservables' that affect student achievement. This is because unobserved teacher-effort or motivation is captured (albeit imperfectly) through some of these variables. For example, more effective or motivated teachers may plan their lessons in advance, spend more time quizzing their pupils and be more interactive by involving students during lessons by asking questions. However, it is not possible a priori to sign the coefficients on the process variables as the effectiveness of the variable is presumably highly 'teacher-dependent'. Finally, we also tested all the sample teachers in a small test of English. Their test scores present additional measures of the potential 'quality' of teaching they provide to the students they teach.

Discussion of results – peeking into the black-box of the achievement function

Table 11.1 describes the variables used in subsequent equations while Table 11.2 shows the process variables by different teacher characteristics. Table 11.2 highlights some very interesting differences in how teachers of different genders, in various cohorts and with diverse education and teaching experience teach. For instance, younger and more educated teachers are more likely to plan their lessons in advance while older teachers appear more confident in asking more questions in class. More experienced teachers and those with higher tenures are less likely to adopt the more 'innovative' techniques such as quizzing students and this could reflect both the government-school teaching style and outdated teacher training.

Table 11.1 Description of variables used

Variable	Description
Individual characteristics	
READING	Pupil's score in language (Urdu or English test), maximum score 25
MATHS	Pupil's score in mathematics test, maximum score 25
STDMARK	Standardised mark
AGEYRS	Pupil's age in years
AGE2	Age squared
FEMALE˙	Dummy variable, equals 1 if female, 0 otherwise
NUMSIS	Number of sisters
NUMBRO	Number of brothers
EDUWISH	Child's educational aspirations, index from 1 to 6, for example 1 = aspires to complete grade 8 only, 2 = aspires completion till grade 10 etc.

168 *M. Aslam and G. Kingdon*

MEDYRS	Mother's education (completed years)
RAVEN	Score on Raven's ability test, maximum possible 60
TIRED	Index of how often child feels tired in class, 1 = very rarely, 2 = sometimes, 3 = quite often, 4 = most of the time
BOOKS	Number of books in child's home (divided by 1,000)
LOGINCOME	Natural log of father's income (Rupees/month)
HOMETUITION	Number of hours of paid home tuition taken by child (divided by 1,000)

Teacher characteristics

FEMTEACH*	Teacher is female = 1, 0 otherwise
FEMALE_TEACH*	Interaction between FEMALE and FEMTEACH
TSALARY	Teacher salary (Rupees/month)
TLOGSALARY	Natural log of teacher's monthly salary
TEACHER_MA	Teacher has MA/MSc. Or MPhil. Or PhD (equals 1, 0 otherwise)
TTRAINYRS	Years of teacher training
TEXP	Years of total experience
TEXP2	Teacher experience squared
TTENURE	Teacher's experience in current school
TTABSENT	Total days of absence in past year (including paid/unpaid sick/ other leave)
TOTHJOB	Equals 1 if teacher has evening/weekend job, 0 otherwise
TSCORE	Teacher's score in English language test, maximum 5
TSPECIAL*	Teacher 's highest degree is in subject she teaches currently in school
MINS_QUIZ	Minutes per week spent in quizzing students on past material (divided by 10)
MINS_HWORK	Minutes per week spent in discussing homework given to students (divided by 10)
LESSON_PLN*	Equals 1 if teacher plans lessons in advance, 0 otherwise
EXPLAIN*	Equals 1 if teacher explains in-class questions while lecturing, 0 otherwise
QUESTIONS*	Equals 1 if teachers asks a lot of random questions while teaching, 0 otherwise

School Characteristics

GIRLS_SCHOOL*	Equals 1 if school is a girls school, 0 otherwise
RESOURCE	Index of school resources
LENGTH_STUDY	Minutes per week school time is spent in studying (excluding breaks etc.), divided by 1,000
CLASSIZE	Actual class size of 8th grade pupils, divided by 100

Note: Variables marked by * are 0/1 indicator variables with Yes = 1 and No = 0.

Table 11.3 shows the results from OLS achievement production functions estimated separately for language and math. For each subject, three specifications are reported. In the first specification (column 1 under each subject), the baseline OLS regression is estimated using a rich vector of individual, household, teacher and school-level variables. The vector of teacher variables includes the standard variables such as teacher certification, training, experience, etc. that are usually available to researchers. The second specification (column 2) extends the stand-

Table 11.2 Process variables by teacher age, gender, experience, education and tenure

| | Teacher's: | | | | | | | | | | | | | |
| Process Variables: | *Gender* | | *Age* | | *Experience* | | | | *Education* | | | *Tenure* | | | |
	Male	*Female*	*Young*	*Old*	*<5 years*	*5–10 years*	*10–20 years*	*>20 yrs*	*College or less*	*Bachelors*	*Masters or more*	*<1 year*	*1–5 years*	*5–10 years*	*>10 years*
MINS_QUIZ	46.8	46.8	55.1	40.2	56.8	46.9	47.4	28.6	55.0	46.3	42.5	51.8	46.3	44.7	48.4
MINS_HWORK	42.8	40.2	42.9	39.5	38.1	47.2	39.4	42.5	51.0	42.1	34.0	42.5	35.7	45.7	45.4
LESSON_PLN	0.21	0.12	0.25	0.10	0.28	0.17	0.08	0	0.07	0.08	0.27	0.12	0.25	0.11	0
EXPLAIN	0.44	0.44	0.55	0.35	0.52	0.43	0.40	0.35	0.39	0.36	0.55	0.18	0.52	0.36	0.42
QUESTIONS	0.64	0.66	0.59	0.70	0.62	0.59	0.70	0.70	0.68	0.66	0.62	0.39	0.61	0.64	0.81

Note: A 'Young' teacher is defined as someone aged 35 or less and old otherwise.

Table 11.3 OLS (across school) achievement production functions by subject

Pupil characteristics	LANGUAGE						MATHEMATICS					
	(1)		(2)		(3)		(1)		(2)		(3)	
	Coefficient (Robust t)		Coefficient (Robust t)		Coefficient (Robust t)		Coefficient (Robust t)		Coefficient (Robust t)		Coefficient (Robust t)	
AGE_YRS	−0.109		−0.071		−0.033		0.063		0.049		0.059	
	(−0.4)		(−0.2)		(−0.1)		(0.2)		(0.2)		(0.2)	
AGE2	0.001		0.000		−0.002		−0.002		−0.001		−0.002	
	(0.1)		(0.0)		(−0.1)		(−0.2)		(−0.1)		(−0.2)	
FEMALE	0.243		0.220		0.234		−0.392	***	−0.389	***	−0.322	**
	(0.9)		(0.8)		(0.9)		(2.7)		(−3.2)		(−2.5)	
NUMSIS	−0.038		−0.038		−0.038		−0.057		−0.065		−0.061	
	(−2.0)	**	(2.1)	**	(−2.1)	**	(−4.0)	***	(−4.6)	***	(−4.3)	***
NUMBRO	−0.028		−0.024		−0.027		−0.005		−0.014		−0.008	
	(−1.5)		(−1.3)		(−1.4)		(−0.3)		(−0.8)		(−0.5)	
EDUWISH	0.106		0.118		0.113		0.073		0.083		0.073	
	(3.7)	***	(5.1)	***	(4.3)	***	(3.8)	***	(4.0)	***	(3.7)	***
MEDYRS	0.004		0.004		0.002		0.009		0.011		0.009	
	(0.6)		(0.5)		(0.3)		(1.7)	*	(2.0)	**	(1.7)	*
RAVEN	0.035		0.035		0.034		0.034		0.034		0.033	
	(10.7)	***	(10.9)	***	(11.2)	***	(9.9)	***	(9.8)	***	(9.7)	***
TIRED	−0.114		−0.138		−0.129		−0.007		−0.002		−0.015	
	(−3.7)	***	(−4.7)	***	(−4.6)	***	(−0.3)		(−0.1)		(−0.5)	
BOOKS	0.146		0.135		0.119		0.245		0.266		0.234	
	(2.2)	**	(2.3)	**	(2.2)	**	(5.2)	***	(5.8)	***	(5.6)	***
LNFINCOME	−0.010		−0.010		−0.012		−0.002		0.011		−0.001	
	(−0.6)		(−0.6)		(−0.8)		(−0.1)		(0.7)		(−0.1)	
HTUTAKEN	−0.065		−0.079		−0.091		−0.160		−0.209		−0.148	
	(−0.7)		(−0.9)		(−0.9)		(−1.8)	*	(−2.3)	**	(−1.7)	*

Teacher characteristics

	(1)	(2)	(3)	(4)	(5)	(6)
FEMTEACH	0.422 (1.4)	0.264 (0.8)	0.289 (0.9)	−0.085 (−0.6)	−0.176 (−1.3)	−0.061 (−0.4)
FEMSTUDTEACH	−0.204 (−0.6)	−0.081 (−0.2)	−0.079 (−0.3)	0.309 (1.6)	0.327 (1.9) *	0.156 (0.9)
TMA_PROF	0.117 (0.8)	0.143 (0.9)	0.100 (0.6)	−0.028 (−0.3)	−0.061 (−0.7)	−0.003 (0.0)
TTRAINYRS	0.031 (0.2)	−0.075 (−0.6)	−0.060 (−0.5)	0.046 (1.0)	0.038 (0.7)	0.035 (0.6)
TEXP	0.019 (0.5)	0.034 (0.9)	0.043 (1.1)	0.012 (0.7)	−0.012 (−0.7)	−0.001 (0.0)
TEXP2	−0.001 (0.7)	−0.002 (−1.2)	−0.002 (−1.4)	−0.001 (−1.4)	0.000 (−0.3)	0.000 (0.6)
TTENURE	0.007 (0.5)	0.022 (1.6)	0.015 (1.0)	0.024 (2.4) **	0.029 (2.8) ***	0.025 (2.2) **
TTABSENT	−0.003 (−1.9) *	−0.002 (−1.6)	−0.003 (−1.9) *	0.000 (0.0)	−0.006 (−1.3)	−0.003 (−0.5)
TOTHJOB	0.115 (0.9)	0.046 (0.3)	−0.030 (−0.2)	−0.006 (−0.1)	−0.012 (−0.1)	−0.046 (−0.4)
TSCORE	0.089 (0.9)	0.005 (0.0)	0.022 (0.2)	0.045 (0.5)	−0.023 (−0.3)	0.020 (0.2)
TSPECIAL	−0.039 (−0.2)	−0.085 (−0.5)	−0.094 (−0.5)	0.205 (2.5) **	0.302 (3.6) ***	0.210 (2.2) **
MINS_QUIZ/10	—	0.040 (2.4) **	0.030 (1.8) *	—	−0.020 (−1.2)	−0.011 (−0.7)
MINS_HWORK/10	—	−0.021 (−0.9)	0.002 (0.1)	—	0.002 (0.1)	0.010 (0.7)
LESSON_PLN	—	0.236 (0.9)	0.291 (1.0)	—	−0.296 (−1.6)	−0.192 (−1.0)
EXPLAIN	—	0.211 (1.6)	0.242 (1.6)	—	0.366 (2.6) ***	0.328 (2.1) **

QUESTIONS	—	−0.266 (−1.3)	−0.278 (−1.4)	—	0.004 (0.0)	0.042 (0.4)
School characteristics						
GIRLS_SCHOOL	0.070 (0.3)	—	0.061 (0.3)	−0.112 (−0.6)	—	−0.030 (−0.2)
RESOURCE	0.002 (0.4)	—	0.004 (0.8)	0.012 (3.1) ***	—	0.009 (2.0) **
LENGTH_STUDY/1000	0.439 (1.3)	—	0.567 (1.7) *	−0.318 (−1.6)	—	−0.472 (−2.9) **
CLASSIZE/100	0.007 (0.0)	—	0.070 (0.2)	−0.499 (2.2) **	—	−0.368 (−1.5)
CONSTANT	−1.344 (−0.6)	—	−2.293 (−1.0)	−1.990 (−0.9)	—	−1.511 (−0.7)
N	1353	1353	1353	1353	1353	1353
R2	0.3702	0.3877	0.3978	0.4547	0.4633	0.4633

How pedagogic practice influences achievement   173

ard production function by including a parsimonious set of 'teaching process' variables. These measure classroom practices and are aimed at capturing teacher effectiveness. Column 3 includes school-level variables.

Focusing first on columns (1) and (2) without and with teacher process variables (under each subject), we see that among the individual and family characteristics, most variables have expected signs. For example, more aspiring and able pupils (EDU_WISH and RAVEN) perform better. Physical tiredness reduces pupil achievement while the home learning environment (proxied by the number of books at home) improves learning significantly. Interestingly, a higher proportion of sisters reduce language achievement significantly while there is no such effect with a higher proportion of brothers. No teacher or school characteristics other than teacher absence are significantly associated with language achievement, but math learning profits from having teachers with longer tenure and specialist teachers, i.e. those who themselves had a degree in the subject they teach – in this case math. Students' language skills benefit from a larger number of minutes spent by teachers in quizzing them and maths skills benefit from having teachers that take time to explain concepts. Including school characteristics in column (3) does not change the coefficients in (2) much.

The first cut achievement regressions in Table 11.3 reveal some interesting findings – one of the key results is that while standard teacher variables do not appear to determine students' language and numeracy skills, some 'process' variables clearly matter depending on the subject: while quizzing benefits language scores, explaining and involving pupils in discussions appear to benefit mathematics skills more. However, these 'across-school' results suffer from biases and we now discuss the main results of this chapter presented in Table 11.4.

Table 11.4 presents the achievement production function estimates by pooling both subjects. Achievement functions are estimated:

1   across-schools;
2   *within* schools using school fixed-effects; and
3   *within* pupils using pupil fixed-effects.

In each case, two specifications are reported – without and with the vector of process variables. We report only the parameter estimates of the teacher variables. The similarity of the results in the school and pupil fixed-effects columns (without and with process variables) is unsurprising; they would have been identical had it not been for an unbalanced panel since there is no variation within the school which is also not within the pupil. This is because in each school we only sampled one section of grade 8. Had we sampled at least two sections, teacher characteristics could have been pupil-specific rather than subject-specific provided the two sections were taught by different teachers within a school. This limitation implies that we cannot test whether a school fixed-effects model based on data from more sections of grade 8 within a school would differ from a pupil fixed-effects one.

It is conspicuous that the coefficients of some variables change a great deal when moving from OLS to school fixed-effects estimation. This can happen if in

Table 11.4 Achievement production functions (two subjects, pooled without and with 'teaching process' variables)

	OLS			School fixed effects				Pupil fixed effects			
	(1)			(2)			(3)		(4)		(5)		(6)
	Coefficient (Robust t)		Coefficient (Robust t)		Coefficient (Robust t)		Coefficient (Robust t)		Coefficient (Robust t)		Coefficient (Robust t)	
FEMTEACH	−0.014		−0.016		−0.388		−0.486		−0.427		−0.537	
	(−0.1)		(−0.1)		(−2.7)	***	(−3.8)	***	(−5.8)		(−7.1)	***
FEMSTUDTEACH	0.274		0.222		0.560		0.610		0.656		0.733	
	(1.9)	*	(1.7)	*	(4.7)	***	(4.8)	***	(6.7)	***	(7.3)	***
TMA_PROF	0.035		−0.008		0.005		−0.076		0.008		−0.075	
	(0.4)		(−0.1)		(0.0)		(−0.6)		(0.1)		(−1.2)	
TTRAINYRS	0.000		−0.069		0.038		0.016		0.043		0.022	
	(0.0)		(−1.2)		(0.6)		(0.2)		(1.5)		(0.8)	
TEXP	0.014		0.027		−0.035		−0.020		−0.036		−0.022	
	(0.8)		(1.6)		(−2.0)	**	(−1.4)		(−3.8)	***	(−2.1)	**
TEXP2	−0.001		−0.001		0.001		0.001		0.001		0.001	
	(−1.3)		(−1.7)	*	(1.2)		(1.4)		(2.3)	**	(2.2)	**
TTENURE	0.021		0.019		0.018		0.010		0.018		0.010	
	(2.8)	***	(2.6)	***	(3.1)	***	(1.7)	*	(4.9)	***	(2.4)	**
TTABSENT	−0.001		0.000		0.000		0.000		0.000		−0.001	
	(−0.4)		(0.0)		(0.2)		(−0.5)		(0.3)		(−0.7)	
TOTHJOB	0.064		0.069		0.085		0.169		0.086		0.170	
	(0.7)		(0.7)		(0.6)		(1.5)		(1.6)		(3.3)	***
TSCORE	0.116		0.092		0.087		0.095		0.086		0.092	
	(1.7)	*	(1.1)		(1.8)	*	(2.0)	*	(3.0)	***	(2.8)	***
TSPECIAL	0.179		0.129		0.029		−0.044		0.024		−0.048	
	(2.3)	**	(1.5)		(0.4)		(−0.6)		(0.7)		(−1.2)	
MINS_QUIZ/10	—		0.032				0.030				0.030	
			(3.1)	***	—		(2.2)	**	—		(3.8)	***

	(1)	(2)	(3)	(4)	(5)	(6)
MINS_HWORK/10	—	−0.012 (−0.8)	—	−0.020 (−2.0) **	—	−0.021 (−3.8) ***
LESSON_PLN	—	0.144 (1.1)	—	0.219 (1.4)	—	0.230 (2.7) ***
EXPLAIN	—	0.141 (1.6)	—	0.040 (0.5)	—	0.043 (0.9)
QUESTIONS	—	−0.161 (−1.7) *	—	0.210 (2.1) **	—	0.210 (3.8) ***
Subject Dummy	Yes	Yes	Yes	Yes	Yes	Yes
Pupil Variables	Yes	Yes	Yes	Yes	No	No
School Variables	Yes	Yes	No	No	No	No
N	2706	2694	2706	2694	2706	2694
R2/R2 within	0.3879	0.4048	0.1988	0.2114	0.0825	0.1197
No. of Groups	—	—	50	50	1353	1353
F (p-value)	23.31 (0.000)	37.86 (0.000)	43.24 (0.000)	33.68 (0.000)	11.57 (0.000)	11.97 (0.000)

176   M. Aslam and G. Kingdon

OLS the coefficient of a variable is 'picking up' the effect of omitted variables. For example, it appears that female teachers are actually less effective (than male teachers) for boys, but are more likely to be working in the schools that are in better neighbourhoods, i.e. which have higher achieving boys in them. If so, the coefficient on the female teacher dummy variable in the OLS equation is biased upwards (i.e. is a smaller negative than its true negative effect size) since it picks up the effect of quality of neighbourhood.

Focus first on the pupil fixed-effects results in columns (5) and (6) as these are of most interest to us. Comparing the estimates without and with process variables, among the significant coefficients, the inclusion of classroom practice variables causes the coefficient on TTENURE to decline from 0.018 to 0.010. This suggests that it may not be tenure per se which generates an improvement in pupil achievement; it may be the adoption of certain teaching practices by teachers with more experience in a given school that increases pupil achievement. Alternatively, teachers who adopt certain teaching techniques and are more efficient may also have their contracts renewed (and hence have greater tenure). Disentangling which of these two effects may be operating is not possible in this study.

Focus on column (6) in Table 11.4. One of the most striking findings is that a student's standardised mark in a subject taught by a female teacher is 0.5 standard deviations *lower* than if the same student were taught by a male teacher. Female students, however, appreciably benefit from being taught by same-sex teachers – their standardised mark increases by about 0.2 standard deviations. The results suggest that in the Pakistani schooling system, there are large effects of having 'a teacher like me' (as in Dee, 2007). A number of explanations can rationalise this finding (Holmlund and Sund, 2005). First, the 'preferences' explanation suggests that teachers of a given sex have preferences for students of the same gender, and may reward same-sex students in terms of higher grades. A second, 'stereotyping', explanation argues that teachers' own stereotypes may influence their evaluations of pupils. Although these two explanations can be ruled out by arguing that the tests taken by pupils in this sample were neither administered nor graded by their teachers, we cannot rule out the possibility that 'preferences' or 'stereotypes' influence the *way* in which knowledge is transmitted to students of different genders. Finally, a third – 'role-models' – explanation, argues that students of the same gender may perform better by being taught by same-sex teachers viewed as role models. This hypothesis is convincing in light of cultural norms in Pakistan where adolescent girls suddenly face strict mobility restrictions and may see female teachers as effective role models. While highlighting possible hypotheses, this chapter does not delve into which one best explains this result in Pakistan.

Teacher certification has no bearing on pupil's standardised achievement. This finding corroborates international evidence (see Hanushek and Rivkin, 2006 for a summary and Kane *et al.*, 2008 for a recent study). Note that variables such as teacher experience and tenure (TEXP, TEXP2 and TTENURE) are included merely as control variables as they are likely to be jointly determined with pupil achievement and we do not discuss their coefficients. For example, the positive coefficient on teacher tenure could reflect that more time spent in a given school

How pedagogic practice influences achievement 177

(hence greater teacher experience in that school) raises pupil learning (causation from tenure to achievement) or it could reflect that teachers who are more effective in raising pupil achievement are also more likely to have their contracts renewed (causation from achievement to tenure). Arguably, however, by including a large number of process variables potentially capturing some elements of teacher 'effectiveness' typically unobserved, this bias may be considerably reduced.

The headline story in column (6), however, is that a large number of 'process' variables are significant determinants of achievement. Being taught by a teacher with another job (in addition to the teaching job in the school) substantially benefits a pupil compared to being taught by a teacher who doesn't have any other job. This could be because more 'effective' or better teachers are also able to find secondary employment. Alternatively, as a large percentage of school-teachers are employed as tutors in evening coaching centres or give extra home tuition to pupils, the positive externalities of teaching different pupils or practice may be passed on to daytime pupils. It is worth noting that this surprising result (positive benefits of moonlighting) is context-specific. As demonstrated later in the chapter it is an entirely private-school phenomenon: in government schools there are no positive effects for student learning of teachers having a second job. The effect of a teacher's English test scores is also significantly positive – a pupil taught by a higher scoring teacher scores, on average, 0.09 standard deviations higher than when being taught by a lower scoring teacher. Among the 'process' variables, the largest positive effects on pupil achievement are from being taught by lesson-planning teachers and teachers who ask pupils many questions during lessons. For instance, being taught by a teacher who plans lessons raises pupil achievement by 0.23 standard deviations. The effect of asking questions is of a similar magnitude. Though the size of the coefficient is small, quizzing on past lessons also raises student mark. Finally, increased time spent reviewing homework is inimical to achievement (though the effect is small) perhaps because it takes away from time that could have been spent learning new material.

Summarising the results so far, pupil fixed-effects estimates showcase several interesting findings. First, most of the standard teacher variables believed to determine pupil achievement (such as certification and training), and often used to guide education policy, have no bearing on a student's standardised mark. Second, gender interaction effects suggest that girls benefit from being taught by female teachers and this has important policy implications. However, this study doesn't delve into potential explanations for this effect (i.e. whether it is because of stereotyping or because female teachers act as role models for impressionable female adolescents). Finally, the study also finds that it is the often un-captured teaching 'process' variables that impact student achievement – lesson planning, involving students through asking questions during class and quizzing them on past material all substantially benefit pupil learning.

Past studies have often focused on determining the effect of teacher characteristics on pupil achievement in across-school equations such as our estimate in column (1) of Table 11.4. Given our methodology, we are interested in how results change when moving to a *within-pupil* analysis compared to an across-school one.

178 M. Aslam and G. Kingdon

Moreover, because we have a rich list of 'process' variables, we compare columns (2) and (6) in Table 11.4 that include them in the specification. Comparing the two columns, being taught by a female teacher has no effect on pupil learning in across-school estimation, the effect is large and significantly negative in a within-pupil framework. And while the coefficient on FEMALE_TEACH is significantly positive in (2), it more than triples in size and becomes even more precise in column (6). Among the process variables, the size and even the significance of a few coefficients changes – for example while minutes spent discussing homework is negative and insignificant in (2), the effect almost doubles and becomes significant in (6). Similarly, while lesson planning has a positive and insignificant effect in (1), a student taught by a lesson-planning teacher benefits a large and significant improvement in achievement if taught by a lesson-planning compared to a non-lesson planning teacher. Finally, while in column (1), QUESTIONS is negative and just significant indicating that pupils taught by a teacher who asks many questions suffer a 0.16 deviation reduced standardised mark compared to when being taught otherwise, this is completely reversed in the within-pupil estimates where we find that the same pupil taught by a teacher who asks many questions *benefits* from a 0.21 standard deviation improvement in test scores compared to being taught by a teacher asking few questions. Clearly, across-school results are often quite dramatically different from with-pupil ones. As the former estimates are often confounded by the correlation between teacher characteristics and pupil and school unobservables, they may give misleading results. Within-pupil estimates are more powerful as they control at least for all subject-invariant pupil and family-level unobservables that may generate biases in estimation.

Note that teacher pay is absent from the above estimates despite it often being of significant policy interest. The appeal of this variable rests in the conviction that higher teacher pay may result in improved pupil achievement either through increased teacher effort, or by attracting a better pool of applicants in a given school or by creating an incentive for teachers to retain their more valuable jobs (Kingdon and Teal, 2007). If true, this provides a rationale for schools to adopt 'performance-related-pay' mechanisms, and offers a tool for policy-makers to channel constrained resources to improve pupil learning (Ballou, 2001, notes that 'merit-pay' mechanisms often do not work when teacher unions are strong). A key challenge, however, is in identifying the causal effect of teacher pay on student achievement. Even within a pupil fixed-effects framework, this is complicated because of the various biases (omitted variables and simultaneity bias) associated with the inclusion of this variable. While reduced, through the inclusion of process variables potentially capturing elements of effort and motivation (often relegated to the error term), biases may not be completely eliminated. Therefore, although we estimated identical equations including the teacher pay variable, the results are not reported in Tables 11.3 and 11.4. We also note that the inclusion of teacher salary in logs (TLOGSALARY) did not change any of the results in the two tables and the variable itself was often insignificant. While suggesting that increasing teacher pay may not be a potent tool for improving student achievement (at least in Lahore), it does raise an interesting question – if higher teacher

How pedagogic practice influences achievement 179

pay is not associated with improvements in students' test scores, how *efficient* is the pay schedule in schools across Lahore? That is, are teachers rewarded by schools for possessing characteristics that improve students' performance? We explore this question later in the chapter.

Finally, two further points must be noted. First, the identification strategy used in this chapter rests on the assumption that student ability across subjects is constant and a failure of this assumption could introduce bias in the estimated results if students are sorted to teachers on the basis of subject-specific ability. A potential problem with the results in column 6 in Table 11.4 is that teachers in a particular subject having a certain style of teaching a given subject could systematically be assigned to teaching students of a higher ability, for example. These teachers' process variables may be picking up this unobserved student ability effect, generating a particular kind of endogeneity bias. While this kind of 'tracking' by ability is relatively uncommon in South Asian countries in general and Pakistan in particular, nevertheless it could create a bias if it were there. Second, the 'language' test used in our survey tested students either in Urdu, the National language, or English depending on whether the school was 'Urdu-medium' or 'English-medium' in teaching. A majority of the students in the sample took the test in Urdu (72 per cent). The use of two languages to measure one language score is potentially another source of bias. To address this and the previous problem, we introduce Table 11.5. Columns (1) and (2) replicate columns (5) and (6) from Table 11.4 for ease of comparison. Columns (3) and (4) replicate the specifications on a sub-sample of students who took the language test in Urdu. Moreover, we restrict the sample to students in schools with *one* section of grade 8 in the entire school. If the concern is that schools may systematically allocate students of a particular ability in a given subject to teachers who are better at teaching that subject, then this 'sorting' issue does not arise in schools where there is only one section of grade 8 – all students of whatever ability level in a subject would be allocated the same teacher in that subject. As we are interested most in the 'process' variables, we note that with the exception of LESSON_PLN, the sign and size of the effects is largely unchanged in the regression based on this restricted sample where we can rule out sorting by subject ability. Thus, we can be relatively confident that the results are not driven by the non-random matching of students to particular teachers within the school or biased due to the choice of testing in a particular language.

Conclusions

The objective of this chapter was to delve into the black-box representing 'teaching' to uncover the teacher characteristics and teaching practices that matter most to pupil achievement. To do so, we exploited a unique identification strategy – within-pupil variation was used to estimate the effects of teacher characteristics on student achievement. This was done by utilising data from Pakistan that permits the matching of students' test scores in language and mathematics tests to the teachers that teach those subjects, allowing examination of whether the

Table 11.5 Robustness check – achievement production functions (Urdu and mathematics, with 'teaching process' variables)

	Pupil fixed effects (full sample)	Pupil fixed effects (restricted sample i.e. schools with only one sectio,n of class 8 and where the language test was taken in Urdu only)		
	(1) Coefficient (Robust t)	(2) Coefficient (Robust t)	(3) Coefficient (Robust t)	(4) Coefficient (Robust t)
FEMTEACH	-0.427*** (-5.8)	-0.537*** (-7.1)	-0.084 (-0.68)	-0.230 (-1.2)
FEMSTUDTEACH	0.656*** (6.7)	0.733*** (7.3)	.410** (2.2)	0.212 (1.1)
TMA_PROF	0.008 (0.1)	-0.075 (-1.2)	-0.000 (-0.0)	-0.030 (-0.1)
TTRAINYRS	0.043 (1.5)	0.022 (0.8)	0.028 (0.4)	-0.236 (-1.6)
TEXP	-0.036*** (-3.8)	-0.022*** (-2.1)	-0.002 (-0.1)	0.062* (1.8)
TEXP2	0.001** (2.3)	0.001** (2.2)	0.001 (1.0)	-0.001 (-1.1)
TTENURE	0.018*** (4.9)	0.010*** (2.4)	-0.033* (-1.9)	-0.019 (-0.74)
TTABSENT	0.000 (0.3)	-0.001 (-0.7)	-0.003 (-0.3)	-0.009 (-0.7)
TOTHJOB	0.086 (1.6)	0.170*** (3.3)	-0.259* (-1.9)	-0.275** (-2.0)
TSCORE	0.086*** (3.0)	0.092*** (2.8)	0.011 (0.1)	0.069 (0.3)
TSPECIAL	0.024 (0.7)	-0.048 (-1.2)	-0.127 (-1.5)	-0.053 (-0.3)
MINS_QUIZ/10	—	0.030	—	0.052

		(3.8)	***		(2.2)	**
MINS_HWORK/10	—	−0.021		—	−0.034	
		(−3.8)	***		(−2.1)	**
LESSON_PLN	—	0.230		—	0.433	
		(2.7)	***		(0.7)	
EXPLAIN	—	0.043		—	−0.253	
		(0.9)			(−1.3)	
QUESTIONS	—	0.210		—	0.214	
		(3.8)	***		(1.7)	*
Subject Dummy	Yes	Yes		Yes	Yes	
Pupil Variables	No	No		No	No	
School Variables	No	No		No	No	
N	2706	2694		798	798	
R2/R2 within	0.0825	0.1197		0.100	0.102	
No. of Groups	1353	1353		399	399	
F (p-value)	11.57 (0.000)	11.97 (0.000)		3.21(0.000)	3.29(0.000)	

182 M. Aslam and G. Kingdon

characteristics of different subject teachers are related to a student's marks across subjects.

Apart from the innovative identification methodology used in this study, a further unique feature is that the data also allow us to test the importance of classroom practices and teaching techniques rather than confining attention only to teachers' characteristics, i.e. qualifications, experience and training. Finally, instead of imposing a universal achievement production function, we provide separate estimates for government and private schools.

The pupil fixed-effects estimates reveal some striking results. One of the findings of interest is that most of the standard teacher résumé characteristics (such as certification and training) often used as measures of teacher quality and used to guide education policy have no bearing on a student's standardised mark. However, despite this we find that teachers are largely rewarded for possessing these characteristics, which have little to do with improving pupils' achievement. Thus, teacher salary schedules appear to be inefficient. While this is true more for government schools, private school salary structures appear relatively more flexible although even here more qualified teachers receive higher salaries when teacher qualifications are not a significant determinant of student learning.

Another interesting finding is that girls benefit from being taught by female teachers, a finding with interesting policy implications. We also find that the usually un-measured teaching 'process' variables impact student achievement strongly – lesson planning, involving students by asking questions during class and quizzing them on past material, all substantially benefit pupil learning.

We conclude this chapter with the caveat mentioned before, namely that differences between teachers in unobserved characteristics still remain a source of endogeneity and undermine the ability to attribute causality to observed teacher variables. However, we also note that the biases associated with this source of endogeneity may be somewhat reduced in this chapter. By including process-type variables which may be correlated with unobserved teacher effort, ability and motivation, we have been able to reduce, though not necessarily eliminate, some of the biases generated with this source of endogeneity.

Note

1 This chapter is extracted from a longer paper: Aslam, M. and Kingdon, D. (2011) 'What can teachers do to raise pupil achievement?', *Economics of Education Review*, **30:3**, pp. 559–574. For more detailed considerations of the methodology used reference should be made to the original paper.

12 Pedagogical renewal and teacher development in Sub-Saharan Africa

Challenges and promising paths

Martial Dembélé and Bé-Rammaj Miaro-II

Education for All emerged as a global imperative from the 1990 International Conference on Education, held in Jomtien, Thailand. Ten years later, precisely in April 2000, about 1,100 participants from 164 countries gathered in Dakar, Senegal, to take stock of progress made towards meeting this imperative. At the Dakar summit, it was established that there had been remarkable progress in terms of increased access, but that quality, measured by achievement scores in reading, writing, arithmetic and problem-solving (i.e. the basic learning tools) and internal efficiency among others, was abysmally low, especially in Sub-Saharan Africa. Various evaluations, e.g. UNESCO's Monitoring Learning Achievement (MLA), the Programme d'analyse des systèmes éducatifs de la CONFEMEN (PASEC) and the Southern African Consortium for Monitoring Education Quality (SACMEQ), have shown that most students in this part of the world leave primary school with very limited or even no mastery of the basic learning tools. As well, because of its current nature, school does not help them learn how to learn and tends to alienate them from their socio-cultural environment. Such findings are all the more preoccupying as for the vast majority of these children, primary school is involuntarily a terminal cycle (note that a significant number of them drop out before reaching grade 6). In other words, one can argue that the current school systems are preparing future illiterates. The cost of this wastage is estimated at more than 25 per cent of financial resources allocated to primary education. It is therefore not surprising that quality was the dimension most strongly emphasised by the Dakar summit in pursuing the new goal of EFA by 2015 (Ndoye, 2002).

The emphasis thus placed on quality has heightened the dual challenge of improving the quality of basic education while increasing coverage and retention. Pedagogical renewal and teacher development are critically important in this context, as ultimately educational quality is obtained through pedagogical processes in schools, and particularly in classrooms. Indeed, it is at the school and classroom level that various inputs come or are brought together to foster student learning; and the coming or bringing together of inputs depends primarily on the knowledge, skills, dispositions and commitments of the adults in whose charge children are entrusted, i.e. teachers and school heads. As constituent elements of the practices of these adults, i.e. teaching and school leadership, knowledge, skills, dispositions and commitments cannot be static. As Eraut put it in his preface to

184   M. Dembélé and B.-R. Miaro-II

Day's 1999 comprehensive review of teachers' learning and the factors which affect it:

> [t]he quality of teaching clearly depends on teachers continuing to learn as teaching contexts, pupil behaviour and expectation of teachers change. Even if there was less change the challenge of adapting to the needs of individual pupils and seeking to improve the quality of one's teaching and associated professional activities would require continuing professional development.
>
> (p. ix)

The same can be said of school heads. As a matter of course, they too have to adjust to changing work contexts, teacher and pupil behaviour, and role expectations. In other words, growth in practice for both teachers and school heads is of supreme importance if the children under their charge are to learn effectively. We can enlarge the circle to include the professionals who are mandated by the educational establishment to supervise and support schools and the adults who work there. In Sub-Saharan Africa and in other parts of the world, one finds two principal categories of such professionals, namely inspectors and pedagogical advisors/staff developers. They too have needs to grow in practice.

This chapter is about pedagogical renewal and teacher development in Sub-Saharan Africa, in the drive towards EFA by 2015.[1] We begin with clarifying the key concepts and a discussion of the issues at hand. This is followed by a brief historical background on teaching and learning, a summary of research on teaching and learning in Sub-Saharan Africa, and an overview of promising paths to pedagogical renewal in developing countries. The chapter closes with a summary of lessons learned from this review.

Concepts and issues

Defining and problematising pedagogical renewal and teacher development

We take pedagogical renewal to mean 'planned qualitative change toward desirable teaching practices, i.e., practices that ensure hoped for student learning'. This is a seemingly simplistic or narrow view of pedagogical renewal; but it is one that has far-reaching implications as will be discussed below. There is agreement on what practices are not desirable, namely rigid, chalk-and-talk, teacher-centred/dominated, lecture-driven pedagogy, which places students in a passive role and limits their activity to memorising facts and reciting them back to the teacher. For a summary description of the overall situation in Africa, see Kellaghan and Greaney (2003, p. 33). This kind of of pedagogy is generally labelled 'traditional' teaching. There is also principled agreement on what practices are desirable, namely participatory, more interactive, child-centred, adventurous pedagogy characterised by cooperative learning and inquiry, with a view to foster conceptual understanding, critical thinking and problem-solving skills. These desirable practices fall under

Teacher development in Sub-Saharan Africa   185

the general category of 'open-ended' instruction. Between traditional teaching and open-ended instruction, Gauthier *et al.* (2003) advocate explicit teaching – a combination of direct instruction and strategy instruction – with advance organisers, modelling, guided practice and independent practice as central features.

The intellectual background of open-ended instruction can be traced back to the work of scholars such as John Dewey. It has gained in popularity since the 1980s, to some extent in reaction to the basic skills movement. But it is proving extremely difficult to implement practices associated with open-ended instruction on a large scale, even in developed countries where certain conducive conditions exist, including small class size, abundance of teaching and learning materials, a teacher corps with university education, etc. In fact, taking good educational practice, however defined, to scale remains a puzzle for educational policy makers and administrators, and an issue of continuous investigation by educational researchers.

Interestingly enough, there is an emergent international experience base of successful implementation of such practices in the developing world. This emergent experience base will be introduced in the fourth section of the chapter. It is taking place in both formal and non-formal educational settings. It goes against the grain in that it challenges what Tyack and Cuban (cited by Farrell, 2002) call a standard 'grammar' of schooling, i.e. 'a set of expected patterns we have historically constructed regarding what a "real school" is. Anything that deviates substantially from that "real school" or "grammar-of-school" image will, by [Tyack and Cuban's analysis] be resisted by teachers, parents and students' (Farrell, 2002, p. 252). Farrell further argues that the mechanisms that central governments around the world can control, e.g. 'build schools, train, employ and pay teachers, supply furniture, textbooks and other learning materials, alter curriculum documents . . . do not alter the traditional model . . . nor . . . alter the "core" of the process, the teaching and learning that occurs in thousands of classrooms. Change at that level is *not* what central governments or outside agencies do well' (p. 252).

This takes us back to the argument we made in the introduction – that teachers and classroom processes are central in any attempt at pedagogical renewal. It is therefore understandable that teacher development is a key component of most, if not all, pedagogical renewal initiatives.

Teacher development has a double meaning:

> On the one hand, it refers to the actual learning opportunities which [prospective, beginning and experienced] teachers engage in – their time and place, content and pedagogy, sponsorship and purpose. [It] also refers to the learning that occurs when teachers participate in those activities. From this perspective, professional development means transformations in teachers' knowledge, understandings, skills, and commitments, in what they know and what they are able to do in their individual practice as well as in their shared responsibility.
>
> (Feiman-Nemser, 2001, p. 1038)

186   *M. Dembélé and B.-R. Miaro-II*

Pedagogical renewal will, in the last analysis, depend on these transformations as well as on teachers' adherence to that which is introduced to renew pedagogy. Teacher knowledge, skills, dispositions and commitments will always serve as filters for any change initiative (their own or others') that bears on classroom processes.

It is worth noting that there are no clear-cut, definitive answers to the question *How best to prepare teachers for teaching and provide for their further development in service?* In fact, there may never be such answers, as schooling, teaching and teacher education must, in principle, adapt to societal changes. However, the literature is replete with useful conceptual frameworks for thinking about and designing teacher education. As well, the literature contains promising practices that can inspire. From a conceptual perspective, what we know can be stated in a nutshell as follows:

- *Learning to teach involves the dual task of constructing a practice and a professional identity.* In more practical terms, it entails learning (to accomplish) the central tasks of teaching and the professional norms and ethics associated with desirable practices. Notwithstanding the fact that desirable practices in teaching are context-bound, it is agreeable that the central tasks of teaching include planning for instruction, managing instruction (including the learning environment) and assessing student learning. Each of these tasks can be further broken down and associated with particular aspects of 'what teachers need to know, care about, and be able to do in order to promote substantial learning for all students' (Feiman-Nemser, 2001, p. 1016). Some of these aspects can be found in the following characteristics of effective teachers, defined as:

  Effective teachers at a mature stage of development tend to:

  - know their subject matter;
  - use pedagogy appropriate for the content;
  - use an appropriate language of instruction, and have mastery of that language;
  - create and sustain an effective learning environment;
  - find out about and respond to the needs and interests of their students and communities;
  - reflect on their teaching and children's responses and make changes to the learning environment as necessary;
  - have strong work ethics;
  - are committed to teaching; and
  - care about their students.

  (Craig *et al.*, 1998, p. 12)

- *Constructing a practice is not a one-time event; hence the need for opportunities to learn as one practices.* Given the ever changing nature of schools and

Teacher development in Sub-Saharan Africa   187

teaching, one must periodically reconstruct one's practice. But the reconstruction of practice is hard because it requires changes in deep-rooted ideas that form the basis of one's practice. This has implications for in-service teacher education, beyond the early years (Elmore, 1996; Lieberman and Miller, 2001).

- *Constructing a professional identity or learning the professional norms and ethics associated with desirable practices requires being in a community of practice and being enculturated into that community.* This also has implications for teacher education. In particular it implies thinking differently about practical experience at the pre-service level and makes a case for structured induction (Britton *et al.*, 2003; Feiman-Nemser, 2001).

The challenge of pedagogical renewal and teacher development in Sub-Saharan Africa

The sheer number of teachers needed to achieve Universal Primary Education (UPE) in Sub-Saharan African countries makes the challenge a formidable one, not only from the perspective of the financial resources that this will require but also from the perspective of human resource availability; for even if financial resources abound, how to attract and retain talented individuals in the teaching profession remains an issue. This is especially true in a context where the profession's image has been adversely affected by a set of interconnected factors: deteriorating working and living conditions due to a decade plus of economic hardships and structural adjustment, widespread dissatisfaction with the current situation of schooling (and with teachers by extension), and the creation of a second class (in the double sense) of teachers in several countries.

The latter factor takes on a special significance at a time when many countries in the subcontinent, such as Burkina Faso, Chad, Guinea, Cameroon, Mali, Niger, Senegal, Togo, etc., are having to resort massively to contract, volunteer or community teachers, in response to teacher shortage and economic hardships. Indeed, this category of teachers has outnumbered regular teachers rapidly in several cases as countries strive to achieve UPE by 2015.

It is important to think prospectively about how to deal with the consequences of this unavoidable situation (see e.g. Dembélé *et al.*, 2005). These include, among others, the changing composition of the teaching force and the potentially harmful instability of the teaching staff in many schools, especially in areas where there are competing job opportunities. In this respect, the experience of Senegal is worth looking at. This country has since the mid 1990s resorted to volunteer teachers to face a severe teacher shortage. Initially, there was no career plan for these teachers, many of whom had completed three or four years of higher education. Pressure from various stakeholders, including the critical mass of volunteer teachers themselves, led to the establishment of a career ladder. This retention incentive has financial, administrative as well as legal implications. How these implications will be handled in the long run remains an open question.

188 *M. Dembélé and B.-R. Miaro-II*

In their case study of the new primary teacher preparation programme in Guinea, Diané and Grandbois (2003) recommend a career plan as a strategy for making teaching an attractive career, sustaining the enthusiasm of prospective teachers, and retaining them in teaching upon graduating from the programme. What the foregoing suggests is that the hiring of contract, volunteer or community teachers is not a panacea to the problem of teacher shortage and the financial burden that teachers place on the budget of the education sector. Countries considering this solution need to be cognisant of its limitations and consequences.

At any rate, redressing the image of the teaching profession stands as an important strategic direction towards UPE. Unsurprisingly, enhancing the status, morale and professionalism of teachers was adopted as one of the 12 main strategies for achieving the objectives set by the Dakar summit. The framework for action reads:

> Teachers are essential players in promoting quality education, whether in schools or in more flexible community-based programmes; they are advocates for, and catalysts of, change. No education reform is likely to succeed without the active participation and ownership of teachers. Teachers at all levels of the education system should be respected and adequately remunerated; have access to training and ongoing professional development and support, including through open and distance learning; and be able to participate, locally and nationally, in decisions affecting their professional lives and teaching environments. Teachers must also accept their professional responsibilities and be accountable to both learners and communities.
>
> Clearly defined and more imaginative strategies to identify, attract, train and retain good teachers must be put in place. These strategies should address the new role of teachers in preparing students for an emerging knowledge-based and technology-driven economy. Teachers must be able to understand diversity in learning styles and in the physical and intellectual development of students, and to create stimulating, participatory learning environments.

Obviously, the implementation of this strategy poses different challenges to different countries in Sub-Saharan Africa in the pursuit of pedagogical renewal. Assuming that understanding what goes on in the region's schools and classrooms is a necessary step towards successful pedagogical renewal, we review the current situation below. We set the stage with a brief historical background.

Teaching and learning in Sub-Saharan Africa: historical background

In 1968, the Organization of African Unity (OAU) and UNESCO called a 'Conference on education and scientific and technical training in relation to development in Africa'. Held in Nairobi from 16 to 27 July, this was a major event concerning the education sector, after the meetings in Addis-Ababa (1961), Paris (1962), Tananarive (1962), Abidjan (1964) and Lagos (1964). In total,

Teacher development in Sub-Saharan Africa   189

33 out of 39 independent African countries (80 per cent), sent delegates to this conference.

The Conference acknowledged the rapid expansion of the education systems in terms of increases in school enrolments and constructions, and felt proud of the progress made, but at the same time, it was pointed out that African countries had failed to reach the enrolment targets for primary and secondary education set in 1961 at the Addis-Ababa Conference. The shortfalls for the two levels were respectively 1.1 million and 387,000. Looking for the causes of the failure, the Conference saw inadequate funding as a result of countries' financial constraints generated by the world economic crisis. However, the Conference pointed out that financial limitations could explain an enrolment slow down, but not poor quality of education as evidenced by dropouts, massive grade repetition and low outputs of the educational systems. Studies showed that, of 100 pupils enrolled in the first grade, only 32 per cent completed their sixth year. Furthermore an increasing number of higher education graduates were often unemployed. It should be recalled that the top priority set by the 1961 Addis-Ababa Education Plan was to train the African manpower in order to modernise and boost the post-colonial economies. All the shortcomings mentioned above pushed the costs of schooling up, hence, jeopardising all education policy measures put forth at the Addis-Ababa Conference.

Unable to come up with the true causes of the above major problems, the Conference concluded as follows:

> It therefore appears that while there is an obvious need for seeking additional financial resources for the purposes of educational development, African countries are faced with the problem of rethinking the organization and content of their educational systems in relation to their economic and social conditions and requirements.
>
> (UNESCO, 1968, p. 9)

As recommended by the Conference, countries had to rethink, i.e. to re-examine and modify, according to their economic, social, cultural and political needs and aspirations, the organisation of their education systems as well as the substance of the education given to their population including the youth. Organisation refers to structure, planning and management of human, material and financial resources, while substance means what to teach, how to teach it and what to expect in terms of outcomes.

The experts pointed out that only careful studies of learning and teaching strategies will help to adapt the curriculum content in various specific conditions:

> There is a need for careful experimental investigation of the learning and the teaching strategies most appropriate to making the curriculum viable in different situations. For example, in many countries, many teachers are either untrained, or poorly trained, school buildings and equipment are entirely inadequate, and financial resources are strictly limited. Under such

190 *M. Dembélé and B.-R. Miaro-II*

conditions what special technique can be evolved and used to improve the quality of education?

(p. 15)

The question of what pedagogies (we prefer that term to 'special technique') to use to improve the quality of education is still of supreme importance for Sub-Saharan Africa (and indeed for other parts of the world) and was at the heart of The Challenge of Learning (COL) study. In the next section, we attempt to provide a response to this question. We draw extensively on research on teaching and learning in Africa, and resort to research from elsewhere as appropriate.

Research on teaching and learning in African classrooms: an overview of the evidence

As it appears in the foregoing, concern about the quality of education in Sub-Saharan Africa is not new. It has simply gained more prominence, unfortunately in response to declining quality indicators. One of the main explanatory factors put forth by both African and non-African scholars has to do with language of instruction. The problem of teaching African pupils to learn to read, write and compute through English, French, Portuguese or Spanish, all foreign languages, without caring about their mother tongues and families' traditional education systems, was pointed out in the early 1970s by Pierre Erny in his book *L'enfant et son milieu en Afrique noire* (1972). According to this author, who worked as a primary school teacher during the late 1950s and early 1960s in Haute Volta (now Burkina Faso), in Congo Brazzaville, and in 'Haut-Katanga industriel' (a region of the now Democratic Republic of Congo), ignoring the African child's cultural background in the process of modern education is an enormous nonsense.

Research on teaching and learning in West and Central Africa

Under the auspices of the Educational Research Network for West and Central Africa (ERNWACA or ROCARE in French), Maclure conducted a review of 1,056 research papers by African students and scholars on the education sector over a period of 30 years (Maclure, 1997). The papers were from seven out of the 12 ERNWACA member countries: Benin, Burkina Faso, Cameroon, Ghana, Mali, Togo, Sierra Leone.

The overall conclusion one can draw from the studies on learning is that the students' levels in reading, spelling, writing, oral communication and mathematics and science are low, and could be graded 'C' and 'C-' for spelling, in a grading system where 'A' corresponds to mastery of the subject learned and 'C' to the lowest level of learning. This suggests that these students have not developed or are not developing the prerequisite skills and competencies in the basic school disciplines.

Teaching reading and learning to read. According to the researchers, the students were weak in reading because there were not enough books in their schools

Teacher development in Sub-Saharan Africa 191

and homes for reading practice. This is a common problem in the vast majority of schools in Sub-Saharan Africa. In fact the issue runs across all school subject matters. There is a chronic lack of reference books even for teachers. Most primary and secondary schools do not have libraries. In addition to lack of books, we surmise that reading instruction may be principally at fault. Rote-memorisation of facts prevails in reading as well in classrooms worldwide, including in Africa. Students working on a second language in such classrooms often memorise sentences and recite them back to the teacher without understanding what they are saying. Teachers seem primarily preoccupied with correct pronunciation of words, correct intonation, and respect of punctuation and link ups as evidence of their students' ability to read. They typically focus marginally on *comprehension* in assessing students in this area. And this has gone unchallenged in many places up to now.

Educators, including teachers, acknowledge that the ability to read is critical to the extent that it is a learning tool. 'La lecture est la clé du savoir', i.e. reading is the key to knowledge, is a saying one often hears teachers use in Francophone Africa. There is also a robust research base in support of this claim. Indeed, ability to read is reported to be one of the best predictors of educational achievement. Juel (1991), for instance, reports that a student who has reading difficulties at the end of his or her first year of formal schooling has nine chances out of ten to be at risk at the end of grade 4; and the probabilities that this student will have difficulties at the secondary level are as high as 90 per cent. Because reading permeates all other subject matters, it is arguable that a student who is behind in reading at the end of grade 1 is a potential dropout (Carnine, 1998).

In light of the foregoing, one cannot insist unduly on the need to improve reading instruction and learning in Sub-Saharan Africa. There are already promising practices in several countries. These can be sources of inspiration for others. They include:

- the experience of *Bilingual Education in Burkina Faso* (see Ilboudo, 2003);
- the *Nouvelle Approche Pédagogique in Cameroon* (see Yakouba, 2003);
- the *'eclectic and play-play methods' in Cameroon* (see Ayuknso Nkongho Ashu, 1997);
- Mali's experience with *Pedagogie Convergente* (see Fomba and Keita, 2003); and
- the *Zambian Primary Reading Program* (see Sampa, 2003).

Interestingly, three of these experiences involve the use of African languages as media of teaching and learning, in addition to French or English. Bilingual education appears therefore as one of the promising paths to follow for improving the quality of basic education in Sub-Saharan Africa.

Teaching and learning mathematics and science. All four studies reviewed by Maclure attribute low student achievement in these two subject matters to poor teaching and limited content knowledge on the part of teachers. One of the studies carried out in Togo demonstrates that there is a correlation between weak language skills and corresponding results in mathematics and science (Maclure,

192   *M. Dembélé and B.-R. Miaro-II*

1997, p. 39). According to Maclure, these conclusions bring to light 'a vicious cycle where poorly-trained teachers provide students with less than satisfactory quality of teaching; and several of these students will subsequently be recruited as teachers' (p. 39).

A recurrent recommendation of all the studies reviewed has to do with curriculum reform. To improve curriculum relevance and thereby the quality of education, the researchers put forward the following actions:

1   providing more space for African languages in reading materials and as media of instruction and learning;
2   adapting school curricula to local socio-economic and socio-cultural realities particularly for rural areas; and
3   strengthening collaboration between local communities, especially student parents' associations, and the leadership of schools.

Looking more closely at teacher characteristics and teaching behaviours. Teacher characteristics and teaching behaviours embody the core external factors influencing student learning. Maclure's 1997 review of research included 173 studies pertaining to this strand of investigation, of which 140 (81 per cent) are end-of-training or degree programme memoirs, theses or dissertations. The studies showed that West and Central African teachers do not have the know-how, nor the minimum knowledge of the subject, to be able to teach effectively. Furthermore they do not master the foreign languages of instruction, i.e. English, French or Portuguese. In sum, these studies suggest that poor quality teaching is due to poor teacher qualification. Teachers are not effective because they are ill-prepared for their job. Their preparation is insufficient or irrelevant, or sometimes both (Maclure, 1997, pp. 58–60). Unfortunately, these studies do not show why pre-service and in-service teacher education cannot produce good teachers. Are they too long or too short? Are the curriculum and pedagogy of teacher education appropriate? No clear answers are given because investigations were not designed to address these specific issues.

Research on teaching and learning in Eastern and Southern Africa

Our information base for this sub-section is constituted primarily by the annotated bibliographies and limited literature reviews that ERNESA – the Eastern and Southern counterpart of ERNWACA – carried out in the framework of the COL study. Although it may not be representative of educational research in all the countries in the two sub-regions, it corroborates most of what is reported above about teaching and learning in West and Central Africa. Educational quality is reported to be below desired standards in both Eastern and Southern Africa. The explanatory factors/conditions that account for this situation are set out below.

• Instructional practices in various subject matters are said to be predominantly teacher-dominated and drill-oriented in both sub-regions (Ackers *et al.*, 2001; Ansell, 2002; O-Saki and Agu, 2002; Tabulawa, 1998).

Most countries in the two sub-regions are yet to resolve the issue of language of teaching and learning, even largely monolingual countries such as Burundi, Rwanda and Swaziland, as well as countries like Botswana and Tanzania where a national lingua franca exists (Arthur, 2002).

- Literacy levels are reported to be low, which negatively affects learning achievement in other subject matters (Qorro, 1997, 2001).
- Teacher quality and motivation are persisting issues (Kimane *et al.*, 2000).
- The need to improve teacher education, or to reform it altogether, appears consensual (Polonyana, 2000).
- There are numerous calls for strengthening continuous teacher development systems and making teacher development school-based and responsive to teachers' felt needs (Anderson, 2002).

One striking feature of pedagogical renewal in the two sub-regions has to do with attempts to switch to child/learner-centred, activity-oriented pedagogy, away from teacher-dominated instructional practices (van Graan, 2003). The experiences of most, if not all, countries can be summed up as follows: attempts to institutionalise child-centred pedagogy both in schools and teacher education institutions have produced inconclusive results so far. Tabulawa (1997) provided a compelling explanation of why it is proving so difficult to implement child-centred pedagogy in Botswana. In his view, the inconclusive results have often been rationalised in simplistic, technicist terms such as lack of resources and/or poorly-trained teachers, whereas the real explanatory factors have to do with teachers' assumptions about the nature of knowledge and how it ought to be transmitted, their perceptions of students, and what they consider to be the goal of schooling. Students' epistemological assumptions as well as social factors such as authoritarianism inherent in Tswana society must also be factored in. These assumptions (teachers' and students'), Tabulawa argued, are incongruent with the basic tenets of child-centred pedagogy; taking them for granted when affecting change in classroom practices can lead to disappointing results. This is congruent with an assertion made earlier in this chapter: breaking the mould of 'traditional' teaching to embrace and use open-ended instructional approaches is extremely difficult for teachers because it requires changing deeply rooted beliefs about knowledge, teaching, learning, learners and the purpose of schooling.

This explanation by Tabulawa does not mean, however, that complaints about the absence of enabling conditions such as teaching materials and equipment, and about large class size and strenuous record-keeping workloads, are unfounded. Indeed, most innovations fail because the enabling conditions were not in place or were underestimated by designers; and also because of their typically top-down nature, which results unsurprisingly in designers and those at the receiving end, i.e. classroom teachers, having different interpretations of what the innovation entails in practice (Fullan, 1991).

We now turn to an overview of promising pedagogical innovations in developing countries, aimed at breaking the mould of traditional teaching in both formal and non-formal education. Our interest in these innovations lies in their common

194 *M. Dembélé and B.-R. Miaro-II*

characteristics. We believe the latter constitute design principles worth taking into account for pedagogical renewal in Sub-Saharan Africa.

Pedagogical innovations in developing countries: an overview of promising paths

Farrell (2002) has been systematically gathering information about what he calls 'radical alternatives' (p. 247). These include, among others:

- the *Escuela Nueva programme* in Colombia;
- the *Non-Formal Primary Education programme* of the Bangladesh Rural Advancement Commission (BRAC);
- the *Escuela Nueva Unitaria programme* in Guatemala;
- the *Fe y Alegria schools* in Latin America;
- the *multi-grade programmes* in Guinea and Zambia;
- the *Convergent Pedagogy* in Mali;
- the UNICEF-sponsored *Community Schools* programme in Egypt;
- the *MECE Rural programme* in Chile; and
- a Network of 'education for production' programmes in Latin America.

Typically, [these alternatives] have some or all of the following characteristics:

- Child-centered, rather than teacher-driven, pedagogy.
- Active, rather than passive, learning.
- Multi-graded classroom with continuous-progress learning.
- Combinations of fully trained teachers, partially trained teachers and community resource people . . . heavily involved in the learning of the children and in the management of the school.
- Peer tutoring [among children].
- Carefully developed self-guided learning materials [for children].
- Teacher- and student-constructed learning materials.
- Active student involvement in the governance and management of the school.
- Use of radio, correspondence lesson materials, in some cases television, and, in a few cases, computers.
- Ongoing and regular in-service training and peer mentoring for teachers.
- Ongoing monitoring, evaluation and feedback systems . . .
- Free flow of children and adults between the school and the community.
- Community involvement that includes attention to the nutrition and health of young children long before they reach school age.
- Locally adapted changes in the cycle of the school day or the school year.
- A focus for the school that is much less on 'teaching' and much more on 'learning'.

(Farrell, 2002, pp. 255–256)

Teacher development in Sub-Saharan Africa   195

As already noted, it is proving quite difficult to implement child-centred, active pedagogy as a desirable practice on a large scale. Teachers are typically unprepared and lack needed support from school heads and supervisors to espouse and enact such a practice. In fact, in most cases, the latter may not be better informed about child-centred pedagogy than the teachers themselves. This does not mean, however, that the idea(l) of child-centred pedagogy should be abandoned. It is simply a call to be cognisant that implementation of such a pedagogy poses formidable challenges, even in contexts where the requisite conditions are in place. It should also be noted that most of the above-listed radical alternatives are in their infancy and on a small scale. There is therefore still much to learn about sustaining them and enlarging their scale. It may well be that the heart of the matter is not child-centredness per se, but how best to help children learn more than unconnected facts. For sure, teaching as information delivery is not effective in this respect.

What lessons have we learned?

What lessons could be learned from the various reviews of African and international research and experiences with respect to 'Pedagogical Renewal and Teacher Development'? What can be done to improve teaching and learning in schools in Sub-Saharan Africa? How to raise the quality of education in terms of developing the intellectual capacity and competencies of the learners, with a view to improving school learning and reducing grade repetitions and dropouts?

First, we believe that the research base for understanding pedagogic processes and teacher development in the region is limited. Many studies have conceptual and methodological limitations. Addressing these limitations and the paucity of research calls for strengthening the research units in higher education institutions and within ministries of education. This is all the more important as there are encouraging signs that research focused on pedagogic quality could have significant policy pay-offs. The international community has a role to play in this matter. It may mean, for instance, helping replicate studies such as the one conducted in Pakistan by Aslam and Kingdon (2007), looking at the ways in which pedagogic style rather than teacher qualification level is the main determinant of learning achievement. Gillies and Quijada's (2008) analysis of high impact strategies for improving educational outcomes in developing countries is also pertinent here.

Second, teacher effect is consistently reported across studies carried out in both developing and developed countries. There is also a consistent finding across studies that school has a stronger influence on student achievement than home and other external factors in developing countries, compared with developed countries. Despite a cautionary note about the methodological quality of the studies that led to this finding, it makes sense, considering the fact that sources of school-sanctioned knowledge and skills are more varied in developed countries than in developing countries. For developing countries, and Sub-Saharan Africa in particular, this has implications for policy and planning in two apparently opposed ways. On the one hand, assuming that schooling is maintained in its present form, this finding calls for considering the school as the best level of intervention for

196   *M. Dembélé and B.-R. Miaro-II*

improving the quality of education. On the other hand, one can take the option to transform schooling in Sub-Saharan Africa with the dual aim to reduce the discrepancy between school-sanctioned knowledge and skills and out-of-school knowledge and skills, and thus create a situation where sources of school-sanctioned knowledge and skills are varied. Taking either option means pushing decision-making to lower levels of the organisational structure of the education sector and strengthening school leadership and community participation.

Third, and this may be redundant, reading ability stands as a sine qua non condition for learning other subject matters. It is also a strong predictor of educational 'survival'. Reading must therefore be considered a priority area in efforts to improve the quality of basic education in Sub-Saharan Africa. In fact, it appears that countries worldwide accord substantial space to language and reading in their curricula. The difference in achievement may lie in how effectively time for teaching reading and learning to read is used in the classroom. Opportunity to learn to read stands therefore as an area where more investigation and special policy measures are needed. Ongoing bilingual education programmes, using African and foreign languages, appear to be good sites for such investigation and for trialling such policy measures.

Note

1 The chapter is an abridged and slightly updated version of a thematic synthesis produced by the authors (see Dembélé and Miaro-II, 2003) as part of The Challenge of Learning study (Verspoor, 2005), commissioned by ADEA (Association for the Development of Education in Africa) for its 2003 biennale. Permission was granted by ADEA to publish this shorter version.

Section 4

New strategies for teacher education and teacher development

Introduction

A number of recurring themes, identified in the earlier contributions to this book, are of particular importance to any discussion of teacher education and development. The first is that the scale of need goes beyond the capacity of existing teacher education institutions in most, if not all, developing countries. This challenge has been apparent for some while and, as the case studies in Section 2 illustrate, a number of governments have been intervening to provide new modes of provision. A second theme is the importance of in-service professional development to improve the effectiveness of teachers. Here the evidence about good quality teaching is becoming compelling. Again these are ideas that have circulated for some time. Successful teachers use specific pedagogic strategies that engage children more actively in the learning process. Qualifications do not guarantee the use of such strategies. Content mastery also appears important, although only very limited opportunities to develop this aspect of education and training exist.

A third theme is that the evidence about the lives of teachers is rarely used, even where it is understood, in the planning, structure and content of teacher education programmes. Many programmes appear monolithic and distant from the working lives of teachers, particularly women.

A final theme relates to the first. Just as it is difficult to secure the supply of teachers in many countries, so a similar problem arises to find sufficient teacher educators with the necessary qualifications and experience.

Taken together, these four themes provide an important point of departure for rethinking the way teacher education is organised. Yet, and this is one of the main arguments that can be addressed to policy makers, the forms of such rethinking are often constrained by the assumptions that go with conventional provision. The predominance of traditional campus based models of training has also influenced research. The MUSTER programme, for example, referred to in some detail in Chapter 1, whilst providing a highly insightful critique of teacher education, did so very much through the 'training college' perspective. There is only limited reference of the effectiveness of new approaches to teacher education, for example of the sort that is suggested by a number of the global monitoring reports. Equally, the type of research enquiries being pioneered by people such as Esther Duflo at MIT's Poverty Action Lab have rarely been applied to teacher education interventions. As a number of contributors to the book have suggested,

200   *Introduction*

such interventions will need to start from the premise that most teachers will only be able to access education and training from a school base. This premise, different from those of the MUSTER and related projects, has significant implications for policy formulation.

In this final section of the book these themes are drawn on to explore different ways of thinking about teacher education and to examine the new types of courses, including those exploiting new communication technologies. These include new forms of open and distance learning. It should be stressed, however, that despite the experience of many of the contributors with this form of provision, the analyses presented do not represent a simple advocacy for open and distance learning. If there is any advocacy to be derived from the contributions to this book it is around the need to think beyond the training institution model to a more school based approach. Such a move involves rethinking the curriculum and reassessing the way education and training is provided. Through this process open and distance learning and new communication technologies could have a significant role.

The research base to these new approaches needs to be strengthened and some indicators about how this might be achieved is given in the final chapter of the book. Here the themes identified above are used to develop seven interrelated factors that policy makers in particular, as well as the wider research community, need to address if well conceived reform of teacher education and training is to be successful.

13 New modes of teacher pre-service training and professional development

Jophus Anamuah-Mensah, Frank Banks, Bob Moon and Freda Wolfenden

Makano's phone bleeps. An SMS originating in the University of Pretoria 300 miles away links her with a mini lecture on multi-grade teaching. Another bleep a few minutes later reminds her that an assignment is due at the end of the week.

John settles into a chair at the end of a day's teaching practice in northern Nigeria. As a College of Education student on teaching practice he uses the classroom to prepare the following day's lesson. The College has provided him with a textbook created from the Teacher Education in Sub-Saharan Africa (TESSA) programme. A network of institutions across nine countries working through a web environment: www.tessafrica.net.

Masuda takes a break from her class. She uses the time to look at her Apple iPod and watch a small video demonstrating how role play can be used in the teaching of English.

These three teachers are fortunate to be profiting from innovative teacher education programmes, in South Africa, Nigeria and Bangladesh respectively. New forms of communication technologies are beginning to open up ways of connecting teachers to teacher education support programmes. As we will discuss below, significant new possibilities are being opened up by innovations in technology, particularly mobile technologies. However, we believe that the structures of teacher education in the twenty-first century needs to be rethought in fundamental ways if the potential of technology is to be realised and if significant improvements in quality and access are to be achieved.

Existing teacher education provision substantially reflects the structures and systems set up in the first part of the twentieth century. Campus based, often residential institutions provide for pre-service education. Regional district authorities take responsibility for in-service professional development programmes. In many countries pre-service education is provided or validated by local universities. Initial teacher education and training globally has increasingly been taken over by the higher education sector. This happened in the United States in the 1920s and 1930s, in most European countries between 1970 and 2000 (Moon, 1998) and in some countries, for example South Africa and Ghana, in the first decade of the present century. The university has varying degrees of autonomy but commonly comes under a ministry of higher education rather than the ministry responsible for schools.

202   *J. Anamuah-Mensah et al.*

Although the costs of the different modes of teacher education and training are difficult to disentangle, the biggest consumer of resources by far is pre-service initial teacher training with its institutional staffing and infrastructure and cost-intensive residential provision. The length of pre-service training varies but many countries aspire to provide a degree level programme extending to three or four years.

The dominant model for in-service professional development is a series of 'out of school' courses provided through regional centres. These may vary in length from one or two days to two weeks. Specialist staffing in the form of advisors or inspectors takes responsibility for such programmes. Certification is rare and links to pre-service providers are generally weak. In some countries the cost of transportation and subsistence associated with in-service activity take up the bulk of the resources available. This type of provision is expensive. Millions of teachers have no access to it.

Data and information on the effectiveness of pre-service and in-service programmes in low income countries is limited. One substantial study of teacher education in a range of African and Caribbean countries, the University of Sussex MUSTER project, reported (Lewin and Stuart, 2003):

> Though the detail is complex, the MUSTER conclusions are clear. The Millennium Development Goals (MDG) relating to education cannot be met unless the supply of teachers is adequate to keep pupil–teacher ratios within reasonable limits, and the quality of their training is sufficient to result in minimum acceptable levels of pupil achievement. The costs of existing methods of training are such that simple expansion of existing capacity is often not financially viable. Improvements in efficiency and effectiveness are needed that can lower costs and expand output within sustainable budgets. It may also be necessary to consider alternatives to two or three years full-time, pre-career training. Traditional teacher education programmes are heavily 'front-loaded' with most investment at the beginning of a teaching career. Their unit costs can exceed those of university education and may be 50 or more times the annual cost of a primary school place. If the average length of teachers' careers is declining, as it is in some cases as a result of HIV/AIDS, and if the numbers which have to be trained are much larger than current capacity, teacher education programmes with lower costs are needed. The alternative is to revise MDG targets for universalising access and achieving gender equity in primary schooling.
>
> (p. ix)

The MUSTER analysis of provision is detailed and critical. A number of policy concerns are identified, including:

- the lack of coherent national policies towards teacher education, particularly in relation to changing demographic trends;
- the weakness of budgetary systems, including the excessive costs and boarding related costs;

- the limited co-ordination between pre-service and in-service providers; and
- the unwillingness to consider financing through non-governmental sources.

The reports of the surveys of nine large developing countries summarised in Chapters 2 and 3 of this book suggest that, a decade on, little has changed. The MUSTER study is particularly critical of what is taught:

> The MUSTER analyses of teacher education curriculum issues lead to many insights into the quality and relevance of material for existing programmes. The picture these paint is one that suggests that investment in curriculum development is long overdue and that much which is currently available falls short of what is needed and what is possible. Large parts of the teacher education curriculum seem to have been adapted from the academic curricula of school or university, rather than designed for adult learners or for the acquisition of professional knowledge and skills. They seldom recognise the role of relevant experiences, nor the different motivation and learning styles of adults. The curriculum needs to be reconceptualised, but in ways that keep in touch with local context and realities.
>
> (Lewin and Stuart, 2003, p. 28)

The process of reconceptualisation, it is suggested, should involve significant slimming down with focussed use of theoretical frameworks that link to the practical tasks of the teacher. Too often, the MUSTER analysis reports 'Foundation' type courses try to teach far too much theory using texts and research drawn exclusively from rich country contexts. The MUSTER analysis posits these future scenarios, more of the same, managed evolution and radical reform, but it warns against the power embedded in the comfort zones of the old. The first scenario it suggests is only possible if there is a reasonable balance between supply and demand for new teachers and the quality of training is regarded as appropriate. We quote the MUSTER study at length because it is the major piece of research about teacher education in recent years and because its comprehensive analysis of the problems seems substantially similar today.

The research for MUSTER was, however, carried out in the early years of the century. The expansion of EFA programme and the growth in both the number of teachers and the number of unqualified teachers is putting even greater pressure on systems, particularly in countries with large and growing populations. This is reflected in the more recent University of Sussex led CREATE programme (CREATE, 2011) which returns to some of the teacher education themes of the MUSTER study and argues again for reform of teacher education as a priority area. It does so again, however, from within a frame of reference that has the training institution or 'college' as the main focus.

In this context we believe that the 'bricks and mortar' campus institutions, created to train teachers for the twentieth century, will be wholly unable to meet the demands of the present century. That is not to say there is no place for such institutions (and here we are referring to both pre-service and in-service institutional

204   *J. Anamuah-Mensah* et al.

structures) but the role will need redefining. Our view is that if teacher education and training is to have any impact on existing levels of achievement in schools then policy and practice must move to a school-based approach.

The vast majority of teachers in low income countries, for the foreseeable future, cannot hope to access appropriate programmes of qualification, upgrading or professional development through 'out of school' training. Even if the evidence was strong, which it is not, that such provision was effective in improving practice the availability of places is far outstripped by the numbers of teachers now requiring support. Unless a school based approach is adopted, millions of teachers will lose contact with all forms of education and training. Advocacy of a school based approach does not presuppose one particular form or model of such training. Some school based approaches to such training that have gained currency recently involved peer support, mentoring by experienced teachers and other strategies that would not be possible given the context of many low income country school systems. However, building training approaches around the school is now, we believe, an urgent priority.

A recent analysis of teacher development in developing countries (Schwille and Dembélé, 2007) has pointed to the great benefits of using school based training to reduce the gap between what is taught in formal training institutions and the world of schools although it points out how many different models of school based training exists with, as yet, very little evaluative evidence of what works best.

Advances in learning theory and organisational effectiveness also challenge prevailing models of educating teachers. Socio-cultural and constructivist approaches to learning stress the importance of context. Some seminal texts (Brown *et al.*, 1989; Lave and Wenger, 1991) have argued strongly that learning should be situated within the context of practice. Learning is an interpretive process reinforced by past and future experience. The related concept of distributed learning has also achieved some prominence:

> today's most successful communities [businesses, schools] have one thing in common. They know how to transform individual expertise into collective knowledge. They are places where each individual contributes their particular expertise to a shared learning history. The creation of new knowledge is everyone's most important work: joint learning leads to innovation and growth as well as creativity and the development of self-esteem on the part of individuals. Researchers often refer to this as distributed learning.
>
> (Leach and Moon, 2008, p. 74)

These ideas have precipitated a wealth of debate around the notion of workplace learning (Smith, 2003). The concept of school based teacher development, developed as learning, reflects some of this thinking. These ideas, however, do seem to support the idea of an education and training that is much more focussed on and in the school and classroom.

The logic of the analysis points to the need for new models of teacher education and we set out the way this might be approached in the remaining part of

New modes of pre-service training 205

this chapter. But three preliminary points need to be established. The first is that whilst the three (or even five) year full-time preparation is set as a gold standard, any other proposal seems second best. This is unfortunate for we believe many aspects of the new approach ought to be in place even if there was not the contractual pressure of numbers now being experienced. Second, we think it important to be realistic about the nature and profile of those being recruited into teaching. In many countries teacher recruits would not gain a college or university place even if there were places available. For many unqualified teachers the organisation and curriculum of teacher education programmes that treats them as a qualified entrant to higher education is problematic. Our third point is an important qualification. Whilst we believe the structure of teacher education needs rethinking, we are not suggesting that a place does not exist for campus based colleges or universities. We believe that the role of such institutions could be important although it would have to be different than it is today, as we discuss below.

Parameters for new models of teacher education

We believe our analysis points to a range of new parameters through which new teacher education policies and practices can be developed. We want to identify six that seem of sufficient strategic importance to gain the attention of the policy and research communities:

- building one structure for teacher education;
- the necessity of redesigning the teacher education curriculum;
- a needs analysis approach in programme design;
- the creation of flexible forms of teacher education and training;
- developing a networks, hubs and banks concept;
- designing new forms of planning and costing.

Building one structure for teacher education

Existing arrangements for teacher education in many low income countries exhibit a series of increasingly dysfunctional inter-relationships. Thus:

- pre-service education, often provided with a less than adequate curriculum, fails to reach the capacity demands of growing school systems;
- the same pre-service providers take on the task of qualification upgrading of existing teachers (unqualified in part because of the capacity problem identified above) but do so through part-time study (sometimes through distance education) that replicates the less than adequate curriculum currently being taught through campus based pre-service programmes;
- in-service professional development providers are almost all failing to meet even basic needs and demands, however these are defined, and what programmes are offered are almost always unrelated to pre-service or upgrading courses.

206   *J. Anamuah-Mensah et al.*

Some consequences of this situation are highly disruptive. Pre-service providers, for example, resist expanding or foreshortening programmes under the banner of 'maintaining standards' thus creating the conditions in which thousands of unqualified teachers enter the classroom. A significant number of graduates from the pre-service programmes fail to enter teaching thus further increasing the number of unqualified teachers entering the school system. The unqualified teachers, fortunate enough to gain entry to a part-time upgrading, take courses almost wholly unrelated to their daily teaching tasks. Part-time upgrading courses make little reference to prior experience (a point also made in the MUSTER study) and predominantly adopt a 'one year full-time = two years part-time' model. A serving teacher may have to study part-time for six or eight years in order to reach the qualification level of those taking campus based pre-service courses. On achieving that qualification teachers may then use it to gain another occupation thus further increasing the number of unqualified teachers entering schools and wholly wasting the resource input to improve teacher quality.

In-service professional development programmes suffer similar problems although in recent years a number of countries have attempted more systemic approaches. Kenya, for example, invested in a large scale open and distance programme to upskill teachers and improve the quality of head teachers. The United National Relief and Welfare Agency (UNRWA) which has responsibility for schools in the Palestinian refugee camps across the Middle East has undertaken a similar programme. But usually a teacher's experience of professional development is spasmodic with one experience having no connection to the next. And illogical arrangements can be found. In more than one context, for example, unqualified teachers who are in particular need of professional development are not permitted to join their qualified colleagues on in-service courses because they are unqualified!

In terms of professional development, it is rare to find any form of curriculum structure. More common is a list of topics (investigations in primary science, for example) that have no sense of overall purpose or progression. The entitlement of teachers to participate in professional development is rarely articulated.

We would argue strongly that the education provided to teachers needs to be thought of in a holistic way. There would be many ways in which this could be achieved, but all would have the aim of offering an integrated service. There would, also, be many advantages in aligning the structures and responsibilities for teacher education with those that deal with supply, retention and deployment. The need for integration, we suggest, applies at all levels, local, stage/region or federal. Such a holistic approach does not necessarily entail the creation of new agencies or bureaucracies, but it does require coherent planning with clear demarcations of responsibility and accountability. Within such an overall framework there could be possibilities of both public and private forms of provision. More holistic planning presupposes a shared understanding of the purposes of teacher education and how it relates to a teacher's career development.

Redesigning the teacher education curriculum

Globally there have been significant changes in the curriculum of teacher education to make it more practice and competence focussed. A teacher education curriculum more focussed on practice offers the opportunity to conceive of teacher learning in terms of progression and competence rather than merely knowledge acquisition.

This would require some formulation of what the core components of such a curriculum would be. In the preparation of teachers for the primary, basic school the teaching of literacy and numeracy would be essential components. The curriculum in this way becomes school focussed, if not school focussed from the outset. This would be of particular value to teachers undertaking upgrading programmes. It would also provide greater practical relevance and motivation to campus based trainees.

Curriculum designers would be required to think through the relationship between the school curriculum and the forms of teacher subject knowledge required. More often in existing programmes subjects are taught without any reference to the structures and forms and content areas that are to be found in the school curriculum.

We are deliberately avoiding any attempt to suggest a prescription for what a practice focussed curriculum should be. This is contested territory that has to be worked through in specific contexts (not the least almost certainly involving those most concerned, the teachers). Without such a model, however, attempts to move to an integrated model of teacher education are likely to be problematic.

We also believe that the social role played by teachers in local communities should be given greater prominence. The role model dimension of the teacher's task, although perhaps seen through rose-tinted spectacles by some, still has a moral resonance in many contexts, particularly when the school offers the only opportunity to acquire the knowledge and studies necessary for social and economic advancement.

A needs analysis approach in programme design

An integrated approach to teacher education with an explicit curriculum allows a more individualised approach to teacher learning. Most models of a teacher education curriculum are essentially 'one size fits all'. A teacher gaining entry to an upgrading qualification usually follows a curriculum as if they were a beginner. There are a number of reasons why this is unacceptable. First, recognising existing and prior experience and knowledge is one of the central tenets of contemporary ideas about learning. It surely makes sense, therefore, to use a teacher's knowledge in the building and construction of courses. Second, the 'one size fits all' approach mitigates against the upgrading process that contributes directly and immediately to context specific classroom improvements. Third, it is grossly inefficient in the use of resources. Many teachers studying part-time to upgrade their qualifications have to follow a rubric that requires two years' part-time study to

208   *J. Anamuah-Mensah* et al.

equate to one year full-time. This is applied across the board to teachers irrespective of the time they have already spent in the classroom. We believe that some teachers could be fast-tracked to an upgraded qualification with benefits to them and with significant resource savings. Others might need longer.

We have found few examples of such a needs analysis approach. If allied to new models of curriculum and within a more flexible organisational structure, needs analysis could be an important cost-effective approach to improving both pre-service and continuing professional development programmes.

Creating flexible forms of teacher education and training

New modes of provision should, we want to argue, be more flexibly organised. This would assume, as we discuss above, a practice-focussed curriculum and an element of needs analysis. For example, it would be possible to define such a curriculum in terms of levels rather than year studied. Level 1 would cover a range of basic competences, with the associated skills and knowledge base, that would be at the core of a teacher's task (literacy and numeracy, as we have suggested, in the primary school, for example). Structured in terms of modules or units this could well comprise of core curriculum for pre-service, upgrading and in-service programmes. It would be relevant to a newly enrolled student but, crucially, it would be of direct relevance to either a teacher upgrading their qualification or a teacher undertaking a professional development programme. Given the evidence on school performance and pupil achievement in many countries there is a strong case for most teachers in the coming decade participating in competence-based, classroom and school-focussed training.

A teacher education course that is modular or unit based but with curriculum defined in terms of practice and competence rather than the traditional discipline or fields of study could be assessed and recorded through a teacher individual record or portfolio. For serving teachers, we believe the majority, this record would be shared within the school and acknowledged explicitly as both a qualifying and professional development resource. If teacher education systems could seek to achieve successful outcomes universally across a first phase or level of training then significant improvements could be achieved. This would represent a foundation curriculum upon which a level 2 and 3, perhaps 4, could be built.

Education systems would, therefore, be able to monitor progress against a meaningful teacher performance measure. Rather than ask how many qualified teachers the question would be how many have achieved the different levels of practical competence. São Paulo in Brazil is attempting to do this with some success (Bruner *et al.*, 2012). To gain rapid expansion of provision, teachers, singly and in groups, should be able to easily access education and training access. Here, traditional modes of provision could be rapidly expanded in the future by the use of new communication technologies. But without changes in curriculum and course structure such technologies will struggle to find a significant role.

New modes of pre-service training   209

To be clear about what we are suggesting, let us imagine two scenarios, first the traditional approach. John Moanga teaches in a small town, 250 kilometres from a large regional city centre. He is taking an upgrading course and this year is studying a distance programme that carries two credits in Education Administration and Child Development. He attends a tutorial, travelling 60 kms by bus, every six weeks. Neither course relates to the classroom tasks on a daily basis although they do contribute to his awareness of the educational context in which he works. He has to travel to the city to take examinations at the conclusion of each credit.

Second, the emergent new model: Christine Aguti is attending a 'new mode' teacher education upgrading programme. Her portfolio shows that she needs to complete three units at level 1 of the curriculum. Two other teachers in her school have similar needs and they are working together. The three units have the title:

- working with parents;
- using the school environment for basic science;
- the role of story telling in literacy development.

Each unit involves completing four classroom based activities and writing them up. There are resource booklets explaining what they have to do, but Christine is also able to access the resources and correspond with her tutor via her new mobile phone. Every 12 weeks they have a visit from a course tutor.

These are two simple examples of the sorts of shifts in provision that a more flexible and integrated approach to teacher education could involve.

Networks, hubs and banks

New modes of provision need new structures in which to become established. We need a more networked approach that brings teachers and schools together in supported forms of education and training (McCormick *et al.*, 2010).

Essentially we suggest three component parts of teacher education provision. *Clusters* of schools and teachers forming the component parts of the system, *Hubs* that provide the support and *Banks* where resources can be deposited for use by those in the clusters and hubs. What constitutes a cluster, hub or bank would vary according to context. A cluster might comprise the staff of two or three schools, or be much larger. A hub might be a College of Education, university or regional training centre. A bank might be a locally produced set of resources or an international Open Education Resource[1] bank such as the Teacher Education in Sub-Saharan Africa (TESSA) programme (www.tessafrica.net).

Equally the means of communication across the system could be wholly face to face, or involve a combination of new technologies and traditional seminar-tutorial support. Our inclination is to suggest that given the scale of need it is the latter that is likely to be the most feasible and effective over the coming decade. The rapidly evolving potential of interactive electronic, especially mobile, communication systems could play a vital role in this.

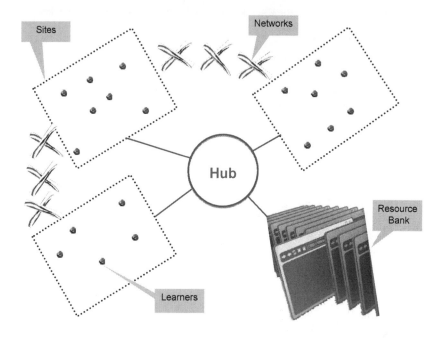

Figure 13.1 A networks, hubs and banks model for teacher development

Designing new forms of planning and costing

The policy process around teachers is often weak. This is particularly true when the rhetoric of purpose has to move into the realms of policy implementation. In our experience systems can be strong on policy formulation but very weak about implementation. There are very substantial barriers to change that can intimidate policy makers.

If reform is to be realised, more sophisticated forms of planning and accountability needs to be in place. Costing (see Chapter 3) is a key component of this, particularly if sustainable systems and programmes are to be successfully set up. We have had some recent experience in looking at the cost structure of teacher education programmes in different countries. Our preliminary experience showed that the designers of programmes often had little knowledge and understanding of the cost consequences of decisions being made. For example, in looking at accredited courses we found the costs of assessment varying from 50 per cent to 5 per cent across upgrading courses with very similar purposes. There needs to be a more explicit modelling of costs and work is in progress to develop tools for this.

The balance of costs going into different elements of programme or course design needs careful consideration. Almost all such activity involves major areas of design:

New modes of pre-service training 211

1. *teams* – through attendance at study centres and/or through open and distance learning resources;
2. *support* – through local and in school systems;
3. *quality assurance* – perhaps delivered through the support system;
4. *assessment* – particularly on accredited courses, but also in some form of professional development programmes generally.

Attention to costing, in our experience, markedly improves the quality of planning. Where external donor funding is supporting reform, then planning and costing models may well exist, but these often fail to extend to detailed planning, costing and implementation. There is much work and research to be carried out in this relatively neglected aspect of teacher education.

In setting out these issues, we do not seek to prescribe a particular type of course structure or provision. We do suggest, however, that each of these six parameters has to be considered in course design. And we strongly believe that the starting point for rethinking teacher education is the school. The argument for this is logistical, in terms of meeting the scale of need and educational in looking at the most appropriate learning context for the teacher's professional development. We do not suggest that the school should work in isolation and hence our interest in clusters and networks, enhanced by the sorts of communication technologies now available to us. Neither the teacher or the school can function effectively in isolation but more creative and innovative ways of linking the school to expertise and experience urgently need to be explored.

Note

1 Open Educational Resources, pioneered by the Massachusetts Institute of Technology (MIT) in the United States, are web-based resources freely available for any user to adapt, if relevant, for their own use in their own context.

14 The 'new' new technology

Exploiting the potential of mobile communications and open educational resources

Tom Power

Introduction

Education is increasingly seen as 'the' core component of international development (UNICEF 2005); indeed Gordon Brown, a former British prime minister, identified education as the key to the ultimate development goal: the empowerment of the poor, and of the world's poorest countries (Steer and Wathne 2009). But there are multiple and complex challenges in providing free, high quality education to all the world's children; in most developing nations, there are issues of grade repetition, low leaving age, teacher absenteeism, teacher shortages, building shortages, double shifts and large class sizes (Glewe and Kramer 2005), as well as a predominance of under-trained or untrained teachers (UNESCO 2005).

These challenges are often most acutely experienced in rural areas, where 70 per cent of the world's poor live. Of the 72 million children in the world who have no access to even the most rudimentary education, estimates suggest that around 80 per cent of these live in rural areas (Mulkeen 2005; UNESCO 2007). Rural teachers face substantial challenges beyond those encountered by their urban colleagues, including isolation, lack of access to reference and other teaching materials, and poor management and support. Indeed, for many, the prospect of teaching in rural communities is sufficiently difficult and daunting that trained teachers try to avoid rural placements or relocate to towns and cities and soon as they are able: 'people are going to kick against posting to the very places where their services are needed' (Hedges 2002).

In poor rural communities across Sub-Saharan Africa and South Asia, there is a pressing need to increase both the number of teachers and the quality of teaching. In order to achieve Universal Primary Education (UPE) by 2015, another 1.9 million teachers will be needed, with more than half of these needed in Sub-Saharan Africa (Education for All 2011); some estimates have suggested figures approximately an order of magnitude higher (Global Campaign for Education 2006). But increasingly, the focus of attention is moving from simply increasing the numbers of teachers, to improving the quality of teaching. 'One of the most pressing, and neglected dimensions has been the critical issue of quality. The right to education is not merely the right to a place in the school-room, but the right to learn' (Global Campaign for Education 2008).

The 'new' new technology   213

There is a pressing need to consider how best to train teachers, in order to provide even a basic quality of education; models of Teacher Professional Development (TPD) must be able to operate at sufficient scale, pace and cost to provide the necessary numbers of teachers to meet the need, but must also adequately equip teachers with knowledge and skills such that their classroom practices create genuine opportunities for student learning, agency and growth. This applies equally to creating new teachers through pre-service training (PRESET), and to up-skilling the large numbers of currently unqualified or under-qualified teachers through in-service training (INSET).

Even if it were possible for conventional schools, colleges or universities to physically accommodate the number of teachers to be trained or up-skilled, traditional approaches take new or current teachers away from the classroom for significant amounts of time (Deane 2006), potentially for up to four years.

There is also some evidence that centre-based 'face-to-face' training may not be particularly effective in changing classroom practices. Within the educational research literature, there are very few examples of TPD programmes that are able to show evidence of improving students' learning outcomes (see reviews by Lawless and Pelligrino 2007; Wilson and Berne 1999). Whilst there are many other contributing or limiting factors affecting students' learning outcomes, one possible explanation may be that traditional TPD programmes have limited impact upon classroom practice, and therefore limited impact upon student learning activities and outcomes. For example, in reviewing the outcomes of long-term TPD for English Language Teaching (ELT) amongst rural teachers in Bangladesh, Rahman found 'most reform attempts have suffered from a lack of planning . . . not providing supportive resources . . . *In spite of a general improvement in Teachers knowledge about ELT . . . there is little evidence of much difference in classroom practice*' (Rahman *et al.* 2006. Emphasis mine).

As we enter the second decade of the twenty-first century, there are many who would argue the need for a new architecture of TPD, in order to train sufficient numbers of teachers to meet the challenges, and to adequately equip these teachers so that they are able to create spaces or settings in which quality learning activities may take place. Moon (2007b) outlines possible foundations for such architecture, with four important assertions:

1.   The 'bricks and mortar' institutions of twentieth-century TPD cannot hope to meet the needs of the twenty-first century.
2.   Most TPD will happen in schools, not in TPD institutions.
3.   To impact on student achievement, TPD will be practically focussed on improving the day-to-day work of teachers.
4.   New technologies, particularly new forms of communication, have the potential to transform professional learning.

The first three assertions beg the question 'what might a programme of practically focused, school-based TPD look like?', whilst the final assertion leads us to ask 'how might new communications technologies support, enhance or transform such a programme of TPD?'.

Power et al. (2009) describe a school-based model of TPD as a particular instance of Open and Distance Learning (ODL). They argue that a school-based ODL approach to TPD enables student-teachers to study in their own time, and allows them to keep their employment, continue to care for their families and to hold their responsibility in their community. Such models of TPD allow teachers in remote areas to participate, whereas attending a conventional course would involve long travel (often slow because of poor rural infrastructure), extra cost and further time away from personal commitments and responsibilities. For these reasons, they argue such an approach is particularly suited to female students (Deane 2006), possibly reducing barriers to, and improving representation of, women in the profession.

Walsh and Power (2011) offer an evolution of this idea, describing a school-based model of TPD not as an instance of ODL, but rather as a specific form of work-based learning. Participation in *new classroom activities* is at the heart of teachers' professional development in this model, being the primary driver for transforming both their professional knowledge and practice.

There are two layers of support provided to teachers, to enable their participation in such activities:

- The first layer of support is always 'on hand' to the teacher while they are in their school; such support includes teaching resources to be used directly within the new classroom activities, and professional development resources for teachers to engage with in preparation for, or reflection upon, carrying out the new classroom activities.

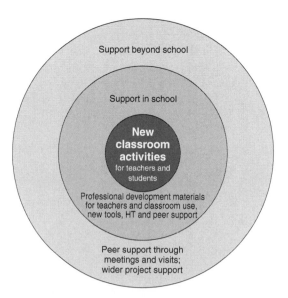

Figure 14.1 EIA's work-based model to support changes in classroom practice (after Walsh and Power 2011)

The *'new' new technology*   215

- The second layer provides more traditional *support beyond school*, in the form of workshops and cluster meetings, providing an ongoing programme of training in community language teaching practices, and providing a forum for sharing, reflecting and problem solving amongst a wider group of teachers.

In such a representation of school based TPD, teachers learn primarily through carrying out new activities in their professional practice. They are supported in this by their peers (in school, and in local networks around their school), and through the materials and tools provided. This is not traditional 'open distance learning' as it is not primarily 'self study', nor is it traditional 'teacher training' in which the training and support is offered at a centre that is physically and conceptually 'distant' from the teacher's context of practice: their classroom. Rather, in this representation of TPD, most of the teachers' learning is very 'close' to the context of their practice – their classroom and their school – and support is provided within that context, or close to it.

These examples provide some hints as to what a practically focussed programme of school-based TPD might look like, which will be expanded upon further in the subsequent case studies. But what of the communications technologies: in what ways might they have a transforming role within TPD? I suggest three distinct, but potentially inter-related, roles for new communications technology:

1. Supporting the collaborative design of TPD course structure, content, activities and resources, enabling institutions operating in diverse contexts to collaborate (Power et al. 2009), whilst retaining 'authentic pedagogy' (Leach and Moon 2008) for their own student-teachers.
2. Supporting the delivery of, and participation in, TPD courses to student-teachers (Leach *et al.* 2005; Walsh and Power 2011), providing them with materials and tools for:

   a. Teachers' own professional learning, providing access to new subject, pedagogic and school knowledge (Banks *et al.* 1999), as well as tools for planning and reflecting upon teaching practice.
   b. Integral use within new classroom practices with students.

3. Supporting teacher professional networks (Leach *et al.* 2005; Power and Sankale 2009).

There is a need to consider the deployment of ICTs in support of such roles with significant thought and care. Many approaches to the use of ICT in development have focussed upon technology, rather than the social practices and contexts in which the technology is intended to be used; these are typically spectacular in their failure to deliver educational outcomes, with some going as far as to suggest projects which over-invest in procurement of technology rather than development of content and practices should be subject to investigation (Pimienta 2007). Beyond the mere financial wastefulness of inappropriate uses of ICTs, some have suggested a more insidious effect: ICTs, particularly computers, are imbued with

216　*T. Power*

so many positive connotations that they may take on an almost totemic value, as symbols of 'modern' or 'quality' education. When *computers in schools* are deployed in ways that fail to deliver positive educational outcomes, this can do significant harm to the self-esteem of teachers and communities, and contribute to a culture of blame (Power and Porteous 2009).

By contrast, the case studies considered in the next section both show uses of communications technology that are driven by the social practices being engaged in, and which are appropriate to the settings in which they are used. In the remainder of this chapter, I focus upon the first two roles identified above. Whilst the third role is well researched and evidenced (as computer mediated communication) in resource rich contexts, most current studies in development contexts are largely restricted to the somewhat limited affordances of SMS text messaging.

The following case studies illustrate how both the collaborative design and the delivery of practically-focussed TPD programmes have been enabled through two particular forms of communication technology: Open Educational Resources (OERs) and mobile phones.

Case studies

Case study 1: Teacher Education in Sub-Saharan Africa (TESSA) and OERs

> Perhaps the most successful of all the OER projects we have heard about is TESSA, the consortium on mainly African institutions that are using OERs to empower teachers and change pedagogy in countries all over Africa.
>
> (Sir John Daniel, 2008)

TESSA represents Africa's largest teacher education research community, extending across 13 Teacher Training Institutes (TTIs) in Ghana, Kenya, Nigeria, Rwanda, South Africa, Sudan, Tanzania, Uganda and Zambia, together with international organisations. TESSA's key purpose is to use the power of this Africa-wide consortium to improve access to, and raise the quality of, all aspects of teacher education and training. Specifically, the TESSA OERs (including text, audio and other media) focus on developing teachers' classroom practice in the key curriculum areas of language, mathematics, science, social studies and the arts, and life skills. To achieve this, the TESSA consortium has developed an extensive range of high quality, multilingual OERs and systems. At their heart are activities for teachers to carry out in classrooms, to improve teaching and learning. The resources are designed to support all teachers, including those with little or no formal training.

The TESSA OERs provide a number of starting points for active experimentation within teachers' own classrooms, the site of teachers' learning. The activities extend teacher's understanding of the fundamental principles of effective learning. They offer connections between ideas, strategies and subjects, and emphasise the importance of teacher's own reflections on their experiences.

The 'new' new technology 217

Although some teachers have accessed TESSA OERs directly through the project website (www.tessafrica.net) and used them in their practice, most of the almost half a million participating teachers do not have regular access to computers or the Internet. Instead, TESSA teachers typically come across the materials in print, as an integral part of the training they receive through their participating TTI.

> I have enjoyed using the materials because they make classroom activities simple and easy . . . Pupils are now improving in their performance and it has helped me improve my teaching skills.
>
> (student teacher, Nigeria)

TESSA, using communications technologies and OERs primarily at the level of institutional collaboration and course design, required only minimal access to computers and the Internet for those designing and implementing the materials, and no access to technology for participating teachers.

What is particularly interesting is the way in which the use of OERs enabled TTIs to collaborate and pool their strengths, whilst at the same time being able to adapt the materials to their own particular settings and purposes. Collaborative materials creation started with an initial core of study units across the five curriculum areas. In each curriculum area, a multi-national team of authors worked to create the first iteration of the TESSA materials. Teams drew on case studies, experiences and existing resources from across the region. Curriculum authoring teams were facilitated by a team leader from an African institution, supported by a partner from the Open University, who worked together to ensure consistency and progression within the materials.

These draft materials were refined through consortium workshops and developmental testing in each of the nine countries and subject to rigorous quality assurance procedures. A key feature of this common core is its highly structured nature. This is designed to enable efficient creation of materials, as well as cost-effective and easy localisation for particular contexts.

> The TESSA materials are easily located in the environment around us without having to travel long distances at high cost, thereby having first hand experience at less cost.
>
> (teacher, Tanzania)

The original core materials have then been contextualised or localised into ten country formats, including versions in Arabic, French and Kiswahili. The localisation, undertaken by teams of teacher educators in each country, adapted the materials to reflect the local place and culture, curriculum, school environment and language. In total the TESSA consortium has created 750 study units.

The capacity and flexibility of TESSA OERs allows for a wide variety of implementation models, for both pre- and in-service courses and at informal, institutional and national levels. Through the TESSA collaboration, all consortium

218   *T. Power*

institutions have well developed plans for integration and use of the TESSA OERs into a range of different courses and programmes, involving up to 500,000 teachers in 2009 to 2010.

> Using these resources is the best way to teach . . . I have used group discussions which resulted in good responses from my students, who have thoroughly understood the lessons . . . I have found myself as a teacher.
>
> (student teacher, Sudan)

Case study 2: English in Action (EIA) and mobile phones

English in Action is a nine-year DFID funded programmed, requested by the Government of Bangladesh, to improve the English language competence of 25 million people in Bangladesh, with approximately half of those being adult learners in the general population, and half being students in primary and secondary schools. The BBC World Service Trust is delivering broadcast, newsprint and online services for adults; the Open University is working with local partners to deliver school-based TPD, with overall project management by BMB Mott McDonald.

Materials for adults are provided through a low-cost Interactive Voice Recognition (IVR) service 'BBC Janala', available through any mobile phone, and also through the mobile website www.bbcjanala.com. Janala, which provides brief English language learning audio clips and activities on demand, has proved extremely popular, with over 750,000 calls being made to the mobile phone service in its first month alone (December 2009). Janala currently has over two million users.

Whereas in Janala, EIA uses the mobile phone to provide breadth (providing small amounts of audio content to large numbers of people – anyone with a mobile phone), in its TPD activities, EIA uses the mobile phone to provide depth (providing extensive content in audio and video, but only to participating teachers).

For primary teachers, principal teaching resources are a series of audio materials on the Nokia C1-01, a cheap and relatively basic mobile phone developed primarily for African and South Asian markets. The audio resources are pre-loaded onto a micro-SD memory card, providing several gigabytes of storage capacity; this enables EIA to provide audio resources designed to accompany every lesson in the national textbook series, for all five years of the primary curriculum. In total, each primary teacher has access to 355 audio files on their mobile phone, including dramatisations, songs, stories and a cast of characters from a fictional school. In some ways, the audio resources for primary are similar to those that might be used in Interactive Radio Instruction (IRI), but with much greater emphasis on teacher and pupil agency, creativity and independence than typical IRI materials. Teachers have a printed 'activity guide' for each year, that suggest a range of activities for each lesson, to do before and after using the audio resources; these activities have also been developed for every individual lesson. Additionally

The 'new' new technology   219

teachers have associated 'hard copy' classroom materials, including posters and flashcards. All of the materials are designed to accompany and extend the lessons in the national textbook series, and to help teachers adopt a more communicative approach to covering the proscribed content.

For secondary teachers, the main teaching resources are also audio files, representing all of the English readings within the textbook series, and enhanced by additional stories, songs and other materials; the secondary materials bear no resemblance to traditional IRI materials, and are simply resources for teachers to use in classroom activities. To this extent, the mobile phone plays the role of 'the classroom in your pocket' (Power and Thomas 2007), providing a rich range of classroom resources that teachers can carry 'in their pocket'.

In addition to the classroom resources described above, there are further teacher professional development materials, provided in audiovisual form on the mobile phone. These include examples of 'classroom language'; videos showing suggested activities, making explicit possible approaches to classroom management and organisation; and examples of techniques being carried out effectively, or problematically, for teachers to see and discuss. To this extent, the mobile phone acts as the 'trainer in your pocket' (Walsh 2011).

The first cohort of 700 EIA teachers (2010–2011) took part in an extensive research, monitoring and evaluation programme seeking to:

1.   understand views and experiences of teaching and learning English;
2.   monitor changes in classroom practice;
3.   independently evaluate any gains in the ability to communicate in English.

Studies focussing upon teachers included quantitative observations of almost all teachers' classroom practice, together with in-depth observations, interviews and questionnaires with approximately a fifth of the teachers taking part. In addition to this, over 1,500 secondary students responded to a questionnaire, and 900 students took part in individual and group interviews.

Findings indicate some success in changing views on English language teaching and learning, establishing the necessary preconditions for a more communicative approach: most teachers now agree that the focus of their English classes is on communication, explaining grammar as necessary to aid understanding (EIA 2011a).

Furthermore, there is strong evidence of basic changes to classroom practice, including substantial increases in the use of spoken English (now accounting for 71–88 per cent of all speaking in English lessons, by teachers or students, across primary and secondary phases), with student talk time increasing from minimal levels to approximately a third of all lesson time (EIA 2011b).

Perhaps most strikingly, there is also strong evidence of improvements in teachers' and students' proficiency in spoken English. Assessors from Trinity College carried out diagnostic (GESE) interviews of English language competence, providing a comprehensive baseline and post-intervention assessment of almost half of the teachers and over 1,000 students. Findings show statistically significant improvements in teachers' and students' oral/aural communication in English language (EIA 2010a, 2010b, 2011c), as shown in Figures 14.2 and 14.3.

In 2012, a further 5,000 teachers will begin TPD with EIA, making it one of the largest ELT TPD projects in the world. By 2017, EIA aims to have trained over 100,000 teachers in Bangladesh.

Analysis

In the first case study, we see that OERs have provided a mechanism through which TTIs from diverse countries, languages and cultures have been able to work together to collaboratively develop 'practically focused' TPD activities and materials. I would suggest that working in such a collaborative manner has enabled each institution to contribute to the production of a quantity and quality of

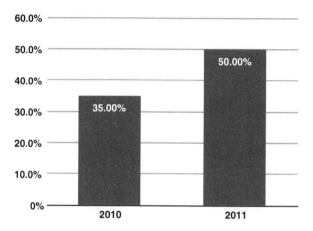

Figure 14.2 Primary student's GESE pass rate pre-/post- EIA

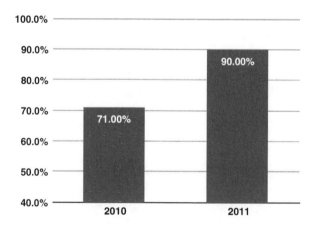

Figure 14.3 Secondary student's GESE pass rate pre-/post- EIA

The 'new' new technology   221

materials and activities that would have been almost impossible for any individual institution to achieve. But the flexible nature of OERs has meant that whilst the essence of each module or activity would be the same, in whichever institution's materials a teacher might encounter them, much of the exemplification and illustration has been adapted to fit the particular culture and context of that institution. However, whilst the power of OERs underpins much of the design and development of TESSA resources, and any teacher with access to the Internet may access the resources, most teachers using TESSA materials do so through print materials, made available through their TTI.

Since the early days of TESSA materials development, a number of other OER initiatives are being developed for African educators, perhaps most notably OER@ AVU (http://oer.avu.org), a project hosted by the African Virtual University, and recently voted 'best emerging initiative' in the OpenCourseWare 'People's Choice Awards' (Education-Portal 2011). The Commonwealth of Learning is also currently developing materials for a new project, 'OERs for ELT', working in partnership with institutions throughout Africa and the Commonwealth to develop OERs in multimedia and traditional text formats to support school-based training for teachers working in the upper basic education sector.

However, whilst the power of OERs to support the collaborative development of practically-focussed, school-based TPD programmes is increasingly recognised, most of the teachers who might benefit from using such OERs, at least in Sub-Saharan Africa and South Asia, are currently unlikely to have individual access to the tools (computers and the Internet) that these OERs are currently designed to be accessed through. Instead, teachers typically access the OER materials in traditional printed text formats, or through occasional use of Internet cafes or IT centres within TTIs.

By contrast, EIA has designed multimedia materials specifically to be accessed through the communications technology that most of the target audience do have regular independent access to: the mobile phone. It is evident from the literature that mobile technologies offer significant flexibility in relation to 'anytime/anywhere' learning (see Naismith *et al.* 2004; Leach *et al.* 2005). Some have also suggested that language learning may be one of the disciplines particularly likely to benefit from widespread ownership of mobile devices such as phones and media players (e.g. Kukulska-Hulme 2006; Power and Shrestha 2010).

Yet whilst the use of mobile phones for TPD may hold significant promise, particularly in development contexts, it is largely absent from the literature. Most studies demonstrating the potential of mobile phones are outside the field of education, with notable exceptions such as the work of Hendrikz (2006) or Sankale (Power and Sankale 2009), both of whom have explored the use of SMS for student support.

EIA has powerfully demonstrated at least a 'proof of concept' for a fuller use of mobile phones as a learning technology within school-based TPD programmes. EIA is already operating at large scale, at least by the standards of educational studies, and should soon be operating at a scale proportionate to the ELT TPD need in Bangladesh.

222 T. Power

The question I want to explore in the final section of this chapter is whether or not the power of OERs and mobile phones might be combined in supporting TPD within a development context. To address this question, I will hypothetically apply aspects of the TESSA and EIA methodologies to the current ELT TPD needs of South Sudan.

Application

Why South Sudan? As the most recent nation state to be recognised by the United Nations, emerging from the longest running conflict in Africa, with arguably one of the poorest performing education systems in the world, the challenges facing South Sudan exemplify issues that are common to many settings in Sub-Saharan Africa and South Asia. I have also had the opportunity carry out fieldwork immediately before and after South Sudan's very recent independence, reviewing some of the current donor funded education initiatives and scoping the ELT needs for possible future funding (Power and Simpson 2011).

In a listing of net primary enrolment rates, South Sudan is ranked second lowest; and for secondary enrolment, South Sudan is the lowest ranked of 134 countries, with only 34,000 secondary students in the country. Half of all 18-year-olds have never attended school. The situation for girls is predictably worse, with just 37 per cent of primary students and 12 per cent of teachers being female. In a system that should offer eight years of primary education, only 13 per cent of schools

Figure 14.4 Classroom damaged by fighting and neglect, but still in use for teaching 47 primary children in P4

offer the whole primary cycle. Sixty per cent of teachers did not complete primary education themselves (UNESCO 2011b).

Many schools were abandoned or damaged over decades of fighting. Figure 14.4 below shows a typical classroom in such a school. The classroom is still in use, for primary grade 4 children. You can see the teacher being interviewed in this class at http://youtu.be/H8cFomBMdVg.

In most states there are over 500 school-aged children for each classroom; in Jonglie state, there are over 1,000 children for each classroom; in Unity state, there are over 2,000 children for each classroom. The national Education Management Information System (EMIS) estimates that of the 24,000 primary teachers supported by the Ministry of Education, 96 per cent have no formal teaching qualifications, and 63 per cent have had no teacher training of any kind (Power and Simpson 2011).

In the period following Sudanese independence in 1956, English played a role as the medium of instruction in most schools in the southern states until, under immense pressure from Khartoum, it was supplanted by Arabic in the mid-1990s. In the newly independent South Sudan, the constitution refers to English 'as a major language of South Sudan', positioning English as an official working language, and as the medium of instruction in schools. Yet South Sudan is linguistically very diverse: although four major ethno-linguistic groups (Dinka, Nuer, Zande and Bari) account for two-thirds of the population, there are some 50 mother tongues present. In addition, there is a continuum of Arabic running from north (Khartoum Arabic) to south (Juba Arabic, a creole).

Although the language education policy is for children to be schooled in two languages – the mother tongue and English – there may be insufficient learning materials or trained teachers to implement either aspect of such a policy effectively at this time. Whilst utilising English may represent the easiest choice for government, in so far as it allows for a uniform set of teaching materials to be produced in a single language for the entire population, most teachers do not have adequate English language skills to benefit from pre-service or in-service training related to the new curriculum, or to engage with new curriculum materials written in English.

The lack of English language skills amongst the teaching workforce is likely to be a significant obstacle to implementing the new curriculum. In four of the ten states (Upper Nile, Western B.E.G., Unity and Warap), up to 80 per cent of teachers are reported to be Arabic trained, with very low-level English language skills.

Windle Trust International (WTI) is the largest provider of ELT TPD, currently working with approximately 3,000 teachers. WTI use face-to-face training with groups of 25–30 teachers, typically running over three months, during which time teachers attend two hours of training at the end of each school day. From observation, much of the training provided appears to be in the form of 'grammar translation'; the teachers I spoke to found it difficult to identify any changes in their practice as a result of the training.

Participating teachers (many of whom are 'volunteers' receiving no salary from the state and only a small 'contribution' from the community via school fees) typically have significant journeys to and from the training each day. WTI offer support through the funding of bus-fares or the provision of bicycles. Most of the teachers I spoke to at one WTI training session had spent around two hours cycling from their schools to attend the training; this suggests teachers are spending approximately 20 hours per week travelling, in order to participate in five two-hour training sessions, after finishing their morning teaching.

The South Sudan Interactive Radio Instruction (SSIRI) service, provided through the Education Development Centre, has also worked with a cumulative total of about 3,000 teachers, although the project director notes that there is high 'churn' amongst the teaching workforce, believing many who had participated may have moved out of the education system.

SSIRI hope to participate in the English language component of USAID's forthcoming Teacher Professional Development Initiative (TPDI), which is likely to reach about one-third of the current teaching workforce (9,000 out of 26,000) over the next three years.

According to the national EMIS, South Sudan has approximately two million children of primary school age, and 26,000 primary teachers, including volunteers. Therefore, to reach the government target ratio of one teacher to 50 students, 14,000 additional teachers would need to be trained. There are some notable TTIs involved in INSET, including Yei, Kotobi, and there is an established English Language Centre at Juba University, but current rates of training are barely above replacement, and are insufficient to begin to close this gap within the foreseeable future.

Figure 14.5 WTI teachers' bicycles, outside a training session

The 'new' new technology   225

In addition to this, a further one million school-aged children are expected to be added to the population in the coming years, as refugee families return to South Sudan following independence. This would suggest a 50 per cent increase in the teaching workforce, just to maintain current student–teacher ratios.

So, in such a context, might practically focussed school-based TPD, OERs and mobile phones be of any relevance?

I think perhaps the most important thing to note is the significance of Moon's first assertion: in such a context, traditional 'bricks and mortar' institutions, and 3–4 year full-time teacher training courses, are simply incapable of meeting the scale of need presented. Such an approach alone would struggle even to maintain replacement, and cannot realistically hope to either keep pace with likely student population growth, or reduce the student–teacher ratio. The need for an alternative architecture for TPD in South Sudan is both real and pressing.

Some form of school-based TPD seems essential, in order to reach the numbers of teachers required (both INSET and PRESET), within a reasonable timeframe and cost. A school-based programme of TPD may save teachers enormous amounts of time, vastly reducing opportunity costs, compared to centre-based training, freeing up perhaps 20 hours of teachers' time per week, compared to the most common current format of ELT TPD. Such an approach may also be significantly more likely to result in improved classroom practices, than current TPD initiatives.

At the moment, approaches appear quite piecemeal – there are a number of different donors, projects and interventions, all with various strengths and weaknesses, but all tackling similar challenges. If the various TTIs, NGOs and donors could be brought together, in a similar way to the collaboration within the TESSA consortium, there is a possibility that they could all 'punch above the weight' of any individual institution or project, whilst significantly lowering the costs of materials development, and thereby increasing the value for money of their own TPD activities. Yet as demonstrated by TESSA, the flexibility of OERs may allow the same 'core' of materials to be adapted to the needs of centre-based full-time PRESET in TTIs, school-based INSET supported by NGOs, and even school-based PRESET.

The growing 'OER movement' in Africa means that an the institutions and projects operating in South Sudan need not take on such challenges alone. They could potentially also draw upon the strength of other institutions across Africa and beyond, perhaps through existing OER networks such as TESSA, OER@ AVU or COL.

EIA demonstrates the potential of the mobile phone as a delivery mechanism for bringing audiovisual TPD and classroom materials into the hands of rural teachers. Within an appropriate context of support (see Figure 14.1), these materials have contributed to substantial changes in classroom practice and learning outcomes. If donor funding were used to support the participation of Sudanese institutions and NGOs in developing OERs for ELT and TPD, the resulting audiovisual materials should be developed from the outset with the intention of being used flexibly by teachers, through their mobile phones, for 'anywhere/anytime'

226 *T. Power*

learning, and for use with students. This would mean that teachers and students could have exposure to appropriate model language, and new classroom practices, directly in their school setting.

Summary

The argument for a 'new architecture' of TPD for development seems compelling; in some contexts, such as South Sudan, it is hard to see how traditional twentieth-century approaches to teacher training could provide a response that is appropriate to the scale of need. At the end of the first decade of the twenty-first century, there are a number of large scale projects emerging, that are beginning to provide some indication both of the nature of this new architecture, and the potential scale and impact that such approaches may be capable of.

School-based approaches to TPD, which leverage the power of OERs to facilitate institutional collaboration, and of affordable mobile phones to facilitate delivery and support new classroom activities, have the potential to reach a very large scale (TESSA materials are currently reaching approximately half a million teachers; EIA aims to reach over ten million students), whilst driving down per-capita costs of training, in comparison to predominantly face-to-face methods.

However, whilst reaching a large scale, TESSA also shows the importance of ensuring local relevance of TPD materials: that a 'one size fits all' approach is neither desirable, nor necessary. In EIA, the TPD materials are *highly* localised to the particular culture and context of the Bangladeshi teachers, and very tightly adapted to the national textbook series. OER collaborations may provide a means for national institutions, NGOs and projects to tap into the expertise and effort of wider Pan-African and global endeavours, yet produce materials that have the 'flavour' of their own country.

Of course, the most significant issue for TPD is whether or not it is effective in changing the knowledge, beliefs and practices of teachers, and through that, the learning outcomes of students. EIA at least demonstrates a 'proof of concept' for practical school-based TPD being effective in changing teachers' minds and practices, and students learning, at scale.

Further work is needed to continue the conceptual and practical development of this new architecture for TPD, through projects and collaborations operating at appropriate scale to deliver impact.

Current OER projects for TPD in the African context (e.g. AVU, COL ELT) should research and develop ways that their audiovisual materials, currently requiring computer access to the Internet, could be adapted for access by teachers through mobile phones.

Future projects must ensure they have robust, independent research, monitoring and evaluation, to be able to demonstrate impact on classroom practice and learning outcomes, and further work is required to explore the comparative costings and cost-effectiveness of school-based TPD against traditional face-to-face methodologies.

15 Reorientating the agenda around teacher education and development

Bob Moon and Abdurrahman Umar

Globally there is an almost insatiable demand for teachers. The needs in the schooling sector have been well recorded. Successive Global Monitoring Reports from UNESCO, the World Bank and other international organisations point up the shortfalls and the large number of para-professionals recruited to make up the shortfalls in qualified teachers. The figures supplied from national offices are not always reliable or up to date but the trends are clear. The expansion of school systems in low income countries is going to continue unabated for the foreseeable future. The basic education sector, despite much progress, still has some way to go in achieving Education for All and meeting the Millennium Development Goals. Population growth will also play a role in expanding provision at this level. The growth in basic education and the wider economic context is fuelling demand for secondary and higher education. There is also a significant interest in expanding pre-school education. All emergent economies are seeking to expand vocational education and training.

The increased need for teachers comes just as the pool of available teachers appears insufficient to meet demand. In economies growing at the rates of Brazil, China, India and Sub-Saharan Africa new structures of employment are appearing. The sort of person who traditionally became a teacher is now lured away to other knowledge-based occupations. Those who become teachers are subject to similar temptations. The teacher retention rates in many school systems hover around 50 per cent or thereabouts after five years. Many qualification upgrading courses, rather than contributing to the improvement of the school system, function as a bridge to higher paid jobs, with improved status, outside education.

These sorts of issues are not confined to developing world contexts. In some of the richer parts of the world teacher shortages are endemic, particularly in times of economic growth. Such shortages are particularly acute in some subject areas at secondary level. Mathematicians and scientists are in very short supply almost everywhere (Moon 2003). These trends are unlikely to be reversed. This is especially true in those countries likely to experience considerable economic growth in the coming decades.

With growing demand but limited supply teacher quality has become a major concern of governments. This is not confined to policy arenas. Parents and local communities are beginning to give voice to concerns about quality. Again, this is

228   *B. Moon and A. Umar*

a worldwide phenomenon. Political leaders like Bill Clinton and Tony Blair made community misgivings about the quality of schooling a major plank of their election manifestos. This was more than just a political idea. They were tuning into a concern amongst parents and the wider community that was already there. The same can be seen in South Africa today as the Mandela Foundation report (2005) on education in rural communities, Emerging Voices, graphically recounts. In India pupil and parental demonstrations in demand of adequate teachers are not uncommon. One web photo collection shows a graphic picture of girls in Rajasthan protesting the lack of qualified teachers (www.mattconsidine.photoshelter.com).

This growing concern about teacher quality reflects complementary forces at work. It seems inevitable that with the expansion of schooling the newly educated will become more critical and preoccupied with the quality of schooling their children receive. At the same time parents, even those with minimal schooling, see the social and economic benefits of education in the new employment structures. Given these pressures concern about the quality of schools and teachers will almost certainly grow, not diminish.

The earlier chapters in this book provide more detailed accounts of these trends and the implications for teacher education and teacher quality. This chapter seeks to distil the descriptions and analyses in ways that provide indicators for policy makers about the way these challenges can be addressed. Some researchers and commentators have expressed concern about the capacity of policy systems to respond (Lewin and Stuart 2003) but it does seem that the modes of analysis and frames of mind necessary to meet, sometimes acute, demands have only just been emerging. We see the GMR for 2005, for example, as particularly significant. It chose to focus on quality in a way that brought together a range of gathering concerns. And it set the agenda for debate in national systems and international organisations which have acquired considerable momentum. Teacher education is at the core of the quality debate.

The evidence and analyses in this book point, we suggest, to the clear message that 'business as usual', to use Paul Bennell's phrase (Bennell 2004) for teacher education and training is not an option. Without change the numbers and proportions of unqualified teachers, in many countries, will rise and there will be little improvement in the access serving teachers have to upgrading and professional development opportunities. The need for teachers resonates with the 'supply side' responsibilities of government and recent analyses have suggested that refining the process of top-down governmental intervention does have significant long-term consequences for educational improvement (Banerjee and Duflo 2011). Look, for example, at the situation in India. As Chapter 5 indicated there are 5.7 million teaching posts across the country. Currently 523,000 are vacant. Government policies in place to reduce class sizes and ensure universal access to primary education require an additional 510,000 over and above current vacancies. Well over a million extra teachers are required. The scale of in-service professional development need, if it is to have any impact on literacy and numeracy levels and primary school completion rates, is significantly larger. Overall figures mask glaring regional inequalities. The Bordia Report (2010) in India set out the figures state by state. In Delhi the proportion of unqualified teachers is 0.08 per cent, whilst in Arunchal Pradesh (a state with minimal teacher training capacity) it is 71.21 per cent. In Bihar the teacher training capacity is currently just under 7,500 places whilst the need in the coming few years is well over 300,000 teachers. And, in addition, in Bihar, 45 per cent of existing teachers are unqualified. Similar statistics apply to states such as Orissa, Uttar Pradesh and West Bengal, areas of high population, demographic growth and rural poverty.

These sorts of figures, as the case studies in this book indicate, are to be found in many parts of the world. Policy systems, however, have often failed to keep pace with the scale of need and demand. Teachers do not feature in the Millennium Development Goals. The MDG's Task Force interim report on universal primary education (Birdsall *et al.*, 2005) did make a strong plea for a focus on teaching and learning and there have been signs that this is increasingly recognised (see Chapter 7 for example). But overall it would appear that the policy options around teacher education remain orientated to the institutional structures of the last rather than present century. This is also true of research which has tended to focus on institutional training rather than other approaches. The MUSTER programme, for example, highly important and influential as it was, stayed very much within the parameters of conventional training models. We suggest that there are seven interrelated factors, looking beyond traditional institutional structures, that have to be addressed if significant reform and progress is to be achieved; these are:

- recognising that solutions to the problem of qualifying, upgrading and providing ongoing professional development opportunities must go beyond existing institutional structures (*the numbers analysis*);
- re-examining the length of pre-service training that is feasible and necessary and linking it to in-service continuing professional development (*the education and training coordination analysis*);
- rethinking the organisation and structures of qualification upgrading programmes (*the catch up analysis*);
- revising the content of teacher training to assess its relevance and effectiveness (*the teacher education curriculum analysis*);
- reforming the professional staffing structures of pre-service and in-service education and training (*the teacher educator analysis*);
- reappraising the way teacher education and training can support teachers, particularly women, in rural communities (*the support and gender analysis*);
- remodelling the education and training approach to develop more appropriate teacher attitudes and commitment (*the teacher education values and development analysis*).

The focus of these analyses is education and training. It is important to make the caveat that to markedly improve school systems requires the complementary development of programmes and interventions of which education and training is one. Teacher salaries and career structures, teacher deployment policies, conditions of

230 B. Moon and A. Umar

service support (housing, travel to work, security, for example), salary payment on time and pension arrangements are just a few of the issues that numerous studies have identified as important in school reform and teacher improvement. Some of the earlier chapters have addressed these issues. Teacher attendance, identified as a major concern in many countries, is an issue for teacher education and training (as we discuss under the teacher education and values analysis below) but it cannot be simply an educational issue. There is strong evidence that governments are now addressing the challenge of teacher numbers and quality in a more systemic way than previously. Each of the country case studies illustrates this. The evolving Brazilian model of incentives and accountabilities offers one example. But there is still some way to go in the international community, as well as in national systems, to ensure the teacher issue is seen as equally important as the building of schools. The summary of seven key teacher education issues below, as well as the varied analyses presented throughout this book, is intended as a contribution to this process.

We have tried, in bringing out these issues, to present them succinctly in a way that policy makers (and also researchers identifying important foci for future investigation) might use in looking at their own context. The discussion is generic although we believe, given that it derives from the previous chapters in this book, it would be recognisable across many contexts.

The numbers analysis

It is clear that the 'bricks and mortar' institutions built to train teachers in the last century cannot meet the huge demand of the present century. This is a recurring theme throughout the book. The numbers analysis does seem an important first priority in planning teacher education and training. However a number of difficulties arise. In some countries data on teacher supply and retention is patchy. This is true of overall numbers and important subsets of data (the qualification, age and gender profile of existing teachers for example). Some countries (Rwanda is a recent example) are now introducing teacher registration processes which will provide a much stronger basis for planning pre-service and in-service education and training provision.

Whatever the data many governments, or regional authorities in large states, have begun to respond piecemeal to make up the shortfalls. This takes a number of forms. The recruitment of unqualified, contract or para-professional teachers is the easiest option. The introduction of shorter pre-service training is another. Each of these options precipitates opposition. Teachers unions have resisted, rather unsuccessfully, the large numbers of contract teachers entering school systems. The teacher training institutions, sometimes supported by teacher unions, have proved strongly resistant to the foreshortening of training. In some countries (Malawi and Tanzania are two examples) early attempts to reform and shorten the training period were closed down by pressure from existing institutional interests. In both the countries quoted similar measures are being reintroduced to expand recruitment.

Reorientating the agenda 231

Recent Global Monitoring Reports have argued the need for rethinking training entry points. In some countries the unwillingness to consider new modes of provision sees a minority of entrants to teaching experiencing a three year pre-service training with a majority of recruits going into the classroom wholly unqualified. There is no logic in this.

One answer, being anticipated in some schemes, is to shorten the pre-teaching training (residential or otherwise) but introduce a much stronger induction school element of training. This would involve new roles for many training establishments, including significantly expanding their outreach role to embrace much more liaison work with schools and local districts than has previously been the case. It almost certainly means embracing some forms of open and distance learning if the support at the school level is to be effective.

This has been the case in Brazil with the federal government encouraging new modes of training through grant and regulatory frameworks that can be implemented, using a variety of approaches, at the regional level. Much of the activity is focussed on unqualified teachers already in the system but the same approaches (using distance education and part-time study) could be applied to the pre-service context.

This seems a highly important option, particularly as old ideas about distance education are being supplanted by new, online, school focussed approaches. Changing the length of training has curriculum and other consequences and we discuss those below. In some parts of the world (England and the United States, for example) governments have diversified the routes into teaching. This has usually meant loosening the control held by the higher education and university sector and allowing other providers (groups of schools working as a consortium, for example) to play a role. These new providers could be public bodies or private organisations. There are dangers in this. One element in bolstering the rather precarious status of teachers has been through increasingly stronger training and education association with the university. However, given the scale of demand, we believe that new forms of provision need to be put in place.

The important point is that policy makers and planners ought to have long-term options that are integral to, not separate from, the existing established institutional structures of education and training. Over the last two or three decades this has not been the case. Importantly these long-term options need to embrace much more rigorous analysis of costs (see Chapter 3). New modes of provision, less reliant on heavy infrastructure and salary costs, have the potential to expand access in much more cost-effective ways than traditional 'bricks and mortar' provision. Existing institutions, however, especially those within the higher education, university system, have incrementally strengthened a hold on the policy system. Within new bureaucratic and administrative structures former teachers and teacher educators have been particularly influential. Attempts to address the numbers analysis by the introduction of new types of courses are often short-term and short-lived. It seems inevitable that governments will be required to create new, enabling frameworks, within which a range of providers, both public and private, might contribute (see the example of Brazil). The issue however is, as we

232   B. Moon and A. Umar

have suggested, a long-term challenge and new, sustainable structures need to be in place to allow the policy system to adequately respond. Chapter 12 set out some models about how this could be achieved.

The education and training coordination analysis

In almost all countries pre-service and in-service education and training is separately administered. It is not uncommon for the former to come under the responsibility of a ministry of higher education and the latter a ministry primarily concerned with schools. This is not unique to developing country contexts. However, where resources are constrained and the need for new modes of provision paramount, such structures work against coordination. There are two dimensions that would benefit significantly from being more closely interlinked. The first follows from the numbers analysis above. If pre-service training is to be extended to greater numbers, without significant increases in resources and infrastructure, and with campus-based institutions playing a lead role, then courses must be restructured. Attendance in colleges or universities has to be foreshortened with an accompanying strength of a full-time school based component to the education and training process. To be successful this would almost always involve significantly new and extended forms of cooperation between training institutions and the local and regional agencies and authorities responsible for in-service professional development programmes. There is, for example, much discussion about the nature and forms of induction programmes for newly qualified teachers. There is a strong argument for incorporating pre-service and induction phases to both make a more effective use of resources and to join a stronger practical pedagogical dimension to the teacher preparation process.

The second dimension relates to unqualified teachers. We know that there are very large numbers of under-qualified or unqualified teachers in many school systems. The next point of analysis addresses this group specifically. But in terms of coordination this group appears particularly vulnerable. In many contexts a teacher will embark on an upgrading programme that in no way connects to other forms of professional support in schools. In many schools other teachers, even head teachers, may be unaware of a teacher's participation in a programme. In such cases an important opportunity has been lost. The potential for using the upgrading teacher, with all the resources that the investment in upgrading commits, to influence ideas and practices amongst other teachers is a significant one but almost always wholly missed.

National and regional systems could gain economies of scale and effectiveness if better coordinated. This is an area where realignments could bring important returns in raising the qualities of teachers. Such coordination, especially in large countries where regional groups may be associated with independently minded social and political groupings, can be problematic. In the context of educating and supporting teachers the effective working of national and local bureaucracies is, we believe, crucial.

The catch up analysis

Millions of teachers aspire to gain qualified status. The benchmark for this varies between education systems. Most require a minimum training requirement (usually two to three years full-time equivalent) and recently an increasing number of systems have introduced teacher competence assessment processes at qualification (South Africa is an example). Many donor programmes support upgrading programmes that attempt to provide education to the hundreds of thousands of unqualified or under-qualified teachers in the school system. We have already suggested above that problems of coordination often leave upgrading programmes isolated in the contribution they make to school and teacher development. But there are further issues that constrain the effectiveness of such programmes. We want to point to five that require policy rethinking.

The first is the almost universal rule that an unqualified teacher taking a part-time upgrading course must complete two years of part-time study for every one year full-time equivalent. A three-year diploma, therefore, takes six years to complete. Second, there is rarely any acknowledgement or accreditation of prior learning or experience. Unqualified or under-qualified teachers, even those with years of experience, are deemed similar to an 18–20 year old embarking on a qualifying course. Third, there is rarely any recognition that the structure and form of the upgrading teacher education curriculum needs to reflect the in-school experience of the participating teacher, a point we return to in the next analysis point. Fourth, we have observed some bizarre interpretations of course regulations as they relate to part-time upgrading courses. In a number of institutions, for example, teachers have to leave their classes in order to carry out the teaching practice requirements in a school close to the training institution providing the course. Finally there is often little linkage between the commitment to resourcing an upgrading qualification and subsequent retention in the sector. Data on this is difficult to come by but the weight of anecdotal evidence points to upgrading being a route out of teaching rather than a contribution to teacher and school improvement. Upgrading programmes will be running at scale for many years to come. The necessity of thinking through appropriate structures and curriculum is urgent.

The situation of unqualified teachers in relation to in-service professional development can also be ambiguous. It is not uncommon for such teachers to be denied a training place because they are unqualified! There are only rare instances of teachers in this category being given any special or priority attention. In many parts of the world the unqualified just fall outside established systems. Given the numbers involved and the likely impact on pupil and school achievement this is an important policy concern.

The teacher education curriculum analysis

The last decade has seen significant debate about the content and form of the curriculum of pre-service education and training in most parts of the world. We have seen in earlier chapters that in Europe, North America and Australasia there have been increasing intervention by governments in teacher training (Moon 2003). There has been a similar concern in many developing countries. The example of South Africa has already been quoted.

The main trend in relation to teacher education has been to strengthen the practical relevance and appropriateness of programmes. It seems difficult to deny the thrust of this. There is increasing evidence, as Chapter 11 by Monazza Aslam and Geeta Kingdon suggests, that it is the quality of pedagogic practice rather than the level of teacher qualification that determines effectiveness in the classroom. There is some evidence that this is particularly true in developing world contexts where pupils do not access other educational opportunities in the same way as more resource-rich contexts. The teacher variable is more important and more easily observed.

There appear very strong arguments, not least in the emerging research evidence in the field, for identifying a number of core pedagogic skills and understandings and seeking to ensure that these are prominent in the education and training curriculum. Initiatives like the TESSA programme referred to in Chapter 12 adopt this position. Yet many curriculum structures do not give priority to pedagogic practice. There are different trends in curriculum design often reflecting colonial antecedents. Many courses still give pride of place to general courses in educational foundations (the history of education, child psychology) at the expense of a strong focus on practice.

If the availability of 'education and training time' is scarce then we would argue that primacy should be given to core teaching skills. In the basic education sector where there is currently so much concern about quality, we believe this should focus strongly on literacy and numeracy. Unqualified teachers, teachers with limited training, need a strong grounding on the classroom practices that support the achievement of these fundamental curriculum purposes, a process, as discussed in Chapter 1, which has such implications for socio-economic development and poverty reduction.

There would also need to be an alignment of pre-service, upgrading and in-service curriculum structures and content. Through flexible and modular structures the early phases of an upgrading programme should focus on improving classroom practice, an in-service aim and one that could also be reflected in the first semesters of campus based training. By planning curriculum in an integrated way the teacher in school should be able to build competence to qualification without the constraints associated with campus based courses. There are many ways of achieving this, and many curriculum planning techniques that can be deployed, once it is accepted that a practice focussed curriculum should be put in place. And this is an area where significantly more research and monitored experimentation could take place.

The teacher educator analysis

Within the teacher education community there is, as we have observed, a resistance to change. One important reason for this is the experience and background of teacher educators. There are a number of factors at play. The same pressures that are impacting on the teaching profession work through to teacher educators. Many systems are finding it difficult to recruit teacher educators with the necessary background and experience. This is exacerbated in the basic education sector by the number of teacher educators who have never taught in the sector. In many countries secondary teachers move into primary teacher training. Graduates of diploma or degree courses may go directly into training teachers. This applies at pre-service level, through college or university staff, and at appointments to in-service training positions. Many staff appointed to teach a curriculum based on education foundation, subjects rather than direct pedagogic practices, are finding their skills and knowledge less relevant as the curriculum changes. The education and training of teacher educators (including retraining) is rarely discussed in policy forums yet would seem to be a key element in the improvement of teacher education.

Raising the quality of teacher educators is a long-term undertaking. In the meantime the provision of high quality resources for teacher educators could become a policy priority. The development of new communication technologies and Open Educational Resources as described in Chapters 13 and 14 offers opportunities to supporting the teacher educator as well as teacher role. Currently many education and training systems are premised on the assumption that an expert cadre of teacher educators exist who, primarily through word of mouth, will be able to convey ideas of new practice and advise about their implementation. This is demonstrably not the case and new structures of support need to be put in place to take account of this.

The support and gender analysis

The working conditions of many teachers are very demanding. Two of the chapters in Section 3 (8 and 10) focus on female teachers who across the globe make up the majority of teachers in the basic sector. There are some exceptions to this gender imbalance (the Malawian teaching force is predominantly male) but they are few in number. The message from the analyses presented here is that teachers need a package of support of which one important part is professional development opportunities.

There is some interesting thinking now, represented in Chapters 8, 9 and 10, that draws on the current interest in capability theory to suggest the development of teacher education indexes. This seems an important idea that gives much greater conceptual grounding to the sort of recommendations about teacher role formulated by UNESCO in 1966 and discussed in Chapter 1. Such an index would have to take account of local and national contextual variables, one aspect of which would be access to professional development. If such an index could be made operational it would give policy makers a framework around which a more holistic approach to support could be adopted.

A particular concern for teacher professional development is place and location. The new modes of school based professional development which could increasingly embrace new mobile communication technologies offer a significant improvement in the professional development opportunities for women teaching in many countries, including those working in the more remote rural communities. Rurality is a considerable challenge for policy systems. Rural teachers are far more likely to be unqualified than urban teachers. Rural children are more likely to drop out or achieve less than their urban peers. The inequalities suffered by rural communities go well beyond the issue of teacher education. There is a role, however, that education and training can play. One main challenge for policy makers is persuading teachers to work in rural areas. There is a great deal of data that shows that teachers deployed to rural communities do not stay long and whilst there are frequently absent. The problem could be couched in different terms. Rather than thinking about deploying to rural areas it is possible to consider recruiting and developing teachers who live, and wish to remain living, in rural communities. The Scottish government, working with the TESSA consortium (tessafrica.net) is educating and training 500 Malawian women a year who live in rural areas to be able to teach in local primary schools. An earlier programme in Nigeria, the DFID community education programme, was successful in achieving similar aims. As yet, however, this perspective has not been incorporated into the mainstream of teacher education provision.

One concern in the discussion of place is the sense of association and commitment teachers have to their employing authority in the district or administrative area where they work. Patrick Chabal, in his study of *Africa: The Politics of Suffering and Smiling* (2009), has spoken of the weak sense of belonging that many people have to the districts in which they live. Family and ancestors, non-administrative groupings (Luo, Kikuya in Kenya or Zulu, Xosa in South Africa) may have greater legitimacy. Yet the structure of teacher support and teacher professional development, along with aid flows, are directed to rather arbitrary and historically recent political boundaries. This analysis is derived from Sub-Saharan Africa but we discern in many development contexts weak commitment to the 'school district' within which teachers work. New forms of support, including perhaps the sort of social networking associated with the most recent forms of electronic communication, offer opportunities to build a sense of belonging amongst teachers. And for this the sorts of social commitment that might be expected of a teacher could grow. Interventions in this area, however, need to take account of the conditions in which teachers live and work and the lives they lead. Education and training will need to become more flexible. It will also need to become more professional and shed some of the 'training challenge' preconceptions that still tend to dominate all forms of provision.

Education, training and support can also extend to the resources currently made available to teachers. Here the orthodoxy of tradition bites hard. The prime resource made available to teachers is the same as a century ago, the textbook. The writing, production and printing of textbooks is a challenging task. In many schools few textbooks can be found. There is now growing evidence that textbooks provide a useful resource for the higher achievers in a class but for the majority they have little impact. Glewwe *et al.* (2009) illustrated this in a study in Kenya.

One interesting development is the idea of 'open schooling'. Both at primary and secondary levels structures are put in place to create essentially schools that function in ways similar to open universities. This is not a new concept. The Open School system in British Colombia in Canada has been in existence since 1919 and has gone through a number of technological transformations (it is today essentially online). The resources created for open schools can also support teachers in conventional school situations in ways that go significantly beyond textbook type provision. The Commonwealth of Learning in Vancouver currently has a programme, funded by the William and Flora Hewlett Foundation, to develop the open schooling concept with particular reference to developing countries (www. col.org/progServ/programmes/education/Pages/openSchooling.aspx).

There are some obvious advantages. It is unlikely that the expanding secondary systems of Sub-Saharan Africa will ever have sufficient mathematics or science teachers. Adoption of open school type courses has considerable potential. But the same could be true in primary schools with teachers who find the subject knowledge required to teach mathematics and science, perhaps other areas as well, difficult to acquire. There is a need for more research and development work on this issue. This is also an area which would benefit from the sort of controlled investigations that Esther Duflo and colleagues have been developing at MIT and through the Poverty Action Lab.

The teacher education values analysis

The Mandela Foundation investigation of teachers in rural communities (Nelson Mandela Foundation 2005) has been referred to a number of times. It is an interesting 'in country critique' of teacher attitudes and values and it highlights a growing community disillusionment with the quality of teachers. There are other documents addressing the same issues. The South African government's 2003 Plan of Action: Improving Access to Free and Quality Education for All directly addresses the growing concerns.

We have educators [teachers] whose accomplishments exceed even the high expectations placed on them by the system and community. They are the heroes of our schooling system and there are many of them . . . Sadly we also have a minority of educators [teachers] who not only fail to give their best in the classroom, but contravene school rules by, for instance, arriving late at work in the morning, and engaging in criminal acts such as improper with learners and sexual abuse. The harm that such behaviour inflicts on our schooling system, in the reputation of the teaching fraternity and on the next generation of South Africans is very high.

This quotation is taken from a study (Buckler 2012) which has looked in depth at the lives of teachers in a number of Sub-Saharan African countries. Buckler's analysis points to the importance of looking beyond the representation of teachers in terms of numbers (insufficient) or quality problems (unqualified, poor attenders) to try to gain some understanding of how the lives and priorities of teachers today influence this practice and the attitudes they bring to their classrooms.

238 *B. Moon and A. Umar*

It does appear that the sense of vocation that has been traditionally associated with the role of the teacher has been eroded through changes in economic and social structures and by the strains associated with the rapid expansion of big and small education systems. And yet the values dimension to the teachers' task seems every bit as important today as ever, if not more so. The discussion around the power that teachers have through their pedagogic practice (Leach and Moon 2008) to open opportunities for children and young people rarely features in the curriculum of teacher education or in the different forms of engagement that teachers have with their employing authorities. The evidence that now exists about the links between school completion, learner attainment and future health and economic well-being is more commonly represented in the dialogue of the international policy community than in the professional deliberations by teachers about their role and purpose. This is more than just a teacher education curriculum issue. A more substantive engagement with the development agenda requires a change in the discourse within which and through which teachers lead their professional lives. To achieve such a change in discourse, to enlist teachers in the development process requires sustained commitment and cooperation across the range of authorities and influences that impinge on the lives of teachers and schools.

In developing these seven points of analysis we seek to provide parameters against which existing institutional structures and policy procedures towards the education and training of teachers can be evaluated. Although there are a variety of institutional structures, and whilst contexts vary enormously, we suggest that each of our points of analysis would have relevance to any teacher education structure. These points derive from analyses and critiques in this book. Most, however, have been identified and well documented for some considerable time. The impetus and urgency around national and international action to expand and raise the quality of school systems is putting teachers at the centre of the reform debate. A plethora of new ideas, new insights and new modes of working exist. The task now is to take the overarching analysis and use the evidence of reform success to significantly remodel the structures and processes through which teachers are educated, trained and supported through professional development opportunities throughout their careers.

References

Aaronson, D., Barrow, L. and Sanders, W. (2003) *Teachers and Student Achievement in Chicago Public High Schools*. Chicago: Federal Reserve Bank of Chicago.

Ackers, J., Migoli, J. and Nzomo, J. (2001) Identifying and addressing the causes of declining participation rates in Kenyan primary schools. *International Journal of Educational Development*, 21, 361–374.

Adagiri S. (2009) A comparative study of teachers continuing professional development in Nigeria and England. Paper presented at the BERA New Researchers Conference, 2–5 September, Manchester.

Adeboyowale, O.F. and Osuji. S.N. (2008) Record keeping practices of primary school teachers in Orido state: implications for successful implementation of the Universal Basic Education Programme in Nigeria, *eJournal of Education Policy*. Available at: www.4.nau. edu/cec/jep.

Adelabu, M.A. (2005) *Teacher Motivation and Incentives in Nigeria*. Available at: www. dfid.gov.uk/r4d/PDF/Outputs/PolicyStrategy/3888Teacher_motivation_Nigeria. pdf (accessed January 2010).

Adeyemi, B. (2010) Teacher-related factors in correlates of pupils' achievement in Social Studies in Southwestern Nigeria. *Electronic Journal of Research in Educational Psychology*, 8(1), 313–332.

Afe, J.O. (2002) Reflections on becoming a teachers and the challenges of teacher education. Inaugural lecture 64, University of Benin.

Ahmad, J., Devaraja, S. and Khemani, S. (2005) *Decentralization and Service Delivery (Policy Research Working Paper 2603)*. Washington, DC: World Bank.

Akyeampong, K. and Furlong, D. (2000) Ghana: a baseline study of the teacher education system. Multi-Site Teacher Education Research Project (MUSTER), Centre for International Education, University of Sussex Institute of Education, 67.

Akyeampong, K. and Stephens, D. (2000) On the threshold: the identity of student teachers in Ghana. MUSTER Discussion Paper 4. Centre for International Education, University of Sussex.

Akyeampong, K., Furlong, D. and Lewin, K. (2000) Costs and financing of teacher education in Ghana, Centre of International Education. MUSTER Discussion Paper 18.

Alarky, M. (2009) Former Coordinator of Curriculum, Sudan National Centre for Curriculum and Education Research (NCCER), Sudan. Interview conducted at NCCER, 5 February.

Alkire, S. (2002) *Valuing Freedoms: Sen's Capability Approach and Poverty Reduction*. Oxford: Oxford University Press.

Alvarez, B., Gillies, J. and Bradsher, M. (2003) *Beyond Basic Education: Secondary*

240 *References*

Education in the Developing World. Washington, DC: World Bank Institute and Academy for Educational Development.

Ammermüller, A. and Dolton, P. (2007) Pupil-teacher gender interaction effects on scholastic outcomes in England and the USA. Center for European Economic Research (ZEW) Discussion Paper No. 06-060.

An, X., Hannum, E. and Sargent, T. (2007) Teaching quality and student outcomes: academic achievement and educational engagement in rural Northwest China. *China: an International Journal*, 5(2), 309–334.

Anamuah-Mensah, J. and Benneh, M. (2009) Particular issues of teacher education in Ghana. Presentation to the High Level Expert Meeting, UNESCO.

Anderson, S. (2002) *Improving Schools through Teacher Development: Case Studies of the Aga Khan Foundation Projects in East Africa*. Amsterdam: Swets & Zeitlinger.

Andrabi, T., Das, J. and Khwaja, A. (2006) Students today, teachers tomorrow? Identifying constraints on the provision of education. Harvard University Working Paper.

Anikweze, C.M. (2008) Teacher supply, retention, preparation and career long development in Nigeria. Unpublished paper prepared for the UNESCO E-9 Ministerial meeting, Bali, March.

Ansell, N. (2002) Secondary education reform in Lesotho and Zimbabwe and the needs of rural girls: pronouncements, policy and practice. *Comparative Education*, 38(1), 91–112.

Arong, F.E. and Ogbadu, M.A. (2010) Major causes of declining quality of education in Nigeria from administrative perspective: a case study of Dekina local government area. *Canadian Social Science*, 6(3), 183–198.

Arthur, J. (2002) Perspectives on educational language policy and its implementation in African classrooms: a comparative study of Botswana and Tanzania. *Compare*, 31(3), 347–362.

Aslam, M. (2008) The relative effectiveness of government and private schools in Pakistan: are girls worse off? *Education Economics*, 17(3), 329–353.

Aslam, M. and Kingdon, G. (2007) What can teachers do to raise pupil achievement? CSAE Working Paper Series, Centre for the Study of African Economies, University of Oxford.

Aslam, M. and Kingdon, G. (2012) How teachers' pedagogic practice influences learner achievements: a study in the Punjab, Pakistan. In R.E. Moon (Ed.), *Teacher Education and the Challenge of Development: A Global Analysis* (Chapter 11). London: Routledge.

Attar, M. (2000) *Curriculum Reforms in Ghana*. Paris: UNESCO.

Ayuknso Nkongho Ashu, E. (1997) The effects of pedagogic factors on the development of reading readiness skills of class one pupils. End of Course Dissertation (DIPEN II). Yaoundé – Cameroun: Ecole Normale Supérieure.

Bai, M. (2008) Rural distance education in primary and secondary schools in Gansu, China. *International Journal of Technology and Distance Education*, 5(7). Available at: www.itdl.org/Journal/Jul_08/article02.htm (accessed 8 November 2011).

Baker, G. (2002) Distortion and risk in optimal incentive contracts. *Journal of Human Resources*, 37, 728–751.

Ballou, D. (2001) Pay for performance in public and private schools. *Economics of Education Review*, 20(1), 51–61.

Ballou, D. and Podgursky, M. (1997) *Teacher Pay and Teacher Quality*. Kalamazoo: W.E. Upjohn Institute for Employment Research.

Ballou, D. and Podgursky, M. (2002) Returns to seniority among public school teachers. *Journal of Human Resources*, 37(4), 892–912.

References 241

Ballou, D., Sanders, W. and Wright, P. (2004) Controlling for student background in value-added assessment of teachers. *Journal of Educational and Behavioral Statistics*, 29(1), 37–66.

Banerjee, A.V. and Dufloe, E. (2011) *Poor Economics: A Radical Rethinking of the Way to Fight Global Poverty*. New York: Public Affairs.

Banks, F., Leach, J. and Moon, B. (1999) New understandings of teachers' pedagogic knowledge. In J. Leach and B. Moon (Eds), *Learners and Pedagogy*. London: Paul Chapman.

Barrett, A. (2007) Beyond polarisation of pedagogy: models of classroom practice in Tanzanian primary schools. *Comparative Education*, 43(2), 273–294.

Barrett, A. (2007) Capturing the *difference*: primary school teacher identity in Tanzania. *International Journal of Educational Development*, 28(5), 496–507.

Bates, R. (2007) Developing capabilities and the management of trust. In M. Walker and E. Unterhalter (Eds), *Amartya Sen's Capability Approach and Social Justice in Education*. New York: Palgrave Macmillan.

BBC (2010) India unveils prototype for $35 touch-screen computer. 23 July. Available at: www.bbc.co.uk/news/world-south-asia-10740817. (accessed 9 August 2010).

Bean, M., Banks, F. and Hutchinson, S. (2011) Open learning for open societies: the role British institutions can play in the Indian human resources revolution. In J. Johnson and R. Kumar (Eds), *Reconnecting Britain and India: Ideas for an Enhanced Partnership*. New Delhi: Academic Foundation.

Beard, C. and Wilson, J.P. (2007) *Experiential Learning*. London: Kogan.

Bénabou, R. and Tirole, J. (2000) Self-confidence and social interactions. NBER Working Paper No. 7585. Cambridge, MA: National Bureau of Economic Research.

Bénabou, R. and Tirole, J. (2003). Intrinsic and extrinsic motivation. *Review of Economic Studies*, 70, 489–520.

Bennell, P. (2002) The impact of the AIDS epidemic on teachers in Sub-Saharan Africa. World Bank. Available at: http://gametlibrary.worldbank.org/FILES/671_The%20impact%20of%20the%20AIDS%20epidemic%20on%20teachers.pdf (accessed November 2010).

Bennell, P. (2004) Teacher motivation and incentives in Sub-Saharan Africa and Asia. Knowledge and Skills for Development, Brighton. Available at: www.eldis.org/fulltext/dfidtea.pdf (accessed January 2011).

Bennell, P. and Akyeampong, K. (2007) Teacher motivation in Sub-Saharan Africa and South Asia. Education paper prepared for DFID, Brighton, Knowledge and Skills for Development.

Bennell, P. and Mukyanuzi, F. (2005) Is there a teacher motivation crisis in Tanzania? Brighton, Knowledge and Skills for Development, 55.

Bentaouet-Kattan, R. (2006) Implementation of free basic education policy (No. 7). Education Working Paper Series. Washington, DC: World Bank.

Biggeri, M. (2007) Children's valued capabilties. In M. Walker and E. Unterhalter (Eds), *Amartya Sen's Capability Approach and Social Justice in Education*. New York: Palgrave Macmillan.

Birdsall, N., Levine, R. and Ibrahim, A. (2005) *Toward Universal Primary Education: Investments, Incentives and Institutions*. London: Earthscan.

Black, P. and Hosking, S. (1997) The teacher crisis in South Africa: quitting, shirking and 'inferior substitution'. *South African Journal of Economics*, 65(4), 232–236.

Bof, A.M. (2004) Distance learning for teacher training in Brazil. *International Review of Research in Open and Distance Learning*, 5(1), 1–11.

242 *References*

Boissiere, M., Knight, J.B. and Sabot, R.H. (1985) Earnings, schooling, ability and cognitive skills. *American Economic Review*, 75(5), 1030–1061.

Bonder, C. and Sardenberg, S.M. (2000) Introducing gender-awareness to elementary school teachers in rural Bahia, Brasil. In *Knowledge, Education and Extension for Women in Rural Areas*, proceedings of Fourth International Conference of the Centre for Women in Rural Development, (Berlin: Humboldt Universitat zu Berlin.

Bordia Report (2010) *Report of the Committee on Implementation of the Right of Children to Free and Compulsory Education Act, 2009 and the Resultant Revamp of Sarva Shiksha Abhiyan*. Delhi: Ministry of Human Resource Development.

Boyd, D., Grossman, P., Lankford, H. and Loeb, S. (2006) How changes in entry requirements alter the teacher workforce and affect student achievement. *Education Finance and Policy*, 1, 176–216.

Breen, M. (1989) The evaluation cycle for language learning tasks. In R.K. Johnson (Ed.), *The Second Language Curriculum*. Cambridge: Cambridge University Press.

Breidlid, A. (2005) Education in the Sudan: the privileging of an Islamic discourse. *Compare*, 35(3), 247–263.

Britton, E., Paine, L., Pimm, D. and Raizen, S. (2003) *Comprehensive Teacher Induction: Systems for Early Career Learning*. Dordrecht: Kluwer.

Brown, G. and Benn, H. (2005) Foreword. In *Keeping Our Promises: Delivering Education for All*. London: DFID. Available at: www.dfid.gov.uk/Pubs/files/education-delivering-promises.pdf.

Brown, H.D. (2001) *Teaching by Principle: An Inventive Approach to Language Pedagogy*. Second edition. White Plain: Pearson Education.

Brown, J.S., Collins, A. and Duguid, P. (1989) Situated cognition and the culture of learning. *Educational Researcher*, 18(1), 32–42.

Bruns, B., Cruz, T. and Amorim, E. (2011) *Inside the Classroom in Brazil. What We Can Learn from Comparative Classroom Observations*. Washington, DC: World Bank.

Bruns, B., Evans, D. and Luque, J. (2012) *Achieving World Class Education in Brazil: The Next Agenda*. Washington, DC: World Bank.

Buckler, A. (2009) The whole classroom is smelling bad. *Guardian*, 23 July.

Buckler, A. (2011) Reconsidering the evidence base, considering the rural: aiming for a better understanding of the education and training needs of Sub-Saharan African teachers. *International Journal of Educational Development*, 31(3), 244–250.

Buckler, A. (2012) The professional lives or rural women teachers in sub-Saharan Africa: a capability perspective. Unpublished PhD Dissertation, Open University.

Carnine, D. (1998) The metamorphosis of education into a mature profession. Sixth Annual Meeting, Park City, June, Utah. Available at: www.edexcellence.net/library/carnine.html.

Carr-Hill, R. (2009) Issues in data and monitoring evaluation. Mid-Term Evaluation of the EFA Fast Track Initiative Working Paper 3(a), 28 June. Available at: www.camb-ed.com/fasttrackinitiative/.

Carron, G. and Chau, T. (1996) *The Quality of Primary Schools in Different Development Contexts*. Paris: UNESCO.

Carter, R. and Nunan, D. (2001) *The Cambridge Guide to Teaching English to Speakers of Other Languages*. Cambridge: Cambridge University Press.

Caucutt, E.M. and Kumar, K.B. (2007) Education for all: a welfare improving course for Africa? *Review of Economic Dynamics*, 10(2), 294–326.

Chabal, P. (2009) *Africa: The Politics of Suffering and Smiling*. London: Zed Books.

References 243

Chadhury, N., Hammer, J., Kremer, M., Karthik, R. and Halsey, F. (2006) Missing in action: teacher and health worker absence in developing countries. *The Journal of Economic Perspectives*, 20(1), 91–116.

Chapman, D. (1997) Improving instructional practice in developing countries: the teachers' dilemma. In J. Lynch, C. Modgil and S. Modgil (Eds), *Education and Development: Tradition and Innovation. Vol. 3, Innovations in Delivering Primary Education*. London: Cassell.

Chapman, D.W. and Miric, S. (2005) *Teacher Policy in the MENA Region: Issues and Options*. Washington, DC: World Bank.

Chen, W.Q. (2010) Rationality and morality: the ideal and the reality of removing substituted teachers policy (Lixing yu daoyi: daikejiaoshi qingkuang zhengcede lixiang yu xianshi; 理性与道义：代课教师请退政策的理想与现实). *Education Development Research* (Jiaoyu Fazhan Yanjiu; 教育发展研究), 15–16, 92–96.

Children's Investment Fund Foundation (2009) Sector landscape analysis: educational achievement, 8 October. Available at: http://ciff.org/assets/landscape/Education-Landscape-2009-10.pdf.

China Broadcast Network (2011) Available at: www.cnr.cn/china/gdgg/201111/t20111126_508837400.shtml.

Chinese Internet Network Information Centre (CINIC) (2009) *24th Statistical Report on Internet Development in China*. Beijing: CINIC. Available at: www.cnnic.net.cn/uploadfiles/pdf/2009/10/12/114121.pdf (accessed 8 November 2011).

Clotfelter, C., Ladd, H. and Vigdor, J. (2006) Teacher-student matching and the assessment of teacher effectiveness. NBER Working Paper No. 11936, January.

Clotfelter, C., Ladd, H., Vigdor, J. and Aliaga Diaz, R. (2004) Do school accountability systems make it more difficult for low-performing schools to attract and retain high-quality teachers? *Journal of Policy Analysis and Management*, 23(2), 251–271.

Cohen, L., Manion, L. and Morrison, K. (2007) *Research Methods in Education*. Sixth edition. New York: Routledge.

Colclough, C., Al-Samarrai, S., Rose, P. and Tembon, M. (2003) *Achieving Schooling for All in Africa: Costs, Commitment and Gender*. Aldershot: Ashgate.

Commission for Africa (2005) *Our Common Interest*. London: Commission for Africa.

Coolahan, J., Santiago, P., Phair, R. and Ninomiya, A. (2004) *Attracting, Developing and Retaining Effective Teachers – Country Note: Korea*. Paris: OECD Education and Training Policy Division.

Cooper, J.M. and Alvarado, A. (2006) *Preparation, Recruitment and Retention of Teachers*. Paris: IIEP & IAE, UNESCO.

Cox, C. (2003) *Las politicas educacionales de Chile en las ultimas dos decadas del sieglo XX in Politicas educacionales en el cambio de siglo: la reforma del sistema escolar en Chile*. Santiago: Chile Editorial Universitaria.

Craft, A. (2000) *Continuing Professional Development: A Practical Guide for Teachers and Schools*. London: Routledge.

Craig, H.J., Kraft, R.J. and du Plessis, J. (1998) *Teacher Development: Making an Impact*. Washington, DC: World Bank.

CREATE (2011) *Making Rights Realities: Researching Educational Access, Transitions and Equity*. Falmer, University of Sussex.

Crouch, L. (2005) South Africa equity and quality reforms: possible lessons. *Journal of Education for International Development*, 1(1).

Daniel, John (Sir) (2008) *5th Pan-Commonwealth Forum on Open Learning*. Commonwealth of Learning, July, London.

244   *References*

Darling-Hammond, L. (2000) Teacher quality and student achievement: a review of state policy evidence. *Education Policy Analysis Archives*, 8(1), 1–44.

Das, J. and Zajonc, T. (2008) *India Shining and Bharat Drowning. Comparing Two Indian States to the Worldwide Distribution in Mathematics Achievement*. Washington, DC: World Bank.

Davidson, E. (2007) The pivotal role of teacher motivation in Tanzanian education. *The Educational Forum*, 71(2), 157–166.

Dawson-Brew, E., Oduro, G.T. and Ankoma-Sey, V. (2009) *Distance Education and Teacher Development: Perspectives from the University of Cape Coast*. Distance Education and Training in Africa (DETA). University of Cape Coast.

Day, C. (1991) Quality assurance and professional development. *British Journal of In-service Education*, 17(3), 189–195.

Day, C. (1999) *Developing Teachers: The Challenges of Lifelong Learning*. London: Falmer Press.

Day, C. and Sachs, J. (eds) (2004) *International Handbook on the CPD of Teachers*. Maidenhead: Open University Press.

Deane, M. (2006) *Achieving Development Goals through Cost-effective Open and Distance Learning in Sub-Saharan Africa: What Costs, How Effective?* Fourth Pan Commonwealth Forum, 30 October – 3 November. Ocho Rios, Jamaica. Available at: http://pcf4.dec.uwi.edu/viewpaper.php?id=275.

Dee, Thomas S. (2007) Teachers and the gender gaps in student achievement. *Journal of Human Resources* 42(3), 528–554.

Dee, T. and Keys, B. (2004) Does merit pay reward good teachers? Evidence from a randomized experiment. *Journal of Policy Analysis and Management*, 23(3), 471–488.

DeJaeghere, J.G., Chapman, D.W. and Mulkeen, A. (2006) Increasing the supply of secondary teachers in sub-Saharan Africa: a stakeholder assessment of policy options in six countries. *Journal of Education Policy*, 21(5), 515–533.

Delannoy, F. and Sedlacek, G. (2001) *Brazil: Teachers Development and Incentives: A Strategic Framework*. Washington, DC: World Bank.

Dembélé, M. and Lefoka, P. (2007) Pedagogical renewal for quality universal primary education: overview of trends in Sub-Saharan Africa. *International Review of Education*, 53(1), 531–553.

Dembélé, M. and Miaro-II, B.-R. (2003) Pedagogical renewal and teacher development in sub-Saharan Africa: a thematic synthesis. Prepared for ADEA in the framework of *The Challenge of Learning* study, commissioned for the 2003 biennale (Mauritius, 3–6 December). Paris: ADEA.

Dembélé, M., Mellouki, M., Gauthier, C., Abillama, F., Grandbois, A. and Gladys-Bijang, S. (2005) *Étude sur la formation et la gestion des enseignants du primaire en Afrique de l'ouest (Burkina Faso, Mali, Niger et Sénégal): Rapport de synthèse comparative*. Washington, DC: Banque mondiale.

DFID (2010) *Learning for All: DFID's Education Strategy 2010–2015*. London: DFID.

Dheram, Premakumari (2007) Empowerment through enquiry: ESL teacher to educator. *TESL Reporter*, 40(2), 60–75.

Diané, B. and Grandbois, A. (2003) La réforme de la formation initiale des maîtres en Guinée (FIMG): Étude-bilan de la mise en œuvre. Case study commissioned by ADEA in the framework of the *Challenge of Learning Study*. Paris: ADEA.

Dillon, D. and O'Connor, K. (2009) Student cohorts in teacher education: creating pedagogical community. Paper presented at the CSSE Annual Conference, Carleton University, Ottawa, 25 May.

References 245

Doan, T.K.K. and Nguyen, T.H.A. (2005) Teachers' attitudes to classroom research in Vietnam. *Teacher's Edition*, 18, 4–7.

Dolton, P. and Marcenaro-Gutierrez, O. (2008) *If You Pay Peanuts do You Get Monkeys? A Cross Country Analysis of Teacher Pay and Pupil Performance*. London: London School of Economics.

Dos Reis, K. (2007) The influence of gangsterism on the morale of educators on the Cape Flats, Western Cape. PhD Dissertation, Dissertation.com, Florida.

du Plessis, J. and Muzaffar, I. (2010) Professional learning communities in the teachers' college: a resource for teacher educators. Educational Quality Improvement Programme (EQUIP). U. a. A. I. f. Research.

Duflo, E.C. and Hanna, R. (2005) *Monitoring Works: Getting Teachers to Come to School Working Paper 11880*. Cambridge, MA: National Bureau of Economic Research.

Dyer, C. (2009) *Teacher Education and Social Inclusion in India: The Role of Teacher Educators*. Available at: www.eenet.org.

Eckert, P. (1995) Adolescent trajectory and forms of institutional participation. In L.Crockett and A. Crouter (Eds), *Pathways Through Adolescence: Individual Development in Relation to Social Contexts* (pp. 175–196). Hillsdale: Lawrence Erlbaum.

Education for All (2011) *EFA Global Monitoring Report Summary: The Hidden Crisis: Armed Conflict and Education*. Paris: UNESCO. Available at: http://unesdoc.unesco. org/images/0019/001911/191186e.pdf.

Education International (EI) (2003) *Education For All: Is Commitment Enough?* Brussels: Education International.

Education Portal (2011) *OCW Peoples Choice Award Winners: Final List*. News article published 19 August. Available at: http://education-portal.com (accessed 1 September 2011).

Edukuyho, E. (2002) Teaching: the job nobody wants any more. *Vanguard Newspaper*, 6 March 2002, Lagos.

Ellis, C. and Bochner, A. (2000) Autoethnography, personal narrative, reflexivity: researcher as subject. In N. Denzin and Y. Lincoln (Eds), *Handbook of Qualitative Research*. Second edition. London: Sage Publications.

Ellis, R. (2003) *Task-based Language Learning and Teaching*. Oxford: Oxford University Press.

Elmore, R.F. (1979) Backward mapping: implementation research and policy decisions. *Political Science Quarterly*, 94, 601–616.

Elmore, R.F. (1996) Getting to scale with good educational practice. *Harvard Educational Review*, 66(1), 1–25.

English in Action (2010a) *Report on the Assessment of Teachers' Levels of English, 23 February – 4 March 2010*. London: Trinity College London.

English in Action (2010b) *Report on the Assessment of Pupils levels of English, 23 February – 25 March 2010*. London: Trinity College London.

English in Action (2011a) *Perceptions of English Language Learning and Teaching among Primary and Secondary School Teachers and Students Participating in English in Action*. Dhaka: EIA.

English in Action (2011b) *The Classroom Practices of Primary and Secondary School Teachers Participating in English in Action*. Dhaka: EIA.

English in Action (2011c) *Study 3a:2 English Proficiency Assessments (March 2011). Preliminary Report on Findings*. Dhaka: EIA.

Erny, P. (1972) *L'enfant et son milieu en Afrique noire. Essai sur l'éducation traditionnelle*. Paris: Payot.

246 *References*

Evans, H. (1999) Learning to teach; learning from teaching. In M. Brown (Ed.), *Dimensions of Teaching and Learning*. Kingston, Jamaica: Institute of Education, University of the West Indies.

Fanfani, E. (2004) Teaching careers in Latin America. *IIEP Newsletter*, XXII(1). Paris: UNESCO.

FAO & UNESCO (2003) *Education for Rural Development. Towards New Policy Responses.* A joint study by FAO and UNESCO. Edited by D. Atchoarena and L. Gasperini. Published by Food and Agriculture Organisation of the United Nations, Rome, Italy. Available at: www.fao.org/sd/2003/KN12033_en.htm.

Farrell, J.P. (2002) The Aga Khan Foundation experience compared with emerging alternatives to schooling. In S.E. Anderson (Ed.), *School Improvement through Teacher Development: Case Studies of the Aga Khan Foundation Projects in East Africa* (pp. 247–270). Lisse: Swets & Zetlinger Publishers.

Fehr, E. and Falk, A. (2002) Psychological foundations of incentives. *European Economic Review*, 46, 687–724.

Feiman-Nemser, S. (2001) From preparation to practice: designing a continuum to strengthen and sustain teaching. *Teachers College Record*, 103, 1013–1055.

Fernandez, C. (2002) Learning from Japanese approaches to professional development: the case of lesson study. *Journal of Teacher Education*, 53(5), 393–405.

Ferraz, C. and Bruns, B. (2011) *Incentives to Teach: The Effects of Performance Pay in Brazilian Schools.*

Figlio, D.N. and Winicki, J. (2002) Food for thought: the effects of school accountability plans on school nutrition. NBER Working Paper No. 9319. Cambridge, MA: National Bureau of Economic Research.

Figueiredo, M. and Cowen, R. (2004) Models of teacher education and shifts in politics: a note on Brazil. In C. Brock and S. Schuartzman (Eds), *The Challenges of Education in Brazil*. Didcot: Oxford Studies in Comparative Education, Symposium Books.

FME (2003) *Education Sector Status Report*. Abuja: FME.

Fomba, C.O. and Keita, F. (2003) La pédagogie convergente (PC) comme facteur d'amélioration de la qualité de l'éducation de base au Mali: Analyse du développement de l'innovation et perspectives. Case study commissioned by ADEA in the framework of the *Challenge of Learning Study*. Paris: ADEA.

Freire, P. (1970) *Pedagogy of the Oppressed*. New York: The Continuum Publishing Company.

Freire, P. (2000) *Pedagogy of the Oppressed*. 30th Anniversary Edition. New York: Continuum.

Freire, P. and Macedo, D. (1999) Pedagogy, culture, language and race: a dialogue. In J. Leach and B. Moon (Eds), *Learners and Pedagogy*. London: Paul Chapman.

Fry, L. (2002) *What Makes Teachers Tick? A Policy Research Report on Teachers' Motivation in Developing Countries*. London: VSO.

Fukuda-Parr, S. (2003) The human development paradigm: operationalising Sen's ideas on capabilities. *Feminist Economics*, 9(2–3), 301–317.

Fullan, M. (1991) *The New Meaning of Educational Change*. New York: Teachers College Press.

Fuller, B. (1987) *Raising School Quality in Developing Countries: What Investments Boost Learning?* Washington, DC: World Bank.

Gallastegi, L., Wolfenden, F. and Chitsulo, J. (2011) Supporting induction to the teaching profession for women in Malawi. Presented at the DETA (Distance Education and Teachers' Training in Africa) Conference, 3–5 August, Maputo, Mozambique.

References   247

Gao, P. and Zhang, R. (2009) Moving from TV broadcasting to e-learning: contributions of distance education to teacher education in China. *Campus Wide Information Systems*, 26(2), 98–107.

Gasper, D. and Van Staveren, I. (2003) Development as freedom—and what else? *Feminist Economics*, 9(2–3), 137–161.

Gauthier, C., Bissonnette, S., Richard, M. and Djibo, F. (2003) Pédagogies et écoles efficaces dans les pays développés et en développement. Une revue de littérature. Background paper commissioned by ADEA in the framework of *The Challenge of Learning Study*. Paris: ADEA.

Ghana Ministry of Education (2009) Website archives available at: www.ghana.gov.gh (accessed January 2010).

Gillies, J. and Quijada, J.J. (2008) *Opportunity to Learn: A High Impact Strategy for Improving Educational Outcomes in Developing Countries*. Written for EQUIP2 by John Gillies and Jessica Jester Quijada (both Academy for Education Development). Available at: www.equip123.net/equip2/index_new.html.

Glewwe, P. (2002) Schools and skills in developing countries: education policies and socio-economic outcomes. *Journal of Economic Literature*, 40(2), 436–482.

Glewwe, P. and Kremer, M. (2005) Schools, teachers and education. Outcomes in developing countries. CID Working Paper No. 122. September 2005. Centre for International Development at Harvard University. Available at: www.cid.harvard.edu/cidwp/pdf/122.pdf.

Glewwe, P. and Kremer, M. (2006) Schools, teachers, and education outcomes in developing countries. In E. Hanushek and F. Welch (Eds), *Handbook of the Economics of Education*, Vol. 2. Amsterdam: Elsevier.

Glewwe, P., Ilias, N. and Kremer, M. (2003) Teacher incentives. NBER Working Paper No. 9671. Cambridge, MA: National Bureau of Economic Research.

Glewwe, P., Kremer, M. and Moulin, S. (2009) Many children left behind? Textbooks and test scores in Kenya. *American Economic Journal:Applied Economics*, 1(1), 112–135.

Global Campaign for Education (2006) *Teachers for All: What Governments and Donors Should Do*. London: Global Campaign for Education.

Global Campgaign for Education (2008) *At the Crossroads: Which Way Forward for a Global Compact on Education?* GCE briefing for the Education for All High Level Group in Olso, 16–18 December.

Global Gateway (2010) India Education system. Available at: www.globalgateway.org (accessed 4 August 2010).

GNA (2010) Bridge teacher-deficit gap ith off-campus training. *Ghana News Web*. Hohoe.

GOI (Government of India) (1985) *The Teacher and Society, Chattopadhyaya Committee Report (1983–85)*. MHRD, GOI, New Delhi.

GOI (Government of India) (2009) *The Right of Children to Free and Compulsory Education Act 2009*. New Delhi, 26 August.

GOI Planning Commission (Government of India) (2008) *Eleventh Five Year Plan (2007–2012) Social Sector Volume II*. New Delhi: Oxford University Press.

Goldhaber, D. and Brewer, D. (1997) Why don't schools and teachers seem to matter? *The Journal of Human Resources*, 32, 505–523.

Gough, I. and McGregor, A. (2007) *Well Being in Developing Countries: From Theory to Research*. Cambridge: Cambridge University Press.

Govinda, R. and Josephine, Y. (2004) *Para Teachers in India: A Review*. Paris: UNESCO.

248   *References*

Govinda, R. and Josephine, Y. (2005) Para teachers in India: a review. *Contemporary Education Dialogue*, 2, 193–224.

Gu, J.G. (2008) Problems and suggestions on our national free normal education (Woguo mianfei shifanjiaoyu zhidu cunzaide wenti jijianyi; 我国免费师范教育制度存在的问题及建议), *Higher Education Development and Evaluation* (Gaojiao fazhan yu pinggu; 高教发展与评估), 24(5), 38–43.

Gu, L. and Wang, J. (2006) School-based research and professional learning: an innovative model to promote teacher professional development in China. *Teaching Education*, 17(1), 59–73.

Guthrie, G. (1982) Reviews of teacher training and teacher performance in developing countries: Beeby revisited. *International Review of Education*, 28(3), 291–306.

Hannum, E. and Adams, J. (2009) Beyond cost: rural perspectives on barriers to education. In D.S. Davis and F. Wang (Eds), *Creating Wealth and Poverty in Postsocialist China* (pp. 156–171). Stanford: Stanford University Press.

Hannum, E. and Park, A. (2006) Academic achievement and engagement in rural China. In E. Hannum and A. Park (Eds), *Education and Reform in China* (pp. 154–172). London and New York: Routledge.

Hanushek, E. (1986) The economics of schooling: production and efficiency in public schools. *Journal of Economic Literature*, 24(3), 1141–1177.

Hanushek, E. (2002) The failure of input-based schooling policies. NBER Working Paper No. 9040. Cambridge, MA: National Bureau of Economic Research.

Hanushek, E. (2003) The failure of input-based resource policies. *Economic Journal*, 11(485), F64–F68.

Hanushek, E. and Rivkin, S. (2004) How to improve the supply of high quality teachers. In D. Ravitch (Ed.), *Brookings Papers on Education Policy*. Washington, DC: Brookings Institution.

Hanushek, E. and Rivkin, S.G. (2006). Teacher quality. In E. Hanushek and F. Welch (Eds), *Handbook of the Economics of Education*, Vol. 2. Amsterdam: Elsevier.

Hanushek, E.A. and Woessman, L. (2007) The role of education quality for economic growth. World Bank Policy Research Working Paper, 4122. Washington, DC: World Bank.

Hanushek, E., Kain, J., O'Brien, D. and Rivkin, S. (2005) The market for teacher quality. NBER.

Hayhoe, R. and Li, J. (2010) The idea of a normal university in the 21st century. *Frontiers of Education in China*, 5(1), 74–103.

Hazans, M. (2010) Teacher pay, class size and local governments: evidence from the Latvian reform. Discussion Paper No. 5291. IZA Discussion Paper Series. Bonn: Institute for the Study of Labour (IZA).

Heckman, J.J., Heinrich, C. and Smith, J. (2002) The performance of performance standards. *Journal of Human Resources*, 37, 778–811.

Hedges, J. (2002) The importance of posting and interaction with the education bureaucracy in becoming a teacher in Ghana. *International Journal of Education Development*, 22(3–4), 353–366.

Hendrikz, Johan (2006) Mobile phone technology as an instrument for student support. 4th Pan-Commonwealth Forum on Open Learning. 30 October – 3 November. Ocho Rios, Jamaica.

Hendrikz, J. and Prins, G. (2009) The use of mobile phones in enhancing academic performance in distance education: an African perspective. International Council for Open and Distance Learning Conference, Maastricht, 7–10 June.

References 249

Heneveld, W. (1994) *Planning and Monitoring the Quality of Primary Education in Sub Saharan Africa.* Washington, DC: World Bank.

Holmlund, H. and Sund, K. (2005) Is the gender gap in school performance affected by the sex of the teacher? *Labour Economics,* 15(1), 37–53.

Holmström, B. and Milgrom, P. (1991) Multitask principal-agent analyses: incentive contracts, asset ownership and job design. *Journal of Law, Economics and Organization,* 7, 24–51.

Hopkins, D. (2001) *School Improvement for Real.* London: Routledge/Falmer.

Hoxby, C. (1996) How teachers' unions affect education production. *Quarterly Journal of Economics,* 111(4), 671–718.

Hoxby, C.M. (2002) Would school choice change the teaching profession? *Journal of Human Resources,* 37, 846–891.

Hoxby, C.M. and Leigh, A. (2004) Pulled away or pushed out? Explaining the decline of teacher aptitude in the United States. *American Economic Review,* 93, 236–240.

Hurst, P. (1981) Some issues in improving the quality of education. *Comparative Education,* 17(2), 185–193.

IBM (2005) Improving India's Education System through ICT, International Business Machines India Ltd, Bangalore, India.

Ilboudo, P.T. (2003) L'éducation bilingue au Burkina Faso. Case study commissioned by ADEA in the framework of the *Challenge of Learning Study.* Paris: ADEA.

ILO (2009) Impact of the global economic recession on education (SECTOR Notes). Geneva: ILO.

ILO (2011) Update of sectoral aspects in the context of economic recovery: education and research (Fourth Item on the Agenda No. GB.310/STM/4). GB 310th Session. Geneva: ILO.

ILO/UNESCO (1966) Recommendation Concerning the Status of Teachers, adopted by the Special Intergovernmental Conference on the Status of Teachers, Paris, 5 October 1966.

IMF (2010a) Coping with the global financial crisis: challenges facing low-income countries. Washington, DC: IMF.

IMF (2010b). World Economic Outlook. Washington, DC: IMF.

Independent (2010) Cameron & Co woo India as demand for retail goods rockets. 1 August. Available at: www.independent.co.uk/news/business/analysis-and-features (accessed 2 August 2010).

*info*Dev (2010a) Survey of ICTs for Education in India and South Asia, Extended Summary, PricewaterhouseCoopers, Delhi, India.

*info*Dev (2010b) Survey of ICTs for Education in India and South Asia, Country Studies, PricewaterhouseCoopers, Delhi, India.

Ingersoll, R.M. (2004) Four myths about America's teacher quality problem. In M.A. Smylie and D. Miretsky (Eds), *Developing the Teacher Workforce* (pp. 28–40). Chicago: University of Chicago Press.

Jackson, W. (2005) Capabilities, culture and social structure. *Review of Social Economy,* 63(1), 101–123.

Jacob, B.A. and Levitt, S.D. (2003) Rotten applies: an investigation of the prevalence and predictors of teacher cheating. *Quarterly Journal of Economics,* 118(3), 843–877.

Juel, C. (1991) Beginning reading. In R. Borr, M. Kamil and P. Mosenthal (Eds), *Handbook of Reading Research,* vol. 2, chapter 27. London: Longman.

Kane, T.J., Rockoff, J.E. and Staiger, D.O. (2005) Identifying effective teachers in New York City. Paper presented at the NBER Summer Institute.

250 *References*

Kane, T.J., Rockoff, J.E. and Staiger, D.O. (2008) What does certification tell us about teacher effectiveness? Evidence from New York City. *Economics of Education Review*, 27(6), 615–631.

Kanu, Y. (2007) Tradition and educational reconstruction in Africa in postcolonial and global times: the case for Sierra Leone. *African Studies Quarterly*, 9(3).

Kellaghan, T. and Greaney, V. (2003) Monitoring performance: assessment and examinations in Africa. Background paper commissioned by ADEA for its Biennial Meeting (Mauritius, 3–6 December). Paris: ADEA.

Kellaghan, T. and Greaney, V. (2004) *Assessment Student Learning in Africa*. Washington, DC: World Bank.

Kimane, S., Matsoso, L. and Lefoka, J. (2000) Lesotho country study on basic education: OSISA Initiatives Final Report. Maseru.

Kingdon, G. (1996) Student achievement and teacher pay: a case-study of India. STICERD Discussion Paper No. 74. London: London School of Economics.

Kingdon, G.G. (2006) Teacher characteristics and student performance in India: a pupil fixed effects approach. Global Poverty Research Group Working Paper 059.

Kingdon, G. and Sipahimalani-Rao, V. (2010) Para-teachers in India: status and impact. *Economic and Political Weekly*, XLV(12), 59–67.

Kingdon, G. and Teal, F. (2003) Does performance-related pay for teachers improve student performance? Some evidence from India. Working Paper. Oxford: Department of Economics, University of Oxford.

Kingdon, G.G. and Teal, F. (2007) Does performance related pay for teachers improve student performance? Some evidence from India. *Economics of Education Review*, 26(4), 473–486.

Kingdon, G.G. and Teal, F. (2010) Teachers unions, teachers pay and student performance in India. *Journal of Development Economics*, 91 (2), 278–288.

Kingdon, J.W. (1995) *Agendas, Alternatives, and Public Policies*. New York: Longman.

Knight, J. and Sabot, R. (1990) *Education, Productivity and Inequality: The East African Natural Experiment*. Oxford: Oxford University Press, Oxford Lavy.

Komunte, B. (1996) *Situation of Primary School Women Teachers During the Economic Crisis in Tanzania*. Dar es Salaam: AGSC.

Konadu, D.A. (1994) Improving the deployment of teachers: the Ghanaian experience. International Institute for Education Planning. Paris: UNESCO.

Kremer, M., Muralidharan, K., Chaudhury, N., Rogers, H. and Hammer, J. (2005) Teacher absence in India: a snapshot. *Journal of the European Economic Association*, 3, 658–667.

Kukulska-Hulme, A. (2006) Mobile language learning now and in the future. *Från vision till praktik: Språkutbildning och Informationsteknik* (From Vision to Practice: Language Learning and IT). Swedish Net University (Nätuniversitetet).

Kyrili, K. and Martin, M. (2010a) The impact of the global economic crisis on the budget of low-income countries (Research Report). London: Oxfam.

Kyrili, K. and Martin, M (2010b). Monitoring the impact of the financial crisis on national education financing: a cross country study (Paper commission for the EFA Global Monitoring Report 2011). Paris: UNESCO.

Lave, J. and Wenger, E. (1991) *Situated Learning: Legitimate Peripheral Participation*. Cambridge: Cambridge University Press.

Lavy, V. (2002) Evaluating the effect of teachers' group performance incentives on pupil achievement. *Journal of Political Economy*, 110, 1286–1317.

Lavy, V. (2004) Performance pay and teachers' effort, productivity and grading ethics. Working Paper No. 10622. Cambridge, MA: NBER.

References   251

Lavy, V. (2007) Using performance based pay to improve the quality of teaching. *The Future of Teaching*, 17(1), 87–109.

Lawless, K.A. and Pelligrino, J.W. (2007) Professional development in integrating technology into teaching and learning: knowns, unknowns, and ways to pursue better questions and answers. *Review of Educational Research*, 77(4), 575–614.

Lazear, E. (2003) Teacher incentives. *Swedish Economic Policy Review*, 10, 197–213.

Leach, J. and Moon, B. (1999) *Learners and Pedagogy*. London: Paul Chapman.

Leach, J. and Moon, B. (2008) *The Power of Pedagogy*. London: Sage.

Leach, J., Ahmed, A., Makalimo, S. and Power, T. (2005) DEEP IMPACT: an investigation of the use of information and communication technologies for teacher education in the global south. Researching the issues. DFID Research Series. London, Department for International Development.

Leithwood, K. (2007) Teacher working conditions that matter. *Education Canada*, 47(2), 42–45.

Lewin, Keith M. (2002) The costs of supply and demand for teacher education: dilemmas for development. *International Journal of Educational Development*, 22(3), 221–242.

Lewin, K. (2011) Making rights realities: researching educational access, transitions and equity, CREATE (Consortium for Research on Educational Access, Transitions and Equity), Sussex, UK.

Lewin, K.M. and Stuart, J.S. (2003) *Researching Teacher Education: New Perspectives on Practice, Performance and Policy*. London: DFID.

Li, B. (2009) The use of e-learning in pre-service teacher education. *Campus Wide Information Systems*, 26(2), 132–136.

Li, Y., Zhao, D., Huang, R. and Ma, Y. (2008) Mathematical preparation of elementary teachers in China: changes and issues. *Journal of Mathematics Teacher Education*, 11(5), 417–430.

Lieberman, A. and Miller, L. (2001) *Teachers Caught in the Action: Professional Development That Matters*. New York: Teachers College Press.

Lockheed, M.E. and Verspoor, A.M. (1991) *Improving Primary Education in Developing Countries*. Oxford: Oxford University Press for the World Bank.

Loeb, S. and Reininger, M. (2004) Public policy and teacher labor markets. East Lansing: Education Policy Center at Michigan State University.

López-Acevedo, G. (2002) Teachers' incentives and professional development in schools in Mexico. Policy Research Working Paper No. 2777. Washington, DC: World Bank.

Louzano, P., Moriconi, G., Rocha, V. and Portella, R. (2010) *Who Wants to be a Teacher in Brazil? Are Teachers Being Well Prepared for the Classroom? Attractiveness, Selection and Training of Teachers in Brazil*. Fundącao Lemano and Instituto Futuro Brasil, Sao Paulo.

Mackenzie, N. (2007) Teacher morale: more complex than we think? *The Australian Educational Researcher*, 34(1), 89–104.

Maclure, Richard (1997) *Négligée et sous-estimée: La recherche en éducation en Afrique centrale et Afrique occidentale. Une synthèse d'études nationales du ROCARE.* avec le soutien de SARA, HHRAN, USAID/AFR/SD.

McCormick, R. (1992) Distance higher education in the People's Republic of China. Unpublished PhD thesis. Milton Keynes: The Open University.

McCormick, R., Fox, A., Carmichael, P. and Proctor, R. (2010) *Researching and Understanding Educational Networks*. London: Routledge.

Macdonald, D. (1999) Teacher attrition: a review of the literature. *Teaching and Teacher Education*, 15(8), 835–848.

252 *References*

McEwan, P.J. and Santibáñez, L. (2005) Teacher and principal incentives in Mexico. In E. Vegas (Ed.), *Incentives to Improve Teaching: Lessons from Latin America, Directions in Development* (pp. 213–253). Washington, DC: World Bank.

Makkawi, Ibrahim (2002) Role conflict and the dilemma of Palestinian teachers in Israel. *Comparative Education,* 38(1), 39–52, 1.

Menezes-Filho, N.A. and Parzello, E.T. (2007) Do teachers' wages matter for proficiency? Evidence from a funding reform. *Brazil Economics of Education Review*, 26, 660–672.

Menon, G., Chennat, S. and Sharma, G. (2010) *India One Million: Feasibility Study*, UK Open University and Plan International, Delhi, India (unpublished).

Mestry, R., Hendricks, I. and Bisschoff, T. (2009) Perceptions of teachers on the benefits of teacher development programmes in one province of South Africa. *South African Journal of Education*, 29, 475–490.

MHRD (2010) *Sarva Shiksha Abhiyan*. Ministry of Human Resource Development, Delhi. Available at: http://ssa.nic.in/ (accessed 3 August 2010).

Michaelowa, K. (2002) Teacher job satisfaction, student achievement and the cost of primary education in francophone sub-Saharan Africa. HWWA Discussion Paper No. 188. Hamburg: Hamburg Institute of International Economics.

Miller, Jane (1995) Trick or treat? The autobiography of the question. *English Quarterly,* 27(3), 22–26.

Ministry of Education (2008) *Primary and Secondary Teacher Education Plan 2008* (Jiaoyubu 2008 nian zhongxiaoxue jaoshi peixun jihua qidong shishi – 教育部 2008 年中小学教师培训计划启动实施). Available at: http://sn.ifeng.com/article/show. php?itemid=382 (accessed 8 November 2011).

Ministry of Education (2009a) *Educational Statistics Yearbook of China 2008*. Beijing: Department of Development and Planning, Ministry of Education.

Ministry of Education (2009b) *Notice on How to Implement 'Rural School Master Teacher Plan in 2010'* (教育部关于做好2010年"农村学校教育硕士师资培养计划"实施工作的通知 Jiaoyubu guanyu zuohao 2010 'Nengcun xuexiao jiaoyushuoshixhi zi peiyang jihua' shishi gongzuode tongzhi). Available at: www.edu.cn/pei_yang_810/20091012/t20091012_411975.shtml.

Ministry of Education (2010) National economic accounting. In *China Statistical Yearbook 2009* (in Chinese). Available at: www.xbjcyc.cn/year/qg/2009/indexch.htm (accessed 8 November 2011).

Ministry of Education (2011a) *Special Teacher Recruitment Plan* (特岗教师计划Te gangjiaoshi jihua). Available at: http://tg.ncss.org.cn/ (accessed 3 February 2012).

Ministry of Education (2011b) *Kindergarden Teacher Specialism Standard [Trial] (*幼儿园教师专业标准（试行） *Youeryuan jiaoshi zhuanye biaozhun [shixing]; Primary school teacher specialism standard (Xiaoxue jiaoshi zhuanye biaozhun [shixing]* 小学教师专业标准（试行）; *Middle school teacher specialism standard [trial] (Zhongxue jiaoshi zhuanye biaozhun [shixing]* 中学教师专业标准（试行）. Available at: www.cnr.cn/china/gdgg/201111/t20111126_508837400.shtml.

Ministry of Education (2012) *The Notice about how to Implement 'Rural School Master Plan in 2010'*. Available at: www.edu.cn/pei_yang_810/20091012/t20091012_411975.shtml.

Ministry of Education and Culture (2001) *Education Sector Development Programme: Primary Education Development Plan 2002–2006*. Dar es Salaam: United Republic of Tanzania

Mizala, A. and Romaguera, P. (2005) Teachers' salary structure and incentives in Chile. In E. Vegas (Ed.), *Incentives to Improve Teaching: Lessons from Latin America, Directions in Development*. Washington, DC: World Bank.

References   253

Moon, B. (1998) The English exception? International perspectives on the initial education and training of teachers. UCET Occasional Paper, No. 11. London, UCET.

Moon, B. (2000) The open learning environment: a new paradigm for international developments in teacher education. In B. Moob, S. Brown and M. Peretz (Eds), *Routledge International Companion to Education*. London: Routledge.

Moon, B. (2003) A retrospective review of the national case studies on institutional approaches to teacher education. In B. Moon, L. Vlasceau and L.C. Barrows (Eds), *Institutional Approaches to Teacher Education within Higher Education in Europe: Current Models and New Developments*. Bucharest: UNESCO.

Moon, B. (2007a) School-based teacher development in Sub-Saharan Africa: building a new research agenda. *Curriculum Journal*, 18(3), 355–371.

Moon, B. (2007b) The global teacher crisis – meeting the challenge through new technologies and new modes of teaching and learning. Keynote presentation to the 12th Cambridge International Conference on Open and Distance Learning, Cambridge, UK. 28 September. Available at: www2.open.ac.uk/r06/conference/BobMoonKeynote-Cambridge2007.pdf.

Moon, B. (2008) Re-thinking the role of the university in teacher education: the Teacher Education in Sub-Saharan Africa (TESSA) experience. Hyderabad, Presentation to the ACU Conference of Executive Heads, 12.

Moon, B. and Buckler, A. (2007) Conceptualising a research agenda: teachers and the development of rural communities. Paper presented at the BERA Conference, 5–8 September. The Institute of Education, The University of London, UK.

Moon, B. and Leach, J. (2008) *The Power of Pedagogy*. London: Sage.

Moon, B. and Nhlanganiso, D. (2002) Challenging the assumptions about teacher education and training in Sub-Saharan Africa: a new role for open learning and ICT. Second Pan-Commonwealth Forum on Open Learning, 29 September – 2 August, Durban, South Africa.

Moon, B., Ben Peretz, M. and Brown, S. (Eds) (2000) *Routledge International Companion to Education*. London: Routledge.

Mpokosa, C. and Ndaruhutse, S. (2008) *Managing Teachers: The Centrality of Teacher Management to Quality Education. Lessons from Developing Countries*. London: VSO and CfBT.

Mulkeen, A. (2005) Teachers for rural schools: a challenge for Africa. Ministerial Seminar on Education for Rural Peoples in Africa: Policy Lessons, Options and Priorities, Addis Ababa, 7–9 September.

Mulkeen, A. (2006) Policy planning, utilization and management of rural primary school teachers in Africa. Report of the Maseru Workshop 2005. Washington, DC: World Bank.

Mulkeen, A., Chapman, D., Dejaegghere, J. and Leu, E. (2007) Recruiting, retaining and retraining secondary school teachers and principals in Sub-Saharan Africa. World Bank Working Papers 99, African Human Development Series. Washington, DC: World Bank.

Mundy, K. and Dryden Peterson, S. (2011) *Educating Children in Conflict Zones: Research, Policy and Practice for Systemic Change*. New York: Teachers College Press.

Muralidharan, K. and Sundararaman, V. (2009) Teacher performance pay: experimental evidence from India. NBER Working Paper No. 15323. Cambridge, MA: National Bureau of Economic Research.

Murnane, J. and Cohen, D. (1986) Merit pay and the evaluation problem: why most merit pay plans fail and few survive. *Harvard Educational Review*, 56, 1–17.

254 *References*

Murphy, R. and Johnson, D. (2009) Education and development in China – institutions, curriculum and society. *International Journal of Educational Development*, 29, 447–453.

Mwamwenda, X. (1995) Job satisfaction among secondary school teachers in Transkei. *South African Journal of Education*, 15, 84–87.

Naismith, L., Lonsdale, P., Vavoula, G. and Sharples, M. (2004) NESTA Futurelab Report 11: literature review in mobile technologies and learning. Bristol: NESTA Futurelab. Available at: http://archive.futurelab.org.uk/resources/publications-reports-articles/literature-reviews/Literature-Review203.

National Bureau of Statistics of China (2012) *China's Total Population and Structural Changes in 2011.* Available at: www.stats.gov.cn/english/newsandcomingevents/t20120120_402780233.htm (accessed 20 January 2012).

National Council for Teacher Education (NCTE) (2009) *National Curriculum Framework for Teacher Education Report.* New Delhi: NCTE.

National Population and Family Planning Commission of China (2010) Available at: www.npfpc.gov.cn/en/about/detail.aspx?articleid=091124092450625020 (accessed 8 November 2011).

National Professional Teachers' Organisation of South Africa (2002) Educator morale in South Africa in 2002. Report on findings.

NCCE (2004) *Research Report on Tracer Study on NCE Graduates in Nigeria from 1999–2003.* Department of Planning, Research and Statistics, Abuja, NCCE.

NCERT (2005) Position paper of the national focus group on Teacher Education for Curriculum Renewal, Delhi, NCERT.

Ndoye, M. (2002) Reaching schools: where quality starts. *ADEA Newsletter*, 14(3), 1–2.

Nelson Mandela Foundation (2005) *Emerging Voices.* Cape Town: HSRC Press.

Nleya, P.T. (1999) Perceptions of Botswana primary teacher educators on selected teaching skills. *International Journal of Educational Development*, 19, 147–156.

Nordstrum, L.E. (2011) Private educational expenditure, cost-reduction strategies and the financial barriers that remain after fee abolition: assessing patterns of household primary school spending in 12 low- and middle-income countries, and policy implications for EFA. Background paper prepared for 2012 EFA Global Monitoring Report. Paris: UNESCO.

Nussbaum, M. (2000) *Women and Human Development: The Capabilities Approach.* Cambridge: Cambridge University Press.

Nussbaum, M. (2003) Capabilities as fundamental entitlements: Sen and social justice. *Feminist Economics*, 9(2–3), 33–59.

Nussbaum, M. (2006) Education and democratic citizenship: capabilities and quality education. *Journal of Human Development*, 7(3), 385–395.

Observer (2010) Nigeria highlights world's failure to tackle global education deficit. 19 September, p. 19.

O'Connor, K. and Dillon, D. (2008) Pedagogical relationship as curriculum in a teacher education program. Paper presented to the American Association for Advancement of Curriculum Studies, Columbia University, New York, 23 March.

Odden, A. and Kelley, C. (1997) *Paying Teachers for What They Know and Do.* Thousand Oaks: Corwin Press.

OECD (2011) *Education at a Glance 2011.* Paris: OECD.

OECD-DAC (2010) *International Development Statistics: DAC Annual Aggregates.* Paris: OECD Development Assistance Committee.

OED (2010) *Oxford English Dictionary.* Oxford: Oxford University Press.

References   255

Ogiebaen, S.E. and Uwameiye, R. (2005) Analysis of factors influencing negative attitudes towards teacher education in Nigeria. *Education*, 126(2), 292–303.

Olatunji, B. (2010) What teacher education policy will achieve. allAfrica.com, 27 April.

O'Malley, B. (2007) *Education Under Attack*. Paris: UNESCO.

Omo-Ojugo, M.O. (2009) Demand and supply of teachers for primary schools in the 21st century in Nigeria. *European Journal of Social Sciences*, 7(3), 149–156.

Omotor, D.G. (2004) An analysis of federal government expenditure in the education sector of Nigeria. *Journal of Social Sciences*, 9(2), 105–110.

OPHI (2010) New poverty index finds Indian states worse than Africa. Oxford Poverty and Human Development Initiative, University of Oxford, Oxford, England.

O-Saki, K.M. and Agu, A.O. (2002). A study of classroom interaction in primary schools in the United Republic of Tanzania. *Prospects*, 32, 103–116.

Osokoya, I. (2010) Teacher education in Nigeria: past, present and future challenges. *Academic Leadership Journal*, 8(4). Available at: www.academicleadership.org.

O'Sullivan, M. (2002) Reform implementation and the realities within which teachers work: a Namibian case study. *Compare*, 32(2), 219–237.

Paine, L. and Fang, Y. (2007) Dilemmas in reforming China's teaching: assuring 'quality' in professional development. In M.T. Tatto (Ed.), *Reforming Teaching Globally* (pp. 21–53). Oxford: Symposium Books.

Park, A. and Hannum, E. (2002) Educating China's rural children in the 21st century. *Harvard China Review*, 3(2), 8–14.

Pedder, D., Storey, A. and Opfer, D. (2008) *Synthesis Report. Schools and Continuing Professional Development (CPD) in England – State of the Nation Research Project (T34718). A Report commissioned by the Training and Development Agency for Schools*. Cambridge/ Milton Keynes: Cambridge University/Open University. Available at: www.tda.gov. uk/cpd-leader/effective-cpd/~/media/resources/cpd-leader/effective-cpd-research/ cpd_stateofthenation_report.pdf?keywords=State+of+the+Nation+Research+Project+ (accessed 8 November 2011).

Pham Hoa Hiep (2006) *Researching the Research Culture in English Language Education in Vietnam*, TESL-EJ, Volume 10, Number 2. Available at: www.tesl-ej.org/word-press/issues/volume10/ej38/ej38a10 (accessed 19 January 2011).

Pimienta, D. (2007) Digital divide, social divide, paradigmatic divide. *International Journal of Information Communication Technologies and Human Development*, 1(1), 33–48.

Podgursky, M. and Springer, M. (2007) Credentials versus performance: review of the teacher performance pay research. *Peabody Journal of Education*, 82(4), 551–573.

Podgursky, M., Monroe, R. and Watson, D. (2004) The academic quality of public school teachers: an analysis of entry and exit behavior. *Economics of Education Review*, 23, 507–518.

Polonyana, M.A. (2000) An evaluation of the effectiveness of the in-service teacher training programme at the National Teacher Training College (NTTC), Lesotho. Unpublished M.Ed Dissertation, Roma: National University of Lesotho.

Pouzevara, S.L. and Kahn, R (2007). Learning communities enabled by mobile technology: a case study of school-based, in-service secondary teacher training in rural Bangladesh. Innovative information and communication technology in education and its potential for reducing poverty in the Asia and Pacific region. Asian Development Bank.

Power, T. and Porteous, K. (2009) Is there a role for Information and Communications Technologies (ICTs) in the education and development of disadvantaged rural communities? In C. Vrasidas (Ed.), *ICT, for Education, Development, and Social Justice*. Charlotte: Information Age Publishing.

256 References

Power, T. and Sankale, J. (2009) Mobile technologies: current practice, future possibilities. In C. Vrasidas (Ed.), *ICT, for Education, Development, and Social Justice*. Charlotte: Information Age Publishing.

Power, Tom and Shrestha, Prithvi (2010) Mobile technologies for (English) language learning: an exploration in the context of Bangladesh. In: IADIS International Conference: Mobile Learning 2010, 19–21 March, Porto, Portugal.

Power, T. and Simpon, J. (2011) *Scoping Mission for an English Language Training (ELT) Programme in South Sudan. Final Report*. DFID Human Development Resource Centre, Cambridge.

Power, T. and Thomas, R. (2007) The classroom in your pocket? *The Curriculum Journal*, 18(3), 373–388.

Power, T., Deane, H. and Hedges, C. (2009) *Equipping Language Educators at Scale: Open Educational Resources and Institutional Collaboration for Professional Development and Practice*. 8th International Language and Development Conference. Dhaka: British Council.

Prendergast, C. (1999) The provision of incentives in firms. *Journal of Economic Literature*, 37, 7–63.

Pritchett, L. and Filmer, D. (1997) What education production functions really show: a positive theory of education spending. Policy Research Working Paper No. 1795. Washington, DC: World Bank.

Psacharopoulos, G., Valenzuela, J. and Arends, M. (1996) Teacher salaries in Latin America: a review. *Economics of Education Review*, 15(4), 401–406.

Qorro, Martha (1997) The role and place of language in education and society: the case of Kiswahili and English in Tanzania. *Papers in Education and Development*, 18, 129–144.

Qorro, M.A.S. (2001) The language medium of instruction in secondary schools. In A.F. Lwaitama, E.G. Mtalo and L. Mboma (Eds), *The Multi-dimensional Crisis of Education in Tanzania: Debate and Action* (pp. 105–117). Dar es salaam: University of Dar es Salaam Convocation.

Rahman, A., Kabir, Md. M. and Azore, R. (2006) *Effect of BRAC-PACE Training on English Language Teachers of Rural Non-Government Secondary Schools*.

Ramachandran, V., Pal, M., Jain, S., Shekar, S. and Sharma, J. (2005) Teacher motivation in India. Jaipur, Educational Resource Unit, 41.

Ramsey, G. (2000) Teacher-driven curriculum or curriculum driven teachers? A new look at an old dilemma. Quality Teaching Series, Paper no. 3. Australian College of Education, ACT, Australia.

Reddi, U.V. and Sinha, V. (2003) India – ICT use in education. In G. Farrell and C. Wachholz (Eds), *Meta-survey on the Use of Technologies in Education in Asia and the Pacific 2003–2004*. Bangkok: UNESCO.

Rivkin, S., Hanushek, E. and Kain, J.F. (2005) Teachers, schools and academic achievement. *Econometrica*, 73, 417–458.

Rizvi, M. (2008) The role of school principals in enhancing teacher professionalism: lessons from Pakistan. *Educational Management Administration and Leadership*, 36(1), 85–100.

Robeyns, I. (2003a) *The Capability Approach: An Interdisciplinary Introduction*. Pavia: Third International Conference on the Capability Approach.

Robeyns, I. (2003b) Sen's capability approach and gender inequality: selecting relevant capabilities. *Feminist Economics*, 9(2–3), 61–92.

Robeyns, I. (2005a) The capability approach: a theoretical survey. *Journal of Human Development*, 6(1), 93–114.

References   257

Robeyns, I. (2005b) Selecting capabilities for quality of life measurement. *Social Indicators Research*, 74(1), 191–215.

Robinson, B. (2008) Using distance education and ICT to improve access, equity and the quality in rural teachers' professional development in western China. *International Review of Research in Open and Distance Learning*, 9(1), 1–17. Available at: www.irrodl. org/index.php/irrodl/article/view/486 (accessed 8 November 2011).

Robinson, B. and Yi, W. (2008) The role and status of non-governmental ('*daike*') teachers in China's rural education. *International Journal of Educational Development*, 28, 35–54.

Robinson, B. and Yi, W. (2009) Strengthening basic education: an EU–China joint project in Gansu province. *European Journal of Education*, 44(1), 95–109.

Rockoff, J. (2004) The impact of individual teachers on student achievement: evidence from panel data. *American Economic Review*, May, 247–252.

Ross, S. (1973) The economic theory of agency: the principal's problem. *American Economic Review*, 63(2), 134–139.

Round, A. and Lovegrove, G. (2005) ICT professionals in the UK and offshore outsourcing. Council of Professors and Heads of Computing, Swindon, England.

Sampa, F. (2003) The Zambian Primary Reading Programme (PRP) 'Improving access and quality education in basic schools'. Case study commissioned by ADEA in the framework of the *Challenge of Learning Study*. Paris: ADEA.

Santibáñez, L., Martinez, J.F., Datar, A., McEwan, P.J., Setodji, C.M. and Basurto-Davila, R. (2007) Breaking ground: analysis of the assessment system and impact of Mexico's teacher incentive program 'Carrera Magisterial' (No. TR-458-SEP). Technical Reports. RAND Corporation.

Scheerens, J. (2000) *Improving School Effectiveness*. Paris: UNESCO, International.

Schultz, L. (1998) Being and becoming a woman teacher: journey through Nepal. *Gender and Education*, 10(2), 163–183.

Schwartzman, S. (2004) The challenges of education. In C. Brock and S. Schwartzman (Eds), *The Challenges of Education in Brazil*. Didcot: Symposium Books.

Schwille, J. and Dembélé, M. (2007) *Global Perspectives on Teacher Learning: Improving Policy and Practice*. Paris: UNESCO.

Sen, A. (1987) The standard of living. In G. Hawthorn (Ed.), *The Standard of Living*. Cambridge: Cambridge University Press

Sen, A. (1990) Development as capability expansion. In K. Griffen and J. Knight (Eds), *Human Development and the International Development Strategy for the 1990's*. London: Macmillan.

Sen, A. (1992) *Inequality Re-examined*. Cambridge, MA: Harvard University Press.

Sen, A. (1999) *Development as Freedom*. Oxford: Oxford University Press.

Sen, A. (2011) Quality of life: India vs. China. *New York Review of Books*, 12 May, pp. 44–45.

Serrao, A. and Sujatha, B.R. (2004) *Birth Registration: A Background Note*. Community Development Foundation, Bangalore, India.

Shalem, Y. and Hoadley, U. (2009) The dual economy of schooling and teacher morale in South Africa. *International Studies in Sociology of Education*, 19(2), 119–134.

Shi, X. and Englert, P.A.J. (2008) Reform of teacher education in China. *Journal of Education for Teaching*, 34(4), 347–359.

Sifuna, D. and Kaime, J. (2007) The effect of In-Service Education and Training (INSET) programmes in mathematics and science on classroom interaction: a case study of primary and secondary schools in Kenya. *Africa Education Review*, 4(1), 104–126.

258 References

Sinada, M. (2009) Professor of Education at the Open University of Sudan. Interview conducted at the Open University of Sudan, Khartoum, 5 February.

Smith, P.J. (2003) Workplace learning and flexible delivery. *Review of Educational Research*, 73(1), 53–88.

Socialbakers (2011) Available at: www.socialbakers.com/facebook-statistics/india#chart-intervals (accessed 23 January 2011).

Sprietsma, M. and Waltenberg, F. (2005) The impact of teacher's wages on student's performance in the presence of heterogeneity and endogeneity – evidence from Brazil. Université catholique de Louvain, Département des Sciences Economiques Working Paper 2005008.

Stacki, S. (2002) *Women Teachers Empowered in India. Teacher Training Through a Gender Lens.* New York: UNICEF.

State Council (2010) *The Internet in China.* Beijing: Information office of State Council of the People's Republic of China. Available at: http://china.org.cn/government/white-paper/node_7093508.htm (accessed 8 November 2011).

Steer, L. and Wathne, C. (2009) *Achieving Universal Basic Education.* London: Overseas Development Institute.

Stuart, J. and Tatto, M.T. (2000) Designs for initial teacher preparation programmes: an international view. *International Journal of Educational Research*, 33, 493–514.

Sudanese Federal Ministry of Education (1999) Sudan Report to UNESCO.

Sudanese Federal Ministry of Education (2004) National Report on Education.

Sumra, S. (2004) The living and working conditions of teachers in Tanzania: a research report. Dar es Salaam: HakiElimu and the Tanzania Teachers Union.

Tabulawa, R. (1997) Teachers perspective on classroom practice in Botswana: implications for pedagogical change. 3rd Biennial National Conference Of Teacher Education Gaborone, 25–29 August 1997.

Tanuri, L. (2000) Historia de Formacao de Professores. *Revista Brasilleira Educacao*, 14, 61–88.

Tao, S. (2005) *Reflective Journal from Engosengiu Primary School.* Arusha, Tanzania.

Tao, S. (2009) Applying the capability approach to school improvement interventions. In *Tanzania EdQual*, Working Paper No. 11, University of Bristol.

TI (2005) *Stealing the Future: Corruption in the Classroom.* Berling: Transparency International.

Times of India (2009) RTE bane: 12L teacher vacancies. 25 December. Available at: http://timesofindia.indiatimes.com/india/RTE-bane-12L-teacher-vacancies/ (accessed 25 October 2010).

Transparency International (2009) *East African Bribery Index.* Available at: www.transparency.org.

UKNARIC (2007) Analysis report on teacher training system in Sudan. Refugees into Teaching Project.

Umansky, I. (2005) A literature review of teacher quality and incentives: theory and evidence. In E. Vegas (Ed.), *Incentives to Improve Teaching: Lessons from Latin America, Directions in Development* (pp. 21–62). Washington, DC: World Bank.

UNESCO (1966) *Recommendation Concerning the Status of Teachers.* Paris.

UNESCO (1968) *Final Report of Conference on Education and Scientific and Technical Training in Relation to Development in Africa. Jointly organized by UNESCO and the Organization of African Unity.* Paris: UNESCO.

UNESCO (2000) *Increasing the Number of Women Teachers in Rural Schools.* Bangkok: UNESCO PROAP.

UNESCO (2001) *Sudan Basic Education Sub-Sector Study*. UNESCO and UNDP, 137.

UNESCO (2005) *Global Monitoring Report: The Quality Imperative*. Paris: UNESCO.

UNESCO (2006) *Teachers and Educational Quality: Monitoring Global Needs for 2015*. Montreal: UNESCO Institute of Statistics.

UNESCO (2007) *The EFA Global Monitoring Report 2008. Education for All by 2015. Will We Make It?* Available at: http://portal.unesco.org/education/en/ev.php-URL_ID=49591&URL_DO=DO_TOPIC&URL_SECTION=201.html.

UNESCO (2008) *EFA Global Monitoring Report 2005: Education for All by 2015 – Will We Make It?*

UNESCO (2009) *Overcoming Inequality: Why Governance Matters. UNESCO Education for All Global Monitoring Report*. Paris: Oxford University Press.

UNESCO (2010a) *EFA Global Monitoring Report: Reaching the Marginalized*. Oxford: Oxford University Press and UNESCO.

UNESCO (2010b) *National Progress Report on Education and Training of Teachers in China*. Beijing: Ministry of Education.

UNESCO (2011a) *EFA Global Monitoring Report 2011: The Hidden Crisis: Armed Conflict and Education*. Paris: UNESCO.

UNESCO (2011b) Why education will foster stability in an independent South Sudan. Press briefing.

UNESCO (2012) *National Progress Report on Education and Training of Teachers (update of 2010 report)*. Beijing: Ministry of Education.

UNESCO Institute for Statistics (2011a) *Financing Education in Sub-Saharan Africa: Meeting the Challenges of Expansion, Equity and Quality*. Montreal: UNESCO-UIS.

UNESCO Institute for Statistics (2011b) *Global Education Digest 2011: Comparing Education Statistics around the World*. Montreal: UNESCO-UIS.

UNESCO/TTISSA (2008) *Teacher Education Policy Forum for Sub-Saharan Africa*. UNESCO-ADB-ADEA, UNESCO/TTISSA.

UNICEF (2005) *Annual Report 2005*. Available at: www.unicef.org/publications/index_34144.html.

UNICEF (2010) *Progress Evaluation of the UNICEF Education in Emergencies and Post-Crisis Transition Programme*. New York: UNICEF.

UNICEF (2010). *Protecting Salaries of Frontline Teachers and Health Workers*. Social and Economic Policy Working Briefs. New York: UNICEF.

UNICEF (2012) Available at: www.unicef.org/india/education_1551htm.

Unterhalter, E. (2003a) The capabilities approach and gendered education: an examination of South African complexities. *Theory and Research in Education*, 1(1), 7–22.

Unterhalter, E. (2003b) Education, capabilities and social justice. In *EFA Global Monitoring Report*. Paris: UNESCO.

Unterhalter, E. (2007) Gender equality, education, and the capability approach. In M. Walker and E. Unterhalter (Eds), *Amartya Sen's Capability Approach and Social Justice in Education*. New York: Palgrave Macmillan.

Unterhalter, E. and Brighouse, H. (2007) Distribution of what for social justice in education. In M. Walker and E. Unterhalter (Eds), *Amartya Sen's Capability Approach and Social Justice in Education*. New York: Palgrave Macmillan.

Unterhalter, E. and Walker, M. (2007) Conclusion. In M. Walker and E. Unterhalter (Eds), *Amartya Sen's Capability Approach and Social Justice in Education*. New York: Palgrave Macmillan.

Unterhalter, E., Challender, C. and Rajagopalan, R. (2005) Measuring gender equality in education. In S. Aikman and E. Unterhalter (Eds), *Beyond Access*. London: Oxfam.

260 References

USAID (2009) Basic education in Ghana: progress and problems. Available at: http://ddp-ext.worldbank.org/EdStats/GHAdprep09.pdf (accessed July, 2011).

Valk, J.-H., Rashid, A. and Elder, L. (2010) Using mobile phones to improve educational outcomes: an analysis of evidence from Asia. *International Review of Research in Open and Distance Learning*, 11(1).

Van der Berg, S. and Louw, M. (2007) Lessons learnt from SACMEQ 11: South African student performance in regional context. Working Paper 16/07, University of Stellenbosch, Department of Economics and Bureau for Economic Research.

van Graan, M. (2003) Practising critical reflection in teacher education: case study of three Namibian teacher development programmes. Commissioned by ADEA in the framework of *The Challenge of Learning Study*. Paris: ADEA.

Vegas, E. (2007) Teacher labor markets in developing countries. *The Future of Teaching*, 17(1), 219–232.

Vegas, E. and Umansky, I. (2005) Improving teaching and learning through effective incentives: lessons from education reforms in Latin America. *Incentives to Improve Teaching: Lessons from Latin America, Directions in Development* (pp. 1–19). Washington, DC: World Bank.

Verhagen, S. and Tweedie, L. (2001) They've got class! A policy report on Zambian teachers' attitudes to their own profession. *VSO Valuing Teachers*. Lusaka, VSO, 39.

Verspoor, A. (2005) The way forward: emerging priorities for action. In A. Verspoor (Ed.), *The Challenge of Learning: Improving the Quality of Basic Education in Sub-Saharan Africa*. Paris: ADEA.

Villegas Reimers, Eleonora and Reimers, Fernando (1996) Where are the 60 million teachers? The missing voice in educational reform around the world. *Prospects*, 26(3), 469–492.

VSO (2002) *What Makes Teachers Tick? A Policy Report on Teachers' Motivation in Developing Countries*. A VSO Sharing Skills, Changing Lives Publication, UK, 57pp.

VSO (2007) Teachers' voice: a policy research report on teachers' motivation and perceptions of their profession in Nigeria. *Valuing Teachers*. VSO Nigeria, 72.

VSO (2008) Listening to teachers: the motivation and morale of education workers in Mozambique. *Valuing Teachers*, VSO Mozambique, 80pp.

VSO (2009) How much is a good teacher worth? A report on the motivation and morale of teachers in Ethiopia. *Valuing Teachers*. Addis Ababa, VSO Ethiopia, 64pp.

Walker, M. (2006) Towards a capability-based theory of social justice for education policy-making. *Journal of Education Policy*, 21(2), 163–185.

Walker, M. and Unterhalter, E. (eds) (2007) *Amartya Sen's Capability Approach and Social Justice in Education*. First edition. London: Palgrave.

Walkerdine, V. (1990) *Schoolgirl Fictions*. New York and London: Verso.

Walsh, C. (2011) e-Learning in Bangladesh: the 'trainer in your pocket'. IADIS e-Learning Conference. Italy, pp. 165–172, July.

Walsh, C. and Power, T. (2011) Going digital on low-cost mobile phones in Bangladesh. Annual International Conference on Education and e-Learning (EeL). 7–9 November, Singapore.

Ward, L. (2003) Teacher practice and the integration of ICT: why aren't our secondary school teachers using computers in their classrooms? Paper presented at NZARE/AARE, Auckland, New Zealand, 29 November – 3 December.

Wei, R. (2008) *China's Radio & TV Universities and the British Open University: A Comparative Study*. Nanjing: Yilin Press.

Welmond, M. (2002) Globalization viewed from the periphery: the dynamics of teacher identity in the Republic of Benin. *Comparative Education Review*, 46(1), 37–65.

References 261

Wentworth, M. (1990) Developing staff morale. *The Practitioner*, 16(4), 1–8.

Willis, J. (2002) General education in the Sudan. *Durham Education Papers*. Durham, The University of Durham, 1.

Wilson, S.M. and Berne, J. (1999) Teacher learning and the acquisition of professional knowledge: an examination of research on contemporary professional development. In A. Iran-Nejad and P.D. Pearson (Eds), *Review of Research in Education, 24, 1999* (pp. 173–209). Washington, DC: American Educational Research Association.

Wolfenden, F. and Buckler, A. (2011). Adapting OERs for professional communities: the teacher education in Sub-Saharan Africa experience. In A. Okada, T. Connolly and P. Scott (Eds), *Collaborative Learning 2.0: Open Educational Resources*. IGI Global, PA.

Wong, I.R. and de Carvalho, J.A.M. (2004) *Age Structured Transitions in Brazil – Demographic Bonuses and Emerging Challenges*. Committee for International Co-operation in National Research in Demography.

Wong, J.L.N. and Tsui, A.B.M. (2007) How do teachers view the effects of school-based in-service learning activities? A case study in China. *Journal of Education for Teaching*, 33(4), 457–470.

World Bank (1990) *Conditions of Service among Primary and Secondary Teachers in Tanzania*. World Bank.

World Bank (2001) *Brazil: Teacher Development and Incentives, a Strategic Framework*. Report no. 20408 BR.

World Bank (2004) *World Development Report 2004: Making Services Work for Poor People*. Washington, DC: World Bank.

World Bank (2010a) *Education Strategy 2020*. Washington, DC: World Bank.

World Bank (2010b) *Achieving World Class Education in Brazil: The Next Agenda*. Washington, DC: World Bank.

World Bank (2011) *Report on Education in Ghana*.

World Bank Independent Evaluation Group (2006) *From Schooling Access to Learning Outcomes: An Unfinished Agenda. An Evaluation of World Bank Support to Primary Education*. Washington, DC: World Bank.

Wößmann, L. (2010) Cross-country evidence on teacher performance pay. CESifo Working Paper No. 3151. Category 5: Economics of Education. Munich: Institute for Economic Research, University of Munich.

Xie, A. (2006) Institutional innovation and systematic construction of teacher education in the transformational period. *Frontiers of Education in China*, 1(2), 201–211.

Yakouba, Y. (2003) L'implantation de la Nouvelle Approche Pédagogique (NAP) dans l'enseignement primaire au Cameroun. Case study commissioned by ADEA in the framework of *The Challenge of Learning Study*. Paris: ADEA.

Yan, H.B. (2009) Current situation of teacher e-training in China and a more practical model: e-training community. *Campus-wide Information Systems*, 26(2), 114–121. Available at: www.emeraldinsight.com/journals.htm?articleid=1779148&show=abstract (accessed 8 November 2011).

Yu, S.Q. and Wang, M.J. (2006) Modern distance education project for the rural schools of China: recent developments and problems. *Journal of Computer Assisted Learning*, 22, 273–283.

Zeichner, K. and Dahlstrom, L. (1999) *Democratic Teacher Education Reform in Africa: The Case of Namibia*. Boulder: Westview Press.

Zhao, J. and Hu, W. (2007) *China Country Case Study (Country Profile Prepared for the Education for all Global Monitoring Report 2008 Education for All by 2015: Will We Make*

262 References

It?). UNESCO. Available at: http://unesdoc.unesco.org/images/0015/001555/155595e.pdf (accessed 8 November 2011).

Zhong, C. (2008) Interpreting and considering the development of the goal orientation in the transformation of Chinese Normal Universities. *Frontiers of Education in China*, 3(4), 594–606.

Zhou, J. and Reed, L. (2005) Chinese government documents on teacher education since the 1980s. *Journal of Education for Teaching International Research and Pedagogy*, 31(3), 201–213.

Zhu, X. and Han, X. (2006) Reconstruction of the teacher education system in China. *International Education Journal*, 7(1), 66–73.

Zhu, Z.T. and Gu, X.Q. (2007) An e-Education approach to teacher professional development in China. *Digital Learning*, 3(6), 17–19.

Index

Aakash tablet 84–5
Aaronson, D. 40
absenteeism, teacher 27, 41, 137
acceptance and adherence to reforms 136, 139–42
accommodation/housing 27, 73
accountability 72, 89, 210
achievement production function 164–5, 167–82
action education model 70
active learning 193, 194, 195
Addis-Ababa Conference 188, 189; Education Plan 189
Adichie, C.N., *Jumping Monkey Hill* 7
African Virtual University 221
age of teachers 61–2
agency 144–6; achievement 145; freedom 145
aid, plateauing of 34
Alkire, S. 147
Anikweze, C.M. 99
Anweshana Experience 82
Arabic 223
Aslam, M. 12, 40
attainment, pupil *see* pupil achievement
attitudes, teachers' 229, 237–8
attrition 23–4, 41
authority 158–60

Bai, M. 62–3, 69
Ballou, D. 41
Bangladesh 25, 194; English in Action 218–20, 221, 225–6
banks 209–10
basic capabilities 143
BBC Janala 218
BBC World Service Trust 218
belonging, sense of 236
bilingual education 191, 196
Blackboards 5
bonus payments 109

Bordia Report 228–9
Botswana 193
boys, women teaching 160–2
Brazil 24–5, 28, 30, 53–4, 101–10, 231; Educational Development Plans 103; Everyone for Education Commitment 107; Institutional Scholarship Programme for Teacher Initiatives 107; Law for Guidelines and Basis of National Education 103, 106; Maintenance and Development Fund for Basic Education and Education Professionals 106; National Education Council (NEC) 103; National Fund for Basic Education 102; National Network for the Continuous Professional Development of Teachers in Basic Education 107–8; national office for education research and statistics 102; National System for Graduate Education Evaluation (SINAES) 106; Programme for the initial formation for Elementary and Secondary Education teachers 107
Bronte, C., *VIllette* 6
Brown, G. 212
Bruns, B. 109
Buckler, A. 15–16, 237
budgets, supplementing in rural areas 73

Canada 237
capability approach 15, 113, 129–49; descriptive analysis of teacher behaviour 132, 135–42; monitoring teacher development 132, 146–8; selecting capabilities for teachers 132, 142–6; situational analysis 133, 133–42; variety of uses 131–2
Capanema, G. 102
career satisfaction 156–8
career stream 108–9
Caucutt, E. 11

264   *Index*

central–local balance 16–17, 30, 53, 78;
India 89; Nigeria 16–17, 92, 99–100
Central Radio and Television University
(CRTVU) 68
Chabal, P. 236
Chad 5
Chattopadhyaya report 81
child-centred pedagogy 139, 140, 193,
194, 195
Children's Investment Fund
Foundation 13–15
Chile 5, 194; National System of School
Performance (SNED) 28
China 5, 30, 53–4, 55–75; education
system 57–9; general background 55–
7; international lessons 74; Master
Teacher Plan 72; National Teacher
Education Network 28; national system
of teacher qualification registration 25;
National Teacher Training Plan 73–4;
reforms to support rural education 71–
4; Special Teacher Recruitment Plan
(STRP) 72; teacher education 64–71;
teachers 59–64
choices 133–5; teacher behaviour 136–42
class sizes 27, 59–60, 61
Cohen, D. 44
Colclough, C. 27
collaborative design 215–21
Colombia 6, 194
Commission for Africa 24
commitment 229, 237–8
'commonly criticised' teacher
behaviour 136–9
Commonwealth of Learning 221
communication technologies *see*
information and communication
technologies (ICTs)
community 17–18, 207; in-service teacher
education and 127–8
community of practice 187
community teachers 187–8
competence, levels of 208–9
competency-based pay 45, 47
competitive society, building a 156
condition-based pay 45, 47
constructing a practice 186–7
context for teacher education 4, 19–31;
policy formation 29–31; teacher
retention 23–5; teacher supply 20–3;
teachers' working conditions and
effectiveness 25–9
contract teachers 26, 95–6, 187–8, 230
conversion factors 132, 133–5; teacher

behaviour 136–42
coordination of pre-service and in-service
training 229, 232
core teaching skills 234
corporal punishment 138
costing 210–11; *see also* economic and cost
constraints
Craig, H.J. 186
CREATE programme 8, 203
critique of teacher education policy 3–4,
8–10
curriculum: school 192, 207; teacher
education 66, 207, 229, 233–4

daike teachers 63–4
Dakar Summit 183, 188; Framework for
Action 7, 129, 188
Daniel, J. 216
data systems 24–5
Davidson, E. 142
Day, C. 127
decentralisation 99–100
deficit model of teacher professionalism
and status 10
DeJaeghere, J.G. 30
Democratic Republic of Congo 5
Department for International
Development (DfID) 3, 10, 98–9
deployment policies 26; India 83;
Nigeria 95
descriptive situational analysis 132, 133–
42; teacher behaviour 132, 135–42
development: gender, education and
151–2; teachers and the development
agenda 3–4, 5–18
devotion 157
dialogue 18
Diané, B. 188
Dillon, D. 124
distance education 200, 214, 231;
Brazil 107; China 68–70, 73–4;
India 82, 84, 85–6
distributed learning 204
double-shift teaching systems 139, 140
Duflo, E. 199, 237

E9 countries 31; Bali ministerial
meeting 21; survey of 21, 22, 23–5, 28
earnings, educational achievement and 14,
15
Eastern and Southern Africa 192–4
economic and cost constraints 4, 32–49;
fiscal shortfalls 33–4; need for structural
salary reforms 41–3; options for

linking salary and performance 43–5; pay as high proportion of educational spending 35–7; positive lessons for addressing 45–8; qualifications, salary and performance 40–1; teacher quantity and quality gaps 32–4; unit costs of post-primary phase teachers 37–40

economic growth 14; China 55–6; India 78

Education for All (EFA) 8, 116, 129, 183, 227; China's progress towards the goals 59; gender equality 151, 163; Global Monitoring Reports *see* Global Monitoring Reports (GMRs); target date of 2015 3, 8, 31

Education for All by 2015. Will we make it? 13

Education International 150

education systems: China 57–9; India 77, 78–80; Nigeria 92

educational expenditure 34; China 57; proportion used on salaries 35–7

educational production function 164

Educational Research Network for Eastern and Southern Africa (ERNESA) 192–4

Educational Research Network for West and Central Africa (ERNWACA) 190–2

Educational Testing Service (ETS) 166

effectiveness of teachers 25–9; Brazil 104–5

Egypt 194

Englert, P.A.J. 62

English 223

English in Action (EIA) 218–20, 221, 225–6

enrolment rates 21, 22; China 57–8; India 77–8; South Sudan 222

environmental conversion factors 133, 135, 136, 137–8, 140–1, 142

Erny, P. 190

exams: China's exam system 74; exam results and salaries 45–7

experience, teacher 176–7

experimental evaluation 45–6, 49

explicit teaching 185

family expectations 155–6

Fang, Y. 66–7, 72

Farrell, J.P. 185, 194

Feiman-Nemser, S. 185, 186

Ferraz, C. 109

financial support for students 71

fiscal shortfalls 33–4

flexible teacher education 208–9

Freire, P. 17–18

Fry, L. 149

Fukuda-Parr, S. 146–7

functionings 130, 133

funding of teacher education 66

further education 37–40

gaming 44

Gansu, China 69–70

Gao, P. 61, 68

gender: bias in treatment of students 138; education, development and 151–2; women teaching boys 160–2; women teaching girls 160, 161, 162, 176, 178, 182; *see also* women teachers

gender parity index 21, 22

gender-redistributive education policy 163

Ghana 26, 115, 116–17; female teachers' morale and self-esteem 119–20, 121–7

girls, taught by female teachers 160, 161, 162, 176, 178, 182

Global Monitoring Reports (GMRs) 8, 17, 19, 227; education policy 29; teacher supply 20–1; 2005 Report 3, 8, 11–12, 20, 26, 29, 228; 2010 Report 21, 26, 29

governance 16–17; structures 30

'grammar' of schooling 185

Grandbois, A. 188

Guatemala 194

Guinea 194

Gurgel, A. 101

Hannum, E. 12

Hanushek, E.A. 12–13

Hazans, M. 46–7

homework, reviewing 177, 178

housing/accommodation 27, 73

Hu, W. 59

hubs 209–10

Human Development Index (HDI) 132, 146–7

ideal capabilities 146

identity: and morale of teachers 118–28; professional 186, 187

ILO/UNESCO Recommendation Concerning the Status of Teachers 7, 31

imagination 119, 125–7, 128

impossible fiction 153–4, 162–3

improvement, capability analysis as a framework for 132, 142–6

in-service teacher education 29; Brazil 107–8; China 66, 67–8,

266 *Index*

in-service teacher education (*cont.*):
70–1; coordination with pre-service
training 229, 232; Ghana 116–17;
India 82, 83–4; integrated structure
with pre-service education 205–6; new
modes 199–200, 201–11; Nigeria 94–
5; Sudan 117
incentive schemes 28, 42, 43–5, 54;
Brazil 109; positive lessons 45–8, 49
income 130
India 18, 24, 27, 28, 53–4, 76–90,
228–9; Central Institute of Educational
Technology (CIET) 86; contract
teachers 26; education system 77,
78–80; incentive programmes 28,
45–6; Ministry of Human Resource
Development (MHRD) 78; National
Council of Educational Research and
Training (NCERT) 78, 83; National
Council for Teacher Education
(NCTE) 81, 83–4; National Knowledge
Network 85; National Policy on
Education 84; Right of Children to Free
and Compulsory Education Act 76,
78–9, 80, 81, 89; Sarva Shiksha Abhiyan
(SSA) 80, 83; shortages of teachers 16,
19, 80–1
Indira Gandhi Open University
(IGNOU) 84, 85–6
Indonesia 25, 28
induction programmes 231, 232
information and communication
technologies (ICTs) 200, 201, 209;
exploiting the potential of 212–26;
India 84–9; teacher education in
China 68–70
initial teacher education *see* pre-service
teacher education
institutions of teacher education 203–4,
205, 213, 225, 231; China 64–6, 72;
India 81–2, Nigeria 91–2
integrated structure for teacher
education 205–6
interactive radio instruction (IRI) 218
international benchmarking 27–8;
tests 12–13
Internet: access in India 85; online teacher
education in China 68–70; users in
China 70
internship 66
intrinsic motivation 44
Iraq 6

Janala 218

Jomtien Declaration 7, 8; *see also*
Education for All (EFA)

Karachi, Pakistan 150–63
Kelley, C. 45
Kenya 206; Teacher Service
Commission 5
Kingdon, G. 12, 40
Kothari Commission 81
Kremer, M. 41
Kubitschek, J. 102
Kumar, K. 11
Kwara scandal 6
Kyrili, K. 34

language: achievement production
function 168–73, 179, 180–1;
education in South Sudan 223; of
instruction in Sub-Saharan Africa 190;
languages in China 56–7
Latin America 28, 194
Latvia 46–7
Leach, J. 118–19, 123, 125, 127, 128, 204
lesson planning 177, 178, 182
levels of competence 208–9
Lewin, K.M. 202–3
Liberia 24
literacy: China 57; India 77; Sub-Saharan
Africa 190–1, 196; tests 166
local–central balance *see* central–local
balance
location/place: issues in teacher
education 235–6; of professional
development and learning 87–9
Lord's Resistance Army 5

Maclure, R. 190, 191–2
Makhmalbaf, S. 5
Makkawi, I. 150
Malawi 24, 236
Mali 194
market forces 73
Martin, M. 34
mathematics 180–1; achievement
production function 168–73;
skills in Brazil 105–6; Sub-Saharan
Africa 191–2
merit pay schemes 43–5
Mexico's Carrera Magisterial
programme 28, 47–8, 49
migration 23–4, 41
Millennium Development Goals
(MDGs) 3, 7, 8, 116, 202, 227, 229;
gender equality 151

Index 267

minban teachers 62–3, 67
mobile phones 218–20, 221, 225–6
modular teacher education 208–9
monitoring teacher development 132,
146–8
Moon, B. 118–19, 123, 125, 127, 128,
204, 213
moonlighting 177
moral hazard 44
morale, teacher 115–28
motivation 142; intrinsic 44; women's for
becoming a teacher 154–6
multi-grade teaching systems 139, 140
Muralidharan, K. 45–6
Murnane, J. 44
MUSTER project 8, 199, 202–3, 229

Nairobi Conference on education and
scientific and technical training 188–90
national–local balance *see* central–local
balance
Ndwasinde, S. 9
needs analysis approach 207–8
Nelson Mandela Foundation 6, 237
new classroom activities 214
networks 209–10
new modes of teacher education 199–200,
201–11; curriculum redesign 207;
flexibility 208–9; needs analysis
approach 207–8; networks, hubs and
banks 209–10; new forms of planning
and costing 210–11; one structure for
teacher education 205–6
Nigeria 5, 53–4, 91–100, 236;
central–local balance 16–17, 92,
99–100; Child's Rights Bill 96; Federal
Teacher Scheme (FTS) 93; Kwara
scandal 6; National Commission for
Colleges of Education (NCCE) 98;
National Economic Empowerment
and Development strategy 96;
National Teacher Education Policy
(NTEP) 96–7; National Teachers
Institute (NTI) 93, 95; perceptions of
teaching 95–6; primary and secondary
teacher preparation 93–5; reform
strategies 96–9; Special Teacher
Upgrading Programme (STUP) 93–4;
Teacher Education Initiative (TEI)
project 98–9; Teachers Registration
Council 95; Universal Basic Education
Commission (UBEC) 93
Nigerian Certificate in Education
(NCE) 91, 93–4
Nigerian University Central Research

Fund 98
numbers of teachers *see* shortages of
teachers, supply of teachers
numeracy tests 166
Nussbaum, M. 135

O'Connor, K. 124
Odden, A. 45
OER@AVU 221, 225
'OERs for ELT' project 221
Ogiebaen, S.E. 96
OLS achievement production
functions 168–73, 173–6
O'Malley, B. 5–6
online centres 69
online teacher education 68–70
open and distance learning (ODL) 214
open educational resources (OERs) 216–
18, 220–1, 225, 226
open-ended instruction 184–5, 193
open learning 200; Brazil 107; India
88–9, 90
open schooling 237
Open University (UK) 218
open universities (India) 84
oppressed, pedagogy of the 17–18

Paine, L. 66–7, 72
Pakistan 6, 24, 28; teachers' pedagogic
practice and learner achievement in the
Punjab 164–82; women teachers in
Karachi 150–63
Park, A. 12
participant observation 134
participation 158–60
Participative Teacher Education
Programme 82
pedagogic practices 234; influence on
learner achievements 114, 164–82
pedagogical renewal 183–96; challenge of
in Sub-Saharan Africa 187–8; defining
and problematising 184–7; lessons
learned 195–6; promising paths 194–5
pedagogy: attributes of 119, 121–7;
identity, morale and 118–28;
India 83–4
pedagogy of the oppressed 17–18
performance-based pay 42–3, 178;
China 62; Latvia 46–7; options for
43–5; positive lessons from country
salary reforms 45–8
Pernambuco 109
personal conversion factors 133, 134–5,
136, 137–8, 139–42
personal development 158

268 *Index*

personal history and psychology 133, 134–5

Peru 24

Phelps States Commission Report 92

PISA 101–2

planning 210–11

Podgursky, M. 41

policy: formation 29–31; seven interrelated factors for policy makers 200, 227–38

policy streams 30

political stream 30

Portugal 102

post-primary phases of education 37–40

poverty: alleviation 17–18; India 78

Power, T. 214

practice, constructing a 186–7

practice-focused curriculum 207, 234; ICTs and delivery of teacher development programmes 215–21

pragmatic capabilities 146

preparation, lack of 137–8

pre-service teacher education: Brazil 106; coordination with in-service training 229, 232; India 81, 82; integrated structure with in-service education 205–6; new modes 199–200, 201–11; Nigeria 93–4; shortened forms 23, 230–1, 232

primary education: China 57–64; India 78–80; teachers' salaries 38–40

principal-agent theory 42, 43

private teacher education colleges 97–8

problem stream 30

process variables 165, 166–7, 169, 173–82

productivity 158

professional development 29; and female teacher morale in rural communities 115–28; pedagogical renewal and 185–7; see also in-service teacher education

professional identity 186, 187

professionalism 188

Punjab, Pakistan 164–82

pupil achievement 11–15, 28; influence of teachers' pedagogic practices 114, 164–82; teacher salaries and 40–1, 45–7, 178–9, 182

pupil fixed-effects 165, 173–9, 180–1, 182

pupil-teacher ratios 27; China 59–60, 61

qualification upgrading courses 205, 206, 207–8, 227, 229, 232, 233

qualifications 206; Brazil 104, 108; China 60–1, 64, 72–3; Ghana 116–17; Nigeria 91, 93; salaries, performance and 40–1; Sudan 117

qualifications-based pay 41, 42–3

quality of teachers 113–14, 183–4, 227–8; approaches to researching 164–5; influence of pedagogic practices on pupil achievement 114, 164–82; quality gaps 32–4; structural salary reforms and improving 41–3; see also effectiveness of teachers, pedagogical renewal

questions, teachers and asking 177, 178, 182

radio and television universities (RTVUs) 68

Rahman, A. 213

Raven's Standard Progressive Matrices test 166

reading 190–1, 196; see also literacy

Reddi, U.V. 89

regional inequalities 28, 53–4; Brazil 101; China 56; India 80; Nigeria 92–3

registration processes 230

relationships 119, 123–5

religious schools 94

reproductivity 158

resource banks 209–10

resource centres 67, 69–70, 141

retention of teachers 23–5, 227

Robeyns, I. 133, 143, 147

Robinson, B. 63, 69–70

rote teaching 137, 191

Rufa'i, R.A. 94, 96

rural areas 15–16, 16, 212; China *see* China; professional development and female teacher morale in Sub-Saharan Africa 115–28; support for teachers in 229, 235–7

SABER-Teachers 10–11

salaries/pay 25–6, 35–48; China 73; high proportion of educational expenditure 35–7; need for structural reforms 41–3; performance-based *see* performance-based pay; positive lessons from country salary reforms 45–8; post-primary phases 37–40; qualifications-based 41, 42–3; relation to qualifications 40–1; and student achievement 40–1, 45–7, 178–9, 182

São Paulo 108–9, 208

Sarva Shiksha Abhiyan (SSA) 80, 83

Index 269

school-based teacher education 90, 200, 231, 232, 235–6; China 70–1; exploiting ICTs 213–26; new models of teacher education 204–11
school curriculum 207; reform 192
school fixed-effects 173–9
schooling patterns 78
schools: best level of intervention to improve quality of education 195–6; condition of 27; violence against 5–6, 222, 223
science 191–2
secondary education: China 57–64; India 79, 80; salaries 37–40; teacher supply 21–3
secondary employment 177
selection of capabilities 132, 142–6
self-esteem 117–28
self-study materials 88
Sen, A. 15, 76, 130, 132, 142–3
Senegal 187
seven interrelated factors 200, 227–38; coordination of pre-service and in-service training 229, 232; numbers analysis 229, 230–2; qualification upgrading programmes 229, 233; support and gender analysis 229, 235–7; teacher education curriculum 229, 233–4; teacher education values 229, 237–8; teacher educators 229, 234–5
sexual charge in the classroom 161–2
Shi, X. 62
shortage curriculum areas 73
shortages of teachers 16, 32–4, 212, 227, 228–9; Brazil 104; E9 countries 21, 22; India 16, 19, 80–1; meeting 229, 230–2; South Sudan 224–5
shortened pre-service training 23, 230–1, 232
Sibal, K. 84–5
Sidique, A. 18
Sierra Leone 24, 25
Sinada, M. 122–3
Sinha, V. 89
situational analysis 132, 133–42; descriptive analysis of teacher behaviour 132, 135–42
skill-based pay 45, 47
social conversion factors 133, 135, 136, 137–8, 140–1, 142
social interaction 87–9
social justice 17–18
social media 87
social norms and context 133, 134–5

social returns to educational achievement 13–15
solution stream 30
South Africa 6, 9, 27
South Sudan 222–6
South Sudan Interactive Radio Instruction (SSIRI) service 224
Southern and Eastern African Consortium for Monitoring Educational Quality (SACMEQ) 27–8
status of teachers 5–7, 26, 188; China 62–4; Nigeria 95–6; Pakistan 154; Sub-Saharan Africa 118, 126
steep hierarchies 30
'stepping stone' approach 125, 127
Stuart, J.S. 202–3
subject ability, sorting by 179
Sub-Saharan Africa 20, 21, 24, 27–8; history of teaching and learning in 188–90; pedagogical renewal and teacher development 183–96; professional development and female teacher morale 115–28; research on teaching and learning in 190–6; teacher salaries 38, 39–40
Sudan 117, 120–1, 121–7
Sundararaman, V. 45–6
supply of teachers 16, 20–3; Brazil 103–4; *see also* shortages of teachers
support for teachers: beyond school 214–15; in school 214; women teachers in rural communities 229, 235–7

Tabulawa, R. 193
Tagore, R.N. 76, 77
Tanzania 129–49; descriptive analysis of teacher behaviour 135–42; initiatives to improve teacher quality 139; monitoring teacher development 146–8; selecting capabilities for teachers 142–6
Tao, S. 15
teacher behaviour 192; descriptive analysis of 135–42
teacher characteristics 192
teacher development index (TDI) 147–8, 235
teacher development matrix 87–9
teacher education curriculum 229, 233–4; China 66; redesigning 207
Teacher Education in Sub-Saharan Africa (TESSA) 201, 209, 216–18, 220–1, 225, 226

270 Index

teacher educators 89–90, 229, 234–5
teacher effectiveness 25–9, 104–5
teacher experience 176–7
teacher fixed-effects 164
teacher learning resource centres (TLRCs) 67, 69–70
teacher morale 115–28
teacher quality see quality of teachers
teacher registration processes 230
teacher resource centres 141
teacher retention 23–5, 227
teacher shortages see shortages of teachers
teacher supply see supply of teachers
teacher training institutes (TTIs) 216–18, 220–1
Teacher Training in Sub-Saharan Africa (TTISA) initiative 9–10
Teachers Television channel 68
tenure 176–7
test scores, and teacher salaries 45–7
textbooks 134–5, 236
Toole, D. 6
'traditional' teaching 184
trust 123–5
twenty-hour instructional week 139, 141

Uganda 5
UNESCO 23; Education for All see Education for All; Global Monitoring Reports see Global Monitoring Reports (GMRs); Recommendation on teacher status 7, 31; Teacher Training in Sub-Saharan Africa (TTISA) initiative 9–10
UNICEF 6, 11; Child Friendly School Initiatives 95; 25 by 2005 initiative 152
unit-based teacher education 208–9
United Kingdom (UK) 23; DfID 3, 10, 98–9
United Nations Millennium Development Goals see Millennium Development Goals (MDGs)
United Nations Relief and Welfare Agency (UNRWA) 206
United States (US) 23, 41
universal primary education (UPE) 212; Sub-Saharan Africa 187–8
Universidade Aberta do Brasil 107
University of Delhi Bachelor of Elementary Education 82
unqualified teachers 206, 232, 233; India 80–1
Unterhalter, E. 15, 144, 145
urban teachers 73

urbanisation 56
Urdu 179, 180–1
USAID Teacher Professional Development Initiative (TDPI) 224
Uwameiye, R. 96

values 17–18, 229, 237–8
Vargas, G. 102
video replay centres 69
video replay and computer centres 69
violence towards schools and teachers 5–6, 222, 223
vocation 90, 125–6
voice 119, 121–3
Voluntary Services Overseas (VSO) 10, 25, 150
volunteer teachers 187–8

Walker, M. 15, 144
Walkerdine, V. 153
Walsh, C. 214
Wang, M.J. 69
welfare economics 130
well-being 144–6; achievement 145; freedom 145
Wentworth, M. 118
West and Central Africa 190–2
Windle Trust International (WTI) 223–4
withholding content during class 137
Woessman, L. 12–13
women teachers: authority, participation and 158–60; becoming a woman teacher 154–6; lived experiences in Karachi 150–63; morale in Sub-Saharan Africa 115–28; in rural areas 16, 115–28, 229, 235–7; support for 229, 235–7; teaching boys 160–2; teaching girls 160, 161, 162, 176, 178, 182
working conditions 25–9; India 82–3; Nigeria 96
World Bank 3, 101–2; core teacher policy goals 10–11
World Declaration on Education for All (Jomtien Declaration) 7, 8; see also Education for All (EFA)
World Economic Forum 29

Yashpal Committee 81
Yi, W. 63
Yu, S.Q. 69

Zambia 24, 194
Zhang, R. 61, 68
Zhao, J. 59